DATE DUE			
GAYLORD			PRINTED IN U.S.A.

JULIAN GREEN

DIARY 1928–1957

JULIAN GREEN

DIARY 1928 – 1957

Selected by Kurt Wolff

Translated by Anne Green

A HELEN AND KURT WOLFF BOOK

HARCOURT, BRACE & WORLD, INC., NEW YORK

The stanza quoted on page 152 is from "A Summer
Night 1933" by W. H. Auden. Copyright, 1937, by
Random House, Inc. Reprinted by permission of
Random House, Inc. and Faber and Faber Ltd. from
The Collected Poetry of W. H. Auden.

The excerpts from my diary were selected by Kurt Wolff with my approval. Had I made the selection myself, it might have been somewhat different, but the author is not necessarily the best judge in such a case, and I relied, wisely I think, on Kurt Wolff's critical sense.

Julian Green

JULIAN GREEN

DIARY 1928–1957

1928

SEPTEMBER 17. PARIS. This diary, which I intend to keep as regularly as I can, will help me, I think, to see more clearly into myself. I expect to record my whole life in these pages, with complete frankness and accuracy. . . . How will the book turn out? I have no idea, but to know that it exists will be a source of satisfaction to me.

SEPTEMBER 18. If people only knew what lies at the heart of my novels! What a tumult of desires these carefully written pages conceal! I sometimes have a loathing for the furious cravings that give me no peace except when I am working.

OCTOBER 6. I want to begin reading the Bible again every evening as I used to, even if this only gives me a faint help against temptations; the least it can do will be to make me wish for better things.

OCTOBER 14. Have read a lot, dreamed a lot these days. Read *Mark Rutherford*, which I feel tempted to translate. What surprises me, when I come to think of it, is that there is someone in me who wants to write a book of this kind and I am obliged to oppose him. There is not a sentence here that I do not wholeheartedly agree to. I am familiar with these struggles and spiritual lapses. The beauty of this book fills me with a great disgust for this world.

DECEMBER 4. Have begun reading Pepys. It makes me sorry not to have better recorded the events in my own life. But he wrote for the pleasure of talking about himself. Now, I obey the incomprehensible desire to bring the past to a standstill that makes one keep a diary. And this desire came to me rather late. Why didn't I begin at eighteen!

DECEMBER 11. I was thinking today about my holidays at Savannah, in 1920 and 1921. I had fits of piety. I read St. Paul in a small, dark drawing room that looked out on an unpaved yard.

The Presbyterian church blocked the view and cast its shadow over the room; in order to see, I had to turn on the light in broad daylight. The heat was heavy and soporific, but I nevertheless pursued my austere reading. At my elbow buzzed a ventilator. From time to time I treated myself to a swallow of ice water. I believed that I understood every word I read. I had great spiritual yearnings, tried mentally to convey myself to a retreat in the desert where I could be a hermit, and felt happy even though my happiness took a strange form. A little of all this went into *The Pilgrim on the Earth.*

UNDATED. Went to see the Barthou collection this afternoon. I was alone in the gallery that contains fragments of statues, and these, I must say, do not appeal to me much. Yet, I stayed there almost ten minutes, seated on a straw-bottomed chair, before a large head of Bodhisattva that plunged me into a sort of abyss. The face is a fine, rather full oval and the brow a little too broad to seem to me perfect. Under the heavy drooping eyelids steals an almost sly glance. The mouth with deeply chiseled corners seems at times to smile, for if one looks at it closely, the face changes continually. What cannot be expressed is the superhuman intelligence to be read in the features. For a few seconds, I had the keen, disturbing impression that the stone head knew of my existence and that it was aware of the problems in my life. "Too many efforts," it seemed to say. "Too much disorder, too many desires." I left it regretfully, vaguely aspiring to better things, a fuller life, but I am too passionate to listen to Asia's teachings. We must, I think, accept the fate of our race and go up higher according to the spirit of our race.

1929

JANUARY 11. My fifteenth year was one of the happiest in my life. I no longer felt that I lived on earth. I can see myself once more, on a spring day, rue Raynouard, in Father Crété's room. We are leaning out of a window. Before us lie the Champ-de-Mars, Grenelle, and, in a sort of golden dust, the heights of Saint-Cloud.

Birds are singing in the mild air. On the terrace below us, an old blind priest walks up and down telling his beads and Father Crété talks to me about life after death. I am happy, but none of this can be expressed. The earth does not contain joys like these. It perhaps gives as powerful ones, but not of this particular quality.

JANUARY 23. A liver attack kept me in bed for three or four days. During this short illness, I thought my life was about to take a somewhat different turn, become more spiritual than it is at present. An absence of desires coincided with my body's weakness and the soul was allowed a free hand. How to make good use of sickness . . . It gave me a yearning for my stay in Brittany when I was nineteen, a time when I got up at night to say my prayers. Nothing impure in my life then. My visits to the Church of Saint-Melaine, to the cathedral at Rennes. Great spiritual longings and great joys. I was *aspirant* in the 50th Artillery Regiment. Later, I was sent to Alsace and to the Ruhr. Very gradually, a taste for living in the world came back to me and I gave up my plan of going to the Benedictines in the Isle of Wight.

FEBRUARY 10. An evening at Gide's. Present, apart from Robert and myself, were Malraux, Schiffrin, and Berl. A long discussion that I found a trifle academic about the small degree of actuality in contemporary literature. Good gracious! A book worthy of the name always belongs to its period on account of the spirit that quickens it. Descriptions of factory stacks and women with bobbed hair are not what date a 1928 book, but all that lies at the bottom of the book, uneasiness, a need to rebel, etc. When one of us said that in 1845 Balzac wrote novels that took place in 1820, Malraux exclaimed: "Don't let us talk of Balzac!" And everyone seemed to agree that it was impossible to talk about Balzac, without my understanding why.

MARCH 4. A great and furious desire to change my life, to be free, but there is no way out except in asceticism or in pleasure such as I used to know. I cheat the violence that forms the basis of my nature by writing my books. . . . It is madness to live like this, to warp my being.

APRIL 10. Gide wrote me such a nice note that I could not resist the pleasure of going to see him. I find him in his study. He tells me right away that he wants to have a straightforward conversation with me, as the others, those of his fellow writers, as he calls them, do not interest him. He has just finished reading my pamphlet (against French Catholics) and asks me how it should be interpreted. "You should see it," I reply, "not as a profession of faith, but as the expression of what I demand of Catholics." "In that case," answers Gide, "I agree with you wholeheartedly." Once more, he talks to me about the years of great religious fervor he had known and declares himself extremely sensitive to the charm of certain Catholic friends, but that he can resist them, when necessary. "Yet, I had warned Claudel . . . ," he says. Then shaking his head sadly, he adds: "All my friends have been converted: Ghéon, Claudel, Laurens, Copeau . . . this has made it impossible for me to talk to them. . . ."

A little later, I tell him how uneasy it makes me to be ranked among Catholic writers. Too many things separate me from the Church at present for me to call myself Catholic, but it would not enter my head to associate these spiritual difficulties with a novel. And even if I were Catholic, it seems to me that to be labeled a Catholic writer would always fill me with horror. It means cheapening religion. Should I express myself publicly on this point? "I should do nothing of the sort, if I were you," says Gide. "No, I have gone through the same experience. Better not open a debate that might bring you, in spite of yourself, to clearly state a profession of faith." "This would be all the more difficult," say I, "since I couldn't say exactly what I believe." "No more could I," says Gide, and he adds firmly: "At any rate, I know very well what I don't believe." We are silent for a few seconds. I think we both of us feel that this conversation is moving. "How painful it is," I say after a moment, "to feel embarrassed in the presence of people you respect and also love, but from whom you know that you may have to protect yourself some day, in spite of yourself. For some of our Catholic friends answer that description. . . . With the best will in the world, they never see you without a lurking idea of proselytism. They are worried about our salvation. They visibly have it on their minds, even when you talk to them of quite different matters. . . ." "Yes indeed!" cries Gide. "They will use every means to draw you to them. When you are with them, you find yourself in the situation of a woman faced with a man who would harbor *intentions*!" Intentions is said with a sort of emphasis. And Gide amusingly rolls up the collar of his thick black woolen coat.

He then talks to me at length about *The Dark Journey*. He seems to admire the whole of it, with the exception of Mme Londe, a character he finds untrue to life, but congratulates me on having continued to the end, in spite of this part of the book which he thinks unsatisfactory, "and at bottom, what I blame in *The Dark Journey* turns to your credit, for when all is said and done, what matters is to have carried a book like this to its conclusion, even with its defects. . . . It is a projection of yourself on paper." We next talk about what we have been reading. . . . Around four-thirty, he leaves me to order tea. I hear his voice at the end of the passage saying that he wants "the good tea." It is brought together with four crackers on a plate, and while we are feasting he asks me point-blank if I will entrust him with *The Dark Journey* to make a film of it. "I have searched vainly through the whole of contemporary literature for a book that could provide a script. One always reaches a place, a level place where the characters pause before moving on, but with you there is a *falling forward* that the screen would render wonderfully. For instance . . ." And he mentions some ten scenes in my book and then adds with a smile: "I hope you believe me now when I say that I know every hole and corner in your book!"

APRIL 11. I remember that my talk with Gide began by remarks about the present mania for classing the dead in one camp or the other, Catholic or atheist. "This is only of relative importance where the living are concerned," says Gide, "but not for the dead, who can't speak up for themselves. . . . See what happened in the case of Rimbaud, of Rivière. . . ." And he adds that for his part, he is taking precautions to avoid any misunderstandings after his death. . . .

APRIL 27. Plon offers me a contract that would bind me for fifteen years. How many wars and revolutions will have swept away contracts by 1945! It is already a great deal to live five years, ten years, without too much loss. Far from poisoning my life, this idea, which seldom leaves me, gives an extraordinary flavor to the present hour. Any plan for the future seems to me more and more futile. But let us behave as though everything were solid, let us go on working until everything crumbles.

APRIL 29. How I have suffered in this little room! What I took for a religious vocation was born here. The yearnings of my fifteenth year, those immense efforts to go to God . . . And here, too, the first desires and the terrible remorse that harried me . . . I used to mark my faults on the wall, behind a photograph of Murillo's Virgin. How many papers thrown into the fire, because of those small tragedies of conscience that make something so sad of our youth!

MAY I. Maritain to dinner. He is someone rare and exquisite, a truly Christian soul in Catholic armor, an armor that hampers his movements. Oh! I know he would protest if he read this sentence, but I can't express otherwise what I think of him. He stayed until eleven o'clock, talking about everything, passing suddenly from sadness to gaiety and from gaiety to an almost sorrowful tone. "Haven't I made a mistake?" he asks me. "Wasn't I wrong in busying myself with all those men of letters?" And, on leaving me, he looked sad and bewildered, although smiling.

MAY 25. "Victor Hugo was a madman who took himself for Victor Hugo." Cocteau developed this paradox in the most brilliant manner, day before yesterday. How can what he said be said again? One would have to have Jean's voice and expression to bring all this to life. Certain proofs of the great poet's madness fill us with joy: "He wrote three hundred lines of verse at a sitting, swallowed oranges, skin and all, wolfed down lobsters, saying that the shell it was that made the sauce go down. . . . He made pieces of furniture with his teeth. . . ."

Colette listens and laughs with us, munching apples. She contributes her fund of anecdotes and tells about Victor Hugo's armchair that had various secret devices. . . .

As he came in, Cocteau showed us a sick bird he had found on the Champs-Elysées. Colette picks it up, examines it, and wrings its neck in the garden.

SEPTEMBER 24. Gide came to see me yesterday. He talked about old age, about his in particular. "Sometimes," he says, "I have to look at myself in a mirror and tell myself: 'You are sixty,' for I don't believe it." And he goes on—not without a reminiscence of Goethe, I think: "I feel young with young people. They keep me from aging." Then he adds: "If it wasn't for Marc Allégret, I'd have already shriveled up completely." He then talks to me about my happiness and wants to know if I fully realize it. . . . I tell

him how much love made me suffer at the University, and he replies that he himself has never suffered from love, that he doesn't
know what it is, and I can't help thinking this a most extraordinary statement.

OCTOBER 3. Lots of dreams, lots of meditations over the book I
am writing at present. The other day, in listening to the last movement of a trio by Schumann, it seemed to me as though the present were abolished and that the only thing that counted was the
music's extraordinary reality. Such a state of mind is impossible
to put into words. Everything fades away, everything appears
absurd and incoherent. There are times when I feel a great disgust for words. They continually show a man his limitations, and
I scarcely see anything but music that can carry him out of
himself.

OCTOBER 16. For the last few days it has been impossible for me
to apply myself to work, and this for several reasons, the chief
being that I can't manage to *find* the beginning of my book
(*L'Autre sommeil*). This is extremely painful, for when I don't
work I have the impression that my life is useless. Yet, no effort
can make me find the first pages of this book if the time has not
come. What comforts me a little is that the same difficulties occur
with each book. Nevertheless, I go through painful moments of
discouragement.

OCTOBER 20. A visit to the painter Vlaminck in his country house,
which is both like a farm and a studio. He is tall and heavy. In his
broad pink face, a beaklike nose and blue eyes with something
ferocious in them. But Vlaminck is extremely agreeable and brings
out some twenty pictures for our appreciation; I think them very
fine and he himself is quite proud of them. "You're going to see
surprising things," he tells us. "Now, isn't this beautiful? That's
painting for you! Look at this . . . and look at this tragic sky,
this road where something is going to happen. . . ." These comments exempt me from giving the usual praise. He then recites a
little poem he had composed and which he likes so much that he
recites it three times over, looking me straight in the eye the
whole time, and at the end of the poem an enormous burst of
laughter doubles him up. He next treats us to an essay on youth
and speed, where it is proved that the speed which characterizes

our times is a sign of decrepitude. Doesn't a child walk slowly, doesn't it take an hour to accomplish what it will do later in five minutes? The older it grows, the faster it gets about. . . .

A little later, he says abruptly: "My painting is the best." This I like, for that is the way he should think, in order to paint. But I regret his adding: "This probably seems idiotic to you, but if I admired M. Renoir, I could not paint. Douanier Rousseau was very stupid. He wanted to paint like Bouguereau, whom he copied, or thought he copied. . . ."

OCTOBER 29. Yesterday, lunched with Curtius at the café Voltaire, place de l'Odéon. One quickly feels at ease with a man whose manners are so simple. We talk of Catholicism and Curtius thinks me right when I say that religion does not provide the answers to some of the very serious questions that life asks us. I was thinking in particular about physical problems. "We are," then says Curtius, "the victims of political sexual morality, that of Israel, a morality that has passed into the mass of Catholic ideas through the channel of St. Paul. But," he adds (and this finds a deep echo in me), "whatever my attitude to Catholicism, there is a Christian element in me to which I could not be unfaithful without committing real apostasy." As a last resort, the Gospel. God is hidden to philosophers (even Thomists?). We then talk about several writers and Curtius tells me how much he admires Joyce, whom he considers the leading European author. "What about Gide?" I ask. "Gide lacks greatness." I have heard Malraux say the same thing, but in a more brilliant manner. As I tell Curtius of my difficulties in writing a novel, he answers: "You should have been a poet," little knowing how right he is.

NOVEMBER 13. Appendicitis on November 1st and an operation on the 2nd. (Dr. de Martel performed the operation.) The complete annihilation of the being by ether, a drop into a dark, sonorous chasm, a great noise of bells, like those of American trains, and above all, the impossibility of offering any resistance, of clinging on to anything whatever—there must be a little of all this in death. The minute before losing consciousness was, I think, strange but not at all terrifying. My first idea when I woke up was: "So. I am dead and, exactly as I foresaw, I still exist."

For a moment the body, the whole being, lay on some mysterious shore, waiting for the rising tide to carry it back. What was the soul doing, while this was going on? Where was it?

* * *

NOVEMBER 14. Today I can stand as straight as I did before my operation, and without effort. Desires, those tiresome companions, return with health. During the first days after the operation, the soul had little difficulty in soaring and I dreamed of a life where desires did not exist, where flesh was silent. Religion, I now see clearly, being made chiefly for the sick, could not fail to show itself to me under the most attractive colors, without its being possible to distinguish what part it could play in my life from now on. Religion has already succeeded in putting my life in such an alarming state of unbalance that I still fear it, although I have found my bearings once more. People think me pessimistic, but those who don't know that I am looking for happiness, the joy of living, yes, the holy joy of living, don't know me at all.

NOVEMBER 15. When I saw Curtius, I remember telling him of a bad dream I had had (I was being buried) and of my fear of dying in a few hours, of dying, for instance, of appendicitis. "Are you threatened with appendicitis?" he asked. "Not in the least." That was two days before my illness. How often have I noticed that we unconsciously prophesy, as though there were someone in us who knows far more about us than we do ourselves.

Have begun to write again with great joy.

There is someone whom I scarcely ever mention in this diary. Happiness is a story that cannot be told. Love is a story that cannot be told.

1930

MARCH 27. Lunched with Malraux at the Pergola, avenue du Maine. He thinks that I write my books according to plans, following a well-thought-out technique. Useless to explain. I prefer listening to what he has to say. He asserts that what he dreads is not death but the years around fifty and the sexual impotence of that age, an impotence which is a sign of death. We talk about the rising literary generation, the one between twenty and twenty-five, of how little interest their work presents. "What can they do?" asks Malraux. "They grew up in a peaceful era, without feeling the jolt of a war or a revolution that has proved so useful to us." And later he says this, which I find very striking: "Between eighteen and twenty, life is like an exchange where one buys stocks, not with money, but with actions. Most men buy nothing."

MARCH 29. Thought this morning about the story I am writing at present. I stand with my back to the wall. In hesitating to talk about the hero's love for a young man, I falsify truth and seemingly conform to accepted morality, I act with a prudence that will make me lose all self-respect. It is in behaving thus that one finally becomes a man of letters.

JULY 3. Read a life of Savonarola. The reformer is a most pathetic character. His affection for young religious, the games they played together in the country, his innocence. "You ought to play for salads instead of playing for money," he told the Florentines. His ferocity knew no limits where homosexuals were concerned. He talks openly of priests who spent the night with *ragazzi* and then went to say Mass. (*"Pensa come la va!"*) There are interesting details. Boniface VIII had to forbid priests to keep butcher shops, brothels, and to serve as go-betweens for prostitutes. . . .

1931

FEBRUARY 1. Reread Stevenson's *Suicide Club* with pleasure and admiration, but some of the author's literary mannerisms spoil the fine story for me a little. I cannot bear his irony, no matter how light, any more than his tendency to preach. This Scot always has a little sermon in his pocket and I think that, unfortunately, the irony is only there to make one swallow the homily. But the great writer is present at every page. Witness the speech he puts into a coward's mouth: "People trifle with love. Now, I deny that love is a strong passion; it is with fear that you must trifle, if you wish to taste the intensest joy of living. Envy me—envy me, sir . . . I am a coward."

* * *

FEBRUARY 7. Very much absorbed by my novel. There is a truth that must be reached at all costs, the one that lies in the heart "of every man who comes into this world." It is not the truth that can be found in a novel, it is not that air of likelihood that makes amateurs cry out their admiration. No, to discover that truth, one must work against oneself, against one's inclinations, against the skill acquired by habit, against success, against the public, one must suppress every page that has only the reader's amusement in view. Words form a sort of current that one must constantly swim against; whoever gives in to the temptation of following the current, goes straight to failure, for it becomes impossible, after long misusing words, to make them tell the truth.

FEBRUARY 14. This morning I decided to rewrite the second part of my novel. The pages lack intensity; the plot unfolds slowly and is not in itself very interesting. The lighting, that is, the play of contrasts, is too feeble, what the characters have to say does not come from their innermost self, and almost everywhere the deep truth is sacrificed to a conventional truth, the truth to be found in novels. I hope that all my efforts are not lost. I have gone through a painful time, I have had doubts about myself, about my faculty for invention and even the mere power of putting words together in a coherent fashion. I feel calmer and more confident today.

FEBRUARY 17. . . . When I told Gide that I was doing over the second part of my book, he said I was right. "I would have been worried if you had told me that all was going smoothly," he adds. "And you are right to fear habit. The dangerous moment comes when a book begins to move of itself." With a shade of bitterness, he then talks about an English novelist who, it seems, had plagiarized *Les Faux-monnayeurs* and had recently written an article about him entitled: "A Bogus Great Writer." "He is too clever," says Gide. "He gives in to success. He's one of those who should begin their books all over again!"

Regarding certain Catholic writers, he says: "One fine day they will annex Nietzsche. Everything that is tragic becomes Catholic. At any rate, they won't get anything out of Goethe. . . ."

FEBRUARY 18. Gide was telling me the other day that he would have liked to try his luck at publishing one of his books anonymously, but that such an attempt was impossible for his next work, because he had already talked about it, and to too many people. "Then you might put it off until the book after that," I then remark. He throws up his hands. "Do you think I have as many books as that in my brain?" he asks, laughing.

MAY 6. Gide and Malraux have lunch with me. The subject of eroticism came up, I don't remember in what connection. Malraux talks about it brilliantly and maintains that eroticism really appears in full force only in countries where the notion of sin exists. Gide, Robert, and I say very little but listen with interest. A little later, Gide, who has been asked by Malraux for the definition of a Christian, looks at us, saying: "I feel I'm going to flunk it." But Malraux sticks to his guns. "Yet," he says, "you have touched lightly on the subject in your *Montaigne*." "Oh," replied Gide, "I touched lightly, I touch lightly on everything!"

After Robert leaves, followed by Malraux, I remain alone with Gide, who tells me about his plans in a friendly manner and—I think I can use the term—about his discouragements. He wants to write a novel in which he himself would be involved and seems unable to do so. He can only create a character that is exterior to his self, or else he falls back on his diary, but finds it impossible to write a novel of which he would be the hero. Proof being, according to him, that he is a real novelist and does not put himself into his books, as certain critics allege, critics whom he refuses to name. . . .

He talks about Bernard Faÿ's brother and quotes the admirable sentence pronounced by this youth who died at twenty-four: "I don't want to go on playing in a world where everybody cheats." "The fact is that you feel at times like someone waiting for a bus who has the last number," adds Gide.[1] "Then you say to the others: 'Go on! Get in!' " He says the last words violently, almost indignantly.

MAY 24. This afternoon, at the Pré Catalan, I watched a young man whose maneuvers intrigued me. He ogled a very beautiful woman of an Asiatic type and, in order to get closer to her, changed his table. Finally, unable to contain himself any longer, although she was accompanied by an old lady, he went up to the

[1] In Paris, people take numbers to get into a bus.

woman and asked her for a dance. It must be said that she too had glanced at him. Yet she refused. He threw her a terrible look that she did not see and bit his lip. He was thin, very white, with a rather delicate nose, pale, staring eyes, an underhung jaw, a skinny nape, and his skull was hollow behind the ears. He did not blush, but moved slowly back, staring at the woman with an expression filled with hatred and greed. It is so rare to find anyone in Paris capable of suffering, or of feeling anything whatever, that the fact is worth noting.

JUNE 22. Finished writing the chapter in my novel: the nightmare of a guilty conscience. How often have I dreamed of a garden that never ended, of a street that continued indefinitely and led straight out of the world! As a child I sometimes felt angry at the idea of limits being imposed to space; a wall, a door, made me indignant.

JUNE 23. At the exhibition of Portuguese Primitives. In a troubled, uneasy period, this austere painting brings us back to reality. For what is called politics has no more reality than a nightmare, even when it is interpreted by uprisings and massacres. The cannon, that big fool, may perhaps kill me, without convincing me for all that of its existence, whereas a few notes of Bach's music seem to bear up the sky. Even if grossness triumphs in Europe, it will never be anything but a dreadful semblance. What is real is beyond all reach.

SEPTEMBER 6. Yesterday evening the fuse burned out and sent us to bed with candles; this reminded me of my childhood and of the terrors of that age, fruitful terrors. At our house in Andrésy, in summer, I dreaded the moment when, once in bed, I had to muster up the courage to blow out my candle. So I would sit on a step in the staircase, my candlestick by me and, on my knees, a shabby copy of La Fontaine's *Fables*. And as I read the little stories—some of which assumed a terrifying meaning to me— I tried to watch from the corner of my eye the fantastic play of shadows on the wall. (For me, the wolf in La Fontaine will always be a nightmarish character.) How wonderful it was to hear the drawing-room door open at last and my parents make ready to come upstairs! I scurried away immediately, having burned half my candle.

* * *

SEPTEMBER 16. As I woke early this morning, I thought about my childhood. There are memories that one scarcely dares touch. I remembered my room in the rue de Passy, at dawn. The sun came through the red cotton curtains and a blackbird whistled in the landlord's garden. I felt so happy that I laughed to myself, in bed.

Later, particularly from the age of fifteen on, I thought only of the future. Everything that I wished for, I located in the future, just as one puts away cherished objects in a cupboard. I carried everything toward a mysterious goal that I wished to reach. And then, when I was about twenty-five, the future suddenly vanished. I can't express this otherwise. Yes, nothing remained but the present. Happiness under all aspects had to be enjoyed right away. The cupboard grew empty.

SEPTEMBER 21. Sadness and disgust made me interrupt this diary. What a false idea it would give of me, if anyone chanced to read it. For there is everything in my life. . . . There is my work, the book that is being created in me at all hours of the day, there is what I read and the thoughts that I keep to myself; and lastly perhaps, what seems to take up such a great place . . . Where is this diary leading me? Toward what darkness, toward what death? What will I be writing in it, in a year? I am filled at times with a terrible uneasiness, but one must go straight ahead.

SEPTEMBER 23. Reading Havelock Ellis. How much more useful his works seem to me than hundreds of novels that teach us nothing about ourselves, that do not help us.

SEPTEMBER 27. In the Trocadéro gardens, I watched men felling a tree. One of them was superb, bare-armed, his broad breast swelling his striped vest. Perspiration glistened on his dark skin. Fine rhythmical movements, a sort of disciplined violence. The ax bit into the base of the trunk and small chips of wood began to fly. At last, the tree began to shake, two men with a rope made it fall to the ground with a great shuddering. The beauty of the scene was with me all that day.

OCTOBER 1. Maritain's visit depressed me. According to him, the world is nearing its end, nay, we are already slipping into the abyss, we are in it; all mystics agree on this point. If there isn't a war, a revolution will take charge and annihilate us. Everything is tumbling down. Germany will perhaps launch into a war without a hope of winning it: her way of committing a sort of suicide. Maritain then talks about Teresa Neumann, whom he saw in her village near Munich. He describes the blood that streams from the woman's eyes and coagulates on her cheeks during the night before Friday. In her visions of the Passion, she repeats Aramaic words that she hears without understanding them, and that specialists have been able to translate. She says that the Franco-German rivalry displeases God and she foretells a catastrophe if a reconciliation does not take place.

I am always moved by Maritain's presence. Everything that is candid and true in the man speaks from his eyes.

OCTOBER 5. When I think that a whole portion of my life has already disappeared completely from my memory, I tremble as though it meant the partial death of my being. Today, I was remembering my solitary holidays at Savannah, in 1920 and 1921. My room, described in *The Pilgrim on the Earth*, my forlorn walks taken with a beating heart under great oaks draped in veils of Spanish moss, my long fits of insomnia in the stifling night. Ah! if it had only occurred to me to keep a diary in such moments, what a liberation it would have been for me, what a benefit!

This evening, I put away old papers and old photographs, all that remains of a shipwreck. . . .

OCTOBER 8. At the Louvre, the "Rape of Europa" by Francesco di Giorgio. I have the impression that the world disappears before such a painting or, rather, that another world replaces ours. Here we step right into a land of dreams. As far as I know, none but the Sienese school can so perfectly achieve this sort of miracle (I am not talking about Oriental art, to which, as a matter of fact, Sienese art is somewhat connected). The Florentines do not take us away from earth, they even make it feel good to us, while Duccio or Sassetta leads us gently away from life. In the same manner, this picture by Giorgio is located beyond the world's borders. On a beach of mauve sand, where footsteps leave no traces, fawns and partridges wander along the banks of tender green water. Quite close to the river, groups of girls, pressed together like flowers in a nosegay, look at the great white bull that rears up majestically, a woven crown over one ear. Europa, in a gold embroidered gown and red stockings, reclines over the animal's flank and neck; she is not frightened, she seems as calm as Peace in Giotto's Good Government fresco. But what use is it to talk about this? It is as though one tried to describe music. Fifteenth-century Siena will always be the country of those who feel exiled in their own times. I regretfully left the picture, weary-eyed and a little heavy at heart. I don't know where we are tending, I don't understand the *usefulness* of what we do. Everything seems to me false and vain, except a few pictures, a few pages of music, and a few poems. I must try, by every means possible, to recover the lost country of which Siena gave me a glimpse today.

OCTOBER 21. For a novelist, there is a conventional reality and a reality that might be called a reality of vision. A man whose profession it is to write stories will conceive what I am attempting to express. Words sometimes gather together of themselves and form images that can have a certain appearance of truth and can take in a bad writer and a careless reader. Truth of vision demands a far more severe effort, a sort of gift of oneself. It is not enough to write, for instance: "She drew back before this look." One should have an inner vision of what these words describe. Otherwise, the following sentence will be a little less true (that is, it will not have the sound of inner truth, which is the only truth), and the sentence that comes next will be even less true and so on until the author has pulled himself together.

OCTOBER 25. I have been to the Louvre almost every day for several years; I have never met anyone there whom I knew.

I owe the Louvre an immense debt. I have the feeling of having been brought up and nurtured by it.

NOVEMBER 12. I am the man who wakes at dawn, his head still filled with the dreams of night, dreams of deliverance perhaps, and who walks to the guillotine; I am the man who leans from his window and sees his house caught in incandescent lava, like a vast stream of precious stones; I am the voyager who sits up in his berth and hears someone cry: "Too late!" on the bridge of a sinking ship; I am the woman who sees the murderer's revolver shine close to her temple, and I am the murderer, I am all that when I read a newspaper.

* * *

NOVEMBER 15. The exhibition of Italian drawings. It seemed to me as though an angel seized me by a fistful of hair and forcibly lifted me above my own self, beyond this world and into a universe where the marvelous reality of art reigned alone.

NOVEMBER 17. I have always admired French craftsmen, but recently my carpenter dazzled me! We had taken him to the Colonial Exhibition to show him a four-poster in Washington's house, a bed that Robert wished to have copied. M. Miot walked around the bed for a moment, looked at it from behind his pince-nez, took a few measures with a yellow yardstick, and without further ado went home. Three weeks elapsed, and this morning the bed is at Robert's. It is as though we had stolen the original at the Exhibition, for if there are any differences between it and M. Miot's copy, I can't see them. It is a great mahogany bed, light in spite of its size, with four very slender columns supporting a white linen canopy. It has the severe elegance of the eighteenth-century American style, that cold, well-bred disdainful something that can be found in certain old houses in Richmond or Charleston.

NOVEMBER 25. Spent almost the whole day with Gide. Robert is with us. We all three have lunch near the Bon Marché and gossip gaily about this and that. Not for an instant did I feel that Gide is older than we are and would not even mention it if he himself hadn't alluded to being sixty. I can never rid myself of the impression that I am talking to a companion of my own age. . . .

As we talked about one of Baudelaire's prose poems, Gide, who happened to have a copy of Schiffrin's edition in his pocket, read aloud the first sentence of the poem and looked at us, his eyes shining with delight. . . .

Concerning *Hamlet*, Gide says that no one ever notices a question that Hamlet asks of Horatio and Marcellus: "And what make you from Wittenberg, Horatio? Marcellus?" A question, according to Gide, that calls for our thinking over the very German quality of the character. "To be or not to be . . ." is more or less Schopenhauer. And that continual hesitancy, that incapacity for action, that infirmity of purpose are neither French nor English, but German.

A little later, we talk about Shakespeare's sonnets and more particularly of the "Portrait of Mr. W. H." "This," says Gide, "is the sole interpretation not only plausible but possible of the sonnets addressed to an unknown man, which form the companion piece to the 'Dark Lady' sonnets."

He tells us of his fear of boring people (I think he said his terror of boring people), a constant anxiety that has led him more than once to shorten the end of his books.

Robert asks him what he thinks of a book that has come out about him and quotes from it an extremely funny sentence. "The author," says Gide, "came to see me just after the book was published and cried on my shoulder. Yes, I had to comfort him for having written his book!"

As I told him that out of carelessness I had left my diary open on my table and that the servants had certainly cast an eye over it, Gide says that the curiosity of servants flatters him and that he purposely leaves unimportant papers on his desk to satisfy their craving to know.

DECEMBER 1. Regarding inversion in literature, Gide talks about the difficulty there seems to be to approach the subject in a work of fiction. What results is more or less successful camouflages. Authors have always resorted to such stratagems. If that is the case, what a number of camouflaged books there is, what a number of semi-confessions that we no longer even understand!

DECEMBER 8. . . . I called up Roger Martin du Gard from Gide's flat, but the telephone rang in vain. "Yet he is there," said Gide, who was by me. "He is wonderful, he knows how to protect his privacy and not answer. . . ." I hung up, saying: "I couldn't, I think I would die of curiosity." "And so would I!" cried Gide. "I answer every ring of the bell!"

DECEMBER 27. This morning I went to see Roger Martin du Gard, who, apologizing for not coming to my house, asked me to call on him. We sit in a little room, forlornly heated by gas. We talk about Gide. I say at one moment in the conversation: "If I described him as I see him, no one would believe me, for his reputation shows him under such false colors." "Yes," replies Martin du Gard, "but he himself would contradict you and maybe prove your most skeptical readers to be right. For he isn't a miser, and yet he is. He doesn't lie and yet he does. . . ." But he asserts that in spite of Gide's being so shifty, he is a faithful and loyal friend. Out of weakness and also out of a desire to please, he sometimes tries to agree with whomever he is talking to, and the day comes when this person realizes that Gide has lied to him out of sheer amiability—and thus his reputation is firmly established. This, at any rate, is the explanation given by Martin du Gard. He also talks about Mme Gide. She has not left Cuverville for the last ten years and no longer reads a word of her husband's books. *Si le grain ne meurt* is a book of confidences, says Martin du Gard, and a book of confidences written for Mme Gide that is unknown to her. This is what he finds "pathetic." "And Gide wanted to talk to her, at a distance, as though he were telephoning, but she had hung up long ago." At Cuverville, Gide's attentions to his wife are "almost embarrassing." "You don't feel cold?" "Is the light just right?" etc. "She buries herself in domestic life, from despair. Gide adores her." Sadness (I think he said remorse) for having made her suffer spoils Gide's keenest pleasures, and if he thinks he has learned between the lines of a letter that something worries her, back he comes from the depths of Tunisia (or elsewhere) to be with her. Martin du Gard adds that Gide never talks of these things except to very intimate friends like himself.

DECEMBER 31. Everything I write proceeds in a straight line from my childhood.

1932

JANUARY 10. The other day, V. and I asked Gide to give each of us a photograph of himself. (V. had egged me on, for of my own accord—never . . .) "I'll think about it," says Gide. And suddenly: "Why, there's a very good postcard likeness of me. For my photograph is sold as a postcard," he adds. "There's real fame for you!"

JANUARY 19. Gide came to see me late this afternoon. Apropos of V.'s lies (childish lies, mere fibs), he talks to me again of truth, one of his favorite topics and one so often repeated that I end by feeling a little embarrassed. "We both have a Protestant heredity that explains this taste for truth," he says, adding that Catholics do not believe that truth is due to everybody and that such subtleness horrifies him. . . . A little later I tell him that I am not satisfied with certain things in the book I have just finished, and he nods approvingly. "Francis Jammes," he says, "is, on the contrary, delighted with everything he writes." This author is supposed to have said: "My *Georgics* are as superior to Vergil's as Christianity is superior to paganism."

JANUARY 21. What keeps me from talking about religion is the fact that in me there lies a fanatic dozing ever so lightly whom I particularly do not wish to rouse. . . .

JANUARY 24. Today I found some old negatives in a trunk. Printed a few snapshots. I saw myself again as I was at fifteen. On looking at a photograph taken at the foot of a big oak in our garden, I had the peculiar impression of being on the verge of remembering a thought that had crossed my mind at the very moment when the photograph was taken, and for a few seconds it seemed to me that a ray of light was about to pierce through the obscure depths of memory. I should have attempted to make my mind a blank, and perhaps, among so many others, that minute in my youth would have found its way to me; my efforts made it run away and fall back into an oblivion from which it was about to emerge. So much of us goes thus to nothingness, so many hours, so many years . . . It is an unpleasant and all but sinister sensation to feel oneself drifting slowly toward definitive unconsciousness, and I can only think with horror of the time when everything that I have known and loved will fade from my memory. What remains of my mother? A few letters, five or six photographs, and memories that will be with me till I die. When we die, my sisters and I, she will die once again and for ever.

JANUARY 28. "B. is a bad painter who someday will paint quite good pictures. They will perhaps be discovered a hundred and fifty years from now, in the depths of a museum in the provinces. Bérard has the charm of his race, and it may be that in constantly hesitating between beauty and fashion, he might finally choose beauty, but he is in danger of tumbling into fashion and staying

there." Who says this? Gertrude Stein. She lies half stretched
out on her black horsehair sofa, her hand buried in her poodle's
white wool. She looks calm and strong as a monolith; she might
be ten centuries old, that is, she has the youth and serenity of a
mountain. She tells me that one day she opened a book of mine
and saw that my sentences were really sentences; she adds that
she read only one sentence!

MARCH 10. I have finished my novel. What am I to do? In spite
of reading, my days seem empty. I dread wasting my time. Who
knows how much of it remains to me? There is pleasure, of
course, but I like it only when it is stolen from my hours of work.
When it is just a way of filling in leisure, it no longer amuses me.

MARCH 15. Saw Gide this afternoon. He tells me that he can
only think about Russia and Communism. What is the use of writing books? This scarcely has any meaning, on the eve of the important events that are taking shape in the world. "Does this disturb you?" I ask. "No, I find it stimulating!"

MARCH 25. This morning, rebelling against pleasure, which it
seems to me impossible to do without, I tried unsuccessfully to
read Pascal. One of Plato's Dialogues would have been as much
help to me. The idea of a religious conversion appears to me at
present as the falsest way of settling moral difficulties. To have
recourse to God against oneself is an expedient for weaklings.
What I looked for in Pascal was the sound of a voice that spoke
to me of another universe than mine. What must be feared is that
pleasure should harden the heart and endanger love.

APRIL 4. Pierre Bost came to question me about my attitude to
politics. I tried to put together the substance of an answer, but
all I think on the subject boils down to this: "I loathe politics.
Because of politics, all that I love is in danger; it is a menace to
individual liberty, a menace to happiness, it disturbs my work. I
wholeheartedly believe in literature and works of art. This belief
is entirely foreign to political preoccupations." Where can my
place be in the present world? I have no idea.

APRIL 7. My book has only just come out and is already being
trampled, as Flaubert expressed it. I went to Bagatelle the other

day, with Robert. The weather was wonderfully fine and we were almost alone. The trees were not yet in leaf, but the lawns were thick with small white flowers. I wanted to be happy, to enjoy the lovely garden, but my book's failure made me a little sad. Why not look things in the face? It is a failure. This grieved me, for I am fond of success, like everybody else. However, I can say that I found something interesting in my very disappointment. I said to myself: "Ah, so that's the way one feels."

I had a good article by Jaloux, who generously defends each of my books when it comes out.

APRIL 29. A visit to Gide. He is back from Switzerland. I thought he looked badly and at first seemed a little weary, a little sad, but a few moments later all his gaiety returned and with it, that extraordinary youthfulness of eye and voice. He reads me most admirably a few pages of Sologub's *Démon mesquin.* His voice reminds one of a bird of prey; it suddenly pounces on a word, swoops off with it, and feasts on it. Then he lowers his book and smiles as though he had really eaten something delicious.

MAY 25. Gide told me the other day about the combined efforts of Jacques Maritain, Abbé Altermann, and Copeau to bring him to conversion. He says that at heart he appreciates this "sort of flirtation." He refuses his soul.

JUNE 13. Reread Renan's *Life of Jesus.* I cannot accept his calling Christ "the charming doctor," or that he should speak of "the orchard of an agricultural enterprise" when he means the Mount of Olives, for this is indeed an insipid way of describing the most sacred spot in this world. Closing the stout volume, I wondered what martyrs Renan's Christ would have called forth. Very few, I should think. The author wished to bring Him closer to us, but instead of bringing Him closer to us, he has lessened Him by wanting to make Him a kindly philosopher and, in order to have us accept Him, reduced Him to our level. I thought of what Blake says:

> The Vision of Christ that thou dost see
> Is my vision's greatest enemy. . . .
> Thine loves the same world that mine hates;
> Thy heaven doors are my hell gates.

UNDATED. Before the war, when I used to take walks with my uncle and when we passed by the Embassy where a fine star-spangled flag waved, I was told to remove my hat. I also tipped my hat to Washington's statue. My uncle bowed gravely. Not content with raising his hat, he held it at arm's length. I did the same, a trifle mystified. And what was more, I recited a few patriotic lines concerning the father of the country and the red, white and blue.

My uncle went back to America and I had almost forgotten the whole thing when one day, passing before the Embassy with my mother and recollecting my uncle's teachings, I ostentatiously saluted the flag. "What on earth is this freak of fancy?" asked my mother. "You've taken to saluting the flag? It's perfectly unnecessary." I tried to explain, but she stopped me by telling about my great-aunt who had braved Northern bayonets rather than bow to the Northern flag. How many times had I heard this story! Soldiers in dark blue surrounding the indignant crinoline, the flag stretched across the street, a bearded officer arguing with the "rebel" lady—this to me was one of the most important scenes in the whole of the Civil War. My mother's native town had been taken by Sherman in December, 1864. To subdue those Southerners who thought themselves superior to everybody, it was considered a good idea to make them pay their respects to the conquering flag. "I will not salute that rag," said my great-aunt. "Madam, you must pass under the flag." "Certainly not, sir!" She also said lots of other things that I have forgotten, but I know that she made such a fuss that she was let alone. . . .

JUNE 21. Saw Gide this afternoon. We had arranged to meet at the Picasso show and went through four rooms of paintings. Gide was full of enthusiasm. "It's amazing," he repeated. "Is there anything in contemporary literature to match this? No, nothing. No one has such boldness." He wants to see everything and does it a little too quickly to my taste, but nothing escapes him. As we talked of Picasso's baffling facility—for nothing seems impossible for the painter to achieve—Gide quoted what Ingres said, without adding any comments: "With talent, you do what you like. With genius, you do what you can."

We then went to the Bonney exhibit. Photographs of the 1900 period. Gide seemed amused at first, then ended by finding the show sad. Whereupon, in came Étienne de Beaumont, who tried to convince Gide that nothing could be prettier than the fashions of that period, but Gide kicked: "No," he said firmly, "they weren't pretty. They were ugly and sad."

We went to have tea, place de la Madeleine. Gide tells me that he has not yet read *The Strange River* but has seen the articles written about the book and in particular that by Th. I said that to my mind, Th. is to be distrusted for certain reasons. Gide immediately agrees with me and picks Th. to pieces. "Yet," he says, "some of the criticisms made about your book are right. You are blamed for creating an imaginary world." At this, I talk to Gide as I don't believe I ever talked to him before. "No one has the right to blame a novelist for creating a world for his characters. Quite the contrary. As regards my pessimism, the reading of any newspaper fully proves that life is at least as black as I say it is." On this point, also, Gide says I am right, perfectly right, and adds: "It is all to your credit that you have created this romantic world. Anyway, you are the only one who is able to do it. I have said so in my diary, but I am glad to hear you protest." He next tells me that the only fault he has to find with *The Dark Journey* is a "certain evenness of flow," due no doubt to its being written day by day. "To work daily is excellent, anyway," he murmurs. And so, if Gide is offered resistance, be it ever so slight, in a conversation, his line of defense breaks down completely, even though he may later fall back into some secret retrenchment or other. We shall see whether or not he will publish the passage in his diary concerning *The Dark Journey*.[1]

JUNE 23. As I was putting away my manuscript a moment ago, a question crossed my mind, one that I have often asked myself. If, instead of writing this morning, I had written after lunch, would I have written the same thing? If I set aside the beginning of this novel and took it up again in a month, would it continue in the way I intend to continue tomorrow? Does one page necessarily bring about another page written in such and such a manner, or does each page enjoy relative freedom that allows it to be what it is, independently of the page that precedes it? I could not but be bored by a book where all the pages would be determined by the first one, and yet I like a work of art to be governed by a certain fatality. The reader should, I think, have the impression

---

[1] The passage did come out in his published diary.

that things could not be otherwise, but in spite of this, something indefinable should hang over the characters, the possibility of something else, the thousand possibilities refused by fate.

AUGUST I. BERLIN. The streets are perfectly quiet. Newspapers give the results of the elections: an advance for the Communists, and for the National Socialists a *Stillstand*. There had been some talk of a *Putsch* for today, but nothing seems to have happened.

Continued reading *The Master of Ballantrae* with very great admiration. If anything could annoy me in the book, it would be its perfection. I would prefer the author's skill not to be always so evident. He sometimes has the air of performing a very difficult task with professional ease.

AUGUST 8. Left Hamburg yesterday aboard the *Oceana*. I sat on the bridge and read *Almayer's Folly*, which disappointed me vastly, probably because I had heard it so highly praised. The most interesting part of its themes is treated very tamely. The author recoiled before a wholly sexual story that might have been magnificent: an unguarded reader can only understand just before the end what all this is really about. Does it require so much courage to say that a man wants to sleep with his daughter? As to the love affair between Nina and Dain, it is at most worthy of an operatic libretto. Some of the dialogues are rather absurdly lyrical, and certain sentences could have been written only by an ardent, ingenuous, and youthful author, such as: ". . . one of those long looks that are among a woman's most fearsome weapons . . . more deadly than a dagger thrust . . ."

As a compensation, I reread a few pages of Claudel's *Connaissance de l'Est*.

AUGUST 9. Around four o'clock this morning I woke and through the porthole above my bed saw the coast of Scotland shrouded in mist. I looked at it for a moment with deep emotion. Childhood memories, which I thought done away with forever, came back in a throng. Then I went back to bed and to sleep and, in one of the clearest dreams I ever had, saw my sister Mary. She walked from one room to another in a small, low, dark house. I remember that she bent her head with an anxious air and that she wore a gray dress with a small white collar of the kind in fashion around 1850. Seeing her dressed like that, I wondered if it were she that I saw, or someone in our family who resembled her. I could not talk to her and she seemed not to see me. The dream was short, but made such an impression on me that it cast a shadow over the whole of the following day.

AUGUST 12. I have no other ambition but to be a man. I rarely feel conscious of belonging to a race, to a country, and in such moments I behave and talk in an artificial manner that shames me. I cannot hate any people and nothing depresses me more than a patriotic ditty. However, this is a point where I have sometimes varied. On August 2nd, 1914, on hearing that day's news, I fell on my German grammar and tore it to pieces. I secretly hoped that the war would rid me of those fiendish declensions and that the enemy's tongue would no longer be taught in France.

SEPTEMBER 7. PARIS. I was thirty-two yesterday and it seems to me as though my life were only beginning. Worked today with great pleasure, but in spite of it, a renewed contact with my book after a rather long interruption makes things somewhat difficult. No one realizes the changes that take place in an author while he is writing a book, even if the book is short. Today, I don't feel quite the same as I did in July.

SEPTEMBER 11. At Souverain-Moulin, in the north of France. It is a seventeenth-century château, squat and severe as a fort, surrounded by water and great trees that stir softly in the gray sky. The wind thunders down the chimneys. I am writing this in a room whose windows look out on the gardens. With its long corridors that run into each other like the paths in a labyrinth, its big rooms with the lingering and delicious odor of country houses, the odor of childhood, this château rises to enchanted regions that one trembles to mention, for fear that the whole thing might vanish. A little while ago, I disturbed all this merely by walking about my room. I must remain completely still in an arm-chair, so that the magic may form around me once more; so that what lives within these walls may not be scared away.

As I did as a child, I amused myself in believing that I lived in 1700, that by leaning out of the window I would see a coach on the road and, for a few seconds, really thought to have succeeded. Some have a longing for future times; but I, more than thirty years old, still cherish an absurd regret for what will never be again, and what I like in Souverain-Moulin is that it belongs completely, not only to the prewar, but to the Old Regime.

SEPTEMBER 18. Around 1905, in the rue de Passy, we lived in a haunted house. You can shrug your shoulders! I remember that my mother's room included a sort of closet where clothes were hung. There, in my opinion, although I told no one of this disturbing secret, the devil elected to live. When I was alone in this room, I stood before the little closet, at a certain distance, and, half dead with fright, called the devil. For the first few minutes, nothing happened, and suddenly I saw something move among the clothes. How often did I indulge in this dreadful game! But I was never brave enough to stay until the end, and ran away howling as soon as suits and overcoats began to stir.

SEPTEMBER 23. I have moments of doubt that plunge me into the deepest gloom. There is really too much of a difference between what I write and what I would have wished to write. At times, when I hear very beautiful music, I imprudently weave it into the novel I dream of giving someday. This is hard to explain, but an author would understand me easily. I have the illusion of possessing tremendous power, until the last chord. Once back at my writing table, I sober up completely. Where are the impulses, the glow of enthusiasm I had a moment ago? I try to write, but have the strange feeling that words hate me and that I put them together against their will.

OCTOBER 3. In a world that goes too fast, I have decided to live slowly. I want to accomplish my task as though a long life were promised me. At table today, we talked about this, but in a vague, insufficient manner. To live slowly is not too easy. It means devoting a whole day to dreaming, when necessary, it means losing one's time to a good purpose. There are days when I long wearily for life in a country house, a life such as could be led at Souverain-Moulin. I would undertake lengthy studies, take up Greek again, I would idle along, I would carry my novels within me far longer, and they would be the better for it. Oh! how I hate the pace at which we all go!

OCTOBER 14. Yesterday, worked almost all day, from ten to twelve and from two to five. Wrote sixty-three lines in all, which is a lot for me. After that, I walked along the Seine as far as the Alexandre III bridge. The weather was delightful, cold with a faint mist and a fine pink sky. Thought the whole time about my work. When I read, I think about my book, when I walk, I think still more about it. Among all the paths open to me in this novel, I am trying to find the right one. I pass without transition from despair to hope. I often feel like giving up this book, then go back to it with a sort of furious rush forward.

NOVEMBER 19. I have been thinking over the article I would like to write about an author's freedom. If a writer were free, would he accept a Rightist or Leftist dictatorship? Neither one nor the other. "But what party do you belong to?" "Not to yours." I am the kind of man who is stood up against a wall and shot in all revolutions. So much the worse. In all the political programs that are offered us, I find nothing that suits me. What sense does it make to call oneself a revolutionary and wish to be killed for a government that has its informers, its *agents provocateurs,* its bureaucrats, like all governments? No, the more I think of it the better I understand that a free writer has no place in the Europe that is being set up at present.

NOVEMBER 23. Monday I went to the Lener concert to hear the thirteenth and fourteenth of Beethoven's quartets. The thirteenth is so full of sadness and sweetness that I am not ashamed to say that I cried. A madman, not far from us, conducted an imaginary orchestra. He had a delicate, sensitive face, red whiskers, hollow cheeks, a big hooky nose, and a famished expression. I watched him with great interest. He loved the music as much as I did and we heard it, perhaps, with the same emotion.

NOVEMBER 24. A naïve, well-meaning person asked me today if there were rules for writing a good book. I answered that I knew of only one, which is to believe strongly in what one writes. And try as I may, this is the only rule I can find that holds good for all literary work. Truth belongs above all to an interior order.

NOVEMBER 26. I listened to Beethoven's sixteenth quartet. Everything in this music seems strange to me. At times, one seems to hear in it the cry of a dumb man who wants to speak a new tongue, a tongue the like of which no one has ever heard. A little more, and wonderful dissonances would burst in these chords—for they are strained to a breaking point.

DECEMBER 18. A moment ago, under one of the Trocadéro colonnades, I paused to look at the Champ-de-Mars vista. The weather was like spring, with a luminous haze floating over the gardens. Sounds had the light quality that they possess only during the first fine days of spring. For two or three seconds, I lived over a whole part of my youth, my sixteenth, my seventeenth year. It gave me a strange feeling, rather more painful than agreeable. Yet I was in such deep agreement with the landscape that I wondered, as I used to, if it wouldn't be delightful to become part of all this and be reduced to nothing, like a drop of water in the sea, no longer to have a body, but just enough consciousness to be able to think: "I am a particle of the universe. The universe rejoices in me. I am the sky, the sun, the trees, the Seine and the houses that border it. . . ." This curious idea has never been very far from me. After all, perhaps something of the kind is what awaits us on the other side of death. And suddenly, I felt so happy that I went home, thinking that I should keep the memory of this great mirage as a rare and precious thing.

DECEMBER 21. Gide and his nephew have lunch with us. How awkwardly the writer behaves! Is this intentional? Or is it natural? He comes in and, I don't know how, makes us all feel ill at ease, for he is stiffer than he ever was. One tries to speak freely without paying too much attention to one's mode of expression, and Gide is there to pick out, one by one, any lapses in grammar, as an expert shot brings down partridges. The conversation wanders this way and that, as it does in *Paludes*. I feel that Gide is hostile today, but why? He sometimes reminds me of an old insect, well equipped by nature with defensive and offensive weapons, but an insect that nature has also deprived of wings, of color, of gracefulness. He highly praises Kurt Weill's *Jasager*, which he thinks very much in the U.S.S.R. spirit, and confides that after his "declaration of love" to the Soviets, he won't write any longer. After lunch, he becomes more and more grumpy. Seated before a self-portrait of Bérard, he asks "what it is," after staring malevolently at it for quite a long time, and declares that he doesn't

like it- which is what no one wanted to know. He irritates me a
little, does Père Gide.

DECEMBER 24. I went to see Gide, rue Vaneau, and there, almost
at his door, slipped and bruised myself in falling. Gide and Yves
Allégret dressed the wound. Gide was charmingly gay and made
me forget the bad mood he was in the other day.

Read Stekel's book on conditions of nervous anxiety, a book
that has taught me a lot about myself. May it cure me of a few of
the phobias that the author describes so well! On thinking it over,
I noted that the most troublesome and most harassing of my
phobias is that of death. It is in all my books. At a time when I
could call myself a Catholic, I did not fear death. I was twenty,
and at that age one doesn't believe in death, or one only believes
in it for others. One talks about it, pretends to fear or wish for it,
but there is nothing sincere in this, it is simply a literary attitude.
So far as I was concerned, the certainty of salvation sheltered me
from all the terrors that I suffered from later. My little *Pamphlet
against French Catholics*, which is a sort of farewell to the religious faith of my childhood, left me, so to speak, unprotected.
And so, the fear of dying immediately came to light in everything
I have written since, and bursts out in the novel I am engaged in
at present. I am at last tackling the subject that attracts, fascinates,
and terrifies me. I am like a man obsessed who throws himself into
the abyss that he dreads.

DECEMBER 26. My wounded knee obliges me to lie on the drawing-room sofa most of the day. I read *Sense and Sensibility* before
a big log fire. Delightful day! A feeling of deep security, very
near to that peace that passes all understanding mentioned in the
Bible. I put down my book, from time to time, to watch the flames
and smell the odor of burning wood. . . .

Jane Austen's method consists in contrasting one moral quality
with another—which quality she strives to personify—and although
I find the method a trifle mechanical, I surrender to the charm of
a writer whose smile is never a grimace and from whom emotion
never draws a scream, for well-bred people don't scream. Jane
Austen always remains a little within the bounds of what she
wants to say, with the exquisite reserve that she alone possesses,
but none the less her delineation is admirably clear. Compared
with her, Charlotte Brontë seems wildly disheveled.

1933

JANUARY 9. This morning, Gide paid me a surprise visit. He talks to me about Roger Martin du Gard, about his house at Bellême which has cost him a considerable amount and where he expected to write all the volumes of the *Thibault* series. A hill obstructed the view from one of the windows. He had it removed. Cost: one million francs. Then he grew tired of his book, of Bellême, and after ten years came to live in Paris. . . . Gide leaves me at twelve-thirty to have lunch with Lacretelle. And for the twentieth time since I met him, asks me on what terms I am with this writer, for Gide has lapses of memory. He declares himself delighted with Stekel's book on anxiety, which I had given him to read. Today, he made a curious impression on me. He gossiped without keeping watch over himself, and I suddenly had the intuition of being with a stranger. . . . He was probably quite different as a young man. But now . . . How is it that I inwardly shrink from him? He was most friendly. He questioned me about my work, but I couldn't help feeling that my answers did not interest him, and immediately talked of something else.

JANUARY 18. The exposition of Impressionist landscape painters; they are marvels at successfully catching the moment that will never return. A minute more and the sky will have changed, the surface of the water not be ruffled in the same way. On the other hand, the landscapes of Claude Lorrain and Poussin are, as it were, nature immutable.

JANUARY 20. In Renoir's painting, the obsession of a beautiful skin is so compelling that it can be found even in his landscapes, where the earth sometimes has flesh tints.

FEBRUARY 5. Read Dumesnil's book on Flaubert. I think it has taught me a lot. But the precepts set forth by Flaubert concerning the way to write a novel do not always seem to me right. What becomes of, not only inspiration, but mere inventiveness in a book where the least fact must find its counterpart in real life, in the author's personal experience? Beyond any doubt, a book like *L'Education sentimentale* can be written so, but you have to be Flaubert to do it. And at the cost of what sacrifices did he work according to such methods? I remember something that Henry James said about Flaubert; he compares him to a knight in magnificent armor, standing at the door of a great palace whose threshold he dared not cross. More exactly, James speaks of a sentry with shining weapons—these weapons must be taken further; there are other doors to open. Flaubert should at least have listened at the door of the soul. (*Essays in London.*)

The novelist invents nothing, he guesses. He will never be wrong if he obeys that inner voice that speaks in each of us and tells us whether we keep within the truth or if we step out of it. The inner truth is the only one that is really essential, the rest, no matter how beautiful, how tempting, is mere accessory.

FEBRUARY 8. Reading Walter Pater's *Plato* made me ponder greatly over myself, and these thoughts are not comforting. I would like nothing in me to obscure my love of truth. Now, pleasure is a danger and I have been carried down a slope where it is most difficult for me to keep from stumbling. That is what worries me, for I believe that the core of one's nature directly affects one's mind. A man who cannot resist everyday temptations can neither think powerfully nor even see things in their true light. I must write better books, I must never swerve from the inner truth. I think that by not giving in to the lures of an easy life, I will finally write a great book, and I hope someday to feel that I have not received more than I have given. I will find peace that day, but at present I am dissatisfied with myself. Who could imagine the difficulties I have encountered? Does one suspect, for instance, every time I describe an irresolute man, a man at variance with himself in my novels, that I have it in for myself? Some pages in my books are like an arraignment of myself.

FEBRUARY 10. Thought over and over a chapter in Pater on Plato's *ideas*. This is indeed a most appealing theory, for it is poetic, but it is also mystical. It affects the senses, but it is none the less spiritual. In my eyes, its attraction lies in admitting a mystery, and this mystery is that, among all *ideas*, beauty is the only thing in this world that is represented in a manner that can satisfy us. Never has physical grace been placed so high. A beautiful body partakes of the divine, but sensual love clouds and soils this divine reflection, and that is what should be told people who believe themselves to be Plato's disciples, because they are slaves to instinct. What appeals to me in this theory, and what holds my attention, is the seriousness of the role of love.

FEBRUARY 21. I am thirty-two, thirty-two times have I passed before the day and hour of my death, as one passes by the door of a house that one will someday live in, without even a thought of glancing at it. But I am getting used to the idea of dying and seeing everything that I love in this world die with me, for it seems reasonable to believe that we are nearing the end of a great cycle. How long will we sleep? It was only in 1900 that the remains of Cretan civilization were unearthed at Knossos. This vanished world had been slumbering for the last three thousand years. . . . Someday a man will stroll about a field and, turning over a clod of earth with his stick, as one sometimes does in country solitude, when the mind is absorbed in dreams, he will hit against a bit of metal and say to himself: "Why, there may have been something here." And if he is inquisitive, learned, and rich, he will excavate the site, and under eight or nine superposed cities he may perhaps discover Paris, as Schliemann discovered Troy. And if this bit of metal does not intrigue him, we will go on sleeping.

FEBRUARY 22. Last night, before going to sleep, I read a few of Milton's sonnets, those I am fondest of, the one where he speaks of his wife, who appeared to him in a dream, the one he dedicated to Cyriack Skinner, and the most famous one of all about his blindness. Around two in the morning, I woke up suddenly, with the feeling of having left a vast, deep, dark temple. The shadows were filled with a long murmuring, like the echo of a chant. All that day, I remembered it with strange emotion.

FEBRUARY 28. Day before yesterday, I went to Dali's to get my picture, as this is my month. (The painter being in financial difficulties, twelve persons had pledged themselves to make him a kind of annuity for that year, in return for which, each of the twelve was to receive a large picture, or a small one and two drawings. We had drawn lots to know which would be our month. To my great joy, I had drawn February, so did not have to wait too long.) I am given the choice between a large painting with an admirable landscape of rocks as a background, but with the foreground taken up by a sort of naked and whiskered Russian general, his head sorrowfully bent to show the shells and pearls that pepper his skull, and a small picture in wonderful shades of gray and lilac, plus two drawings. I choose the small painting. Dali talks to me about Crevel, who is ill, but "estoical." He enlarges greatly on the beauty of his own painting, carefully explains the meaning of my picture, which he calls the "Geological Transformation," and which represents a horse turning into rock in the midst of a desert. He is going to Spain and speaks with terror of the customs formalities and the thousand petty annoyances of a trip by *ferrocarril* (railroad), for he is a little like a child who is scared by life.

The other day, I was walking down a new avenue—mapped out but as yet unbuilt—that has been given the name of Paul Doumer. At the corner of this avenue and the rue de la Tour stood, only a year ago, a Louis-Philippe house that I described in *The Strange River*, a pension in my time, the Pension Mouton where I spent several months in 1914, then in 1916, with my father and sisters. It was in this pension, in the room I shared with my father, that I experienced one of the keenest joys that ever made a human heart beat. I was fifteen, I firmly believed in God and wished for nothing else on earth than to live for Him. When I said my prayers at the foot of my bed, I was carried away by such an outburst of joy that I wished I could die that very minute. Then, lying in bed and on my back, in a posture that I tried to make uncomfortable, I felt so happy that I simply could not sleep. But such feelings can neither be described nor explained. They have all the force of a first love. I was in love with God, with the Church, with the whole of an invisible world that became mine in attracting me to it. I think this happiness lasted almost a year, with intervals of lukewarmness. The first carnal sins and a deeper knowledge of myself put an end—and in the most heart-rending fashion—to the sort of ecstatic dream of my fifteenth year. In 1919, at Rennes, I was *aspirant* in the 50th Artillery Regiment. I had an extraordinary return to fervor, then in America, in 1920 and '21, and, since that time, nothing, but I distinctly remember those happy days, the happiness of a soul when it yearns for none but God.

MARCH 15. Gertrude Stein. She mentally turns over a considerable number of peculiar ideas and displays them forcefully, one hand in the pocket of an ample embroidered waistcoat of the kind worn by eighteenth-century financiers, the other twisting and smoothing her cropped gray hair. Her eyes are large and beautiful, there is something brave and *open* in her expression. She talks to me at great length about an immense novel she wrote around 1907, published in 1920, and which, she says, has been a source of inspiration for several contemporary American writers. And she quotes several very well-known names. "It's a rather formidable book," she tells me, "it moves rather formidably. It is an epic." Her voice is deep and manly; when she laughs, she laughs in bursts that show every tooth in her head. She speaks of Cocteau as an important writer, some of whose work is bound to remain, but what? She does not say, she does not declare herself outright about anything in a precise way. She admires a large painting by Berman that hangs in the sitting room, but does not even look at the other pictures.

MARCH 21. A telephone call from Gide, who asks me to go to see him as he has a curious manuscript that he wants me to read. We were to go afterwards to see a film that a certain Mr. D. is showing in his home. I think Gide looks worried. He hands me two gray copybooks, tells me he will sit by me and write while I read the typescript that has been entrusted to him. But he does not write, he goes from one corner of the study to the other, opens a door, talks to someone, returns, offers me a cigarette, and finally says he is vexed because he has agreed to speak at a meeting organized by the *party* (the Communist party). Lots of German writers exiled by Hitler will be present. "But I am disturbing you. Go on, go on reading." I feel that my very stillness annoys him. He goes off again and talks to someone in another room and, returning, says it is time to leave.

Off we go in the pouring rain. In the taxi, Gide talks about my working methods. "One feels the influence of daily work in the even flow of your books." But I haven't worked in this way for several years. And also, infinitely more gifted authors than myself have worked steadily every day. Dickens, for instance. And even poets. "Ah? Who?" "Why, one of the greatest: Keats." "Only once!" cries Gide with a defiant gleam in his eye. "When he wrote 'Endymion.'" I was about to reply that, precisely, "Endymion" was a long and exacting labor and this strictly proves what

I wish to say, but feeling that Gide is so strangely, so inexplicably moved, I remain silent.

We reach D.'s house. He receives us in a vast, luxurious studio. Big couches strewn with white furs. On a wall, a wonderful Bokhara, the white ground scattered over with large red flowers. But this is only a sort of boudoir. In the studio proper, no other furniture but a sofa with a glass bowl of white lilacs by it, and that is all. Our host is dressed in dark red velvet. He is studiously affable. A Javanese servant appears, closer to a work of art, think I, than a human being; he wears a lovely gaudy costume and a sort of Highlander's cap and, under his sarong, show exquisitely delicate feet. This awe-inspiring person kneels and offers us cigarettes and candied fruits. I can't help smiling and Gide nudges me like a schoolboy. These refreshments over, we go into the next room to see the film, which we had been told about at great length. Not very well taken, but some of the views are excellent. In particular a scene where boys are seen dancing on the banks of the Indus, which is in spate. The river boils, white as the whitest smoke, and flows at a terrific speed. The tops of the trees rise above the waters. The dancers revolve slowly in a ring, in the meadow.

We leave at last. I dine with Gide at the Brasserie Lutétia. He seems once more very depressed. He tells me that Vaillant-Couturier has forced his hand, that he, Gide, had tried to retract his promise only to be informed that it was too late, that the posters were printed. This meeting is to take place at the (Masonic) Grand Lodge of France. Gide is so upset that he cannot eat. I don't think I ever saw him in such a state. He becomes a little livelier and his gaiety returns when I ask for some information about Tunisia, where Robert and I expect to go. In talking of Tozeur, his eyes light up.

MARCH 30. Those who have never waked up at dawn with the agonizing feeling that life is going by, those will not care for my book. I have attempted by means of hints to express the terror of death. In a book like this one, to allude to sickness and death heightens their prestige, if I may say so. I don't wish to know the exact nature of Amfortas' wound, it is enough for me to know that it killed him, and also, in retaining its anonymity, death seems to me far more imposing than if it appeared under a name borrowed from the medical jargon.

It so happens that by giving things a name, an irreparable blow hits them full in the heart. That, for instance, is what makes pornographic novels so poor; the contents of these books are self-destroying.

My last novel is the most extravagant of all those I have written so far, but if I didn't put this folly into my books, who knows if it wouldn't establish itself in my life? My books are perhaps what have allowed me to preserve a semblance of equilibrium. I was in an excellent mood for working this morning. A sentence that I had thought of, over a year ago, fell quite naturally into place; it had occurred to me one day as I watched the rain from my study window.

APRIL 4. In all my books, fear or any other rather strong emotion seems to be linked in some mysterious manner with a staircase. I noticed this yesterday in going over all the novels I had written. For instance, in *The Pilgrim* the old colonel walking up the stairs corresponds, in the hero's mind, to a sort of mounting fear. In *Avarice House*, Emily passes her father's ghost on the stairs. In *The Closed Garden* the heroine pushes her father down the stairs, where she spends part of the night. In *The Dark Journey*, Mme Grosgeorges, in an agony of distress, goes up and down the staircase. In *The Keys of Death* the hero thinks over the murder he has in mind on the stairs. In *L'Autre sommeil* the hero faints on the stairs. In *The Strange River* is a staircase where Philippe trundles his indecision and spies on his wife. Lastly, in the story I am finishing (*The Dreamer*), a staircase is the scene of a sinister and hysterical fit of laughter. I wonder how I could have repeated this effect so often without noticing it. As a child, I dreamed that I was being pursued in a staircase by someone. My mother had the same fears in her youth; maybe something of this has remained in me. I am sure that in many a novelist the accumulation of *memories beyond memory* is what makes them write. They speak for hundreds of the dead, their dead; in fact, they express everything that their ancestors had kept deep in their hearts, out of prudence or out of decency.

MAY 10. Yesterday I laid aside the novel I was writing (*The Dreamer*), to begin another. I am expecting a great deal from this new novel (*Midnight*), and wrote seventy-three lines by working all day. This is the upheaval I have been thinking of for weeks. I want to perform the impossible and finish this book by September 1st.

So-called love-making is the more often a caricature of happiness. Happiness is far greater, far deeper, and far simpler. And because it is simple, it can neither be described nor analyzed. Happiness cannot be told about and there are times when it swoops down on us, for no apparent reason, in the height of illness, or in a dark room where you are moping, or during a walk through the meadows; you suddenly feel absurdly happy, happy to the point of dying, that is, so happy that you would like to die, so as to prolong this extraordinary minute for ever. I felt this yesterday, in a tearoom on the avenue de l'Opéra, then once as I was reading *Sense and Sensibility,* and very often in my early childhood.

JULY 31. Continued reading *Nicholas Nickleby.* Except for the part about Squeers and Dotheboys Hall, genius appears very seldom in this first volume. The funny characters are not always funny and the gentlemen are awful, like most of Dickens' gentlemen. The author does not yet know how to give a clear idea of the spot where a scene takes place, except in the part mentioned above and where you really have a feeling of the country, of winter, and of solitude. Dickens' taste for cruelty transpires in the episodes at Dotheboys Hall, a cruelty that he toned down only too well for fear of his public.

AUGUST 12. Finished *Nickleby.* Squeers punishing Smike in the carriage is one of the most painful and most powerful scenes that I know of in fiction. The character of Nickleby seemed to me of small interest, and also those dreadful girls and their conventional virtues, but in Squeers is a depth of evil that makes up for the book's little imperfections. What wouldn't Dickens have done, had he dared!

SEPTEMBER 8. I often wonder what can be the meaning of life, if it has one, and above all, to what extent the material world exists. What can the present uneasiness of Europe signify, for instance—Germany's excitement, the anguish of so many men and women to whom the future appears black with threats? Obviously, no one can answer the question, but I often have a fleeting impression of living in a world that does not exist, or that does not exist in the way we imagine. Perhaps the material world merely has the value of a symbol. This idea has been familiar to me since I was fifteen. Thus, the universal uneasiness is perhaps the fictitious representation of your own uneasiness. The "crisis" is first of all in you. The disorder of the world corresponds to an interior disorder that you discover within your own self.

OCTOBER 20. After many a hesitation on my part, it has been decided that we will go to America next month. I resisted as I always resist the idea of traveling. How many times have I fallen ill just before going away! Packing my suitcases creates in me an uneasiness that I cannot understand, but that a Stekel would probably explain perfectly. It is perhaps, hidden under this symbolical form, the terror of dying that acts on me. To be afraid to die is absurd, and I know that very well, but my body does not; that is the reason why it conjures up a thousand difficulties at the proper time, does its best to simulate grippe or, as has been the case recently, more serious illnesses. I remember a doctor's exasperation as he said to me: "If you were really ill, I could cure you! But how do you expect me to operate on your brain?"

OCTOBER 28. Yesterday afternoon, at the height of an anxious state that had lasted ten days, I suddenly felt the indescribable presence of happiness. I went to my room, locked myself in, then returned to the drawing room, walked about the hall, and the house had never seemed pleasanter to me. From the windows that look out on the avenue, I watched the rain. The sky was a delicate gray and the light still strong enough to avoid turning on a lamp. Wandering from room to room, I examined the furniture as though I had never seen it before. This extraordinary state of mind did not last long. What curious stratagems things can invent when they guess that we are about to leave them, and when they attempt to detain us. The drawing room seemed unusually beautiful in the twilight; the furniture shone and glinted like metal, and the big prayer rug looked as though it had been laid on the surface of a lake.

OCTOBER 29. Have suffered a great deal these last days for fear of having, as I thought, contracted a disease. I went to see a doctor who said: "What do you want me to cure you of? There's absolutely nothing the matter with you." And off he sends me, but my imagination has broken loose and I return home in a state of mental distress that shames me. For nearly a week, I went through throes of anguish such as I had never yet experienced. Then, day before yesterday, as I lay on my bed a prey to terrible anxiety, I felt suddenly that there was someone in the room with me. Almost at once an inner voice said to me very gently, but with indescribable authority: "Be at peace. You are not ill." I got up immediately: happy, deeply, unutterably happy.

When I feel as heavy-hearted as I was for the last few days, I can only turn to God. But what does that mean? Who is the God that I believe in? I tried to speak to Him, a little while ago, in my room. Never have I felt surrounded by deeper solitude. Pray? I can no longer pray.

NOVEMBER 2. We went aboard ship yesterday at Le Havre. The boat is shaken by a violent pitching that prevents my writing legibly and upsets almost everybody. For my part, it delights me. The sea is a leaden gray; foam spreads its furbelows around the ship. I read Freud's little book on childhood almost at one sitting. Nearly everything in these astonishing pages should be underscored, but no matter how hard Freud tries to explain everything, the mystery subsists in its entirety. Once he has established that the child is in love with its mother, he has only moved back the limits of the unknown a little further, for I am still asking myself this question: Why? Concerning the essence of our being, Freud, like all theorists, is silent.

I had to wait until I was thirty-two before reading a psychoanalytical book. (Stekel's work on anxiety.)

NOVEMBER 28. NEW YORK. Since my arrival here, I have been living a little like a sleepwalker, surprised and often dazzled by everything. If I had time enough, I would talk at length about what I have seen. I will confine myself today to describing the extraordinary sight I witnessed three days ago. W., who pilots us around, had said: "You must go there tonight. I think something will happen." We went with him to Harlem. After a short walk, he takes us to a small bourgeois flat, its three rooms already crowded with men and women. If I understood aright, anyone can come, provided a dollar is paid. And so, we have a little of everything here, men in tuxedos, others in chamois jackets and corduroy trousers, which are the country's national costume since the depression. There are women here too, some of them rather smart. They have come to *see*; they hope, like everybody else, that *something* will happen, but that can only be after some drinking. So people drink and, from time to time, put down their glass to dance to one of the nostalgic airs poured out by the inexhaustible radio. But soon there is no longer room enough, as newcomers appear every minute. In the center of the smallest room, a gigantic sofa groans under the weight of ten or twelve persons seated cheek by jowl, all studiously serious, glass in hand. A young man in white velvet trousers comes up to our friend W. and speaks to him. Long fair locks straggle across his brow and, when he tries to push them back, fall over his nose. He is so intoxicated that one can scarcely hear what he says and his eyes can't focus. This is his first trip to New York. He comes from the West. The friend who made the trip with him is seated at our feet. He too is the worse for liquor, but a little less so. "I like all this," he says to me. "People smiling. Everything is all right." In the hum of conversation, I hear someone close to me say: "Oh, I get enough money all right, but I can't tell you how." Guffaws of laughter greet this semi-confidence. Another man says that the cost of *living* has gone down a good deal and that you can get rid of someone for less than a hundred dollars. I feel too hot and the cigarette smoke stings my eyes. When I suggest leaving to W., he begs me to stay a little longer. "You'll see," he says, "nothing ever happens till one in the morning. They haven't drunk enough yet."

Around twelve-thirty, something does happen. After a discussion which I unfortunately did not follow, someone dared one of the leather-jacketed boys to undress. How could he refuse? Everyone stared at him with a mocking, incredulous expression. If he hesitates, people will laugh. He is a big boy with a violent temper. He begins taking off his clothes, or rather, tearing them off as though they scorched him. As each garment drops, I imagine he will stop at that, but not at all, he even removes his socks and there he stands, completely naked in a circle of dressed people who look at him silently. After the first moment of amazement, a sarcastic voice asks the boy what he is going to do next. Without hesitating, he walks up to one of the women seated on the sofa; she laughs and pushes him away with the tips of her fingers. A man next her laughs louder, and a blow from the boy's fist immediately sends him sprawling on the carpet. This is the signal for an almost general fight. The women scream and faint.

The furniture is smashed. I see a small chair fly over our heads and crash against a wall. "Marvelous!" cries W. "They're sure to begin shooting." Vain attempts are made to separate the brawlers. The naked fellow is extremely powerful and fights everyone indiscriminately. The one I mentioned above, who was so happy, rolls at my feet with the boy in white trousers. The uproar is such that we can't hear ourselves speak. We go to the kitchen and deliberate. The police will be on the spot in a few minutes. Let's go. What surprises me no less than the rest is that the colored man in the cloakroom hands us our overcoats as calmly as if we were leaving after a concert. And as we drive through Central Park, W. leans over and says to me: "Some evenings, it's even more fun."

DECEMBER I. From my bedroom window, I see Central Park. By night, it is studded with lights and seems like a great glittering river rolling its waters through the darkness. By day, with its network of long footpaths, its rocks jutting from the earth, and the delicate spread of its branchy trees, the park reminds you of a landscape in a primitive picture. Charming gray squirrels come up to you begging for the nuts they conceal in miserly hoards under bushes. It appears that around midnight, less timid beggars rove the paths and hold up rash pedestrians. I have also been told incredible stories of murders. . . .

Yesterday I went as far as Washington Square on top of a bus. Robert was with me. As we passed the Rockefeller building, all its windows ablaze, like a huge block of mica, we could not help exclaiming with surprise and admiration, like provincials. But any European arriving in New York feels a little provincial. In each of us, no matter how knowing, lies a greenhorn.

A little later we went to the Public Library, where illuminations ranging from the ninth to the fifteenth century are on show. A page by Girolamo dei Libri engaged my attention for a long time and I looked fondly at it. Mantegna's manner is perceptible everywhere, in the petrified draperies, in the little pebbles on the sand, in the curly waters of the torrent. I felt as though I had found a shelter in this landscape, yes, a shelter against all that overwhelms me in the monstrous beauty of this city. And as I stood before the wonderful Damascus plums by Jean Bourdichon, my heart beat as though the whole of Europe had been given back to me, Europe with its small houses on a human scale, Europe that we are in fear of losing at any moment, Europe with its museums, its cathedrals, its violent and shady politics, its grandeur and its baseness—how far away it seems and how little understood! I had lunch the other day with some New York writers and journalists. They discussed the international situation in an amazing way. Not that they were misinformed, far from it, they knew too much. But from all the facts stored in their memory, they drew conclusions, strictly logical ones, forgetting or not knowing that the gravest European problems present themselves under a supremely illogical form. There are unfathomable whims of fate, the *quid obscurum* that upset all observers' calculations.

DECEMBER 6. I have decided to go south. That is really why I came. I will go to see my friend Jim at Suffolk and we will return to the University. It has been eleven years since I left it, and I wonder if I will be sad or happy to see it once more. No doubt I did not know how to benefit from all it offered me; I did not quite understand the University, and it did not condescend to explain itself. It was only once I had left that I realized how deeply I loved it and was unknowingly immensely indebted to it. But in 1920 I missed France too much. At twenty, in one of the most beautiful landscapes in the world, without a worry for the future, I contrived every day to think myself unhappy. Ah! if everything had to be lived over again, with the experience that I have acquired since! How many friendships were offered me and discouraged by my lack of sociability!

DECEMBER 12. A little before Richmond, I woke in time to see a field of red earth under a pale blue sky and so many memories swept through my mind that I couldn't even begin talking about them. What makes my trip a little melancholy is that it is like a journey into the past. I remembered my holidays at my grandfather's house, a few hours from here. The house was far more than a country house; with the hills in the distance, the great trees that brushed against its walls, the place was, in my eyes, an ideal dwelling. It was a perfect world, locked within itself, carefully guarding its happiness and its peace, removed from the real world by invisible barriers. In summer, the house had a wealth of silence, of coolness, of shade. How good it was to read novels on an old tumble-down sofa in a library that smelled of old books! Gray, with a red roof, almost completely hidden by big firs, elms, and birches, it bore some resemblance to the country houses described by Russian novelists, or so I liked to think. It was built of wood and burned to the ground in one night, in June, 1922. Since then, I have mentally reconstructed it many a time, putting all the vanished objects where they belonged: in the dining room, a copy of Reynolds' "Winetasters"; on the second-floor landing, the big camphor-wood chest where the sheets were kept; in the drawing room, the backgammon board and the ivory hand used as a back-scratcher for the dog, and in the hall, under the stuffed horned owl, the shillelagh my grandfather had brought back from Ireland.

That stick was simply indescribable. One could give an idea of it by saying it looked like a gigantic corkscrew that powerful hands had twisted one way and stretched the other. I think this was the stick my grandfather asked for when, at the point of death, he got up saying he was going for a walk, he was going to Heaven.

There was fighting several times around the house during the Civil War. Bullets grazed the walls. Why didn't I note the stories my father used to tell me! When Virginia was invaded, my grandfather was arrested for helping the Confederates. He was imprisoned at Fort Warren and stayed there a few months. He would most likely have been shot if he hadn't been English. He owned no slaves except a sufficient number to do the cooking and housework and treated them better than a European treats his servants. I doubt for instance whether he would have allowed one of his colored men to sleep in winter in an icy room, such as those existing in almost all Parisian apartment houses, where nothing has been foreseen for the comfort of our servants. Owning slaves was a burden that is difficult to imagine nowadays. As they had no responsibilities, they had to be cared for continually, watched over when they were sick, their children brought up, and you had a whole black family on your hands, with its exactions, its whinings, its domestic feuds. So the abolition of slavery was greeted in the South with the same relief by whites and blacks, for in putting an end to an institution the very principle of which was intolerable, it rid slave-owners of a nightmare.

DECEMBER 14. At the University. She is the same as ever, cordial with that shade of disdain that gives her so much charm. Her vast lawns bordered by Greek Revival columns reflect a peaceful soul, perfectly satisfied with herself. You call on her, a hand is extended with a smile. If you turn away from her, if the whole of America forsook her at the foot of her hills, she would none the less pursue her quiet dream, adorned with classical literature, white frontages, black foliage. From North to South, what could there be for her to envy? Isn't she Mr. Jefferson's daughter?

I met almost all my old professors. The way they received me touched me far more than they could imagine. I believe almost all of them called me by my Christian name, which made me blush with pleasure!

Dr. Faulkner talked to me about the Negro question. He said, and I have always felt as he does on this point, that colored people are looked down on only in the North by whites. And he told me the following story. Four or five men are reading the papers in the lobby of a big hotel in Philadelphia or Boston. In comes a colored traveler who settles down not far from them and also opens his newspaper. After a look at him, all the whites leave the lobby, except one who gets up, goes to the Negro, and asks him where he comes from. "From Virginia." "So do I," says the white man. And they shake hands. What astonished me most is that the memory of the Civil War should still be so vivid.

1934

JANUARY 12. In Savannah. How strange it seems to be here! Last night, I was a long time getting to sleep. I lay in a gigantic bed, almost as big as the fabulous bed of Ware of which Shakespeare speaks. In the semi-darkness I could see the stout oak columns rise to the ceiling and mentally went over what my mother told me about her native town. In this great bed, my mother was born.

Yesterday, I went to see some friends of my family at Wormsloe, quite near here. Wormsloe is an old house hidden in the heart of a dusky park. It is protected by ghostly oaks; these giant trees are covered with Spanish moss that hangs in gray tatters continually stirred by the breeze, and nothing can be stranger than the light that filters through this sort of airy, funereal fabric. The house was built around 1780. Its name would have delighted Poe, its name and all the shadow that moves through the low-ceilinged, silent rooms. Noticed several fine Italian mantelpieces, mutilated by Sherman's soldiers as they passed this way.

Yesterday I showed Robert the house that my grandfather built shortly before the Civil War. To be accurate, it was finished on the day when General Beauregard shelled Fort Sumter, April 12, 1861. It is a vast Tudor house painted a tawny yellow. Sycamores border one side of it, and banana trees half conceal the Gothic porch. The effect is weird. To my mind, the house is both hideous and magnificent. It is one of those things where violent ugliness reaches peculiar beauty, and I think that Christian Bérard would faint with pleasure on seeing the semi-Gothic, semi-Louis XV drawing rooms! The room I prefer is the dark, warm library with its ogival mantelpiece with a blazing log fire, its portraits of Lee and Stonewall Jackson, its plaster busts, its pictures (all a trifle askew), its books in worn bindings. The Gothic moldings are disintegrating, the paint is scaling, and the whole thing remains splendid in a manner that seems peculiar to the Southern states. On the second floor, the room where Sherman slept. It was there, no doubt, that he wrote President Lincoln on December 24, 1864, to offer him Savannah as a Christmas present. It is not true that my grandfather offered the Northern general his house. Sherman exacted it because it was the finest (according to the taste of the period) and the roomiest in Savannah.

After supper, a long conversation with my Aunt Catherine. She talked to me about my maternal grandfather. He was a member of the Confederate Government and a price was put on his head by the Federal Government in 1865, which did not prevent him from dying a Congressman in 1879, aged forty-seven. He had a taste for parties, political activities, and eloquence. His wife is what is called a character in a novel. She spent most of her time in bed reading, believed herself to be ailing, and devoured a book a day.

JANUARY 13. Crossed the Savannah River. An immense river divided into five branches by islands. Its waters are clay red and reflect nothing. Its northern bank marks the boundary of South Carolina. I walked under big oaks draped in moss with its long, restless fringes. Impossible to describe the effect of poverty and magnificence produced by this parasitic vegetation. There is something disturbing about the very quality of its luxuriance. Its color hesitates between pale gray and a dull greenish white; it is both theatrical and sinister, lending a haunting melancholy to Southern landscapes. Seen from a distance, it reminds one of a head of hair. It comes from Barbados, a name that precisely describes its strange aspect. We call it Spanish moss.

Visited the ruins of Sheldon Church. An eighteenth-century church destroyed by fire in 1861. What still stands are the four walls and the brick columns of the porch. A great wood has to be crossed in order to reach it, you pass under giant oaks and there it stands, in a solitude where the only sound comes from a bird as it bursts into a sort of laughter. There stands a tree whose monstrous branches spread about ten yards from the trunk and sweep the yellowing brushwood with their gray fringes. I stood there for a few minutes, listening to the mocking, funereal chattering that came from a treetop. The sun shone at my feet. Never, beyond a doubt, have I ever been in a spot where I more keenly felt that we are nothing, that nature does not even see us. A vague, deep fear seized me suddenly and I ran away.

At the Tomotly plantation, I walked down an interminable avenue of oaks. Always those same long, torn curtains fluttering in the wind. Stout black branches writhe like great snakes inside this gray horror. These trees often give me such an unpleasant feeling that I am filled with a sort of anguish, and yet they attract me, for they seem to give the most beautiful picture imaginable of death. On this plantation, as far as the eye can reach, I see nothing but these huge black trunks raising to the skies arms laden with rags. You feel that by lingering in their shade, all things would become indifferent and that death would be easy. They are like so many old wizards watching over the soil of the South.

Returned to Savannah at sunset. The long avenues and squares seemed bathed in blood-red light. As I walked by the old pink and brown brick houses, I wondered how much and to what extent this town was part of me. I have lived here a lot in memory, but this is impossible to write about. A moment ago, I was obliged to ask my way. I comforted myself for this humiliation by remembering that even in Paris, and in my own quarter, I managed to get lost.

JANUARY 14. In the house where my mother spent her youth, I sat down to look around me and to pretend not to be just a visitor. I am alone. From the window, I can see a pretty Colonial house where Thackeray stayed when he came to Savannah and where he wrote a few pages of *The Virginians*. On the other side of the big shady square, the soft voice of a colored woman selling fruit. Great silence in the house, where everything shines: the tilted mirrors, the dark wood furniture, the black flooring. Yet, thirty minutes away stand those pink columns in the solitude of the woods, and those trees, like vestiges of prehistoric times filled with dread, and at the top of the tallest tree, a bird from the virgin forest laughing ominously in the sun. I don't know why I think of this, seated by the innocent piano that played dances for girls in hoop skirts. But it seems to me that in the South, a barbarous and menacing nature marches almost to the threshold of these frail white-columned houses. It is all around us, with its buzzards and its snakes and its nightmarish vegetation. And a melancholy that seems to spring from the beginning of time.

Yet my mother came from Savannah and she was gay. She was a small woman, witty and good, whose footfall, voice, and peals of laughter will be with me always.

JANUARY 28. Back in Savannah, this time under an assumed name, in order to be free. I counted up that I am related to almost two hundred people in this town. Dark glasses protect me pretty well in the daytime. Yesterday, however, I found myself face to face with one of my cousins at a street corner. I guessed from his expression that he thought I bore a striking likeness to myself, but without turning a hair I went on my way like a somnambulist.

FEBRUARY 4. The other day, to Cypress Swamp, one of the strangest places in the world. Imagine a large wood of gigantic cypresses tall and straight as the pillars of a cathedral and standing in ink-black water. On the borders of the pond, flowering bushes with a heady scent. We rented a boat to go at random through the trees. When we reached the heart of the wood, and the banks were out of sight, I had the feeling of plunging into an immemorial past. In this prehistoric setting, the silence itself seemed filled with secret horror. Here, no bird sings. Their calls could be heard in the distance. I was glad for a fine day, for the sun to shine on my hands, and in spite of the light that pierced the black foliage, I felt very much aware that we were in one of those hidden spots for which death has a special liking.

On the banks grow crocuses and prodigious masses of pink and white camellias.

As we returned, I repeated to myself two lines of Poe's that kept their hold on me for the rest of the day:

> It was down by the dank tarn of Auber,
> In the ghoul-haunted woodland of Weir.

FEBRUARY 8. NEW YORK. The news from Paris has saddened me so much that I haven't had the heart to keep this diary. Hour by hour, during the whole of yesterday, I followed the movement of the riots, listening to detailed and I am sure very often most inaccurate reports in the local newspapers. We are leaving day after tomorrow.

FEBRUARY 13. This morning, I sat in the stern of the ship and looked at the gray sea, the white furrows we left behind us, the bridge glazed with spray and rain. It made me think of such vague, faraway things that I cannot describe them. By looking a long time at certain landscapes, I can sometimes conjure up from the depths of my memory certain recollections without my knowing where they come from. I have always had the power of doing this. It enchanted my childhood. Something of it, but very little, has passed into my books. These are memories beyond real memories, beyond those that can be located, dated, but how can anything so secret be expressed? The more one speaks of it, the greater the mystery. Lately, I mentally listed all the places I have known where these memories awaken. For instance, the charming, neglected garden behind Saint-Julien-le-Pauvre, or the room in the museum at Brussels where one has a view of gray and black roofs. I have never mentioned this to anyone. When I was a child, I used to listen to my sister as she played pieces by Schumann for me, and there was one whose title I liked almost as much as the music: "Distant Lands." Later, I invented a sort of geography of these distant lands. The East did not figure in it, but Edinburgh, Antwerp, and Friesland had a place of honor. Quite recently, looking at a map of the United States, my eyes fastened on Cascade Range, and for a few seconds I once more felt that bygone emotion, the absurd, delightful longing for distant lands. It would be hard to believe if I told what an influence this childish idea had over a whole part of my youth. What is certain is that the habit of situating happiness in distant lands ruled me up to my sixteenth year, or thereabouts. I could not extricate myself from my childhood; real life inspired me with deep distrust and I liked the world only when it fitted in with my extravagant conceptions. Such and such an air of music charmed me because it substituted for the real world—where I could not manage to find a place—an infinitely more real world where I strongly felt that I would be happy. And behind all the ideas that I have forged of death is this one, a remnant of childhood, that, in a word, death is the most beautiful of distant lands.

Finished Woodward's *Life of Washington*. The humorous tone of the book spoils it for me a little, but for all that, it is the work of a man who searched for the truth behind the silly legends that have cloaked the historical character. His Washington appears as a man who was both empty and necessary, great on account of the place he occupied. For it seems as though fate sometimes chooses the most colorless men to assign them the most difficult task. The interesting man, the one whom fate should obviously have selected, was Jefferson. But the fat, heavy, pompous boy called Washington was chosen in preference to any other.

FEBRUARY 27. PARIS. "There will always be a France to love," said Renan. I am afraid that the France I love will end by disappearing. Each day seems to carry away a little of her. In the present commotion, an indefinable world is being born where I can't find my place. A general sadness. I hear of nothing but people who are frightened and want to leave the country.

MARCH 2. A long conversation with a Catholic writer who wants me to see Father Altermann. I refuse. I refuse gently, but refuse. We had been talking about the devil, whose presence I have felt several times since 1923. The writer in question stared and murmured: "But that is nevertheless a grace." A very strange grace indeed. He added rather sensibly: "But where the devil is present, Christ is also there." I thought over this conversation deeply. At the bottom of my heart, faith still remains.

MARCH 14. Anguish. Whoever has not suffered from it could not judge me. On leaving my publisher, where I had been to autograph copies of my book, I was suddenly seized with anguish. As I walked down the rue Garancière, it occurred to me to go to Saint-Sulpice, and there, in this church, I went and hid in the darkest spot, in front of the Lady chapel. I thought as I knelt: "I have not come to make promises that I could not keep. There are things that I cannot give up. I simply want to receive *strength*. Heaven cannot refuse such a legitimate grace to any human being." I said my prayers as best I could and left.

MARCH 24. This morning at Passy, the thought came to me suddenly of all that is inexpressible in what we attempt to say, pen in hand. And this, to such a point that writing, for me, is no more than alluding to what one cannot express—because the words are lacking. . . . Try as we may, something always escapes us. The human tongue does not exceed certain limits.

MAY 2. Went to an exhibition of the Lord's Passion in French art. I was struck with respect and admiration for the stained-glass windows, although I know them so well. I remembered my bygone fervor, my great longing for a pure and Christian life. Have I gained much by rejecting all this? On the human plane, I have developed no doubt, but what of the spiritual? Compared with a saint, what am I worth? Very much moved by the great painted wood Christs from the Sainte-Chapelle. Pondering over all this a little later, I thought that our civilization is stranger than we realize. To see, from childhood to the day of one's death, representations of tortures in churches, in houses, and sometimes in streets, isn't that a really singular fact? A man nailed to two pieces of wood, that is what Christianity shows us at every turn. The Church was born in tortures. A fourth-century Greek child never saw anything in temples but statues of ideally beautiful and happy men and women, but we are offered images of a dying man. If a man who knew nothing of Christianity were taken to the Louvre, he might perhaps leave it, sick with disgust.

MAY 17. Gide looks sad and even a little scandalized on hearing that L., the writer, belongs to the Rightist association of the Croix de Feu. I tell him that for my part, I would never line up with any party because politics disgusts me and also because I know nothing about it. "Neither do I," says he. "I can't make head or tail of it. But if you don't choose, you end by being adopted by one or the other political party." And he talks of an anti-fascist league, among which figure Rivet and other scholars. He reads me a few pages of Kafka's *Trial*, which I don't know, and tells me the book seems most particularly designed for me, even more so than for him. He reads well, but in a theatrical manner, bringing out certain words with excessive emphasis. He tells me that Jouvet insists on my writing a play for him, a fact I very well know. We talk of the training necessary for writing for the stage, always a long process. According to Gide, a master stroke at the very start, so frequent in writing novels, is almost unknown in writing for the stage. As we part, leaning over the banister (I had been to see him), he talks about my drawing room, where he had waited for me day before yesterday, and sees in it a reflection of my personality: "It is an elusive one," he says with a smile and a nod, "and at the same time, a very intense one. Yes, that blue sofa and those red chairs . . ."

MAY 18. Gide was telling me yesterday that he used to know the Uffizi very well. "I was even quite a dab at it," he says, smiling. "But now, this is no longer of interest to me . . ."

MAY 26. How can the world's beauty be expressed? Some days, it crushes me like a tremendous burden. It delights me under every one of its aspects. I used to feel this so keenly that death appeared to me (this is horrible to say) like a sort of liberation from joy, just as sickness, according to Michelet, is convalescence in the opposite direction, and death a sort of recovery from life.

JUNE 1. A lecture by Doctor Jung on the collective unconscious. Doctor Jung is a tall, ruddy-faced old man with a white mustache. He wears a dress suit and talks quietly about amazing things. According to him, we carry within us, in the deepest part of our unconscious self, certain ideas that are a remote heritage common to all races of humanity. Some of the sick people he looks after, on being asked to make sketches, have reproduced, unknowingly, extremely ancient symbolical signs that are familiar only to Orientalists. For instance, *mandalas*, or magic circles ornamented with crosses and snakes. Slides enable us to understand exactly what he means. Certain Tibetan or Hindu drawings correspond to sketches by children aged between seven and twelve.

Cassou and Jaloux were at the lecture. All three of us left together to gossip until 1 P.M. in a café on the place Péreire. They believe that *constants* exist in the human brain that would partly explain these strange drawings. Certain ideas, certain emotions always express themselves in the same manner. However, they make no attempt to explain, through reasoning, certain almost incomprehensible coincidences. For my part, I wonder if these mysterious signs are not an unconscious memory of an antediluvian handwriting. We inherit so many things from our parents and our great-grandparents. Why shouldn't this inheritance go very far back into the past, to the origins of humanity? We are steeped in memories.

UNDATED. . . . The children in my books—there are two or three of them—open their lips only with extreme discretion, and scarcely move, for the simple reason that the man who created them does not feel capable of making them talk, or even act, in a plausible fashion. Why is this? I don't know. I have always had the feeling that the "under sixteen" among my characters make fun of me. They bother me. I feel them watching me. They hope I'm going to make a mistake. It's a pleasure to send them packing. In *The Dark Journey* is a small boy that I chased from the book with a slap in the face.

Yet I am fond of children. I love my childhood and that of others, and I believe that I wouldn't be able to write another line if I lost the memory of my early years. How many of us who think themselves freed for ever of the terrors, hopes, and joys of their tenth year, live until their death on this hidden capital! The child dictates and the man writes.

JUNE 14. In my room, at the far end of the flat, I read the beginning of the Gospel according to St. John in the English version. I read it in a whisper. At the twelfth verse, I was blinded by tears. An extraordinary, unaccountable emotion seized me. I did not feel like kneeling. On the contrary, I got up, I tried to blot out inside me the image of the outer world. I think that in the depth of our being, at the very bottom of our heart, is a spring ready to gush forth. The Son of Man comes and sits by this spring and talks to our soul, the Samaritan woman. I have felt this keenly, at different times, for the last few years. Ah! may nothing ever destroy a love for the divine within us! This is what should survive all religions, whose forms are so often vain. To go through this life trying to establish a balance between body and soul is not enough.

AUGUST 4. I was tearing morning-glories out of a flower bed

when I was handed a letter from Gide about *The Dreamer*. It gave me such pleasure that, having read it once at a gulp, I went to a shady walk to read it over again quietly. Added to his letter was a very detailed list of the mistakes he had noted in the course of reading the book: three in all.

SEPTEMBER 2. The other evening as I went to sleep, I said the prayer that Father Crété had taught me when I was fifteen, when a single impure thought had never yet entered my head: "*Jesu, mitis et humilis corde, fac cor meum sicut cor tuum!*" Never perhaps did I say that prayer with more faith than I did last night. But what is the good? In me is a great desire to change and, I can say so, strange as it may seem, a real love of Christ. However, I don't see how I will be able to undertake the struggle against temptations, since it all comes down to that.

SEPTEMBER 13. In thinking over my life, I see that it has been a rather singular one, although nothing of this shows from the outside. I was very near to renouncing the world in 1918. I hesitated and stayed where I was. I believe I was right. I lost a great deal on the spiritual plane, but I think that a balance will be established someday. I am convinced that few men of my age are tempted as I am. This has already harmed me. I have allowed myself to be beguiled by the created world, but in me are elements of resistance. . . . I was brought to thinking all this by reading several books on Hindu philosophy.

OCTOBER 30. Just a moment ago, we were in my study, having coffee and listening to one of Beethoven's quartets (the third of Opus 59). I was glancing through Father Bruno's book on St. John of the Cross, when I came across these lines, which were already familiar to me:

> *¿A donde te escondiste, Amado,*
> *Y me dejaste con gemido?*
> *Como el ciervo huiste,*
> *Habiéndome herido . . .*

I felt deeply moved, as though a powerful voice called to me in the stillness. For the space of a second, I had an intuition of what a mystical life can be, and what can also be, *seen from the other side*, the life that we lead in the world.

*   *   *

NOVEMBER 6. How can reading the Gospels be reconciled with a life where pleasure nevertheless plays a part? This does not seem to me possible. There are days when I can't open the New Testament without feeling a hypocrite, but should one, from hatred of hypocrisy, suppress all spiritual reading if one can't suppress pleasure, and can one go from one to the other without loathing oneself?

NOVEMBER 25. Reading the *Fioretti* makes me forget the present world and the dark future. I too have experienced the joy known to Brother Masseo, Brother Giles, and the other companions of St. Francis. No doubt this lasted but a few minutes in the whole of my life, but I know what it is, I have had those fervent moments when the world vanishes into mist, I have been in love with Heaven. A vague memory of it returns to me at times, but it is enough to make me happy. No doubt I had a calling.

At the Orangerie. A show of seventeenth-century painters. Dumesnil de la Tour. A marvelous artist, but his candle must not be taken away from him, or the reddish lighting that lends mystery to his painting. His "Nativity" is very beautiful. The Child is more touching than any Infant Jesus in the whole of Italian painting and more *real*. This is where France triumphs, she clings to the truth.

NOVEMBER 28. At the Orangerie. Dumesnil de la Tour delights me. He understood the magic of truth. Nothing seemed to him commonplace. To light a candle in the midst of four peasants was enough for him to enter an enchanted world, but an enchanted world where, by a miracle, truth remains truth.

DECEMBER 4. Yesterday, Raïssa Maritain was telling us what a short time had elapsed since the foundation of Christianity. What are two thousand years in the eyes of God? Scarcely an hour, perhaps. And she added that the coming of Christ was such a momentous event that its consequences are not yet apparent to us. I agree with her there. The Gospels are full of obscure sayings, and what we understand of these books, what we understand with our whole heart, can probably be reduced to a few verses. But I also think that the supposedly eternal churches will have to disappear and be forgotten before all the sayings of Christ find their accomplishment. . . .

❈　❈　❈

UNDATED. Lately, Maritain, speaking of the Concordat between the Vatican and Germany, quotes Pius XI as saying: "If I had to, for the welfare of souls, I would make a covenant with the devil. . . ." As we were talking of "The Night of the Senses" by St. John of the Cross, I thought I saw an immense wall, such as was never built by man; it was perfectly white and rose into a black sky, where it was lost among the stars. This image engrossed me for some time without my finding it possible to divert my attention from it.

DECEMBER 12. Maybe I shouldn't breathe a word about the most beautiful, the most mysterious dream I ever had. I dream it once or twice a year. Suddenly, I see myself on a road that skirts the top of a cliff and I know that the dream is beginning and with it, a feeling of happiness such that human speech cannot give the faintest idea of it. Farther on, there will be a big iron gate, so difficult to turn on its hinges, then the long avenue of trees, then once again the cliff and I pause to look at the sea, but instead of the water I see an immense forest that stretches to the horizon and covers the whole countryside, and at that moment I feel as happy as someone who has passed beyond death. Is that all? It is.

1935

FEBRUARY 4. Read over the pages of this diary from 1928 to 1935. I think that the notebook I am finishing at present will show the signs of an inner change in me, although the circumstances of my outer life remain the same. There are, however, rather long periods of calm (how can this be expressed otherwise? The fever, the agitation sometimes drop) and then what is most serious in me strives for the upper hand. In such moments, these gray notebooks run a certain danger, but I think I would make a great mistake in destroying them, for they describe an experience of life that many people have not had.

FEBRUARY 16. At times I envy, and basely envy, people who can be converted, who throw themselves at the feet of a priest to get rid of everything that troubles them and makes them suffer. For me, this is impossible. To be quits of everything one has done, because one has confessed everything—no . . . Happy is the man who, without violence and without a struggle, manages to lull his desires and go higher.

FEBRUARY 28. I wrote forty lines this morning. . . . Last night, I wondered why I shouldn't portray my characters naked. Yes, that is how I would like to show them, in all their physical truth. As a rule, characters in a novel are reduced to a bust. They talk and wave their arms, but the lower part of their body, except in pornographic novels, is chastely concealed from the reader's curiosity. Yet the body speaks the truth just as much as the face, it has its own particular expression, it is humble, brave, contemptuous, cocky, joyful, pensive; courage can be read in the outline of the shoulders and of the breast, etc. This should be developed.

MARCH 15. These days are so overpoweringly mild that they prevent me from wanting to note the small things that make up my life. This is spring with its neurotic sky, its languor, its foretaste of death. Yet, I worked. There are one or two sentences in my book (*Midnight*) that made me laugh to myself, but I have such a reputation for melancholy that probably no one will notice that I am also fond of gaiety. And after all, maybe these sentences are not amusing.

MARCH 17. Yesterday, very near the Ides of March, Germany told the whole world that she was rearming. This must have been going on for years, or she would not have announced it so openly. So the Versailles Treaty is in shreds.

I don't very well see how peace can last. . . . It is not that I fear death. For the last few months, death has lost many of its terrors as far as I am concerned, but there is so much left for us to do and learn.

MARCH 20. I don't think I shall ever forget these days of anguish. There is an enormous commotion in the world, the repercussions of which make us all suffer. All I can hope for is that the storm will blow over. I dare not even say what I fear. England has just forwarded Germany the weakest of replies. Everything concurs to make Hitler certain that the whole of Europe is afraid of him.

The other day, in one of those moments of anguish that I cannot tell anyone about, I suddenly had an instant of overwhelming joy, a joy mingled with terror, because I did not understand its reason.

APRIL 14. ROME.   At St. Peter's for the Palm Sunday celebrations. The clergy walks through the whole length of the basilica in a cloud of incense. Two choirs answer each other, one with the procession, the other from a gallery near the high altar. An admirable effect. The procession re-enters the nave after having gone around the portico. Suddenly, the choir takes up its chant from the gallery, as though moved by an unexpected inspiration and not according to ceremonial rites. In all this, I cannot help seeing a recollection of the Temple, for the Church is the memory of humanity. I don't mean to say that St. Peter's is a reminiscence of the gold and white building with which Herod the Great crowned Jerusalem, but the *effect produced* must have been the same.

APRIL 17.   At St. John Lateran. The hymns moved me so much that I knelt with everybody else. Yet, an hour earlier, I was thinking of very different things. . . . I note this more in sadness than with irony. In church, I regarded myself as an awful hypocrite, but I had gone there to look at the gilt ceiling and the large mosaics, and the liturgy moved me.

APRIL 30.   This morning, at four, I woke in a state of most painful anguish. I got up, went to the window, and leaned out. It was drizzling. The sky was a fine pale gray, and beneath me the tiled roofs formed a great confused mass of darkish pink. The birds sang in the Pincio gardens. There was such happiness in the air that I could not resist being infected by it for long. My sadness suddenly abated. I had the feeling that the day was dawning within me. These abrupt transitions from melancholy to joy are one of the traits of my character that intrigue me most, and the one that I put up with least easily. I would have liked to be more stable and, yes, more serious. I have moments of ridiculous frivolity, I mean that my sadness is often as frivolous as my joy.

MAY 10.   Yesterday and the day before, I spent a long time in the Roman Forum and the Forum of Augustus. I found more beauty there than anywhere else in this town. These temples, torn to pieces, not by time, but by men, are a model of eternal perfection. No matter how small the fragment of a Roman work, it bears within it a world that to me seems unlimited. I mean that it contains art in almost its entirety where what is essential in art is concerned. After it will be nothing but repetitions, brilliant repetitions, no doubt, but also what a lot of trash! I sat before the bas-relief of the *Suovetaurilia,* where one sees a porker decked with fillets, more ferocious and more formidable than a battleship, a ram, then a bull laden with all the majesty of Rome. Lizards ran about in the sun at my feet. Raising my eyes, I could see the Arch of Septimius Severus and, toward the left, the Rostral column. How much more religious than St. Peter did this stricken landscape appear to me!

MAY 16. Just now, as I was filing some notes, I began to laugh. "What are you laughing about?" asks Robert. "I am thinking of Gide's rhinoceros." I had been to see Gide, a few years ago, on his return from Africa. Curtius was there. Gide talks to us a little about his journey, but briefly, and judging it would amuse us more than accounts and descriptions, he showed us a magnificent insect preserved in a small glass jar. We admire the big black scarab, whose head is provided with a horn, and this leads me to say that it looks like a rhinoceros. "It is not a rhinoceros," says Gide, "it is a . . ." (Here a Greek name that I have forgotten.) "I can see that it isn't, of course," I reply, "but don't you think that horn gives it a family resemblance to a rhinoceros?" Gide and Curtius look at each other. "My dear friend," says Gide, with a shade of surprise in his voice, "I assure you that it is not a rhinoceros." Curtius adds: "No doubt whatever on that score." "Naturally. I wouldn't dream of contradicting you." And I am silent, but think that if Gide were not born in France, he should have been born in Scotland, where every word is taken literally. Does he really imagine that I thought I had seen a rhinoceros under my very eyes, a rhinoceros in a glass container?

Months went by after this astonishing conversation, and someone informed me one day that there is a type of giant scarab called a rhinoceros. I felt relieved.

JULY 10. PARIS. Yesterday, a visit to Gide. I don't know how it was that we talked about our way of living when we travel and how impossible it is for us both to watch over our expenses and to keep accounts.

We go out and he talks of this and that. He tells me that what strikes him most in my books is that the pencil never leaves the paper, that the line is unbroken to the end, and that if he ever writes anything about me, he will stress this particular point. He also says that all that is true in my novels is true in spite of an appreciable disagreement with the reality of daily life. He adds that I have reached a turning point, that my real career will begin on the day when my public will desert me, when my books will be found too much unlike the naturalistic models that the public demands. "The public," he says, "wants novels that resemble those it knows." He further adds that I am not to flinch when the time comes, but to let myself go to my inspiration, to my real temperament—that of a visionary writer. In this regard, he resumes talking about himself and says that at bottom he has never found his real public. "What writer ever really finds his public?" I then ask. "Why, almost all of them. Look at Bourget!" I reply: "Let us talk of great writers. Didn't Charles Dickens appeal to a number of readers to whom he should not have appealed? His real public is being found at present." He agrees with me there and talks of the books he might have written and regrets not having written. "If seventeenth-century writers could have foreseen that they would still be read three hundred years later, they would have written quite differently. One can imagine their returning to this world and saying: 'If we had only known! . . .' For one feels that they could have done better and did not dare to." One can't help thinking of the preface to *The Loves of Psyche and Cupid:* ". . . No matter how little of an assurance a writer can have of talking to posterity," writes La Fontaine, "he should always have this object in mind and try to order matters for its use." I ask Gide what the books he did not write would have been like. "Oh," he says pensively, "works of imagination, novels . . ."

A little later, he tells me that so far I have had an exceptional place in literature, thanks to the element of unreality that is found in my books, "but," he says, "someday you will have to give up this position and take sides." (He is thinking of the great political conflicts that will probably split this country.) "Clashes between the Rightists and the Leftists are almost inevitable. Then you won't be able to confine yourself to literature. You will be forced to choose." "To choose?" I ask. "Choose between Communism and Fascism? And if I don't feel drawn to either party, what am I to do?" Gide shakes his head. "You will have to choose," he repeats firmly. (This from the author of *Les Nourritures terrestres!*) I ask him if he feels free, since his conversion to Communism. (He had said a little earlier that he had become "a representative person," with a slightly mocking laugh to show that he didn't take himself seriously.) He answers no and quotes what Barrès said when asked what irked him most in his parliamentary career: "To vote with my party!" We part soon after this. He asks me to think over the trip to America that we are planning.

JULY 13. Gide was telling me the other day that he did not know how to give an idea of the plots of his books, that he had never known how, and that he believed that people who can give a skillful account of such things are *worthless when they sit down before a sheet of paper.* (This because I had told him of sometimes feeling like acquainting someone with the subject of a novel I am writing and that, at the last moment, I had always changed my mind, for fear of not being able to do it creditably.) He added that when he narrates something, he is always afraid of not holding his audience's interest to the end. If, for instance, he is interrupted in the middle of a story, no one ever asks: "And what comes next?" when the interruption has ceased. He further says that in his books, the end is often unduly abridged; he wonders if this is not a "residue of his youth," the fear of not being listened to until the end.

SEPTEMBER 4. It has been a little over a year since I began to study Buddhism. Has this changed anything in me? Yes, I think so. What terrorized me formerly no longer touches me. I face the idea of death without a tremor, whereas the idea of dying used to be so painful to me that I dared not turn my thoughts in that direction.

SEPTEMBER 19. Once more those inner difficulties that I find so strange. I sometimes have the feeling of being a sleeper eager to wake who dreams of the day when he will be set free. There are moments when I imagine a voice calls me and the sweetness of its call makes me forget all that worries me in this world. What is best in us, in me, is love. Yesterday, in deep inner loneliness, I whispered: "If there is anyone close by who can help me, let him stretch out his hand to me!" But the voice must be obeyed when it orders you to listen. Often, in the midst of reading a book, one hears it with a beating heart, but out of laziness, or for fear of upsetting the whole of life, one waits like a coward for it to hush. That is what happens to me.

SEPTEMBER 24.   A few minutes of deep joy lately at the thought that my liberation depended above all on myself and not on exterior circumstances. "Where lies the kingdom of God?" "Within you." (Ah! why don't we go there right away!) "Where lies Nirvana?" "Where the precepts are observed." So we are there, if we wish it.

Have read the *Gospel of Sri Ramakrishna*. It contains wonderful passages about the personal God and the impersonal God. How much more important this seems to me than the Anglo-Italian controversy!

The Police Department distributes booklets in apartment houses. So thus we know what precautions are to be taken in case of air raids (gas masks, shelters, don't get excited, everything is mentioned). I wonder when and how we will emerge from this hideous period.

OCTOBER 28.   All five of us were seated around the dining-room table. A log fire burned in the hearth and it was so dark that we had to turn on the lights although it was not yet two in the afternoon. There were five of us and we laughed and suddenly I felt that we were far more numerous, that our gaiety had attracted all the missing ones, my father, my mother, and the two sisters I have lost; they sat by us and kept us company until the end of the meal, laughing with us all. I had an impression of great happiness, an impression of deep security, but dared not breathe a word of it.

DECEMBER 20.   For the last few years, I have detached myself from many things. I sometimes feel like a man in a small boat. The boat moves away from shore. I have a clear view of the earth and its flowers, its houses, all that it has to offer me that is beautiful and good, but from time to time a powerful stroke of the oar removes me a little farther from it all. I then have a slight feeling of anguish followed by one of deep security.

The other day, as I listened to music, I had the delightful sensation of the proximity of another world. Behind the impalpable veil, there it is, the world of truth, that kingdom of God that intrigued me so much as a child.

On thinking about my life, I see very little progress. Yet there is a great desire in me to know the truth, but this means setting out on an adventure that requires lots of courage. If ever I get to know this truth, I will share it with those I love. The day will come when we will be ready. Then I will tell what I have learned and we will be far happier. We will know at last, all of us, that death does not exist and we will be together for ever. . . .

1936

FEBRUARY 5. How am I to change my life? From the inside. It is useless to burn books and manuscripts. Detachment is not thus obtained; a new heart is what must be asked for, and the rest is easily accomplished. I am always surprised and a little frightened to see people who imagine that they possess fine pictures, rare furniture, valuable books, whereas, it is just the opposite, I mean that all these objects are the masters of those who believe they own them. How many people might say: "I belong to a bronze by Pollaiuolo, to a couple of large sixteenth-century chests, to a sketch painted by Delacroix . . . etc." And the richer one is, the more tyrannical and numerous are these masters.

UNDATED. After an interruption of more than twelve years, I have gone back to the study of Hebrew. I had begun it at the University. A Polish Jew named Drabkin and I translated the beginning of the *Bereshith*, but I was too lazy to go on with it. What is more, everything touching the Jewish race gave me a feeling of inexplicable uneasiness. I had no hostility toward Jews, but our ground of mutual understanding was very limited and I saw very well that they did not think as we did. Scarcely anyone at the University spoke to Drabkin, aside from his coreligionists. This was the very reason why I tried to be friendly with him, in order to repair or at least lessen what I considered an injustice. But most surprising of all: Drabkin did not suffer at all from the ostracism to which he was subjected. I even wonder if he was aware of it. He laughed gaily over everything. He could neither be saddened nor offended. His ears stuck out on either side of a cap jammed down to the nape of his neck and he was completely lacking in elegance. I was fully aware of his ugliness, his barbarous accent, his contemptuous ignorance of our history, but envied him his knowledge of Hebrew. . . .

APRIL 5. At Ober-Lech, in the Arlberg. The hotel is isolated on a plateau surrounded by mountains. The snow has partly melted, but great patches of it remain. At the right, a wood of fir trees where I sit and read. I like these trees. From the window of my room, I look so long at them sometimes that they assume an indescribable aspect. A child would understand me. It is not that they change their shape or color, but they become different. In the morning, they rise from the valley of the Lech to the vicinity of the hotel, and at night they go down again, like a procession of pilgrims in their black capes. They do not move, but how clearly I can see them marching, swathed in mist! On and on they come, so numerous that some still remain in the darkness.

MAY 9. PARIS. Last Thursday, my first Hebrew lesson with M. Moses V., who had been recommended to me by a bookseller. With amazement, I saw M. Edme walk into my study. [M. Edme is a character in *Midnight*.] He is rather short, with very black hair, a carefully trimmed beard, a straight, delicate nose, shining eyes that look as though they were painted on enamel, thin cheeks, more like an Arab than a Jew. He makes me recite Psalm 23, which we then parse, but I was flurried, as much by the man's learning as by my own ignorance, so I answered wrong. We have begun reading Isaiah. I wondered that he did not make me begin at Genesis, but he probably thinks its Hebrew too easy. The tongue spoken by the prophets is infinitely more varied, with more nuances and more abstractions; the study will demand great efforts from me, but I remember properly only what I acquire with difficulty. At the University of Virginia, the *Iliad* was handed to students who could scarcely recite their Greek alphabet.

SEPTEMBER 20. LONDON. Long hours devoted to studying Hebrew. All that I know of this tongue I owe to M. Moses V., whose name I mention with gratitude. He it is who guided me through the labyrinth of the seven conjugations. The rest is a matter of vocabulary and I can now work alone. Took a great number of notes on Isaiah, also on Genesis. It is the most beautiful of all tongues, the one used by God to create the worlds and call His first servants. . . .

I think that what urged me to resume my study of Hebrew was the divergence of the English, French, and German translations, not to mention the Vulgate, which offers a particular problem. How is it, I wondered, that these translators do not always agree, since they all have the same text before them? Such uncertainties are not to be found in the translations of Homer. Could it be that the Biblical translators faced something untranslatable? I do not say that the essential part of the message has not come down to us, but what could not be rendered was the sound, the noise of the Hebrew sentence. Now, it is enough to read half a page of the Bible in the original to understand the capital importance of the choice of syllables in the drafting of this book, which is mainly a poetical book. A Hebrew poet has never resisted the pleasure of alliteration; it is for him a supreme way of expressing anger, indignation, joy, or fright. With a skill of which the best French translators can give no idea, he multiplies the sibilants and sets in motion the grandiose register of gutturals. The Almighty's powerful breath passes into this tongue and I am afraid that very little of it remains in Abbé Crampon's honest version. I will return to the subject later.

SEPTEMBER 25. Have read Gide's journal. How well I recognize him here, the Gide of 1925, the one we have lost! I continually feel like writing him, forgetting that the Gide who would read the letter would be the Gide of 1936, a Gide surrounded by new comrades; there are too many clenched fists raised around him for me to reach him.

OCTOBER 14. A *new beginning* of my book yesterday, another this morning. To begin a book used not to give me too much trouble. To a certain extent, I wrote what came into my head on the first page (from what depths does this come?), then I followed up this first page blindly to the end. At present, I realize that to go blindly along will no longer lead me anywhere, except to a trail I had already blazed and to a known objective. There is something in me that would drive me to repeat what I have already done, if I did not fight this instinct with all my might. One must carefully avoid being trapped by the snare of words. I ride a horse that knows his way to the stable only too well. If I wasn't more exacting, I would long since have slackened the reins; I try, on the contrary, constantly to set my horse straight. This is something that will be judged if ever these fifteen or twenty beginnings of novels are found among my papers. Some of them are curious.

OCTOBER 16. Dinner at Vyvyan Holland's. H. G. Wells and several less-known novelists were there. . . . As we talked about Germany, Wells says that the Germany of today is, in a way, the materialization of France's fears. . . . Around ten o'clock, after an excellent dinner, comes the time for port wine and limericks, and, regarding the latter, Wells asserts that this kind of literature was invented by Edward Lear around 1850, which surprises me, and he quotes, a little wrong, several of the best-known and most risqué limericks. Peals of laughter followed by long silences, those heavy silences peculiar to these parts and that are almost incomprehensible to anyone who has lived in France, where people practically snatch the words from each other's lips. . . . I have too much admiration for Wells' genius not to be a little disappointed, without quite knowing what I expected, anyway. I probably imagined that he would be brilliant, as brilliant as certain prominent authors in Paris, and now, on thinking it over, I like this great writer's simplicity (I don't say his modesty). As he talked about Lenin and Stalin, I asked him if Stalin spoke English. Not a word: an interpreter had to be called on. Stalin received Wells in a pullover, smoking a pipe, for which he apologized. What about Lenin? Did he know English? "Oh, perfectly. He had lived in London; he went every day to the British Museum. Why, the Russian Revolution was hatched at the British Museum!" A little later, I forget in what connection, someone mentioned the Bible. "A nefarious book," says Wells. "It has done the greatest harm to humanity and in particular to the Jewish race." I would have liked him to explain why. A good deal could be said on the subject, for I believe that a wrong interpretation of the Scriptures has given rise to innumerable false ideas. To quote one instance only among a thousand others, our conception of good and evil regarding physical love, the whole of our sexual morality originated by the Pentateuch and St. Paul . . .

* * *

NOVEMBER 7. At the National Gallery. What painter has expressed better than Rembrandt the majesty of the Jewish people? I am thinking in particular of the portrait of Jacob Trips, his severe face that of one of Israel's elders; a great skinny body wrapped in furs from which emerges a fine, dry, domineering hand grasping a long stick. I am also thinking of the portrait of the Jewish merchant (in this portrait the gray sleeve slashed with black is the finest sleeve I know in painting, even finer than Titian's sumptuous sleeves; yet, looking at it a little closely, one sees that it must have been made of rather poor fabric, although it gives an impression of richness that is difficult to analyze). Dreamed a great deal before these admirably dignified faces. Whether their business was explaining the Scriptures or selling cloth, these men had something royal about their brows and eyes. Yet it was perhaps these same Jews, these doctors of the law and these merchants from Amsterdam, who ill-treated Uriel da Costa. . . .

NOVEMBER 30. PARIS. Yesterday, for a moment, I had a great longing to talk confidentially to someone, to talk of my inner difficulties. For it is not good to remain silent always. But how can one speak of things that are sometimes beyond human speech?
. . . I have come to believe that death does not exist, that there is only a long development of life throughout the centuries, that the body's annihilation is a liberation, that a child at the time of birth imagines it is about to die because it leaves its mother's womb and that the same mistake occurs in our minds when we breathe our last.

DECEMBER 15. A telephone call from Gide. "Don't mistake my silence for coolness," he says. And he adds: "I sometimes dive under. . . ." I go to see him. He seems gay, younger than he has ever been since I knew him. He first talks to me at some length about *Midnight*, which he read at Cuverville. He likes neither the first nor the second part. . . . A little later, he expresses his admiration for English literature (this in connection with Shakespeare's historical plays). "We seem so dry compared with them," he murmurs. And he gives a nod, meaning "Yes, yes, we are!" as though I had protested. The conversation next shifts to politics, he congratulates me on not having made a choice between Communism and Fascism, "since," he says rather sadly, "they are the same thing." And he adds: "You are nonpolitical.

Stay so." He talks admirably of the *réfractaires*—the people who are opposed to the regime—whom he saw in Russia. . . . Portrait of a young German whom he met on a ship, during a journey on the Black Sea: a sort of Rimbaud, almost absurd if his face had not been so beautiful, wearing a leather jacket and carrying a small umbrella under his arm; with that, a wild unsociable expression. Gide asked him if he worked. Answer: "I don't work. I refuse to work." "But what do you do for a living?" "I manage."

Forgot to mention a moment ago that regarding the third part of *Midnight*, Gide reproaches me for having used the word *love* in every place where, according to him, I should have used the word *desire* "to express the panic frenzy in the story."

DECEMBER 21. Just realized that I haven't said a word about Edward VIII's abdication, which set England astir for ten days, but I keep my diary more and more neglectfully. This, I suppose, goes to show that I am gradually being detached from my former self.

1937

JANUARY 2. Long readings of the Bible in Hebrew. For the last months, I have been unable to think of anything but this book and fell gladly under its spell. . . . This immense wealth will probably never be exhausted and we are just beginning to have a glimpse of it, and yet it is ours, it constitutes the dowry given by humanity for its spiritual espousals. . . . Yet we must beware of the translators' counterfeit coins.

JANUARY 8. LONDON. Saw *Hamlet* at the Old Vic. It is at once the most beautiful poem, the most beautiful tragedy, and the most beautiful novel that was ever written. Certain passages, even the best known, appeared to me almost beyond what a man can do, and I left the theater dizzy and as though I were a little tipsy. The part of Hamlet is played by an actor who is a little too conscious of his handsome face, a little too athletic, a trifle too much given to leaping and bounding. Some of his attitudes are hard to excuse.

When he sees his father's ghost, he expresses terror by crawling on the stage and recites a rather long soliloquy on his stomach. An ultra-modern setting. An orgy of cubes and stairways and, in the second act, an endless vista of antlers. Are we at the court of a cuckold? None of these defects struck me during the play, but I had noticed them unconsciously. Shakespeare's lines do away with all that. And what Gide said came back to me: "How dry we must seem . . ." It might be.

JANUARY 26. I sometimes feel a sort of impatience with my body. If it could understand me, I would say to it: "What do I care if you are comfortable? Your happiness is an ever-recurring problem, more and more difficult to solve. Not a day goes by without your complaining. You are bored and you bore me. You have to be amused, taken here and there, your peace and well-being seen to. I protest against your whims but, like a coward, obey your tyrannical caprices, and if anything threatens you, I imagine myself to be unhappy and so I am. Your laziness, your constant kicking, your covetousness weary me. If I work too long, you take your revenge in headaches that oblige me to let you lie down after having drawn the curtains and turned broad daylight into night," etc.

FEBRUARY 5. Anne has been here for the last few days, and I have enjoyed showing her a few churches. These London churches are charming old ladies dressed with puritanical elegance, a white cap on their head, hands folded on their stomach. Thus they stand, lost in a city they can no longer recognize, aloof and disdainful. St. Bride's, which has to be hunted for amidst blackened houses, is one of the most engaging; a narrow garden, dying in the fumes of London, still protects it from the Strand's onslaughts, but the day will come when it will occur to someone that the ground on which the church stands is very valuable, and St. Bride's will give place to some skyscraper. Few strangers visit it. No Frenchman that I know of has mentioned it. Inside, it is white and gold and hesitates, without making up its mind, between being a house of prayer and a ballroom. It is austerely coquettish, with a leaning to Corinthian furbelows. If it followed its inclinations, the church would turn baroque, but it takes refuge in the well-bred graces of the neo-classic style. Its Greek columns relate themselves as best they can to great ogival windows; its height is cut in two by a gallery of black wood. Highly polished brass candelabra and golden flowers are sprinkled all over the church against a background of white walls. St. Bride's is more innocent than prayerful.

FEBRUARY 9.   Last night we went to the Westminster Theater, where Chekhov's *Uncle Vanya* was given. I felt so full of bliss that, for a moment, I believed that *happiness* was near, the only name I can give to a mysterious event that has so little connection with what is usually understood by the word *happiness*. It is not human joy, but human joy sometimes leads to it. Impossible to explain what I mean. This inexpressible something is there, behind the denseness of this world. I did not strain to reach it, knowing only too well that in such cases one should keep a sort of interior stillness, a complete passivity, but the play began and the actors' lines dispersed it all. However, something remained to me of this great inner contentment, a feeling of absolute security.

Chekhov's play made me feel like going home to write. The author's beautiful expression, both sad and tranquil, shows in the matchless simplicity of the dialogue. Everything comes from the heart, from all that is common to mankind. What is human, all that is human in us, at the bottom of that heart of ours that we know so badly. Each is, in himself, the whole of humanity.

MAY 22.   At the University of Virginia. I am writing this in the old library, where I like to think that Poe sometimes came to read and dream. Fifteen years ago, I worked at this very table. I tried to forget Paris and thought of it without cease, instead of profiting from all the happiness that was being offered me. I was in love and unsociable and made myself wretched to my heart's content. Is anyone ever stupider than at that age? I did nothing to discourage my own sadness but cherished it instead; it afterwards developed to an extraordinary degree, threatened to take possession of my whole life; I got rid of it by introducing it into my books.

Visited the new buildings, none of which are fine. The old University is intact, but while it used to be surrounded by woods, meadows, and ponds, as in Mr. Jefferson's time, it now suffocates within a belt of big, commonplace houses. Useless to tell me that the buildings were very expensive, that doesn't give them any more merit in my eyes. No, what happens to cities and universities is what happens to men: wealth kills something in them that can never again be found or replaced. Now that the University has become one of the big American universities, with a gymnasium the size of a railroad station, a dormitory as big as a barracks, etc., it attracts an increasing number of Northern boys, and I find no fault in this, but note that it is hardly any longer a Southern university. Its professors come from all over the country. . . .

MAY 26. Leaving the University, we passed through the finest valleys in the world and I would have liked to linger there, but time is short. Time is always short, from birth to death. Why? Because we don't know how to stop. I scarcely had time to see the Ragged Mountains again from a distance, the mountains which are the scene of one of Poe's tales. It was, I think, during an excursion in these mountains that he predicted to a few of his companions that there would be a war between the North and South.

The day before we left, around ten o'clock at night, in wonderful moonlight, I sat with Jim under the big trees that grow in front of the library and, for a few minutes, I felt the sweetness of living. Memories were perhaps a help, for I don't know what alchemy changes yesterday's sadness into a feeling of happiness, although it is a quiet happiness, a happiness of shades. I wondered if there existed anywhere else in the world a landscape dearer to me than the long stretch of lawn bordered by white columns and black trees. Above whispered the breeze as it stirred the leaves and, higher still, the great stream of stars.

> At midnight, in the month of June,
> I stand beneath the mystic moon . . .

I am sure that Poe thought of the place where I was sitting when he wrote those lines. And yet, this wonderful night, these trees, these white columns were to me the setting of a nightmare, the nightmare of youth. In this very spot, the absurd and degrading thought of suicide crossed my mind. What a child I was!

JUNE 9. NAG'S HEAD, NORTH CAROLINA. Pleasure kills something in us. I have thought this for several years and for several years I have had moments of rebellion against myself, but cannot make up my mind to talk to anyone about it.

. . . Last night, at supper, I suddenly experienced that strange happiness that I cannot define. Through the windowpanes, I could see the pale yellow sand, the turquoise-blue ocean, when something deep inside me told me to go to the beach at nightfall. My heart beat very fast and I could scarcely conceal my emotion. I returned to my room and waited until it grew dark. The sky was torn by long flashes of lightning racing from one end of it to the other. I took advantage of the fact that no one noticed me and went barefoot to the beach. The raging waves roared like a cannonade. Here and there in the darkness shone rotting fragments thrown back by the ocean, dead or phosphorescent fish, and I recognized the carcass of a shark that I had looked at that afternoon. I listened to the great call that came from the open sea and stayed there some time, my heart full of love, with a feeling of deep security. . . . But why talk of what cannot be expressed?

JUNE 24. I shall end by being completely detached from this diary, because I cannot succeed in putting in it what really counts in my eyes. Very few of my inner difficulties show in these pages; I can see very little in them of the constant debate that goes on between what is real (and wishes to rule me) and what is illusive (and fascinates me). In this world, I am like a hypnotized man attempting to return to wakefulness and to full consciousness. I have given in to the glamour of a pure and simple mirage; at present, it is difficult, it is painful for me to wake up.

JUNE 26. I read some letters from General Lee recently. In several of them, he mentions the old house I described in *Avarice House*. The house was really called Kinloch and belonged to my uncle Loughborough Turner. I spent a few days there around Christmas, in 1919. We used to get up very early when it was still night. In the big, dark dining room, my uncle read or recited long prayers, then we threw ourselves on the good, indigestible things that are served for breakfast in America: bread so hot that it burned your fingers, thick pancakes swimming in butter. You could see the bluish hills through the windows. But I have said all that in my book. How could I give that lovely house to a family of misers? I didn't know where to stick my characters, and then, I was tempted by the setting.

JULY 14. IN LONDON. 73 EGERTON GARDENS. Monday afternoon, just after leaving Le Havre, I was lying in my cabin, a little de-

pressed, a little weary of not being quite well again, when suddenly in the heart of silence—for the sea's even murmur was like
a silence that one might have heard, a scanned silence—I distinguished a very singular noise, which was like the very distant cries
of a great multitude. Then I seemed to hear singing, thousands
of voices singing in harmony, but singing one note only, always
the same one, and there was an astonishing variety in this chant
and such that words cannot describe it. At the same instant I felt
carried away by immense joy, I had the impression that the whole
of the universe was bathed in an element that I can only call
happiness, and in this happiness everything was annihilated. For
three or four minutes, I listened to this hymn of glory and suddenly it ended, but a very vivid memory of it remained in me.
I have had experiences of this kind several times in my life. I
don't know what to ascribe them to.

JULY 19. Spent the day with Gide, who is in London for a short
visit. All three of us—Robert, Gide, and I—lunched at Kettner's.
I was afraid that the place would not suit Gide, but he seemed to
like it and admired the Caucasian scabiosas that graced our table.
He is in very high spirits, which does not prevent him from being
extremely pessimistic regarding Europe's future. "Too many reefs
ahead," murmurs Gide, "too many reefs to avoid a shipwreck."
He asks Robert a question which I try not to hear, but how could I
manage not to? "What branch of the army do you belong to?"
Then I hear Robert talk of artillery. "Anyway," says Gide, "a declaration of war would at once be followed by a revolution." An
opinion that Robert does not share. Gide talks bitterly about the
Communist party and the attacks aimed at him since the publication of his last book (*Retouches à mon retour d'U.R.S.S.*). . . .
Robert leaves us after lunch. Gide and I go to Brompton Road on
top of a bus. In the red and blue drawing room (where I recently
resumed writing), I don't know how it came about, but we talk
about the Bible and Gide tells me that he used to read it so much
that it *bewitched* him. As I was remarking how sad certain of
St. Paul's sayings made me feel, Gide quotes Abbé Mugnier's reply
when he confessed how little he cared for the great apostle. Abbé
Mugnier had looked at him for a moment with a smile and then
said: "St. Paul is the backbone of the fish." Gide finds this answer
admirable. "Don't smile," he says, "for it is indeed the backbone
that gives the fish its structure, the ἰχθύς, it is the spine of Chris-

tianity." He then reminds me that St. Paul's epistles were of an earlier date than the Gospels and I am very much struck by his remark.

A little later, as we had gone back to talking about Christianity, he tells me that, for his part, the expression to *seek God* seemed too vague and did not correspond to anything much in his mind. And he added, lowering his voice a little: "I feel far closer to Christ than to God . . ." We parted shortly after this.

JULY 26. PARIS.   I remember an afternoon I spent in Brussels last April. I was sitting by an open window on the top floor of a tall house and looked at Sainte-Gudule as it rested over the roofs like a great, dark bird; behind it, a gray-blue sky filled by the song of a single lark. A view of such rare beauty, a beauty that went to the heart, that I left it regretfully, like something that I would never see again. We had scarcely gone down the stairs when the sky turned cloudy. I will probably see Sainte-Gudule again, but it will be another church. "One never dips twice in the same river." I know that only too well. Only the Eternal really exists.

The Eternal is the most beautiful name that has been given to God. You can think it over until you lose all feeling of the exterior world, and I think that, in a certain manner, it is in itself a way that leads to God. If we seek what is eternal in the sensuous world, all the manifestations of matter vanish from our sight, what is most solid together with what is most ancient, until we reach the limits of what is imaginable in all possible spheres. When I was still a child, I used to think over occasionally the term *for ever and ever* that Protestants add at the end of the *Pater*, and the words finally gave me a sort of mental dizziness, as though by continuing in that direction you would reach something inexpressible, an immense void into which you fell.

JULY 27.   Every time I open the Bible, I find an allusion to my life, to my problems, to the particular form that moral weakness assumes in me. That is why I consider the book a magical book. For what does the second chapter in Jeremiah talk about? About the reader, about no matter what reader who, having opened the book at that passage, reads what I am reading about the wild ass which is never sated, about Israel who prostitutes herself to the *baalim*, just as each of us runs after pagan gods, that is, after all the world's illusions, seeking our joy in what passes away, whereas no joy is true or permanent that is not supernatural. Too many instances of this could be quoted.

Around my twentieth year, I wrote a page about reading the Bible. The page is lost, but I remember trying to point out, with the feeble means at my disposal, that the Jewish people was each one of us and that, in the great tragedy enacted between the Eternal and His people, the role of conscience is held by Moses and by all the prophets who came after him. And so, when the Israelites want to stone Moses, this is an image of human nature in rebellion against grace. The same is true when Jeremiah is persecuted by people at court who force him to go down into a well. . . .

JULY 29. If one wished to be converted, churches should not be resorted to for that purpose, but places that are so-called haunts of pleasure. I scarcely know any but those in Paris: they are the saddest thing in the world, I think, and the ugliest.

OCTOBER 28. A little while ago, I was listening to an air from Handel's *Hercules,* Iola's air, I think. The beauty of the accompaniment is so grave and so profound that I was suddenly startled, as though I had seen a ghost. "The tread of gentle night" coming toward us, walking down some mysterious staircase . . . step by step, the ear follows it in rapture. I wonder if music is not the easiest means of bringing us into contact with ourselves, with that secret part of us, hidden from us by the world—with God, perhaps.

NOVEMBER 8. If we only knew that the whole of Heaven is contained within our breast, that the Eternal rests in us, that the voice of the universe speaks to us at all times, in the whispering of the rain, in the song of a bird, in a few lines sketched on a square of paper by an artist, in a prelude by Bach . . . Only the deaf and blind go through life without being overpowered by beauty ceaselessly renewed.

NOVEMBER 14. In Achim Arnim's *Die Majoratserben,* I copied this sentence: "Each man begins the history of the world all over again, each man ends it." I wandered through the sentence as though it had been a great, shady avenue that led straight out of this life.

* * *

NOVEMBER 15. "Lamia." When I read Keats, I feel like a bear in a stream of honey, for everything there is delicious. I think that Keats, more than any other poet, has the extremely rare gift of conjuring up in a very precise fashion what he barely describes. The whole of the sensuous world seems contained in his verse, but, by looking a little closer in the hope of analyzing this magic, what do we find? A bare shoulder here, a lock of golden hair there, a narcissus . . .

DECEMBER 8. It is hard to work one's way to the top of the spiral that makes us pass so often through the same places. Yet it leads to death and illumination. Even in the darkest hours, when all hope of conquering oneself seems unreasonable, one should remember that above, very far away, shines eternal light. No matter what we do, we are going, sometimes in spite of ourselves, toward a happiness of which our mind can form no idea. What good is it to regret the shadows of this earth? We must think of death with hope and firmness, of the great, shining country that lies beyond the black gate.

1938

FEBRUARY. I think there is in each of us, not only the two men spoken of by St. Paul, but a good dozen persons who rarely agree among themselves and are almost always in contradiction. One of these persons is an eccentric—no, let us speak plainly—one of these persons is a lunatic. All of them hold forth in turn, and the lunatic also puts in a word. His presence is tolerated by his companions, whom he makes uneasy; he enjoys great authority and, in the case of many writers, he shows talent, I might even say that he is their talent.

MARCH 12. Since yesterday, Austria has fallen under German rule. It is the end, in sorrow and in shame, of Europe as we knew and loved it. The German armies entered Austria without firing a shot. Hitler was not put to the expense of a single shell. Neither England, nor France, nor Italy so much as budged. At the present time, it does not appear that a single man in the world dares say no to Hitler. Paris is dumfounded by the news. Each of us can share the general humiliation. Some people are afraid that Germany, intoxicated by her easy victory, will now turn her attention to Czechoslovakia. What would happen then? In spite of everything, no one wants to believe in a war.

MARCH 19. Saw Gide this morning. He looks very badly and the lower part of his face is now that of an old man, but his expression remains youthful. He tells me that he has never felt more alert, intellectually. He had nephritis in Africa, which obliged him to return to Europe. I made him read the parts of my diary that concerned him. He says he is glad that I mentioned his speech at the Grand Lodge of France and how much it disgusted him, talks of a novel that he began with a sort of enthusiasm and of an anthology of French verse he is preparing. It will have twelve hundred pages. He will give "nothing that is not exquisite." He scarcely mentions the European situation except to say that the annexation of Austria is the first chapter only and that it is absurd to talk about this country's rape when it gave itself joyfully to Germany.

MARCH 24. Read Jeremiah in Hebrew. How can I reconcile reading this book with my daily life? Here, in this world, no problem is given a solution. Everything will have to be settled elsewhere.

APRIL 13. Went to Gide's day before yesterday to give him some more of my diary to read, the parts where he is mentioned. He declares himself delighted. "If the whole book is like that!" he cries. Apropos of Victor Hugo, he tells me the story of the Guernsey hairdresser who stretched a sheet under the poet's armchair, cut his hair, and gathered together the locks to make them into a parcel which Hugo took away with him. In Hugo's house, says Gide, was a closet filled with packets of hair and of nail parings. Fetishism, thinks Gide, adding that as hair and fingernails play an important part in magic, the poet no doubt wanted to ward off any danger coming from that quarter. To my surprise, Gide seems to find this rather reasonable. We lunch at Michaud's, rue Jacob, where Robert is waiting for us, and Gide talks about Spain. He believes that once the Civil War is over, there may be a reconciliation between the governmental party and the rebels at the expense of the foreign volunteers, who will be accused of all the ills the country suffers from, and that there will be a crusade to chase out of the country Russians and Italians alike. He gives us an account of a meeting between the Pope and Cardinal Verdier (whom he calls Cardinal Mercier, for his memory fails him at times). Pius XI, it seems, regretted not having taken the hand held out to him by the Communists. "We have been lacking in love," he is supposed to have said as he burst out sobbing. "Ah, Christ would have taken the hand that was offered Him! He would not have spurned it!" At this, it seems, the Cardinal buried his face in his hands. Gide relates this scene with an emotion that makes him forget he is in a restaurant full of people, and he repeats over and over again the sentence about Christ in a manner that did not fail to touch me, and touch me deeply. Regarding the terrible difficulties with which present-day France is struggling, he says: "The men the country needs, well, those men lie in churchyards under wooden crosses." I ask him if this is not true of the whole of Europe. "No," he replies, "Germany knew how to preserve her elite during the last war, whereas France, with her extravagant generosity, gave everything she had, for the sake of the gesture. . . . And so did England. I remember Edmund Gosse speaking to me of England's youth, mowed down by the war: 'All our gallant youth . . .' " He looks old today. His face has taken a grayish tinge, his shoulders are bent, but in moments of emotion, such as he had a little while ago, a sort of flame returns to quicken his body and his features. As we were talking of I forget what passage in my diary, Gide says that I gave a very good sketch of himself and of me. As I hand him a page about Roger Martin du Gard to read, I tell him that I expect to suppress it. "Why?" asks Gide after reading it. "Martin du Gard knows perfectly well that I don't like his play." And the same held good for what he said about Claudel. He no longer withdraws. He does not refuse to see in print what he said in private. How many of us would do the same?

APRIL 23.   Gide's wife died, I think, on Easter day.

MAY 4.   Lunched with Gide day before yesterday. He is in mourning from his tie to his spats, for he wears spats. In a slightly lower voice than usual, he says a few words about his wife's death, a death that must have been a rather peaceful one. At Ferrari's, where we lunch, he talks on all sorts of subjects. He asks me whether I would write a preface to the French edition of the Bible that Schiffrin wants to publish, but I cannot consent to it. It would give a wrong impression of me, would make people think that I am taking a pious turn. Simply, I would feel ashamed. There are too many contradictions in my life and I don't want to be taken for what I am not. Gide presses me a little to accept, but indeed I cannot.

JUNE 7. That deep longing for happiness, that longing I have in me, as we all have, so much so, for instance, that I can't listen without melancholy to a bird singing on a too fine summer day in Paris, where does it come from? It is not merely the longing to possess everything, formerly so strong in me; it is a painful and sometimes pleasant nostalgic longing for a happiness too far away in time for our brief memory to retrace it, something like a recollection of the Garden of Éden, but a memory adapted to our weakness. Too much joy would kill us.

JUNE 10. Dined yesterday at Gide's. He had said to me beforehand: "Mme Van Rysselberghe will be there, and Catherine." "And who is Catherine?" I asked. Gide blushed a little (and this is the very first time I had ever seen him blush) and said: "Why, she's my daughter. I called her Catherine in memory of *Wuthering Heights*, but she doesn't like her name." He accompanies this with a pleasant little laugh. At dinner, Mme Van Rysselberghe talks about a writer and the articles he recently published against the Jews, and it seems that this same author is a trifle ashamed of his own anti-Semitism. Gide says that he has a regard for him without thinking him very intelligent. "Yet," replies Mme Van Rysselberghe, "you have to be intelligent to write as he does, with such a vocabulary. . . ." "Unquestionably," Gide answers at once. "You're right." How often have I seen him give way in matters of small importance, although he sticks to his opinion when the subject is worth while! Gide's daughter looks at us in silence. The upper part of her face is like Gide, but not the lower one. Her very black, very shining eyes are her father's, without, however, that attentive, ironical something that escapes words. She wears her hair in a net and hardly opens her lips.

* * *

JUNE 20.   I try to read a page of the Bible in Hebrew every day. The Books of Samuel, which I am studying at present, scarcely offer any difficulties, but the Book of Job, which I read alternately every other day, is infinitely harder. I am speaking only of the style, of course, the obscurities of the poem itself being proverbial. I will return later to the enormous divergences I have found in the translations that have been made of it, divergences that I think due to the fact that the text suffered greatly before coming down to us. Generations of copyists have multiplied the misreadings of it. The letters that correspond to *D* and to *R* are rather easily mistaken one for the other unless perfectly shaped; the same holds good for *B* and *C*. The *calamus scribae velociter scribentis* of Psalm 35 is responsible for many an error. Doubtless, the context is there to testify, but no sooner is it a question of reestablishing the primitive text than modern translators no longer agree. This is where tradition is the greatest help. But which tradition?

JUNE 23.   I don't think anyone suspects what forms the substance of my sadness. How can I express it? It is impossible to say and would seem ridiculous, but I'm going to say it just the same. I wanted to be a saint. That is all. I can add nothing to this. A great part of my life does not resemble me. I am very keenly aware of constantly passing by the man that I wanted to be, and in a certain way he exists, he is there, and he is sad, and his sadness is mine.

JUNE 26.   Went to see Gide yesterday morning. He wanted me to meet a certain Mr. Cook, a colored professor who teaches at the University of Georgia. A man of about thirty, with a pale yellow skin and short beaky nose; his long feet are shod in white shoes; he turns the tips out widely, as do all the Jews I have known. For Mr. Cook is a quarter Jewish, as he himself informs us. He speaks French admirably, with an accuracy and animation that are far more those of a Jew than of a colored man. I think he gave us both an excellent impression of good will and intelligence. Once he has gone, I talk to Gide about the Negro question. I tell him that, with time, white America will have to absorb this black America whose existence is such a painful problem. . . . "But the Jews," says Gide, "America will never absorb the Jews! The Jews will have to absorb America. Yes, they will. And this will happen everywhere. In 1800, there was one Jew for every six thousand inhabitants in New York. Around 1890, there was one in every six hundred. Now, there is one in every sixty!" A little later, he tells me that he doesn't in the least believe in the superiority of a colored school child over a white school child, in the colonies. The colored child has a better memory, that is all. . . .

We leave the house together. In the street, I tell him that the movement for the abolition of slavery had originated in our Southern states and that, long before the Civil War. To which Gide replies that on his return from Africa, he had been tempted to write an ironical defense of slavery (what a subject for Swift)! He would have stressed the fact that a slaveowner took great care of what had cost him so much money, whereas a boss who directs free workers is far less concerned about their health. He knows that a sick or dead colored man can be replaced at a moment's notice, and cheaply. . . . We go to lunch boulevard Saint-Germain, at a small restaurant near the Légion d'Honneur, and have a rambling, desultory conversation.

I can't remember in what connection I ask Gide if he knows Asia Minor, and he tells me of a disappointing and rather dull trip he made there. "But the landscapes?" (I had in mind certain pages by Renan.) "Oh," says Gide, "a landscape is always fine. Those where there isn't anything to admire are very few. . . ."

After lunch, we walk toward the Champs Élysées. On the way, I ask Gide how his Anthology is getting on. He is reading over the seventeenth-century poets. "I hope you will include one at least of Racine's spiritual hymns," I say. And off we go, reciting verse as we cross the place de la Concorde under a broiling sun.

> *"De la Sagesse immortelle*
> *La voix tonne et nous instruit: . . ."*

"Ah! yes," says Gide and continues my quotation:

> *"Enfants des hommes, dit-elle,*
> *De vos soins quel est le fruit?"*

He considers these lines very superior to the choruses in *Esther* that are so much admired. For my part, I am weak enough to be fond of these choruses, but what is stiff and conventional in the age of Louis XIV is far from daunting me—on the contrary . . .

JUNE 30. We should make a note of the books we read. . . . No matter how much a writer thinks that he is not directly influenced by what he reads, there exists nevertheless a secret but unquestionable connection between the author's works and the books on which he feeds (as there is between our body and what we eat). It may be that such or such a page of a novel has been written in unconscious protest against a chapter read the day before, and this page can change the course of the whole book. We know what Poe read at the University by the librarians' slips.

JULY 2. Where the modern stage is concerned, I think Gide is more lenient than I am, or perhaps he isn't stirred by the wild hopes that seize me when I see the curtain part; consequently, he is less often disappointed. . . . Yesterday evening, we went to see *French without Tears*, or rather the French adaptation of the play, of which I believe it best to say nothing. Gide tells me the story of his gardener (at Cuverville) who threatened to leave him if X, the under-gardener, did not go. After a lengthy investigation, Gide finally learns that the under-gardener casts spells and that the cow had miscarried the very evening when he arrived at Cuverville. "What a subject for a novel!" cries Gide. "*The Outlaw* . . . Imagine the man's life, harried from one country to another because he has the evil eye. You could make something of it, Green. . . . Do you dislike being given the subject of a novel? Yet Pushkin gave Gogol the subject of *Dead Souls*. . . ."

After the play, we went off to drink beer. Gide talks about his diary, which, he says, has all but turned into "a graveyard for stillborn articles." He continues: "It gives a completely false idea of me, for I hardly ever keep it except in moments of discouragement. So I give the impression of being sad, and this is not so. I am neither sad nor unhappy." He tells me that the publication of my diary will have an important effect on me, but does not make himself more explicit. . . .

JULY 15. . . . We believe that we increase our happiness by multiplying our wealth, whereas we are also multiplying sources of suffering. By wealth I don't mean money only, but what money allows us to obtain and, generally speaking, what Satan offered Christ. But to leave this world for a life of contemplation means creating a new and as powerful attachment, an attachment to spiritual things. What then is self-detachment? Once, Maritain quoted to me what a mother superior of a convent said about a

nun who was too much attached to a strict observance of the
Rule: "She will remain a long time in Purgatory on account of
her virtues. . . ."

JULY 17. Just had a telephone call from Gide, who wants me to
meet one of his friends. By some freak of fancy, he speaks English to me, as he does sometimes: "You will find him very interesting," he says, "yes, really. . . ." How I like hearing him speak
English! He is another Gide, a little uncertain of what he is about
to say, a little bashful; he must have been like that at twenty.
Noticing that my unsociability makes me hold back, he then says
in French, turning into the Gide I know: "Oh! I don't want to
bore you!"

JULY 18. Lunched with Gide. He talks about Poe, says that in
England the poet's reputation is considered greatly overrated, that
he is a writer whose imagination is often "coarse and facile." I
find the opinion absurd and say so. "And yet," says Robert, "what
an influence he has had in France in molding certain poets!" An
indirect influence over Valéry, through Mallarmé. "Oh," says
Gide, "in the eyes of many Frenchmen, Valéry does not pass for
being a real poet . . ." And, guessing our thoughts, he adds:
". . . just as many people refuse to see a painter in Leonardo da
Vinci." W. F.'s son is also lunching with us. He is a silent, ob-
serving boy. After lunch, Gide, feeling tired, goes into the next
room to rest. Robert leaves, I remain alone with F., and we have
a little talk. He is a Communist, like his Papa. Seems deeply scandalized that I should think it doubtful that the governmental party
will win in Spain. "My father went over there. He saw the soldiers.
Their morale is excellent." He tells me that there will soon be a
"great uprising in Paris." "Who gave you this information?" "A
member of Parliament." I can't help thinking that in boys of his
age politics takes the place held by religion in many of the youths
of my generation.

   During lunch, Gide remarked that the past played quite a big
part in my diary. "In my case," he says, "when I was young, I
refused all links with the past, from self-esteem. I sold my father's
house for that reason. But since, with age, I have come to care
more for the past."

JULY 27. . . . At Tournai, much admired the cathedral, but the inside, I think, shows too sharp a cleavage between the Romanesque and the Gothic, not to be detrimental to the latter which is frailer and less solid than the Romanesque. The ogival style seems stricken at birth by some mysterious disease. It visibly attempts to *escape*, like some neurotics. That way of sending vaultings higher and higher, in defiance of all reason (see Beauvais), is an act of deep nervous unbalance. In this sort of rush toward the sky lies a contempt for nature, a morbid defiance that the architect of the Parthenon would not have understood.

AUGUST 11. BÅSTAD, SWEDEN. We watch an insect, but does it see us? It is hardly conscious of a shadow in the light above it. We are perhaps unconsciously observed in the same manner by beings of incommensurate size. . . . Maybe there exists a spirit, an angel, a *power*, as the Greek Gospel says, who thinks, as it sees one of us: "This unfortunate insect has tried ten times, a hundred times, to climb that glass pane to find an outlet to the sun and the fresh air. It distinctly sees the sky through this transparent thickness that exists as though it were not, and yet keeps it prisoner, and it can't understand what prevents it from flying into space. Come, we'll open the window for it!"

For the last few years, the problem of the window that won't open has counted more and more in my life. It is, generally speaking, the problem of every life. To escape . . .

Last night, I walked along a road. Looking at the starry sky, I felt such deep joy that all the words I could use would express it badly. I paused, a prey to a mysterious happiness of which nothing can be said. It seemed to me that, very gently, the window opened a little. That is the way it must be at the last, when the body ceases to suffer and the soul stands on the threshold of night.

Night, night, I have always felt that night was favorable to me. For me, it indicates the vanishing of the world of appearances, the world lit up by the sun with its colors and its constant sound of words; in the material field of life it accomplishes what we should be able to accomplish in the spiritual field, and what it offers our eyes of flesh irresistibly attracts the inner eye. Before such a sight, all that has to do with our everyday life becomes insignificant. Our individual fate and the fate of nations are reduced to their true proportions, that is, to nothing.

SEPTEMBER 3. STOCKHOLM. At the Museum of Prehistoric Antiquities. All these vestiges of such a distant age made a curious impression on me, the impression that the whole of humanity marched through me, as though on a highway. It is all of me and I am all of it. I was born on the day when it raised its eyes to the clouds for the first time, I will be part of it to the end, if there is an end. I cannot die, its heart is mine, and this heart is only beginning to beat. What I call living is nothing else but the consciousness that humanity has of itself. I have felt this to such a keen degree that our fear of dying seemed to me suddenly one of the most tragic misunderstandings we have ever suffered from; it doubtless arises from that disastrous confusing of our bodies with ourselves. But how is it possible to talk about this? Such things appear natural to people who know what I mean, because they have *experienced* them. The others would take me for a madman. The characteristics of the thoughts that occur to me, as they will gradually occur to everyone (for nothing separates us from the other, just as nothing separates drops of water in the ocean), the characteristics of these thoughts are that their value is practically nil as long as they remain in the intellectual field; we will have to live them.

SEPTEMBER 12. COPENHAGEN. We are leaving Denmark by the next boat. Indescribable anguish broods over the world. I have my full share of this anguish, but in order to keep up my courage, I have taken my novel out of my suitcase and have set to work again. This does me more good than anything else. Have noticed that our agitation almost always lies on the surface. Deep inside us is a region of quiet, of happiness for whoever wishes it, particularly under such circumstances as these. "The kingdom of God is within you." If we believed this, we would go mad with joy, but our skepticism preserves us from this inconvenience.

SEPTEMBER 29. PARIS. I cannot bring myself to give a detailed account of so many hours of anguish. The most difficult day was the twenty-fourth. Returned on the twenty-fifth to Paris, where everything is in complete disorder. Everywhere, nothing is talked about but a mobilization, an ultimatum. On the 27th, news came that Hitler's ultimatum to Prague expired that afternoon at three. The war then appeared certain, but hopes revived this morning. Hitler, Mussolini, Chamberlain, and Daladier are to meet at Munich.

* * *

NOVEMBER 6. Last night, a familiar nightmare roused me from sleep, the nightmare of being pursued. I was in a rocky landscape. How well I recognized all those steep slopes, those almost vertical paths winding around the gigantic stones! I leap from rock to rock to finally drop shrieking at my enemy's feet. As I woke, it occurred to me that this enemy was my own self and that what my adversary pursued and wished to subdue was my body.

We must go beyond our conception of God, for God is eternally beyond all things.

On opening a window this morning, I breathed the odor of dead leaves brought by the wind. I can't express the happiness that these autumn days give me. It seems as though they brought me news of *elsewhere*, and then I immediately begin thinking that nothing that can happen to us on this earth is of much importance, since the mere idea of what is waiting for us later is enough, even at present, to overwhelm us with joy. "Eye hath not seen, nor ear heard, neither have entered into the heart of man, the things which God hath prepared . . ."

NOVEMBER 15. The other night, in one of the strangest dreams I ever had, I saw a lovely bird of paradise flying about my room and then alighting to walk slowly to the door leading into the passage. Its wings and tail were like sheaves of a cerulean blue. Someone above me said: "This is a bad omen, an omen of death." Then a long silence and another voice said, at a far greater distance: "Yes, an omen. The invisible world has parted open like a big curtain to send this magnificent bird into the lower world. How men fear death! The most comforting of omens terrify them and the messenger bird of joy brings sadness to their ignorant hearts." These words were not spoken; it was more like an exchange of thoughts; silence answered silence.

NOVEMBER 20. This morning I thought: A child in its mother's womb is snug and warm and most likely happy. It believes this small, warm space to be its universe, where it lacks nothing. What suspicion can it have of the world we know? None. Granting that one might enter into communication with an unborn child, what notion could be given it of a book, a house? None whatever. Our situation is the same in regard to the world beyond us, which stretches around us and which as a rule we reach only through death. In reality, we too live in a dark cavity which we like and will only be born screaming when we die. Then we will discover a universe of inexpressible loveliness and will walk freely among the stars.

DECEMBER 13. I saw Gide the other day and for the first time felt a kind of embarrassment in alluding to certain changes that have taken place in my life. I realized that the things I told him were said instead of those I wished to tell him and could not. This pained me. If he had been indifferent to me, I wouldn't have cared in the least.

DECEMBER 15. We were with the Suarèses the other evening and asked to see the cook's blackbird; someone went to fetch the cage and put it in the middle of the drawing room. The bird, disgruntled by being taken out of the kitchen where it was asleep, immediately ruffled its feathers and, when I went nearer to admire it, let out such a furious whistling that we were deafened. Not at all scared to see eight people around it. It leaves its cage in the daytime and wanders about the flat; it has learned the "Marseillaise," but that is a treat reserved to intimates. I would have liked to take it away with me. If the lease allowed it, I would fill our few rooms with animals. I would have several crows, blackbirds, and parrots; cats and dogs too, needless to say; no monkeys with their disquieting faces, but squirrels all free to come and go at will; the windows would stay open. Vasari tells us that certain painters of his times, Sodoma in particular, surrounded themselves with their favorite animals, but we have become so civilized that this is no longer possible.

1939

JANUARY 25. I showed Gide the parts of my diary that concerned him. When he read the account of our day in London, he nodded, saying: "Yes, that day, I felt that we might have talked to each other . . ." To get beyond reticences, what we lacked was not being together long enough. As regards myself, I can say that my talks with Gide are like the snatches of a long conversation that never took place. It is not from lack of confidence on his part or mine, but I require a lot of silence to be able to speak, and I think we are alike on that point. . . . On going home, I reread a part of *Si le grain ne meurt* with such pleasure that I felt like writing to the author as though he had just sent me the book. But I did not do so. I have always been awkward in showing affection.

It was at his house that I saw Gide. He wanted me to go to Egypt with him, but I refused. We talked over our day in London. He said to me suddenly: "You are fond of the mystics. Read Fénelon. Fénelon's letters." As we were about to part, I had a feeling of inexplicable sadness and I believe he had too. Something of it showed in his face and, I believe, in mine.

JANUARY 30. Came across some notes I had taken one day in May, 1938, after a visit from Gide. We were in my study, where I had collected a few books; a log fire brightened the room. I don't remember why we began talking of Flaubert's correspondence and I asked Gide if he recollected the admirable letter about Le Poittevin's death (and Le Poittevin's heart-rending cry as he lay dying: "Close the windows! It is all too beautiful!"). "No," said Gide, "I don't remember the letter well. It has been years since I read the correspondence." After hesitating, he asked: "Isn't the letter you mention the one where Flaubert says that as he watched over his dying friend, he read Kreutzer's *General History of Religions?*"

FEBRUARY 1. I have never had much faith in theories on heredity; their ingeniousness makes me skeptical. And yet, how much there would be to say about my ancestry. . . . I have been molded, at least apparently, by my adopted country, but there is something irreducible in me that comes from elsewhere. In putting away some papers, I found a sheet where I had noted, at a time when the person I am was still of interest to me, how much Irish, Scotch, and English blood ran in my veins and in what proportions. What is impulsive, dreamy, and also carnal in me, I owe to Ireland; to Ireland, too, the fact that I succeed one day and fail the next, everything that urges me to write my books, in a word, what is best and worst in me. I recognize the Scotch share in the religious crises—the most recent of which have not been the least painful—in a deep, unvarying love of the Scriptures, in a long perseverance that has almost always had the better of my innate laziness. From England . . . but this game bores me because of its artificial character.

FEBRUARY 5. I believe that one of the vainest worries for an author who publishes his diary is that of absolute coherence. For a reason difficult to explain, he likes to feel bound to his past, to establish a sort of resemblance between the characters he has successively *gone through* since birth. He tries to blend with them, he imagines that they speak for him, he scruples to disown what they have said for fear of being accused of vacillation. And thus in the heart of his being, slowly dies all notion of moral freedom, all aspiration to living, for the characters we were are now no more than ghosts, and a solidarity with the past is a solidarity with death.

In reading over this diary, I have often been surprised to see what I have put in it. How many gestures I will never make again! How many apparently definitive opinions I am now ready to find erroneous! But I appeal to tomorrow against yesterday, I appeal to the man I will be someday, I appeal to the man I am.

I have varied, I will vary again. At all times, I feel in me a deep aptitude for changing that mingles with the instinct of living. To remain where they are is an unnecessary martyrdom for many people. I am one of these, with all my heart I want to go forward. . . .

Baudelaire deplored that, among the Rights of Man, that of contradicting oneself had been forgotten.

Nevertheless, I won't keep this diary any longer. No sooner do I feel that I am writing for the printer than I wonder whether I would have written thus and so and not otherwise, a little less guardedly, a little more humbly. I regret the former free-and-easiness, and Gide's remark sounds dismally in my ear: ". . . a graveyard of stillborn articles." And then too, can one continue keeping a diary when the figure one cuts in this world no longer interests one? One should have Pepys' admirable lack of self-consciousness to keep a diary worthy of the name, to believe more than I do in the reality of what surrounds us. How remote the years when I wrote at a stretch the material for three or four printed pages of this diary, never tiring of the pleasure of telling myself all about myself! But all that is over now. I was someone talking aloud in his loneliness, it is no longer possible to me to continue if I know I am being listened to.

* * *

FEBRUARY 8. If the mystics are the lords of the invisible world, spiritists are its burglars. The kingdom of Heaven can be taken by violence but not by picking its locks.

What a Gospel could be written by gathering together the words spoken by Christ to His saints! If it belonged to me to do this book, I would give a prominent place to the word received by St. Francis de Sales one day when he was tormented by the idea of predestination: "My name is not the one that damns. My name is Jesus."

And also this to St. Teresa of Ávila, who was grieved not to be allowed the right of reading the Scriptures in the vernacular: "I will give you a living book."

The Gospel is a book that will never close and that is written each day in the heart of contemplatives.

Satan's masterpiece is to make us, of ourselves, tug at the rope until it breaks. To accomplish this, he puts it into our heads to read an increasing number of serious books until they sicken us. In his hands, the writings of the greatest ascetics become instruments of despair. It is easy enough for him to delude us. Who would suspect him of slyly laying on our table such and such a volume of *The Ascent of Mount Carmel* or *Spiritual Life* by St. Vincent Ferrer? Of course there is a certain risk in such expectations, but the old enemy knows only too well that he has little to fear, and he likes to fight Heaven with its own weapons.

The parable of the talents. As a child, not knowing that a talent was a coin, I imagined that this parable applied to writers, to painters, to all those who had received a gift, and today I doubt whether I wasn't right. The saddest thing is that having received a talent from God, we thank Him by paying Him back in false money.

The parable of the wedding guests. I can't help finding it most comforting. Of course, there are those who were bidden to the feast and who will languish in outer darkness because of their "great refusal"; but there are also the tramps who were forcibly made to enter the banqueting hall. *Compelle intrare* . . . Humanity saved in spite of itself.

When I think of my far-distant years of religious fervor, of those spiritual longings that I never mentioned, which all but turned my life in quite a different direction from that it has taken, I am surprised that the pendulum, having swung so far one way, should not have swung farther to the other side. But I was pre-

served from atheism, just as I was spared from walking on all
fours and eating grass. . . . The idea that God might not exist
has never so much as grazed me.

MARCH 15. There comes a time in life when you can't listen to
music any longer, particularly if you have known years of great
happiness and that the future darkens gradually. The other day,
I stopped my radio when it gave out the first notes of a Beethoven
sonata for piano and violin. "To suffer in that manner," I thought,
"is really too stupid." In the same way, I don't wish ever to hear
Don Juan again, for it reminds me too precisely of the time when
I listened to it in the charming Residenz Theater at Munich; or
Schumann's *Faust*, or his Second Symphony, and certainly not a
single note of Schubert's. There may come a day when I may
recover all this once more, but at present, music can only embitter
a sadness I am ashamed of.

Thus ends the eleventh notebook of my diary, interrupted when
I saw that the great European upheaval was about to begin again
and that happiness was no longer possible.

Undated Diary

UNDATED. Although I learned English as a child and have never
ceased speaking it, I can't write in that tongue without feeling
that I am trying to put on a garment that was not made for me;
this garment irks me and I am conscious of not wearing it as well
as I should. It is a uniform that is too tight for me. My dressing
gown, my everyday costume, the one I feel free and happy in, is
French.

Vice begins where beauty ends. If one analyzed the impression
produced by a beautiful body, something approaching religious
emotion would be found in it. The work of the Creator is so
beautiful that the wish to turn it into an instrument of pleasure
comes only after a confused feeling of adoration and wonder.

Music is blended with my whole life and to such an extent that
it is difficult for me to imagine one without the other. I am not
sure that this is entirely good, but it is too late to change anything

about it. With time, I have learned how to free myself from certain musical influences and above all no longer to consider music as a refuge in trying moments; on the contrary, I turn away from it in such moments and don't wish to listen to it now except in quietude and, if possible, in happiness. To coddle one's melancholy by feeding it with all the sadness of Chopin's "Nocturnes" —no.

The first concert I ever heard was given in the old Trocadéro, toward the end of the First World War. The famous echo in this disastrous auditorium first played hide-and-seek with Berlioz' "Hungarian March." Then a lady was heard in an air by Handel, and with relentless fidelity the walls returned the singer's harmonious bleats. The program was varied and copious. After that came something I have forgotten, and next came the intermission. After that, in a deep silence, rose a profound, even murmur and the flight of a dark bird over an abyss: the first measures of the Ninth Symphony, which revealed a new world to me. Until then, I had believed that all religious emotion necessarily belonged to Catholicism, but the voice I heard in this supernatural music spoke to me of an infinitely larger universe than I had suspected; I admitted with surprise that the sense of the divine did not belong exclusively to the Church. Less ignorant, I would not have been so much disturbed. It was not that the Church seemed to me less true, but she became different in my eyes, and the change worried me, for I did not know what would come of it. The following days did not restore my peace. Something worked in me for a long time and suddenly, in an obscure part of my mind, something exploded. The earth that I had learned to despise seemed all the more beautiful and attractive since I thought of withdrawing from the world, but I dared not acknowledge to myself that I had been mistaken and the sufferings I then endured were such that I have never quite recovered from them. What appears to me stranger than all the rest is that having heard the Ninth Symphony time and time again since, I have never been able to recapture the religious character that I had first lent it.

UNDATED. Lunched with Stephen Courtauld at his house in Portman Square, in London. The decoration of the rooms is limited to fillets of gold along the doors and ceilings. One would search vainly for a house more elegant and more simple in the exquisite delicacy of its proportions. Manet's "Bar of the Folies-Bergères" hung in the dining room and I could scarcely keep my eyes off it during the whole meal. What held me was not only the quality of this marvelous picture but also the enigma of the mirror in which a person is reflected and whose back we should see and that is not there. . . . In the drawing room, the "Theater Box" by Renoir and five magnificent Seurats. After looking at the pictures as long as I could, I wondered what this painting gave me, apart from an immediate and very keen pleasure. Has it been a help to me as a writer? There are no colors in my books: nothing there but black and white, effects of light and shade, but they are the books of a man who would like to know how to draw with vigor. My admiration always goes to painters whose pencil stroke shows the most energy.

UNDATED.   The other day I was talking to Gide about my diary and he advised me once more to publish it. "You will easily find a publisher for it," he says (the publication would have been, of course, that of the unexpurgated text). "You need only have ten or twenty copies printed," he continues. "That would be enough to preserve it. Think of what happened to Byron's diary. I thought that his sister had destroyed it, but the one who burned it was his *publisher*." "I will make several copies of mine myself," I then say. "It would be surprising if one at least were not preserved." "No," replies Gide, "that's not enough of a security. You have a family." "My family would not touch it." He makes a gesture, as much as to say: "Ah! you never can tell!"

Continued reading Flaubert's letters. After his twenty-fourth year, they lose all naïveté and become splendid, often harrowing. The little taste he had for happiness, his dread of the future, take on a tragic and sometimes disconcerting expression. I cannot imagine anyone writing to pass the time away, *to make life go by*. . . .

UNDATED.   There are days when I think that I would have liked to know how to talk, and when I say talk, I mean putting words together in such a way as to close my opponents' mouths or to make them open in amazement, in fact to shine, to convince. Instead of which I sometimes mumble in a humiliating fashion. In short, I lack presence of mind. The strange thing is that I express myself with a certain ease when dealing with an absent-minded person; I sink below mediocrity as soon as I feel I am being listened to. So, for many a year, I blushed to the roots of my hair each time I thought of the telephone call the Governor of Virginia honored me with. I can laugh at the whole thing now. The telephone line connecting Virginia to France was to be inaugurated at Richmond, and two weeks before this ceremony I had been advised that the Governor would speak to me on that occasion and that all I had to do was to be at home and wait. There was something paralyzing for me just to imagine that thousands of miles away, such an important person would pick up the receiver and listen to what I had to say, but that would only happen in a couple of weeks. . . . Needless to say, I felt flattered. Soon, only one week remained. Finally came the day itself, then the hour, and the telephone rang. My throat parched, I took off the receiver. I then heard a great noise of water that sounded like the sea, or rather, a stage imitation of it. I was told that this was London. The sound of water began again and, at last, in a Judgment Day silence, the Governor's voice rang out: "Mr. Green?" "At the telephone." "Mr. Green, this is the Governor of Virginia. I am speaking from the Capitol, in Richmond. Can you hear me?" "As though you were in the room. . . ." At that moment, the Governor mentioned, one by one, the people who were with him, to listen to this telephone call from France; there were—can I ever forget it?—the president of a railroad company, the president of one of the large Southern banks, the president of something else that I can't remember, and with each new president (whom I imagined in a white waistcoat, holding a big julep), it seemed as though a little more blood flowed back into my heart. I believe I have managed to forget the sentences that fell from my lips, and the least I can say about them is that they must not have been very interesting, but I do remember sleeping very badly that night, kept awake by an imaginary conversation with the Governor, a conversation in which I shone. . . .

UNDATED. To be able to write a book, I must have an object to look at, a picture to place before me which I could *refer to*. Thus, for *Avarice House* I had the photograph of a room, taken at Savannah, in an unknown house, around 1880; in the center of an unpretentious drawing room, one sees a round table covered by a cloth and on this table, a closed book; torn leather armchairs; on the mantelpiece, a barometer; and on either side of the door, great solemn curtains drawn aside to allow invisible persons to pass. I think that almost all my characters have come out of this room. In writing *The Closed Garden* I had before me the photograph of a painting by Utrillo.

1940

SUNDAY, JULY 21. BALTIMORE. Between the last copybook of this diary and the page I am now beginning, the events we all know of have taken place. I was in America when the war broke out. I returned to France and stayed there until after the armistice. Then I left Europe. I have been here a week. I will be forty in a little more than a month and find myself in more or less the same circumstances as when I was twenty—minus my illusions and minus my enthusiasm—that is, most uncertain of the future. I am a French writer, but cannot live in France, for the time being at least. So consequently I must henceforth write in English. I am not unknown in this country no doubt, but fully realize that almost everything remains to be done, to be done all over again. The idea is more of an incentive than a discouragement. The despoilment I must undergo is not granted to everyone, and it is sometimes a great and fearsome favor to be torn away from one's possessions.

A long effort of liberation has probably been spared me because I was incapable of making it. During the five or six years preceding the war I eagerly probed into all the sayings of Christ regarding poverty. I used then to think that one could remain spiritually detached in the midst of great wealth, that everything depended on the mental attitude adopted toward worldly goods, that the rich could be poor in spirit, and the poor eaten up with avarice. I also wondered if I would ever be able to rid myself of the possessiveness I felt within me. To this an inner voice invariably answered: "Leave that to me." I thought of that voice as I crossed the bridge at Irún which leads from France into Spain. But, no sooner freed from everything that might weigh me down, how will I avoid thinking once more about making the future secure? One earns a few dollars, first one buys a few books, then two or three bits of furniture, then several little things one imagines one wants, and the love of worldly goods is renewed within us. But I have experienced the divine moment when such a love seemed dead in my heart.

JULY 24. There are times when I think that hopes of spiritual freedom are the saddest delusion that can torture the human brain. For I see only too well that I am not one of those who are able to do a necessary violence to their feelings and wonder that others can make such an effort. All I can obtain from myself is not to give up the idea that, when all is said and done, spirit is bound to prevail, but I am afraid that in my case its prey will be no more than a corpse. Perhaps the important thing does not lie in conquering but in fighting on to the end. How sad to think of being one of those who have only had a glimpse of the truth.

I am writing this in a small drawing room with French windows opening on lawns shaded by willows, cypresses, and oaks, and terraces where the grass grows between purposely uneven stones. Not a sound reaches me, barring the thrush's rather melancholy cry; the leaves hang motionless in the scorching air; at my feet pants a big black poodle whose yellow eyes watch my every gesture. Here, in this keepsake setting, imagination refuses to form an idea of the threat that hangs so heavily over the world.

I sometimes wonder what has become of our flat in Paris, and in particular of my study where I spent so many peaceful years without the least intuition of what was going to happen. However, I do remember that one day, as I stood before my bookshelves, I imagined a German officer reading the titles of the volumes and snickering at the fine Hebrew Bible in two volumes which I so much regret having left behind. But I immediately dismissed this premonition—if it was one—from my mind. Last winter, on a very mild and sunny day, I sat in a corner of this study, close to my books, whose gildings shone softly in a ray of light, and felt happy to be there, in my native city, a volume of poems open by me. I asked for nothing more. I could hear the birds in the Champ-de-Mars, the children laughing as they played in front of the house. Had I remained a few weeks longer, I would have heard the enemy dictator holding forth fifty yards from the spot where I sat peacefully drinking coffee.

JULY 25. I am copying, translating as I go into English, the narrative of what I saw in June, 1940, but the work is painfully slow. The English tongue has never prompted me to desire the linear perfection of form that French gives me, and I have the feeling of writing English with a hand that is always afraid of making the sentence run crooked.

JULY 26. The gardens under our windows cannot be discovered at first sight, for they are hidden under canopies of foliage; a network of green paths or grassy flights of steps connect with no other plan but one due to an intelligent whim. On a beautiful morning last winter, in the midst of a setting where nature had been chastened and reduced to a human scale, the finest of the oaks suddenly crashed down on the well-kept lawns; the air was still and unthreatened by the slightest breeze. . . . Although rotten at the core, the tree continued to put forth sturdy leaves and its powerful branches seemed to defy time.

Dined with the Garretts, who have a wonderful estate a few minutes from here. The great stone house is overgrown with ivy, much like a piece of furniture concealed by its loose cover; below it, vast lawns bordered by trees, a lake with a mist arising from it. We had dinner facing a rather fine but overwooded Italian garden; a too luxuriant foliage blurs the design of the paths and here, as in the real South, the virgin forest always tends to resume its rights and turn garden architecture upside down: shaggy nature, itching to go wild, needs a continual haircut. Nothing particular was said at dinner, or afterwards—we are not in France—not a thing to record, just a sort of well-bred good-fellowship. Nothing spiteful either and consequently, nothing amusing. . . . From time to time, the shifting outlines of the trees were etched against the background of a mauve sky shot by flashes of heat lightning. As my neighbor at table talked about the Frick collection, I could not resist saying a few words about the Barna da Siena that hangs in this museum, about the little picture hidden away in a small room, showing Christ in a red robe, bearing His cross. I had a reproduction of it on the mantelpiece of my study in Paris. I liked the mild, very reproachful glance that Christ turned toward me and also thought I read great affection in His eyes. A visionary's Christ . . . After dinner, went to a pretty low-ceilinged room in the middle of which shone a long polished wood table. All the men sat before a glass of brandy, and I with them, very much out of my element and not at all in my place. A bank manager questioned me about the political situation, and I tried to reply in a well-informed manner. . . . At such times, I always see myself as funny, but for one spectator only, myself. When I add up all that I can talk about to a fellow guest at a dinner, the total is small; no one ever asks me about *what I know*.

Most of the ten or twelve guests at this dinner seemed to believe in the possibility of a British victory, or at any rate that the German attack on England would fail; they hope that this country will be able to hold out two or three months longer, which appears interminable.

JULY 29. A chasm now stands between me and my youth: the war. This makes me feel I am aging. Before the war I went slowly toward middle age, and, instead of turning away, my youth continued with me. It followed me, as you go a bit of the way with a departing traveler. I would say: "Let's go as far as that tree together, let's go as far as yonder turning, let's go to the foot of that hill. . . ." It went as far as the Irún bridge, but did not cross the frontier with me.

Yesterday, happiness came in suddenly, as it used to, and remained for a moment in the great, dark, silent drawing room. We were standing by a window, looking at the rain as it spun its web in the lowering sky, and I felt, in spite of all the newspapers could shout at us, that happiness was close at hand, humble as a beggar, magnificent as a king. It is always with us (but we are unaware) knocking at the door to come in and sup with us.

My cousin, who has all sorts of plans in mind, wants me to spend next winter with her. . . . I dare not refuse anything that is offered me under present circumstances. Life is often given to fearsome acts of generosity and will not allow them to be scorned. It seems like a dream to see with what ease God has removed us from a long series of tight corners. I think that the most sinister hour of my life was the one when I burned a whole suitcase of papers at Bordeaux, in the bedroom of a small hotel. I threw bundles of letters into the fire, trying not to understand what I was doing.

JULY 30. Wasted a whole morning dreaming today, and in the worst possible fashion. Annoyed to feel hesitant, and to such an extent. . . . Read a few pages of Rothenstein's memories of life in Paris around 1890, a charming, rather foolish life, the description of which both saddened and charmed me. For I am really too fond of the pleasant side of life, I have none of the

American energy that blows up rock and uproots virgin forests! One of my greatest subjects of amazement is my love of a certain kind of stillness.

My cousin seems most mysterious to me, as mysterious at times as a character in a novel, mysterious as almost all women appear to almost all men. We see each other at meals that are cheerful and rather brief. She stays upstairs until dinner time and I on the ground floor which has been allotted to me. I can hear my cousin pacing to and fro above, and there is something indefinably pensive and preoccupied in her step. Two big black poodles keep her company; they sit at a window and bark deeply if anyone goes down the road, which is very rare, and—what is most curious —they sometimes bark for fifteen minutes without its occurring to their mistress to hush them, although they are so close to her; I wonder if she even hears them.

True order is founded on prayer, all the rest is more or less disguised disorder. The Middle Ages were a huge edifice whose foundations were the *Pater*, the *Ave*, the *Credo*, and the *Confiteor*. All that is built on anything else can only collapse sooner or later into blood and mire.

AUGUST 7. Worked pretty well at the book I am writing about my childhood. That is my way of returning to Paris.

MONDAY, AUGUST 19. Reread a few pages of *Gulliver's Travels*; its sinister beauty has always attracted me. Hatred of the human race gives the author a dark genius that scales the peak of disproportionate grandeur. Certain sentences make you shrink like a cut from a whiplash. A style both icy and vehement, a cold, clear-sighted fury, a scatological and gloomy humor all tend to show the deep, unruffled seriousness of an erotomaniac. When you reduce the whole of life to the performance of a few physical acts which then take on considerable importance, you end by having a view of the world that is, in a way, infernal, although not without beauty. But this beauty is of a terrifying order and not in the least appreciated by those who have never breathed in— be it ever so little—emanations rising from the bottomless pit. Sade is surely related to this great and melancholy author.

TUESDAY, AUGUST 20. A rule I have always tried to follow is to make each day a small life, as complete as possible: reading, writing, listening to music or looking at pictures. Not a bad rule, but one that has resulted in moderating my life's tempo. Thanks to it, nevertheless, I have been able to write more books than my innate slowness would have otherwise allowed. Yet, having formed the habit of building only by slow degrees, how am I to adapt myself to living conditions that suppose rapidly accomplished work, a book dashed off in a few weeks, lectures written in less than a month?

FRIDAY, AUGUST 30. Faces half seen, smiles understood too late, everything that passed me by from 1920 to 1940, and that I did not grasp . . . Yesterday, because of the date inscribed in a book, August, 1920, I began dreaming over my life, over what I was doing twenty years earlier. Have I improved? No. The liberation I vaguely counted on has not taken place. But the yearning for that never visited land should be kept within us, the journey should never be given up: that perhaps is the most important thing.

SATURDAY, AUGUST 31. Some Hindu writer, I cannot remember which, but think it is Vivekananda, compares the sexual instinct to a wild elephant tied down by one foot: sooner or later it ends by breaking its shackle. This instinct brings an element of madness into human life. Nothing indeed comes closer to a frenzied lunatic than a man in a paroxysm of desire. We are bound to earth by the middle of the body.

SUNDAY, SEPTEMBER 8. I was forty, day before yesterday. I am at the zenith of my life. This does not mean, or so I would like to think, that I will go downhill from now on. No, I hope for a long pause on a level stretch, a plateau on which I can stroll about, God willing. The wheat is stirring on this plateau and I may pass by with my sickle—but storms gather over harvests.

I should like to write the story of a man whose appearance showed complete serenity of heart, whereas, actually, this character's loneliness would be made tragic by carnal famishment.

TUESDAY, OCTOBER 1. NEW YORK. Tired of always being my same old self. Has anyone ever said a word about this particular form of sadness? Spiritual man dwells in the top of the face, in the lower part, the carnal man. The lower part of the face must not prevail over the top part, a small portion of the great universal dream should always be retained and nourished within the inner self.

THURSDAY, OCTOBER 10. I finally enjoy being in New York because the city is our last link with the Europe that has been taken from us. Our point of contact with the Old Continent.

FRIDAY, NOVEMBER 1. BALTIMORE. Today, I was foolish enough to go up to the attic where the volumes of my diary are kept, and to open one of the little notebooks bound in gray linen. I sat in a small rocking chair, by a window, and for an hour wandered through the streets of Paris, as I used to. The Paris of happy days, that of 1930. Once more I felt its sidewalks under my feet, heard the boats calling on the Seine, smelled the odor of its trees and its smoke, and hundreds of faces stared at me, as in a dream. I had a rude awakening. I must not read those diaries again, or else let it be over there, in a Paris from which Germany has been chased away. I have suffered too much and suffering wears the soul, just as fatigue exhausts the body.

THURSDAY, NOVEMBER 7. Someday, perhaps, I shall find peace, if not joy. Just as we did not know how happy we were before the war, in the same way we are ignorant today of the extent of our misfortune. I, for one, had placed my happiness in too many exterior things and realize it now. The setting and its accessories had passed on to the essential plane; I needed fine objects, amusements, I mistook pleasure for happiness, I was not sufficiently aware that true happiness takes shelter in an almost inaccessible region, as far as possible from the world.

WEDNESDAY, NOVEMBER 27. No matter how dark life becomes, the current of prayer must not be interrupted, for prayer it is that straightens everything out, even when the game seems lost.

In spite of all weaknesses, we must believe that there is something great within us that will triumph someday, otherwise life would not be worth living. How could anyone wish to live for the pleasure of sending food to the stomach? Not I, for one. My ambitions are less modest.

THURSDAY, DECEMBER 19. My life has changed a little, interiorly. When did I make my choice? I no longer know. Perhaps, even, I never knew. One reaches a decision when the underground work nears completion, when the pros and cons have been weighed and counted once and for all in the mysterious region where such hidden operations are perfected. There came a second when I said yes, but my consent was obtained before I even knew it. And so we grope our way through a world of darkness. This frailty makes me skeptical as to the serious character of some of our errors.

MONDAY, DECEMBER 30. Does our body never weary of desiring the same things? For it always yearns after the same feast while our spirit continually demands something new. There are only two types of humanity that I have ever really understood: the mystic and the profligate, because both fly to extremes, searching, each in his own way, for the absolute; but of the two, the profligate is to my mind the most mysterious, for he never tires of the only dish served up to him by his appetite and on which he banquets each time as though he had never tasted it before. Probably because of this, I have always had a tendency to consider an immoderate craving for pleasure as an accepted form of madness.

1941

WEDNESDAY, JANUARY 8. It is sometimes more rewarding to watch a spot of sunlight travel over a wall than to write business letters, but who can understand that, of the two occupations, one is eminently beautiful and intelligent, the other perhaps base and stupid? A man who thinks thus is necessarily alone in the part of the world where I live, but he might possibly be better understood in China. How can one avoid being disappointed in talking to human beings? . . . In order to find yourself again, you must go to your room and close the door. In 1941, oh, how the outside world throws us back within ourselves, how much the invisible is present there, pleading with us just as angels glow in the night of the senses.

FRIDAY, JANUARY 10. On reading the beginning of the Book of Esther, I was struck by the sparkle of precious stones that dazzles the eye in the first chapter; each verse gleams like emeralds and sapphires. I do not doubt there is a hidden meaning in all this, but in growing older we lose the gift of understanding things with our admiration and thus passing through the gates of astonishment into Israel's great mystical dream. In my opinion, it is more important for me to know the cause of Vashti's fall from favor than to learn it is possible to breakfast in New York and sleep in London, all in the same day; each week finds me a little more deeply out of tune with my century.

SUNDAY, JANUARY 19. In reading over Poe's *Metzengarstein,* I wondered why his country should have been so unfair to him. Over here, readers probably find him morbid and America does not care to be represented by such an unwholesome poet. She disowns him all the more violently since she herself possesses the lack of balance of which Poe's genius is like the dark blossom, the great night-flowering lily held in the hand of Death.

THURSDAY, JANUARY 23. I am trying to write an essay on reading the Bible for Maritain, but such difficulties lie in store for me that I feel discouraged before even facing them. Before flinging oneself into an abyss, one must make sure of knowing how to fly. What I would like to say, in any case, is that the Bible has been a spring where I have drunk freely in times of distress and on the banks of these living waters have lain me down to dream of splendid *elsewheres,* from which all pain has been driven away.

JANUARY 26. One of the secrets of real talent is to see everything *for the first time,* to look at a leaf as though one had never seen one before, for then only can it appear to us in all its *newness.* The power of marveling makes up the genius of childhood, so quickly blunted by habit and education, and no one will ever be able to fit words together in an acceptable order unless he knows a little how to see creation through Adam's eyes. In art, truth lies in surprising.

When one looks at a stone as though it were a miniature mountain, one begins to see it as it really is.

THURSDAY, JANUARY 30. To be ready to die for someone whom one has never seen, whose voice one has never heard, that is the whole of Christianity. A man stands by a window watching the snow fall, and suddenly joy steals into his heart, a joy that has no name in any tongue. At the very depth of this rare moment, he feels a mysterious peace that no material worries can disturb; there lies the shelter, the only one, for Paradise is nothing else but loving God and there is no other Hell than not being with God.

FRIDAY, JANUARY 31. "I led you out of France so that you would come to me." How often have I heard these words in the silence! They have comforted me, may they not judge me!

WEDNESDAY, FEBRUARY 12. SUFFOLK, VIRGINIA. I am back again in a room where I suffered so much and where the hope of returning to France was the only thing that kept me from sinking. Do I still keep this hope? Of course, but what kind of France will I see again, and when? We are not people who have exile in our veins, like the Jews; it is hard for us to adapt ourselves to the presence of certain ideas. But then what could we dare complain of, we who have enough to eat and who sleep under roofs without a fear of their toppling over our heads? I took a walk yesterday afternoon in the surrounding country. The long, rust-colored plains seemed sad to me, but much in tune with my mood. The night before, on the boat that took me from Baltimore to Norfolk, I looked through my cabin window at stretches of water that shimmered milky in the moonlight, and it did me good. It was two in the morning and that night's supernatural peace went to my heart. Many of the sorrows we are sent can be soothed a little by a glance at the stars.

THURSDAY, FEBRUARY 13. Read St. John of the Cross. Very much struck by a passage where he says that as human nature yearns for God, it inevitably happens that this aspiration after good is simultaneously accompanied by a rising flood of carnal desires: as nature forms a whole, it is difficult to curb one side of it, in order to allow the other side to live. This explains why temptations can be so powerful at a time when our greatest impulses toward God are felt.

FRIDAY, FEBRUARY 14. It would require time and great freedom of mind to write a book containing the mystery of trees in a mist, the beauty of children's laughter, rain gleaming on the cobbles of a Parisian courtyard. Yet that was *my* book, the book I wanted to write; fragments of it strew all my novels. The war has brought about a deep and violent separation between the world and myself. Reading newspapers only adds to my confusion of mind each time I try to understand what is happening around us. No peace can be found at present except in prayer. The few minutes we give to God are like a fortress where we can take shelter and where we can be sure that the world will not reach us; no matter how much it roars and batters at the walls, angels are there, mounting guard on the battlements of the *Pater*.

FEBRUARY 28. On beginning *Varouna* in May, 1938, I was still influenced by a long series of books I had been reading as early as July, 1934. My object was the study of Hindu philosophies. India is a field of tares where wheat sometimes grows too. Two or three years ago, I still believed in metempsychosis, one of the great heresies of our times, and the subject of my novel has no other meaning than that. But what took place with *Varouna* is what took place with other books of mine: I began it in a certain mood and changed in the course of writing. Around January, 1939, I happened on St. Catherine of Genoa's *Treatise on Purgatory*, and the work impressed me deeply. I have never believed in chance. The book answered many of the questions I asked myself and overthrew opinions that I thought deeply rooted in me; it determined a new current of ideas in my mind concerning man's spiritual destiny. Soon afterwards, a talk I had with Maritain about Aristotle and Plato dealt a crushing blow to such belief as I gave the dreams of Hindu mystics. This conversation pained me very much at first. Suddenly it seemed that instead of having thousands of years ahead of me to accomplish my salvation, I had only a few hours; it was a very rude shock but, at the same time, I felt that a whole structure of errors had crumbled. My conversion, which resulted from these facts and also from other more personal ones, took place in April, 1939, a few days before I left for America. About half my novel was written and I thought of laying it aside, but being curious to know how it would end, as well as regretful to leave it derelict, I felt I must go on with it. That is why, as early as the end of the first part, which must date from February, 1939 (the manuscript is in Paris), while I was slowly returning to the Church, an almost Christian tone is noticeable, or at any rate one very different from that of the beginning. The second part is already steeped with the spirit of

Ramón Lull, particularly the episode of the celestial lover, and the third is wholly Catholic. In a preface rewritten some ten or twelve times, I have also attempted to adjust inconsistencies that a careful reader might discover in these three narratives. I did my best to cleanse metempsychosis in baptismal waters and, its head covered with Manichaean veils, it looks almost Christian.

SUNDAY, MARCH 2. The other day I went to see Miss W., senior professor of English at Goucher College. I had to settle certain details of the course of lectures I am to give from March 24th on. Miss W. received me at the close of the afternoon in a small flat with windows opening on North Charles Street. On the drawing-room walls were reproductions of stained-glass windows at Chartres and shelves of most honorably well-thumbed books. In the fireplace, a couple of logs burned tidily, a gentle blaze, just the fire for a peaceful-hearted old spinster. Miss W. has a small grayish face, and her wrinkles smiled at me occasionally with a touch of mischievousness. She is learned and handles English cautiously, as though it were a rare and fragile object; one feels that she constantly minds her p's and q's. If a sentence begun seems to strike the ear harshly, she drops it and goes on to another. She told me that I would have fifteen pupils, but not to expect wonders of them, excepting for a little German refugee. "They keep their feet on the ground," she confided. "Then we will start from the ground," I said. What they lack most, it appears, is imagination. We will see soon enough, but how strange all this seems to me, even now!

THURSDAY, MARCH 27. My first class did not go off too badly. The classroom is on the second floor of the college, with two or three windows opening on the street. In the center of the room is a large round table at which eighteen people can sit comfortably. My pupils are between sixteen and twenty years old. Two or three are pretty. They all gaze at me with guarded curiosity. Feeling horribly ill at ease, I took a seat among them and after asking their names, began to talk, referring to the notes that lay in front of me, together with my watch. Contrary to what I dreaded, I was not afraid, but as I continued reading I wondered if what I said was worth while expressing, and this annoyed me. Putting my paper aside, I began improvising, saying with much emphasis several things I did not wish to say. In my flurry, I mentioned Uriah Heep as a character in *Martin Chuzzlewit*; a piping voice firmly corrected my mistake, and I laughed along with everybody else. I said a moment ago that this class did not go off badly, but that is not quite true; I went home discouraged, with a feeling of defeat and, worse than anything, a fear of having bored these children. I told them that they were to write me the beginning of a novel, and read amazement in many a face, but I know of no other rule for writing a novel than sitting down at a table and starting off with Chapter One. If a recipe exists, my pupils and I may discover it, but for the time being, I know of none. They were free to write what they pleased, I said, in the manner they understood best, but advised them to begin by painting a picture of the chief character. And if it suits them to first make a plan of the novel, let them; for my part, I never do. I felt that they were staggered by the latitude I gave them, not knowing what to do with it. I am curious to find out what will come of all this.

Another class on Tuesday. They have begun asking me questions. They cannot understand that I am not exacting a complete plan of the story they wish to relate. I tried to point out that the plot of a book is the characters' work, that the first thing to do is to create living, interesting characters, capable of action. So they must attempt to create a character and we would then see its capacities; the story will result from this. I am sure that they feel I am putting the cart before the horse, whereas it is exactly the contrary. I joked a little, they smiled politely. I asked their advice continually, to encourage them to speak. Have they *accepted* me or not? I would like to win their confidence and help them, teach them to use their brains. As to teaching them to write a novel . . .

FRIDAY, MARCH 28. Perhaps I ought not to write what I am about to write, perhaps it is wrong to preserve the memory of anguish for ever. Yet the moment I wish to speak of has had such a deep repercussion throughout my inner life that I want to mention it in this diary, which is an attempt to guess at the course my life is taking. So I see myself once more on the morning of the 21st or 22nd of September in a hotel bedroom at Rotterdam. The room is bright, commonplace, and white and gives on a street from which arises a ceaseless hubbub. By leaning out of the window, I can see sidewalks jammed with people returning from work, for it is past noon. Facing me, the jagged line of pointed roofs bites into the bright blue of a fine autumn sky. I open my suitcase, just to take out a Bible that I lay on the table and skim through to find words that will bring me peace, but turn the pages, unable to concentrate my attention on a single verse. My mind is like a bird, the terrified prisoner of a small room, my thoughts spin round and round; I kneel, try to collect my wits, but can only tell myself, forlornly: "It's all over, we will never be happy again: war has come." I get up and find I can scarcely stand. My soul does not know what to do with my body; yet I do not fear for myself. . . . A few hours before, I heard children calling out a strange word, whose meaning I finally guessed, for these same children pretended to shoulder a gun: war. It was at Dordrecht, at a canal crossing. War . . . Moloch has opened its nightmarish jaws, perhaps to devour what I hold dearest in this world. At that moment, in the hotel bedroom, my distress was greater than the religious feeling I had counted on to help me bear this trial. *I was not ready.* And the scene was so painful that today even, after an interval of more than two years, *nel pensier si rinuova la paura.*

SUNDAY, MARCH 30.   There comes a second when our whole fate is decided, but that second is the fruit of a long series of actions and we do not realize that they are connected one to the other by secret links. I see well enough, or think I see well enough, the moment that determined my destiny. It was, I believe, in April, 1919, on a mild afternoon as I was returning home from Benediction. The ceremony had taken place in the crypt of the rue Cortambert chapel. Walking up the crypt stairs, I paused for an instant on a step, my heart brimming over with sadness at the thought of the world I was leaving, and also of all it might have given me and that I was refusing in order to enter a monastery. Heaven knows what took place within me at that moment. I felt suddenly that I had made the "great refusal" which was to give my life such a peculiar character. And at that same instant, a huge weight was removed from me: the weight of the Cross.

It seemed to me, in that second of time, that the whole earth had been offered me and, leaving the Middle Ages, I found myself in the midst of the Renaissance. Once more in the street, a street bathed in spring and full of provincial charm, I realized perfectly well that my life had just taken a fresh turn. . . .

I do not know why these memories come back to me. They hurt. The happiest years of my life have been so to speak embroidered on a ground of sadness. And yet, is this quite correct? Behind wonderful, carefree moments, when I was twenty-five, there lurked at times a shade of disquiet, but never of melancholy. Only after death will we know what our life meant.

WEDNESDAY, APRIL 2. Monday, I returned from my class with a headache. I had proved most inferior to myself, although my lecture had been carefully prepared. I intended making a quick sketch of a character as unromantic as could be, in order to show my pupils how to turn an unpromising subject to good account. A stationmaster. "Can you imagine a more uninteresting life than that of a stationmaster?" I asked the girls. "Why yes, we can," they answered, " a stationmaster meets all kinds of people." They were obviously right; my example was badly chosen, so I dropped it and tried my hand at improvising. The ringleader of the class, a plump Jewess, criticized my methods in such a manner that I blushed. "How can you expect us to write a novel? I think your idea is silly. . . ." Amazement kept me silent, but a little later, when I was talking about Jane Austen, my Jewess interrupted me again to inform me that this author's characters all expressed themselves in the same fashion. I then asked her to develop her idea a little and she gradually began to flounder, mutely begging for comments that I carefully refrained from giving. I finally showed her, with the most scrupulous politeness, that she did not know what she was talking about; she bit her lip and retired into silence. A few of the young ladies' papers are curious. One makes her character speak thus: "My father left me ten million dollars. My fortune now amounts to thirty-two millions. . . . I have had lovers. . . . I have loved love, ecstasy, and something else! I live in idle security" (that's easy enough, my girl, with thirty-two million dollars). One or two show a modest amount of talent. What a strange experience I am having!

MAY 20. A man can turn his room into a Paradise or a Hell without budging, simply by the thoughts he harbors.

MAY 23. Books, the exile's last resource. A book is a window through which one escapes.

* * *

MAY 30. On rereading *The Lives of the Desert Fathers,* I felt my fifteenth year thrill within me, a time when I was so madly in love with Heaven that I thought myself about to bound into the Kingdom in a single mighty leap. A recent Catholic, I imagined having a touch of the supernatural fervor that stirred the early Church. I wanted to go to Paradise at a full gallop. The memory of a winter evening has stuck in my mind more clearly than any other instance. It happened in the pension I tried to describe in *The Strange River.* My father and I shared the same bedroom. I was in bed; my father was saying his prayers. All of a sudden, I was seized with an unutterable happiness, a happiness of spirit that tore me free from myself. For a few minutes my soul was completely absorbed in God. I could not have said what was taking place in me, but my thoughts, instead of wandering here and there, as they usually did, came to a standstill in a sort of rapture that I have never experienced since. And the very words I use in trying to describe the indescribable only serve to confuse my memories. And yet, this is not so. What lives in my memory is the feeling of deep security—a little of which still remains—the inexpressible peace enjoyed by the soul when it takes shelter under the all-powerful wing of the Lord.

JUNE 12. Journey through Virginia. We left Baltimore day before yesterday for the Shenandoah Valley. The scenery strongly recalls certain chapters of the Bible: peace, the sweetness of wooded hills where the setting sun casts a pensive light; at the foot of the mountains shines the river like a great sword laid on the grassy meadows. What Nature says is unintelligible to those who are not fond of silence. Be it ever so loud, Nature's voice cannot be heard unless you listen close, and the least chitchat covers the sound of her words. There is a sort of *spiritual majesty* about these Virginia horizons that cannot be expressed. It is a setting for Ruth or the last chapters of the Pentateuch. Looking at the deep valleys where copper-colored beams of light seem to seek shelter against the night, one would like to be silent for ever, like Trappists. Human speech is almost always doomed to such failures and is so often inferior to what it intends to say that you wonder if this is not one of the consequences of original sin. Before that, there must have been other means of communicating thought, something less coarse. I have noticed one particular about human speech: the more it strives to clarify what is obscure, the more it confuses matters and increases chaos, unless inspiration takes a hand. The real word, the word of words, can only be sensed in the heart of silence, but all that I can say is mere confusion.

At the University, toward the close of the same day. All the students have gone; everything is given up to solitude and to memory. We strolled on the big lawn that spreads before the Rotunda: great trees whispered above our heads, rows of white columns glimmered in the twilight, and I had never been struck as now by the simple beauty of the "ranges." I would have liked to linger there for years, but we had to leave, one always has to leave, no matter what or where. And then, what would I have done at the University? Where is my place? Where am I going to live? Where am I going to die? Since Paris has been taken away from us, I seem to wander about without quite understanding what has happened to us all.

JUNE 13. VIRGINIA. Glanced through a copy of *The Strange River*. It is my best book, my most grown-up book, the most difficult to write, the most thoughtful, the richest, and also the most difficult to read. Poor Crevel said it was a revolutionary book; he was right, but what spoils the book in my eyes is that in writing it, I did not see all that I should have seen and so very nearly did. Philippe is a character that spells disaster, a bourgeois who no longer believes in anything, not even in what he himself stands for. In his permanent terror of a great social upheaval, he should have foreseen the days of February, 1934. He should not only have foreseen, but *seen* them, his fear could and should have made a prophet of him. I might have written this and did not and, for this sole reason, the book does not satisfy me, although I prefer it to all my other novels.

JUNE 15. At Williamsburg, day before yesterday. A few years ago, I smiled at it too easily. These brand-new houses mentally and physically lack the film of age. They remember nothing and want to look as though they belonged to a period of which they are completely ignorant, yet they are sometimes beautiful and curious and you wish to believe that the second capital of Virginia was like that. A tunnel is almost finished and ready to whisk away automobiles, whose presence destroys the illusion of being in an eighteenth-century city. How soon will its inhabitants be forced into wearing wigs and hoop petticoats?

To read over a diary is like turning over a sandglass; the sand keeps on running through it, the sand is the same, so is the sand-glass, and everything is different.

JUNE 20. Today, I spent part of the morning and afternoon at the Library. Read the fourth canto of Dante's "Purgatorio" with extreme pleasure. Here we are at last in the field of truth, far from the hideous delusion so minutely depicted for us by news-papers every day! It is faith, an all-powerful faith that lends such amazing density to the great Italian's words. In this immense poem with walls as solid as those of a Romanesque basilica, there is never a cleft in the rock through which doubt can steal.

JUNE 23. Sixth canto of "Purgatorio." One *sees* everything this man says, each line strikes and arrests one's attention. His econ-omy of words is so great that nothing could possibly be de-leted, but his conciseness is surprisingly full of meaning. Certain lines are haunting, such as Pia's cry: "*Ricorditi di me, che son la Pia* . . . , etc." You walk into the terrifying world of *reality*, where Maya ceases, where sensual illusions cease, where the set-ting of this life that conceals the truth vanishes; but in the kind of spiritual landscape through which we move, souls are shown us in such a manner that we see them—as though the poet lent us his sight and we, in turn, saw into the invisible. If one could speak thus without raving, you might almost say that spirit becomes concrete in these verses.

JUNE 25. If we could live a life of holiness, death would no longer be feared, for a holy life brings peace and deprives death of its horrors. From the day—around my twentieth year—when I realized that death would take me when my turn came, my life was, so to say, poisoned. I seemed to see death at each bend of the road, prowling around those I loved best.

Yesterday in Washington, where I spent a couple of hours in the new museum of art (Mellon collection). Almost all Italian painting is represented there. Overwhelmed by the beauty of these pictures. It is a review of painting from Giotto to Piazzetta, and in the unbroken connection of this great vision lies something in-flexible, almost inevitable, even more moving than the perfection of each individual work, for the painters probably had no more than a rather vague idea of the continuity to which they all contributed nevertheless. You can see the genius of the race pursue a dream of superhuman beauty.

Left the museum around two o'clock to sit on a bench in a wide avenue whose name I forget. I read a few *terzine* from the "Purgatorio." The day was very fine, I felt almost happy. If we were not wretched barbarians, what wealth life would ladle us by the handful!

A human being is separated from the rest of humanity by barriers that scarcely ever fall. That is the tragedy of one and all. Words betray us shamefully. We want to speak and no one is there to hear us, even though we talk to twenty people a day. What we think deeply is practically incommunicable. Love sometimes guesses our meaning, but that privilege belongs to love and to love only. God uses this agency to draw us to Him, for He alone understands us perfectly. Talking to a man is to throw a bridge over an abyss, but is there a road that continues the bridge on the other side of the abyss? Very rarely.

JUNE 27. Today I continued reading the "Purgatorio" with the same admiration and astonishment. There is great sweetness in the first *terzine* of Canto VII, an exquisite sadness that contrasts with the tone, so often hard and terse, of Dante's verse. I read and reread them with such keen pleasure that the trial we are undergoing grew easier for me. In Canto XI, the paraphrase of the *Pater* is of prodigious beauty; human speech suddenly rises to heights that we no longer reach; it seems as though this language was intoxicated by grace, but such an inebriation is divine and remains lucid. In Dante, there is no faltering, like that of a mystic coming out of ecstasy: he treads the air as though it were a road.

JULY 4. I went up to the attic the other day to take a manuscript out of a small trunk, an unfinished novel whose future has always appeared so doubtful to me: *The Transgressor*. I sat on the floor and read over several pages. A great many things had escaped my memory. How extraordinary to forget so much of what I wrote with such care. And as I read on, I could see myself doing so, and thought: "What a scene for a novel! To be sitting in a garret, reading a manuscript so peculiar that I do not quite know what I will make of it . . ." And it was really like a scene in *The Transgressor*, so much are our books part of us.

* * *

JULY 17. At Craftsbury Common, in northern Vermont, where we arrived yesterday around 7 P.M. in wonderful weather that reminded me of all the fine days in my childhood at Andrésy, at Conflans-Sainte-Honorine, at Poissy. As we came in sight of Craftsbury, the sun was imperceptibly, almost regretfully leaving the meadows and valleys. The earth seemed to laugh with joy in the golden light. As I gazed at one of the most beautiful landscapes in the world, one that made me think so strongly of France, I pondered over the deep mystery that war represents; it appeared to me in the light of a sinister game that humanity occasionally feels the need of playing, a game of violence and death, something like a *lust for unhappiness,* an irresistible need to suffer in order to restore some equipoise or other, the laws of which are unknown to us.

AUGUST 18. Reread Hawthorne's *Notebooks* sometimes with delight and at other times with boredom. A great writer, but the man himself seems a little slight. He lacked not living in a big city, or better still, in a capital. His generalities about life, the soul, good and evil are those of a provincial, but he is not short of genius. At times, he gives the impression of having taken long walks in the invisible whence he returns with an extraordinary booty of ideas that he expresses in two or three intensely deep phrases. He talks to us too often about his vegetable garden; you can be interested in green peas and salads but the subject is quickly exhausted. There is unquestionable beauty in the author's life, a studious life tinged with boredom, melancholy and austere happiness, but his taste for moral security and spiritual comfort disconcerts me. He fears evil and at the same time has a vague hankering after sins that he knows only imaginatively. I may be mistaken, although I do not think so. I have always felt that I guessed clearly enough the kind of man he was.

AUGUST 22. A curious study could be written about Hawthorne, with whom I have so much in common, as I now see on reading his journal closely. But his thirst for glory is very foreign to me. I have never wished for praise, nor done anything to obtain it (and this perhaps has gone against me). I would have liked Hawthorne to show more pride. "Will the world ever know me?" is a question he should never have asked himself (because he should have known the answer). What endears him to me particularly is

the value he gives to silence and all the invisible. His is a lonely
and mysterious soul, nearer night than day.

AUGUST 25. Read Hawthorne's *French and Italian Notebooks.*
A great disappointment. Hawthorne should have stayed in his
pretty house at Concord or not told us what he saw on the other
side of the Atlantic, for in Paris, Rome, and Florence this great
writer becomes platitudinous. His admirations are often funny. In
his eyes, the lounge of the Hôtel du Louvre is fit for a palace.
(The whole passage should be quoted in all its delectable ingenuousness.) In Italy, he mistakes Giotto for Pinturicchio and,
discoursing on painting, informs us that he prefers the works of
the illustrious Mr. Brown (an American artist of his times) to
those of Claude Lorrain. He blames Italian crowds for not being
crowds but "a collection of individuals" (September 10, 1858),
which is certainly the greatest compliment that could be paid a
crowd. He is embarrassed by the nakedness of statues (this is
rather touching although supremely irritating and ridiculous in a
gentleman of fifty-four; I thought of my friend Benton, who
would not read Baudelaire because he found him indecent and
still remember with remorse his hurt look when I laughed in his
face on that account, in 1922). Strange that Europe should have
made a most experienced author write such nonsense. At the very
bottom of Hawthorne lurked a provincial, brought to light by
this journey. Noted a few passages where he talks at length of
séances in Florence. Someday I will say more about this very
poor book; there is something humiliating in reading it for those
who, like myself, admire the author as one of the greatest writers
of his time.

SEPTEMBER 8. NEW YORK. Spent the morning at the Metropol-
itan Museum looking chiefly at the Flemish primitives, and with
such attention that I strained my eyes a little. What I particularly
wanted to see was how they went about painting a tree. Gerard
Dow gave me the best example of what I was looking for. The
tree, of the horse-chestnut variety, is treated with the leaves in
bunches, the top of each bunch edged with a thin line of light.
So much for the general impression. In detail, each bunch forms
a mass of tiny bright vermiculations on a dark ground, a process
adopted later by Patinir, Isenbrandt and several others. The effect
seems just right to me, showing a more scrupulous observation

than, for instance, the manner of certain Venetians in whose painting trees are hastily sketched for the requirements of a background and look like sprays of feathers. I prefer Gerard Dow's way of seeing nature, which is that of the Middle Ages, to the Impressionist method, in spite of Sisley's and Monet's great achievements, but then I realize more and more clearly that I often look at the outside world with the eyes of a fourteenth- or fifteenth-century man. . . . And it may also be that I sometimes look at the inner world with the eyes of those who believe as people believed in the days of Tauler and Henry Suso. I was deeply moved once more by certain pictures such as "Christ Appearing to His Mother" by Van der Weyden, or the "Annunciation" by Petrus Christus. [Since writing this, the painting has been attributed to Van Eyck.] Such works would lead a man to Paradise if he could listen to what they have to say; they create silence around them (in the next room are the Italian paintings and their screams), but what use is it to talk about what cannot be expressed?

I also wandered about in a landscape by Patinir, trees, meadows, and blue rocks; I was happy for a moment, and that means a great deal, nowadays.

SEPTEMBER 24. BALTIMORE. From my room, the eye looks down into great masses of greenery where the sun touches a branch here, the edge of a leaf there, as though to mark the stages of a mysterious saunter. At times, I feel prisoner to the trees that watch over the house in almost magical stillness; finally so still that you would like the foliage to stir more often, the wind to come down these airy steps, move about whispering through the labyrinths of green. Sleepy nature is maybe more disquieting than when in an angry mood. She is never man's accomplice, she dislikes his presence and would be glad for him to perish from the face of the earth. Ivy's sole ambition is to bury our palaces, churches, and factories under the sinister profusion of its small, black, funereal leaf. The roots of the oak wish to shatter our walls, its blind arms to pierce our roofs. Everywhere, the virgin forest claims her rights to the earth desecrated by man; it was there before him, and will survive the traveler whose passage in this world offends it.

SEPTEMBER 26. What takes place in our brain in the space of a minute should be recorded, if there were time enough to do it. But indeed, there would not be sufficient paper and also, how could the thread of such innumerable and rapid ideas be followed? You might as well attempt to follow the flight of swallows through the air. From one end to the other of life, a torrent of ideas runs through us and only a few of these can be discerned with some vividness. If this is the case, what is a diary, and how much truth can a work contain? The amount we extract to talk about is just an infinitesimal part of a sum that possesses its whole value only if the eye takes it in completely. I am not, nor have I ever been, quite the man of the diary I write. When I reread pages dating back to 1928, or to 1935, or even to 1940, something in me raises a protest. I am better and worse than I have implied, but I have always wished to be truthful. Now, to be truthful is one thing and to be accurate is another.

OCTOBER 6.   The story of the manna gathered and set aside by the Hebrews is deeply significant. It so happened that the manna rotted when it was kept. And perhaps that means that all spiritual reading which is not *consumed*—by prayer and by works—ends by causing a sort of rotting inside us. You die with a head full of fine sayings and a perfectly empty heart.

OCTOBER 16.   Oh, when will the Seine be reflected in our eyes once more?

Yesterday I talked about death with someone. We were walking in a wood of firs, on a carpet of tiny, russet, needle-shaped leaves; the setting sun blazed through the trees. We wondered if such men existed as never thought of death. And although I myself so often think of death, can I even imagine the day when I will no longer walk through city streets or under trees?

I was about twenty when I first thought of death as inescapable. It was in my uncle's orchard, in Virginia. I knew very well, of course, that I had to die, but, as Bossuet said, I knew it but I did not believe it. That day, I had a glimpse of what dying could mean and was seized with a sort of terror. Until then, like all young beings that life smiles on, I believed myself immortal, death was for everyone else but me. It was a kind of interior revelation and I do not think that I ever recovered from it.

OCTOBER 21.   Listening to the *Kyrie* from the B minor Mass, I remembered the day in 1921 when I heard an air by Bach played for the first time. Played is not quite the word for it. A music teacher sat at the piano to talk to us of Bach and with one hand ran over the first notes of that same *Kyrie*. It seemed, listening to this bare and unadorned phrase, as if I entered an unknown world. I had never heard anything like it, nothing that appeared more beautiful to me than the fifteen or twenty notes that rose in the silence; they made me think of footsteps, those of a numberless multitude marching along in a dim light, a humble, sorrowful humanity seeking its way through a great, dark country. It was as though music had been revealed to me in that single moment of time.

OCTOBER 27. It is growing dark. I place a lamp on the table and its light falls straight on the page of Homer with which I intend to fill my solitude. The window sash is half raised, night thickens behind it, but I can still see shreds of mist clinging to branches, and then comes the whispering of rain, a sound delicate as the patter of thousands of bird claws on the leaves, answered inside my room by my watch's tiny chatter. What silence back of all this! You would think that the water muttering in the trees and the ticking of the watch were the very voice of silence, rather than a noise that broke it. The little ebony elephant on the table watches my hand write these lines, and I want to note this peaceful hour as it passes from birth to death: it is five o'clock.

NOVEMBER 8. Some twenty-three or four years ago, in Rome, a friend put a volume of Bloy in my room. It was *Mon journal*, I remember. I was too young at the time to appreciate the merits of a book whose vehemence merely proved an excuse for me to laugh and jeer at it, although I was secretly perturbed by the serious character of its testimony. Such a voice echoes indefinitely through the years. All of us who have read Bloy and learned to love him do not rightly know what we owe him. I am not judging him as an author; he often ranks among the best, although at times he is also inferior to what he wished to be, and the reader suffers as much from this as he did. Nevertheless, he is the bearer of an immense message. In his letter about the conversion of Israel, for instance; the passage is one of terrible and mysterious beauty: a converted Jew is neither more nor less than the Prodigal Son who goes home to his Father, and no matter how he behaved, the Prodigal Son remains his Father's favorite.

* * *

DECEMBER 7. Today [Pearl Harbor], which should have been like all the other days created by God, with the sun triumphantly crowning a blue sky, today was in truth a day garbed in black to be mentioned henceforth with bated breath, as one used to mention August 2nd, 1914. It is a messenger of mourning, one of the veiled and masked ambassadors sent us by fate, bearing terrible and unknown credentials. But we must receive him calmly: "And when these things begin to come to pass, then look up and raise your heads," says the Evangelist.

DECEMBER 14. A moment ago, at the cathedral, I listened with great pleasure to an Advent hymn in which an entire civilization sprang to life, such as it was five or six centuries ago. No one will ever be able rightly to describe the peculiar effect of this music on the soul of a believer. It quickens echoes of a marvelous past that we remember deep within us, for it is our past and one common to all the men of our race. It should never be said that Americans cannot understand it. America stems from Europe, and it was the Europe of long ago singing this morning under the dark vaulting of a none too striking church. From the spectator's point of view, what improved things a little was the faded pink of chasubles striped with pale gold, the candlelight, the great copper cross and, in a word—apart from the spiritual side—everything that lends charm to the Church's ceremonies, everything that "appeals to the feelings," as monks would say.

1942

JANUARY 12. In New York, a few days ago. At the Franciscan church on 31st Street. Although not beautiful, it is really a Catholic church. The monks are responsible for this: their devotion attracts crowds who pray under the dark vaultings and pray kneeling for many long minutes. The crowd is made up of all sorts of people, many of them poor, as well as of cloaked somebodies with weighty Mass books, such as we have in Europe, regular attendants of the supernatural. Candles, barefooted, brown-frocked monks walking to and fro, continual prayer—I recognize

Catholicism in all this, what some would call the Catholic atmosphere, one I have always loved. The church copies one of the chapels at Assisi as best it can; horrible paintings offend the eye, but shadowy twilight improves things a little.

JANUARY 23. I have begun writing my lecture on Péguy. In reading over *Le Mystère de la charité*, I was most deeply moved by the fifteen or twenty pages about the Blessed Virgin at Calvary. It is the picture of the greatest grief that ever was, and one has to go back to the great French primitives to find it described with such power. I may perhaps attempt to translate these lines and read them at the end of my lecture.

FEBRUARY 14. Something new must be done; one's thoughts should not be continually sifted through the sieve of old books.
   The Bible only is eternally young, like a mountain torrent that has been leaping down a slope for thousands of years. Not only is it the youngest of all books, but the most recent, it is in advance of everything that will ever be written. A man writing a thousand years hence is *already* behind Bible time.

MARCH 16. You cannot give an account of love, any more than you can give an account of misfortune. That is why there are so many omissions in my diary.

MARCH 17. Last night, to a performance of *The Magic Flute*, which I had not heard since 1925 or '26 and had then found a little boring. Yesterday, however, although the voices were middling and the settings hideously pretentious, I was thrown into a sort of rapture; it seemed as if all that we are in danger of losing had passed into this music, I mean that all the beauty of our unhappy planet had chosen this ethereal refuge against all our forces of destruction. One can, alas, blow up cathedrals and palaces with bombs: a little training, a gift for aiming straight, are sufficient for that, but Mozart's music is a sort of enchanted castle where a too unhappy soul can still find shelter.

MARCH 18. Alone in the house. I opened *Macbeth*, which I am to see acted tomorrow. The first act brought back all my former admiration—no, not quite; I began to jib at so much bloodshed and, on reaching the third act, closed the book. Psychologically

speaking, it is one of the most *juvenile* of Shakespeare's plays.
The characters' nature is given once for all at the very start, particularly as concerns Lady Macbeth, who will remain exactly
what and as she is: she could pile murder upon murder during
forty acts and still be the same. Macbeth, however, grows somewhat bolder, but his character affords no surprises. He and his
wife are like steam engines driven full tilt along a perfectly straight
track; crime never swerves them; from time to time a whistle
shrills remorse, that is all, and on they go. And then, if you omit
shrieks heard in the darkness, curses, the racket of a storm and
daggers "breeched with gore," what remains is a singularly im-
poverished play. The action is, of course, carried out with great
art and many of the tirades spoken by Macbeth and his wife are
memorable, but I cannot believe that the weaknesses of this play
escaped the author of *The Tempest*. I may change my mind tomorrow evening. In another fifty years, I think, *Macbeth* will have
to be rewritten in modern English, otherwise no one will understand a word of it.

MARCH 19. *Macbeth* is more bombastic on the stage than when
it is read. Yet the chief actor (Maurice Evans) is at least tolerably
good. In spite of all, the mighty blast of genius pervades these
horrific scenes, and the audience listened in perfect silence to
lines that flew and bounded with all the vigor that was theirs three
centuries earlier.

MARCH 24. The other evening, I read my lecture on Péguy to the
nuns of Notre Dame (an Order founded by St. Pierre Fourier).
I sat on a platform and, by me, Father Couturier in his white robe.
Facing me, some thirty nuns in black, and a few pupils. I read
distinctly and noticed that almost all these women were in tears.
What moved them was the passage about the Blessed Virgin in
the *Mystery of Charity*. And so, it suffices to read these few pages
for their eyes to water. How happy you are, Sisters! I walked
home in the beautiful moonlight. As I reached the house and
paused to enjoy the quality of silence in the countryside, I understood suddenly that for years, perhaps, a divorce had been pronounced between my daily and my inner life, I mean that I no
longer have a hold on what mankind calls real life. I felt this very
strongly as, so to speak, I faced the revelation of an obvious fact.
This is what I might call my problem, and that would not be a

problem if there were not a war. I know only too well that the *emergency exit* is within us.

MARCH 31. The state of Christianity in 1942: English children "evacuated" from the coast inland are questioned by grownups. The latter ask them who is Christ. Answer: A swear word. That is all they know. All they know of Christ is this blasphemed name. The real causes of the war are perhaps to be found in facts like these.

APRIL 26. Finished *Memories of Happy Days* yesterday evening at seven. I wanted to call it *Before the Evil Days* (a quotation from the last chapter of Ecclesiastes), but my publishers convinced me that this title, far better to my mind than the former, would create a bad impression on account of the word *evil*.

MAY 11. So here you are, almost forty-two . . . If he could judge you, what would the boy you were at sixteen think of you? What would he say about what you have become? What secret hopes have you not disappointed, hopes you do not even remember? How passionately interesting, though sad, it would be to confront these two beings, one so full of the promises that the other has so little kept. I can imagine the youth harshly scolding his senior: "You've deceived, you've cheated me. Where are all the dreams I gave you to keep? What have you done with all the wealth I so foolishly handed you? I vouched for you, went pledge *for you*. You have gone bankrupt. Far better would it have been for me to leave with what I still had and that you have wasted. I do not admire you, far from it." And what would the elder man say in his defense? He would talk of acquired experience, of useless ideas thrown overboard, he would bring forward a few books, talk of his reputation, look feverishly through his pockets and desk drawers for something to justify him. But he would defend himself badly and I think feel ashamed.

JUNE 6. All the dead are our elders. When a child of ten dies, he is my elder because he *knows*.

JUNE 11. Read Stekel's book on anxiety again. There is a certain amount of uneasiness in the admiration I feel for this work. For these brilliant pages simplify our personality to the extreme, and

I really mean simplify, whereas, conversely, the author forms an exaggerated idea of our mental subtlety. This transformation of "slight repressed desires" into anxiety, in spite of such complicated processes, reduces our physical and moral nature to the role of a machine, or almost. Our brains—I do not say our souls, as this word has no place in these gentlemen's vocabulary—our brains, as well as our hearts, are so many factories where desires of all kinds change into I know not what that is atrocious as well as forbidden. The instinct of murder, or theft, or incest struggles desperately to come into the open and bring about the act of liberation. The borderline between good and evil vanishes, or if it remains it is only at the cost of physical and mental torture. Can it be that the human being is a monster? The answer might perhaps be yes, were it not for grace. One puts the book down with the feeling that we are even more mysterious than we thought, and that is no doubt what is truest in this stout volume—but the truth is there, unbeknownst to the author: it is a valuable one. No sooner does a man imagine that he knows himself, that nothing escapes analysis, than he heads straight into darkness. The sense of mystery should always be retained.

JULY 19. I would like to be able to tell the truth about myself. I know this is very difficult, that it depends not only on an honest purpose, that a particular form of talent is requisite, and above all, a determination to avoid being ensnared by words. I would like to tell *my* truth one day, one hour, or only for a few minutes. . . . The only means I can see of managing this is to write a novel.

JULY 22. If the war ended tomorrow, I would no doubt find myself much the same as I was in 1939, and the fact worries me, for in the spiritual order, this war is meaningless if it does not help part of humanity to improve. And if the operation fails, if the few million men and women whose duty it is to shake themselves free refuse the opportunity offered them—an opportunity that is perhaps a formidable godsend—the war will have to continue or to start up again. Just as each of us is the cause of the war, in the same manner each of us has the power to stop it. As soon as one tries to find the real causes of this war elsewhere than in our innermost selves, one gets lost in the chaos of human reasoning, for war is above all a spiritual tragedy.

*   *   *

AUGUST 10.   This morning's mail brought me a letter from President Roosevelt. It begins with these words: "President Roosevelt to Julian Green, greetings." (This is the usual formula.) It then enjoins me to report at the York Road office in Baltimore, with a three-day change of linen, for, the document goes on to explain, I have been called up and found fit for the army.

AUGUST 26. NEW YORK.   I have just had lunch with Saxton at the Century Club. He had a letter from Thomas Wells in Paris, saying that the city was more beautiful than ever. Could he have any suspicion of the way this remark affected me? In the twinkling of an eye, I saw the Seine once more, Notre-Dame, our deserted flat. . . . After lunch I went to Harper's with Saxton and he presented me with a copy of my book which is to come out in a few weeks (*Memories of Happy Days*). Is it absurd to own that I felt a childish pride as I went off with the book under my arm? That I skimmed through it in the bus that took me home and, what is more, stopped in a tearoom on Fifth Avenue to read over a few chapters?

AUGUST 28.   I went to see Maritain yesterday evening. We spent an hour and a half chatting in his flat on Fifth Avenue. He talked to me about Bloy and Péguy. I wanted to know if Péguy was not a little boring, a trifle too didactic in his conversation, but it seems not, that on the contrary he had great charm, that what he said had none of the labored, determined quality of his written style. I asked Jacques why Péguy had never answered Bloy, who had written him after reading one of his books. . . .

Péguy thought it strange that anyone should live in Montmartre, as Bloy did. To Péguy's formal mind, Montmartre was the equivalent of a night club.

I felt very close to Jacques during our whole conversation. I said that God would overthrow empires to wrest an assent from a soul, and that we see only dimly the spiritual side of great catastrophes.

He told me of an English Carmelite nun who had been ordered to ask that special worship be given the Blood of Jesus, and that as this worship had been refused by mankind, the threat of very great misfortunes had grown more definite. A little later, I said that the supernatural was like an element whose laws we knew badly, that by calling on its intervention, terrible *disorders* might take place—disorders that are really attempts to restore divine order—that those among the bourgeois who knew this, instinctively and by every means protected themselves (by the refusal of all poetry, of all religious mysticism).

SEPTEMBER 7. CAMP MEADE. I would like to note a few aspects of the days I am going through, so that an experience that has been forced on me may be turned to the best account, be it ever so small. I am writing this at the close of a cold, rainy day, seated on a campbed in the tent which I share with my four companions. The place is very badly lighted by a single electric bulb. On a canteen, a little radio plays one of those melancholy airs that the American ear never seems to tire of. The Spaniard, a nice, stout boy, has gone to bed, from despair. The Chinese traces beautiful characters on a sheet of paper, and the curiosity with which I look at them certainly has nothing indiscreet about it; he is a slim, reserved youth, given at times to fits of mysterious laughter. The Canadian, with bulging blue eyes, is probably the most touching of all in his childlike sadness and perfectly helpless attitude toward military life, which he cannot get used to. The American is a very silent, strapping fellow given to sudden fits of expansiveness, when he lets out rather unfortunate things: liquor makes him talk so. He is skinny and ugly, not as bad as might be thought and as he leads one to think. For my part, I am overwhelmed by boredom after a long, perfectly empty day. I talked this morning to a young Jew from Palestine who recited several passages of the Bible to me in Hebrew. A moment ago, I lay on my bed, wrapped in a blanket, and read the New Testament (Segond's translation), which I keep in my pocket. I wonder what meaning my present life can have.

SEPTEMBER 30. Yesterday, I held my first class for officers. There were twenty of them, not counting twenty soldiers and noncommissioned officers I have mentioned elsewhere. My heart thumped as I began to talk, but, as always, my "double" spoke for me. . . .

OCTOBER 7. There is nothing difficult about getting up when all the stars are shining in the black sky. I think, on the contrary, that to see the stars helps me to bear the whole day's burden, but what hurts is to be parted from those I love. However, I believe that if everything that happens is accepted as coming from God, life is wonderfully lightened. I wonder that men can accept a military life, that they see it only as the consequence of a certain policy, without realizing that beyond it all are a will and an intention superior to humanity's tragic whims. And this will must be appealed to, so as not to give in to sadness and fatigue.

OCTOBER 21. I could not sleep last night. Too many thoughts struggled in my mind, and it seemed as though my whole life came back to me in great fragments, like some landscape lit up by sudden flashes of light, in deepest night. At three in the morning, I got up and walked about outside the tent. The sky was a very dark blue and the stars spoke a tongue that words cannot express, a tongue that will always move me, for it appeals to what is truest in us. I lose myself in contemplation of the night sky, as some throw themselves from a bridge, to end it all, but in my case it is to find what I have been seeking since childhood, and when I look at the stars I can never be completely unhappy.

DECEMBER 1. Dog-tired. I don't know how many generals from Washington are coming here for the day, to see how we are doing. I am supposed to hold a four-hour class, so that if the generals happen our way, they will be certain of finding me at work with my pupils. Have just been told I will have to lecture before the Secretary of War. The subject I have chosen is the geography of France.

Moments of horrible sadness. Particularly in the morning, when whistles make us jump out of bed and a phonograph with a loudspeaker blares *gay* tunes of heart-breaking melancholy. I wonder how long I shall be here. I think they are keen on keeping me, alas, although the O.W.I. in New York has asked the army to *lend* me to it.

DECEMBER 31. Demobilized. Returning to Baltimore.

1943

JANUARY 4. NEW YORK. I often wonder how they live, those blameless ones! A pure soul is so mysterious! As I was thinking things over, the other evening, it seemed all of a sudden as though I saw a mental picture such as I have seen several times during the last five or six years. My mind's eye showed me a great city built like a fortress, but low and squat, on a vast plain at twilight. A hazy light rose from the city, and after a time I understood that this city was our soul and the light was the light of grace. A man in armor walked along the ramparts, and this man was human will, which mounts guard on the ramparts of the soul. And in the shadows of darkness, all around the city, was a great ragged mob of dismal faces, moving furtively. When a prowler came near the walls, the armed watchman thrust him aside with his sword, but could not prevent one or two of them from finally gaining entrance, nor could he prevent others from following, nor, after an hour, the whole city from falling into the hands of these ragged prowlers who represented in my mind thoughts of pride and covetousness.

JANUARY 16. Reread St. Augustine's *Confessions*. He seems to have conquered the frenzy of sensual desires at one blow, after his conversion. He talks admirably about these terrible chains he had dragged after him with such delight. During my whole youth, I was obsessed by the thought of an ideal life in which anxieties of a sexual order would not exist, because the pain they continually bred seemed out of all proportion to physical pleasure. It is not by chance that love is called a passion.

A verse from Ecclesiastes has haunted me all day: "God has put eternity in the human heart." [The author here follows the French translation from Crampon, 3:2.] Yesterday, I went to the little church on 62nd Street. It was nine at night. The church was empty; just two women whispering in a corner, a couple of Italians, their heads covered by scarves, and there was also, in the middle of the nave, a dead man in a coffin, under a black drapery. I tried to imagine that I was a corpse and my entire life took on a new light; struck by the smallness of our efforts to go to God, to respond to continual appeals.

JANUARY 24. Reread a few pages of *Le Rouge et le noir*, and in particular the chapter entitled "Le Séminaire." I used to admire this piece more than I do now, when I mostly see in it a sort of frantic dryness that is not unlike Sade. I quite see the beauty of these pages, but no longer enjoy it. It enraptured me formerly, but at present all I see in l'Abbé Pirard is a cassocked scarecrow and he no longer interests me. What a strange seminary the author takes us to! It gives the impression of a seminary for lost souls.

JANUARY 27. The Casablanca Conference. An offensive in Tunisia is expected, perhaps a speedy invasion of Europe. (The word *invasion* is frowned on over here.) The O.W.I. spreads the news throughout the world in twenty-two tongues. . . . How little I feel part of all this! I write my paper every day and take it to 57th Street, where I read it before a *mike*, in a small, empty room. Strange to talk daily to someone who, alas, cannot answer and maybe does not even hear.

FEBRUARY 2. Looking at a photograph of Gattamelata, I wondered how a blind face could be stamped with such strength of character, but that is the way with almost all of Donatello's portraits. Now, what expression can an eyeless face have? The truth is that the eyes are usually what lie in a face: they try to mislead an observer as to the meaning of the long, sad tale told by the lips, the nose, the curve of the cheeks, the lines and wrinkles, in fact the whole of a mask that cries: "I am the face of a miser, of a hypocrite, of a coward, of a pleasure-loving man!"

I recently bought Vigouroux's Polyglot Bible. Yesterday, in the preface to Ecclesiasticus, I read a sentence that plunged me into an endless reverie: "The four manuscripts that have gradually given us these fragments" (this concerns the Hebrew text of the book in question) "would seem to have come out of the *guenizzah*, or storeroom, of the Moses Synagogue in Old Cairo." Oh, the power of the simplest words! This sentence took me into an unknown world, yet one where everything seemed familiar. Thought of the term *Consul romanus*, which stirred Thomas de Quincey's imagination so strongly.

FEBRUARY 20. At Robert's flat on 62nd Street I can look out of the window and, with a slight stretch of imagination, think myself in Europe, in a bygone Europe—but there, in the 57th Street building, what I have at my door and see through the large bay window is my own century with a vengeance. A huge steel bridge, two gigantic gasometers, and a couple of factory smokestacks; so much for the foreground. In the distance beyond, skyscrapers. But in some strange way, the view is tolerable, I mean that these hideous objects compose into a sort of beauty. And in

this hell of stone, brick, and metal, with never a leaf to gladden the
eye, each morning, a bird sings: not for long: just four or five
notes, that's all, but this single trill contains a world of solitude.

APRIL 7. Words cannot express the loneliness created in the soul
by sin, for it estranges God from us, and in the absolute the only
true presence is that of God and real loneliness exists only where
He is not (if these words can have a meaning). Love and sometimes friendship stave off ordinary loneliness, but God alone can
do away with supernatural loneliness.

APRIL 15. I gave a lecture yesterday at a large college for girls.
I was shown a suite of drawing rooms all in the 1860 style, all
very solemn, with heavy curtains and tufted furniture that people
would fight over at the Flea Market. Talked with the professors
until it was time for my lecture; we gravely exchanged platitudes
about the temperature and the war; I have learned to do this with
all the soberness expected of me. Formerly, when I was younger
and less patient, I refused to take part in this make-believe and
lapsed into haughty silence. I read my lecture before two hundred
girls whom it could only have bored to tears and who none the
less applauded vigorously, as one girl, delighted, I imagine, to be
free to run away at last. Never have I felt so gauche. There is so
little reality in my present life, I mean so little that corresponds
to what I am, to what is like me. . . .

MAY 2. I have always dreamed of a life where sensuality would
be absent, not by reason of ascetic discipline, but from the very
nature of this ideal existence. However, doesn't this mean dreaming over the happiness of childhood? If I said this, I would have
psychiatrists against me, I know, for they claim that childhood is
a period of great sexuality and no doubt they are right, but a
child does not suffer from sexuality; he is not even conscious of
it, virtually it does not exist where he is concerned and so he is
able to enjoy the happiness I mention.

(AUGUST, 1948. *Yet who would wish for such questionable hap-*
piness? It stands to reason that the sexual instinct is a cause of
much suffering, but apart from purely physical manifestations, it
is also an element of essential activity that is to be found every-
where, in my opinion, as much in the field of intellect, in literary

creation, as in spiritual life itself. The odium cast on it by Catholic and Protestant writers is one of the saddest errors of puritanism, the origin of which is far earlier than the seventeenth century. And, moreover, a very difficult error to get rid of. Right in the twentieth century, our ideas of religion are so peculiar that one is not religious, in the eyes of the world, without also being ever so little of a puritan. For the devout, enemy number one is the sexual instinct; the only thing he forgets is that this instinct comes from God.)

MAY 3.   There are people who suddenly cease believing in God. Speaking for myself, I am aware of gradually ceasing to believe in humanity. It impressed me for a very long time by its speeches, its laws, its books, but I am beginning to see it in a true light—a very sad one—for humanity is an old lunatic whose fits of cruelty alternate with smiles. Humanity thinks itself majestic and venerable, forgetting its constant taste for blood and an immense thirst for calamity. Do not tell me that it seeks happiness; humanity, and this is only too clear, loves rows and ructions.

MAY 4.   Thoughts have wings, words trudge afoot. In this lies the whole of a writer's problem.

MAY 8.   I have never looked at Dürer's seated Christ without feeling heartsick, for it seems to me that if He is in such grief, it is particularly on my account. To whom would I dare say such a thing without feeling very ridiculous? Yet the little drawing really gives me that impression, and I wonder if this is not the very one it should give. Otherwise, in thinking that such terrible sorrow is caused by the whole of humanity, the sense of personal responsibility is considerably lessened. And as regards this question of salvation, I wonder if God does not wish it to appear to each of us like a great debate between Himself and "me," between Himself and every human being, as though each human being were alone on earth or, better still, as though each human being were in himself alone the whole of humanity.

MAY 25.   Read and reread the metaphysical poets: Donne, Herbert, Crashaw. I have a great feeling for Herbert's subdued poetry, for those nocturnal dialogues with Christ, in an old English vicarage: one can imagine the table with its lamp and papers, hands dropping a quill pen to fold in prayer. This is one of the sweetest and most peaceful moments in the history of the human conscience. When a recluse talks with God, how little does he know that such an hour of recollection sums up the aspirations of a world and that what he is doing perhaps surpasses in importance the clash of armies battling over a province.

JUNE 3. A spiritual void cannot be filled by reading the mystics; that would amount at most to staving off one's hunger. What induces us to buy so many books on religion? This is no doubt a "leaning," but shouldn't it worry us to see so many books around us, so little Christianity in us? I secretly think that a well-prayed *Pater* would teach us as much as the works our curiosity battens on, leaving our hearts thirstier than ever. We wish too much to know for the sake of knowing, instead of knowing in order to improve ourselves. What good are all those books of ours if they do not teach us to love our neighbor?

Taking up Chaucer again. His is the morning freshness of medieval times. In his world, already an old world, he was new. He discovered spring and all its scents, as though it were the first of all springs. We are too weary, too surfeited to pick a rose and smell it with the simplicity of a man of those times. But it must be said that we have also been too much bombed, torpedoed, and exiled. . . .

JUNE 8. Spent yesterday evening at the Maritains'. Lourié and his wife were there, Paulding of the *Commonweal*, Father Couturier. Jacques talked about Father Lamy. He told a number of very beautiful stories, such as the one about Father Lamy climbing a hill with a statue of the Blessed Virgin in his arms that he means to place in his chapel. All the village saints accompany him, climbing with their bare feet a few inches off the ground, passing through trees whose branches remain motionless; all of them have halos differing as to size, and talk to each other, saying: "He is going to send us away. . . ." In the course of conversation someone remarked: "There are no saints nowadays." Father Couturier answered rather gruffly: "Madame, St. Catherine of Siena's mother used to say: 'There are no more saints.' There are, on the contrary, a great many. We have all known some." Followed a discussion on art and religion. I said: "One can imagine a saint painting a picture (Fra Angelico) or composing music. Can one imagine a saint writing a novel?" "Why not?" they asked. "Then name one," I replied. So far, a novel written by a saint remains a sort of theoretical case. I even wonder if the fact of writing a novel would not curb serious spiritual efforts.

JUNE 11.   I was saying the other day that in novels virtue is usually shown up in a ridiculous light, no matter what the author's intentions. What could be more frightfully bungled than Little Nell in Dickens, or Balzac's virtuous young ladies? The most remarkable exception, to my mind, is Mme de Tourvel in *Les Liaisons dangereuses*. What part does irony play in this woman's portrait? I have no idea, but it seems obvious that the character *escaped* Laclos and lives independent of the author. White is a color (if it is one) that novelists use clumsily; they are far more skillful in using black, which is, according to Tintoretto, the most beautiful of colors (if it is one).

JUNE 17.   Wandered around Times Square and its vicinity the other evening, giving in to the longing I sometimes have to mix with a crowd, to be lost in a multitude, for no definite reason. Not that I get tired of books, it is a sudden craving for the streets. To my knowledge, Poe alone has described this feeling well; however, either from innocence or a sense of decency, he does not explain it. With me, it is perhaps the counterpart of a too regular life; a minimum amount of disorder is perhaps necessary to afford a certain balance, or, if the word *disorder* is too extreme, let us replace it by the *unforeseen*. The best that streets can offer is the unforeseen. But I hate crowds and after a few minutes drifted into a movie.

JUNE 18.   My edition of Mallarmé is incomplete (a selection of poems published by Perrin); I am completing it by using a copy of the N.R.F. edition belonging to Robert. Took the greatest pleasure in copying the whole beginning of *Hérodiade*. One cannot imagine how words could say more, or better; with Mallarmé, speech possesses a peculiar quality of extreme transparence combined with great inner complexity; it is like a block of cut crystal that revolves on its own axis; its outline can be seen at times and suddenly the pattern disappears, the sharp edges crisscross and seem to multiply in an apparent disorder out of which light unceasingly flashes. It has been wrongly said that his language is obscure. It is anything but an obscure language, it is a language without the ghost of a shadow and whose mysteriousness seems to be woven with light.

JUNE 30. Writing letters has always bored me to an incredible degree. The shortest note obliges me to make one and sometimes two drafts, which is ridiculous. A letter begun is often set aside, and sometimes for ever. In my drawer are numerous sheets of paper with just these words under the date: *Dear Mr. . . .* or *Dear Mrs. . . .* and that is all, because I have stopped, discouraged by the intense futility of the whole business. I have great difficulty in expressing myself in a letter. I say too much or too little, and the too little does not seem worth while continuing, whereas the too much always exceeds the limits of what was expected. I think I have unfortunately lost more than one friend by not having written a necessary letter in time, but then, what is a friendship that hangs on a letter? I want stouter friendships that stand up better before a trial by silence.

It so happens that one thinks so often and so habitually of God in set phrases that this great reality, which is the only reality, is obliterated by conventional words. We should try to think of God in His *newness*, in His eternal freshness. From time to time, but rarely, we have a confused impression of a huge mystery and then falter a prayer, at times the best of all possible prayers. How many of us have ever had a feeling of the presence of God? We take refuge in the most familiar forms of our religion, I do not simply say of religion, but what we make of it by a daily refusal of holiness . . . We fumble our way along without knowing what we are, or what we are doing, without knowing what is happening within us, because the world has put our eyes out. Money, sensual pleasure, ambition, success, kill in us all feeling of the mystery that surrounds us from birth to death. . . . This feeling should never leave us, the voice of silence should never cease to echo within us, the voice that says: "You are mine, I shall never let you go."

JULY 4. Human speech. Its imperfections are what intrigue me; to realize such insufficiency, it suffices to compare the swiftness and clarity of our thoughts with the heaviness and slowness of the words we use to voice them. There must have been a time (before original sin?) when human thought flew from one brain to the other without the help of this clumsy go-between.

* * *

JULY 11. Read Joergensen's *St. Francis,* which impressed me very deeply. There would be a great deal to say about it. St. Francis' struggles to preserve the original character of his Order seemed most pathetic to me. He failed, he saw his work changed, become jeopardized (some would say: succeed), and that, under his very eyes. The great good period was that when the brothers slept under the stars and all but starved. Later came money, came a desire for knowledge. A school was founded at Bologna, in spite of St. Francis' explicit wish, and he *cursed* the founder. The question would be to know if the first Franciscans were not really the only true evangelical Christians that the earth has seen since the apostles.

JULY 12. My mind is still taken up with Joergensen's book, for I see clearly enough that it passes judgment on our own way of living. We are so far removed from the Gospel that at first sight, one does not quite see how we could return to it. I know that when we kneel to say our prayers we are (in a certain way) with the Gospel, but the rest of the day we are separated from it by chasms. We open our lips, it would seem, only to deny it. We have lost the way to happiness. The life of a Franciscan around the year 1200 appears a martyrdom to us, because we see only its more difficult aspects, against which our idea of *well-being* rebels. We cannot conceive the unutterable interior joy that formed the counterpart of terrible privations (terrible in our eyes). Joergensen says that the English Franciscans, on meeting again after all sorts of difficulties, felt such great joy that they could not speak intelligibly. St. Francis danced as he talked to the Pope. We know that he sometimes pretended to play the fiddle with two sticks of wood and sang until rapture overcame him. These were men intoxicated with joy and such a joy that our wretched pleasures can never come near it. St. Francis was certainly one of the greatest of all poets and to such a degree that we wonder if holiness is not poetry under an absolute form, and if human poetry, even when it crawls on a level with the ground, is not the reflection of spiritual splendor such as we are incapable of imagining. What would sleeping on a board matter to us if Christ and Mary came to visit us? One is appalled at the thought of all we need to spend a short day without discomfort. A gloom is cast over some people by a bad meal, or what they call a bad meal. I have wondered for the last few days if Christ did not offer us His Gospel a *second* time during St. Francis' life. I know, of course, that He offers it to us every day and at every hour of the day, but that time was, if I may say so, a special time, a more particularly pressing exhortation. The world, the whole Christian world, should have followed. It does not appear that this took place.

JULY 20.   Reread a few of Whitman's poems. He is an American after my own heart, a grand person, ignorant, crazy, generous, and inspired. There is something barbarous about his intemperate speech, but a deep feeling for human fellowship and a contempt of all meanness rank him among the very first. When he lays a branch of lilac on President Lincoln's coffin, the gesture is most important, because of the man who makes it and because of Lincoln. Whitman possesses the enormous immodesty of a child, and I am afraid that America is secretly ashamed of the *enfant terrible* she has given the world. Stevenson has written pages of facile irony about this great poet, whom the Scot refused to understand, for it is easy enough to make fun of Whitman's absurdities, which are numerous. His greatness covers it all, his long cape, his vast and so bravely "artistic" sombrero; but in Whitman lies a sort of childlike nobility that Europeans cannot appreciate because a certain type of ingenuousness irritates them. I know very well that Whitman's extravagances can raise a smile, but who could resist his way of clapping you on the shoulder and calling you Camerado!

AUGUST 2.   It is always rewarding to read Stekel, and what I have said in this diary about his book on anxiety calls for several things to be set straight. We should see where he is right in simplifying our nature, in considering it as a mathematician studies a problem in algebra. It may indeed be, as the author says, that a transmutation of feelings is effected in the secret regions of our moral being, but the deep, supernatural causes of our actions cannot but escape an observer such as Stekel for whom the supernatural is a fabrication. Stekel would have challenged the possibility of such a theory as that of God working in us, unbeknownst to us, but we can resent a man of his intelligence denying the reality of religion without even having attempted to experience it; that is what irritates the mind in an otherwise stimulating book. I readily admit that "syphilidophobia" is a disguised fear of moral impurity, that the phobia of poverty is, also in disguise, the fear of not being loved (a fine, deep explanation), but these so-called elucidations only increase obscurity, for when all is said and done, we always end by asking: Why? Why is it so? Why this transformation of one thing into another? The answers he gives to such questions are inadequate, for they do not explain what prompts us to act. The mystery is not even touched on.

AUGUST 11. It is sometimes enough to pray fervently for ten minutes to feel that something is happening, that the soul is struggling to free itself from the world—but the powers of imagination are terrible. All one can hope for is to keep faith to the end, as best one can, as one would shield a lighted candle from the wind with a cloak—but one can never forget that at sixteen, one simply wanted to become a saint; one was right, then: that is the only honorable ambition.

AUGUST 19. John Donne's sermons fill me with great aversion for his doctrine, steeped as it is in death and damnation, but the writer is great. There is something both ringing and low-pitched about his sentences that strikes and arrests attention; they are often affected and grandiloquent, but they have a way of suddenly struggling loose from their draperies, and you feel as though Lazarus stood before you in all the horror of after-death corruption and talking with remarkable authority. Donne seems almost hypnotized by the more brutally painful aspects of death. To say it attracts him is putting it mildly—he is in love with it. There is a sort of firm, icy despair in him, hardly tempered by faith, having more in common with Seneca than with the Christianity that this ex-Catholic claims to be his. A strange character, haunted by memories of his youthful errors and to such a point that one wonders if he is not vulnerable at heart and, in spite of himself, in agreement with this disclaimed part of himself—a great sensualist who somberly and deliciously relishes a regret for his sins, failing sin itself. He shows a frightful zest in talking of moral evil, or the effects of the plague, or the pangs of death.

AUGUST 23. I was at the Co-ordinating Council a little while ago, to hand in a paper I am to read there day after tomorrow. Nailed to the wall of one of the offices was an immense plan of Paris, in admirable detail: every house could be seen; one might almost have counted the windows and chimneys. I immediately looked for and recognized our house on the avenue de La Bourdonnais and the one on the avenue Wilson. All that is over there, and I am here. The thought, so simple that it might seem absurd, plunged me, nevertheless, into a deep melancholy. I looked at that map with an outburst of love, for Paris is in us, in a way that I cannot express: the streets, the lines of the river correspond to something interior. All that has become part of our consciousness, but I think one would have to be deprived of Paris for a long time to understand what I have just written.

OCTOBER 15. I wonder if I shall ever be able to define what I call happiness. I don't mean a feeling that everyone knows, or has known, or thinks he has known, but something else more particular, something almost religious—a paralyzing emotion. I think that I must have been about eight when I experienced it for the first time in a classroom of the Lycée Janson. By looking out of the window I could see the gabled roof of a covered gallery that connected the small lycée with the large one, and it was when I was looking at this roof that a mysterious joy swooped down on me. I think that I remained in this indescribable state for several minutes, no longer quite aware of what was happening around me and, above all, not knowing why I felt so happy. Today, I feel that this unreasoned happiness is perhaps the normal state of humanity when it is torn away from evil, I mean the happiness that humanity would know if it returned to God. Several times later I have known moments such as I have just described and *that never depended on outside circumstances*. This is exactly what distinguishes them from moments of ordinary happiness. I was not happy just because the day was fine, or because things went well, it was because of other things that I could not understand, that I still do not understand. And I have always been struck even by the slightness of the connection between this happiness and that induced by love, for instance. I call it religious on account of its extreme graveness and on account of its mysterious origin.

NOVEMBER 20. Very much struck by reading Hopkins. He wanted to be a saint before being a poet. He believed that a good Jesuit glorified God better than a great poet, and he was both. He attempted to exorcise nature, to see God through it, to separate it from sin and discover it as it was before original sin. His curious, beautiful, forceful language tries to express what lies beyond human speech; a language that seems close to ecstasy, that tries desperately to see what man saw in the Garden of Eden, and that the poet *remembers*. Around 1875, this Jesuit, practically unknown to almost all of his contemporaries, leaped ahead of the most modern of our present poets, who seem to follow after him.

NOVEMBER 27. A little while ago, I was looking from the window of my room at the little gardens back of the house and saw, seated at the window of a small house that faces this one, an old gray-haired woman sewing diligently. I watched her for a few minutes, my head full of childhood memories brought up by the tiny gardens and the woman's even movements, which reminded me of Mlle Goudeau, our old seamstress; and I was anxious to retain all that was true and singular about this moment: the unknown woman wrapped in her little mystery, I in mine, and between us, a sort of bridge thrown from my window to hers by memory.

CHRISTMAS. To the Manhattanville convent yesterday for midnight Mass. The great freezing avenues in this part of New York, an unlovely night in a setting of sordid houses, shattered silence, blown to pieces by passing cars, drunken laughter, hostile colored faces, and then the convent in the solitude of a large park on top of a hill. A sung Mass, like those I used to hear in the rue Cortambert, but this one sung by more proficient voices, disincarnate voices that seemed to pass above humanity rather than mingle with it. About fifty of the black-gowned nuns went to communion; they walked up to the altar and returned with an admirable slowness that showed how little they lived in our times and that their life, wholly turned inward, already partook of eternity; their gait, in an indescribable manner, had the slowness of smoke rising from a wood fire into motionless air. They appeared to float, like people in a dream. It is religious life that teaches such slowness in a world basely enamored of speed. Nothing was more beautiful than these very deliberate and very simple attitudes, this refusal of all haste.

DECEMBER 28. I said good-by a moment ago to my O.W.I. colleagues, for I am going back to Baltimore. We had a farewell glass of port in Lazareff's office. I am writing this in the sitting room of the 62nd Street house; I have had pleasant times here, but it is already taking its place in the past, as one leaves a house long before crossing its threshold for ever, and it has been some days since I really felt present in this place. The flowered curtains are drawn, the large room is quiet, a little mysterious—it has always appeared so to me—the fire glows in the mock-marble fireplace and the wood crackles softly. From time to time, I hear the distant rumble of a train as it thunders by, but night muffles sounds and throws a man back into himself. . . .

1944

JANUARY 12. BALTIMORE. Spent three hours last week in the Washington art museum. Intensely weary, but hope to derive some benefit from this. Thought about what painting says to each of us. It bears witness to the world's beauty, raises a great and violent protest against habit, which gradually blots out from under our very eyes the wonders of daily life. It is the Fountain of Youth where our imagination bathes. Between 1850 and 1900, French painting unconsciously and unceasingly took up St. Francis' "Praises unto the Lord of His creatures": Sister Water and Brother Sun constantly being honored.

FEBRUARY 7. Reread the *Aeneid* in the train that took me to Washington. I found too keen a pleasure in the book not to attempt to discover what it is made of. For months I have lived shut up within myself, and the verses I am reading seem to lend a new radiance, a new force of persuasion to the outside world, and at the same time revive a universe in which grace apparently plays no part. Every one of us is so permeated by Christianity, even unbelievers, that the ancient world always appears more remote and more peculiar than it really was. Some feel a longing for it that is akin to the regret one might have in leaving a country for exile. What takes away from the happiness of some among us is that in the world such as they know it, there exists a book called the Gospel. A book that takes up very little space, that each of us is free not even to open, but it remains none the less true that the book is there, and that the presence of this slim volume causes several to be not so easy in their minds as they would like. They would be far happier but for the few hundred pages that may very well end by keeping them from sleep and disturbing them to the depth of their beings.

FEBRUARY 19. Continued, not without hesitation, *If I Were You,* the novel I began a while ago. What always makes me pause on beginning a novel and what makes me go back on what I have written and start off afresh, is that once the first pages are written, I have to live with the characters described, live with them for three hundred pages, with them and the manias, faults, and pieces of furniture I have bestowed on them.

Read *The Rock,* by T. S. Eliot, with great admiration, particularly the first page and its masterly statements on our ignorance. And these questions: "Where is the wisdom we lost in knowledge? Where is the knowledge we lost in information?" One would like to see such lines inscribed on the fronton of every university in the world.

FEBRUARY 28. A visit from Robert. We walked together on the road. We talked of what we were reading, of the books we would like to write. I told him that he was the only person in the world to know me perfectly and that I could, in consequence, say everything to him and be certain that he would understand. He is always present, whereas most people are partly elsewhere when you talk to them, even if they are fond of you. The head is there, the heart is far away, or the heart is close at hand but the head travels.

MARCH 23. WASHINGTON. Six P.M., a time when children call out to each other in a manner different from that of noon, I mean that their end of the day voice is softer, gentler, touched with unconscious melancholy. It seems as if everything tried to harmonize: the light and the street noises become more subdued, silence itself changes quality.

MARCH 29. Read Dorothy Hewlett's book on Keats with passionate interest. I marvel that, having been dead more than a hundred and twenty years, he should still inspire the reader with love. A boy with cheeks too pink, with black hair, shiny and soft as feathers, they say, whose hazel eyes had "a winelike luster." I like to think that he once crowned himself with laurel, that he put

a wreath of bay leaves on his lovely head for fun and kept it
there in the presence of visitors, refusing to remove it, in spite of
smiles and raised eyebrows. It is said that his ecstatic gaze made
people pause in the street. Beside him, Byron, who insulted Keats
("that dirty little cad," he called him), Lord Byron was nothing
but a coxcomb who smelled of cigars, who dreaded getting fat
above all things, a lady's man, a success, a poet who sold well.
Whereas Keats, Johnny Keats, once upon a time advised by a
weighty critic to "go back to the shop, Mr. John, back to plasters,
pills, and ointment boxes," bore within him all the poetry in the
world.

APRIL 9. Thought this morning that, of the two men living within us (the two men spoken of by St. Paul), each wants to fulfill
his destiny and reach a sort of perfection, the highest possible for
him to attain, but for this to take place, one of the two must kill
the other, as there can never be a lasting peace between them.
There can be truces, but with time the truces become shorter
and shorter and more and more difficult.

Felt depressed this morning on account of the problem I have
just alluded to. Worked hard to forget it and the war as well. I
have counted up that a fifth of my life has already been spent in
war-times.

APRIL 21. Impossible to say everything in this diary. . . . I have
tried to recover a balance that is more and more endangered by
my dual nature. Hosts of questions crop up incessantly. Perhaps
such uncertainties form part of my fate, teach me something that
I must learn. . . . What I lose in all this is my past buoyancy.
My heart is no longer so light, nor my head. I keenly feel the
hypocrisy there would be in attempting to reconcile a life of
pleasure with religious practices. Yesterday, because of a long-
standing promise, I was obliged to go and read a lecture on Péguy
to the Jesuits at Woodstock. I read four poems ("The Holy Inno-
cents," "Sleep," "Innocence and Experience," and "Leprosy and
Mortal Sin"). My audience listened in deep silence; I was afterwards told that it had been much struck by the *newness* of Péguy.
Before reading these poems, I was taken to a room to prepare, to
recollect myself, I suppose (a *prie-dieu* under a portrait of Newman in his old age, a desk, a fine view of the large park). . . .
What is strange and that I note carefully for future reference

(such landmarks are useful) was the effect that reading Péguy's poems aloud produced on me: I was deeply moved, far more perhaps than the "theologians" seated before me (there were also a few "philosophers"). Something told me: "Maybe this is for your own good rather than for theirs" (that is, the journey, all this traipsing)—but could I not have just as well read or reread these poems at home? No, the circumstances I mention lent them a particular quality.

APRIL 24. Once more, I pulled the volumes of my diary out of their box. I should not have done so: it is a mistake that can result only in immense sadness and most useless regrets. Of course, so long as I read them, I am back in Paris, but I wonder if I will keep this diary or if I will not burn it someday. I have always had a mania for flinging troublesome manuscripts into the fire. No one will ever know how many papers I burned in my youth. Nine times out of ten I was sorry for it, but it was then too late.

MAY 6. God should not be sought in books—except in the Gospel, which is not "books" but the book—He should be sought within us, for God is within us long before He is in books, and far more so. He is the one who must be eternally rediscovered, and I say eternally, because our eternity will no doubt be spent in doing this. The definitions given of Him are often obstacles to the knowledge we might have of Him; spiritual books, no matter how excellent, build systems, and not one of these systems is God, but is too often a substitute for Him, in the reader's mind. The feeling that an ignorant man can have for God is sometimes more exalted than what professors of theology say about Him in their books. More and more I distrust people who cannot talk of God without quoting texts, as though a historical character were being discussed.

MAY 8. BALTIMORE. Yesterday, went to St. Mary's, the Sulpician seminary near here, in the country. An immense, very majestic building with an important façade; severely plain except for a great doorway flanked by massive columns and surmounted by a heavy balcony, the whole edifice in the seventeenth-century Spanish style. Finished, I am told, in 1927. It is the finest thing I have seen in America, as far as modern architecture is concerned. A seminarian, Mr. Prime, had invited us to Vespers. So I sat by

Mr. Prime, who wore a surplice over his soutane. The chapel is a long room lit by tall windows. Two rows of stalls faced each other; there were over two hundred pupils and ecclesiastics, all in surplices. I had an extraordinary feeling of happiness when the Psalms were sung, the *Magnificat* and particularly the *Jesu dulcis memoria*. The sun shone softly in the long chapel where the many surplices lent a snowy whiteness. . . . I was no longer in America, I was in France and even in a seventeenth-century France. Very much struck to see how successful the thought of the founders of the Order had been in creating such a powerful illusion thousands of miles away from Paris and at a distance of three centuries. What I had before my eyes was a reflection of the Saint-Sulpice seminary in Paris, or at any rate of something that must have existed over there and been preserved intact through space and time. Perhaps the correct manner in which Latin was pronounced by young and old may have had something to do with it.

MAY 13. Never has the light seemed more beautiful to me. It is like a great hoard of riches tossed by handfuls into the depths of the foliage, depths all a-rustle with cries, songs, and calls. Can it be that I have never looked at it before? It turns the shade into a servant that follows it step by step in wonderful humility. I look untiringly at the lawns where a pattern of branches shifts amid pools of gold; now and then I leave my books and papers to walk on the road and in the woods to watch daylight triumphant.

MAY 24. It is cooler, after last night's storm. Robert, who had never been to Mount Vernon, took me there. For about ten minutes we drove through a vast garden; a wood bordered by lawns. I had been to Mount Vernon ten years before. Memories filled with melancholy came back to me, memories of a time when I knew I would be back in Paris in a few weeks, a time when my life was not, as it is today, sadly unmoored. We sat on the porch behind a row of slender columns. At our feet, beyond great stretches of green, ran the Potomac shrouded in bluish mist, a huge river with straggly shores that could easily bear whole fleets on its titanic shoulders. Indoors, I was once more struck by the countrified look of small rooms indelibly stamped by the simplicity of eighteenth-century American life such as is found almost

everywhere from North to South. I think one should have stood
within these walls to understand a certain America, for Mount
Vernon is like the mother cell of a great hive, of ever increasing
proportions. Looking at a rather dark little parlor whose tiny
window offers an immense view, I dreamed for several minutes,
as though something had at last been explained to me, I imagined
all the reveries, hopes, disappointments, and courage the room
had contained. Walls painted a dull green, polished wood furniture, silver candlesticks, the carpet with its bold floral pattern,
and, in this triumphantly conventional, honest setting, confined in
the narrow window and shattering the whole house, the landscape
like a large gap, and the vast blue river. I would have liked to
make all this perceptible, but such a twofold and contradictory
impression escapes speech; what can be said of it is inadequate
and can only be alluded to.

MAY 27. Read Browning's "Songs from Paracelsus." Beyond a
doubt, these lines were written for me:

> Yet we trusted thou shouldst speak
> The message which our lips, too weak,
> Refused to utter . . .

That is one of the greatest mistakes I will have to answer for
someday, a far more serious mistake, to my mind, than everyday
covetousness. I have held my tongue when I should have spoken
out. And I could have spoken; I had the means, I still have them.
Browning says elsewhere that an artist saves or loses his soul
inasmuch as he uses his gifts. I feel keenly that God speaks to us
through the mouth of those we see every day and through the
mouth of books that fall—and never by chance—into our hands.
  Thought today of what D. H. Lawrence said in a sentence that
contains all this writer's eccentric violence: "We are crucified in
sex." Strangely true of many among us. It used to humiliate me
to have this problem in my life. I supposed that the great men I
admired had not had these difficulties. They simply did not mention them. The sexual question did not fit in with the idea I
wanted to form of myself, a somewhat foolishly solemn idea.

JUNE 6. Heard today that the Allies have landed in Normandy.
It took me some time to believe it or even understand the news-
paper headlines. They are fighting between Trouville and Caen.
We returned to Washington last night.

Passing through Gainesville, we went out of our way to see "The Lawn" (my grandfather's estate). The house, rebuilt after the 1922 fire, looks very good among the old trees. The big cedar, the one I described in *The Keys of Death*, is still there, an old crippled giant still defying storms. All the windows were shut, and I understood that everyone was away. Robert climbed the bank that borders the great lawn and looked over the fence, which is covered with honeysuckle. A moment I shall remember. A vast blue sky, a deep silence, the late afternoon silence in the country, and the trees that talked to me of my twentieth year, of my father with whom I had strolled around the house one day in 1921. I was happy then, a little on account of the absurd, enormous confidence I had in the future.

JULY 4. MILLS COLLEGE. I held my first class yesterday. Spoke without notes for almost an hour, to my own surprise. I sat down at my desk much as one would fling oneself into the water, but with the first words, my anxiety gave way to self-confidence. After an hour of this, I was spent. I talked about the novel, brought up the question of knowing where books come from, but without providing the answer (how could I?). The class listened in admirable silence. A couple of nuns took notes. About twenty people in all.

Went to see the Milhauds after dinner. . . . Darius talked about Satie and his mania for collecting. After his death, ten unused and moth-eaten suits, hundreds of brand-new handkerchiefs, dozens of umbrellas were found in the composer's room. Cocteau is said to have seen him come out of a department store in a shower, an umbrella thrust inside his coat to protect it from the rain, looking up at the sky with hatred. No one ever entered Satie's home during his lifetime, says Milhaud. In front of his house at Arcueil-Cachan is another house, a deserted one on the wall of which some hand (Satie's hand?) had written: "The devil lives in this house."

JULY 20. At table today, several students asked for my views on education. I laughed and answered that I hesitated to tell them, as my views were unconventional and we were in a college. "Oh come!" they cried, "we aren't children!" "Well," I said, "they stuff your heads full of facts, without teaching you to draw useful conclusions from them. Education consists in rousing intelligence, in stimulating it rather than burdening memory. It doesn't matter much that you have read all Spinoza and all Plato (as you are forced to in some colleges) if you don't know how to reason correctly. And rather than make you swallow all these books, it would be far better simply to give you a taste for reading (which you have lost through enforced reading), etc." It was all they could do to keep from applauding. What I said was so unlike what is usually told them.

JULY 21.   If everything could be said . . . But Poe is right: *My Heart Laid Bare* will never be written. "No man dare write it. No man will ever dare write it. No man could write it if he dared. . . ." Or, having written it, he wouldn't dare not throw it in the fire.

AUGUST 5.   Mrs. Stein tells us that she has a great number of letters from Matisse and that she burns them as soon as she reads them over, which makes us all protest in horror. What can be done to prevent her from destroying the letters? She shakes her head, only promising to save one letter which she hands us and that contains the account of a visit Matisse paid Renoir in 1918. I remember this sentence of Renoir's: "I'm just an old fellow who hasn't done much, but what I've done is really mine." Speaking of his painting, he says: "Yes, but it's *not enough like Courbet.*" Mrs. Stein tells us there is too much about stomach-aches in these letters of Matisse. "How could all this interest the public?" How? Of course it would! She smiles and shakes her head. She is going to burn the whole lot, except that single letter.

AUGUST 13.   At Birmingham, Michigan, with my brother Charles.

AUGUST 17.   Yesterday, I walked by myself in the gardens of Cranbrook. I looked at Milles' big, innocent statues mirrored in the water. Also looked at boys and girls bathing in a little lake: that was more beautiful. America's masterpiece is youth: its body is a hymn of glory.
   Had a long talk with Charles. He looks very much like my father as I knew him around 1920. My father was forty-seven when I was born. I particularly remember him when he was fifty-five or sixty. Charles' big gray eyes have Papa's kindness. And he has also inherited my father's courtesy, the meaning of which is scarcely ever understood nowadays, or appreciated. Charles thinks

the war is about to end, but he has two sons in the army and I am afraid this influences his judgment. He has had a hard life. His courage and, above all, his extraordinary trust in God make me feel very close to him. When in difficulties, he is always convinced that God will "straighten" everything out. And, of course, that is what happens. The other day, a neighbor said to him with a smile: "Everyone knows that God protects the Greens in a special way!" I laughed with him, but have always thought so a little too.

AUGUST 23. BEAR TRAP FARM, VIRGINIA. Today, at breakfast, a woman at a table not very far from ours said it would be a good thing if Paris were razed to the ground so as to be done for ever with that impure city. Her neighbors calmed her down at once by remarking that if people began razing all impure cities, they would have to raze Washington, New York, etc. And the lunatic said no more. In this curious hatred of Paris lie so much sensual deprivation, years of repressed desires, frustrated pleasures, long-ings. . . . This is not the first time that I have noticed the mani-festation of a puritanical conscience. "We are at war because of Europe's sins" is an argument that leaks from the talk of the calmest and best-informed people. No one can understand any-thing about an American unless he remembers that even in a lack of religion, the reactions of a religious man still linger in an Amer-ican. The old yeast of puritanism is still what makes the dough rise sometimes.

AUGUST 24. In Hawthorne's diary, his "day-book," as he calls it, I noted this which enchants me: "In an old house, a mysterious knocking might be heard on the wall, where had formerly been a doorway now bricked up." And this too, extraordinarily pene-trating: "A person to be writing a tale, and to find that it shapes itself against his intentions; that the characters are otherwise than he thought; that unforeseen events occur; and a catastrophe comes which he strives in vain to avert. It might shadow forth his own fate,—he having made himself one of the personages." (Pages 15 to 20 in Houghton Mifflin's edition, 1910.)

I am writing this in my room. The wind blows with a great murmuring that passes through the whole sky. Silence over the countryside, silence spread over the countryside like a sheet; yet if one listens closely, the locusts' chirp can be heard in the meadows and the distant creak of a cart going up the road. In the little house where I am staying, the hour is so deeply peaceful that one would like to spend it only in doing beautiful things, in writing, or in praying (if one could). The crowing of a rooster rises from the bottom of the valley, but over all this is silence that masks every noise. I must also note, for memory's sake, that the blue of the hills verges on violet.

AUGUST 26. Yesterday evening, at seven, I heard an American correspondent in Paris; he was speaking from there. His voice was indistinct, but around that voice was the hum of Paris. All I understood was: "This is So-and-so in Paris." And that sentence was enough for me. I listened without catching a word, but delighted and more moved than I can express. And so Paris can be heard once more. The odious gag is off. . . . At supper, in the lovely dining room where old furniture gleamed softly and candlelight flickered on the rafters, ten or twelve of us sat at the long table. Through the window, I could see bluish-gray clouds sail through a pale green sky, chased along by a cold wind from over the hills: there was something violent and gloomy in the great picture that contrasted with the restfulness of the room where we sat, with the soft, peaceful candlelight. After the soup, a maid came in to place a glass of white wine before each of us, then a graying gentleman rose and said a few very simple words; he said: "We must not speak of the fall of Paris, but rather of the rise of Paris," and raised his glass to drink France's health. Someone else added—an old white-haired man: "And we are also thinking of our boys who are fighting." And that was all. After supper, I thanked the man who had spoken. He smiled; he said: "It's three in the morning in Paris. I don't think there's much sleeping there tonight."

AUGUST 27. Reread *King Lear*. When I was twenty, in Virginia, an hour away from the place where I am now, I used to turn storms to account by reading over certain scenes in this play which is, sure enough, the story of a big storm, whose hero is a storm; Lear himself is that storm; all he can do is to rage or weep, he's not a man, he's an element. From the very first scene on, he is mad or doting, but he is a dotard of the violent type. What bothers me greatly is the counterplot of which Edmund is the chief character, for Edmund is a conventional traitor and, owing to him, *King Lear* is a magnificent poem and at the same time a melodrama. The scene where old Gloucester is tortured is almost unbearable, but contains this unforgettable line: once the old man's eyes have been put out and he declares that he wishes to go to Dover, Regan cries with terrible brutality: "Go thrust him out at gates, and let him smell his way to Dover." (Act III, scene 7.) Very much struck by marvelous scene 6 of Act IV, where Edgar is seen as he pretends to lead blind Gloucester to the edge of Dover cliff, whence the old man wants to throw himself, but they stop long before. "You are now within a foot of the extreme verge," says Edgar. Gloucester flings himself forward and falls on the ground. Edgar then feigns to be someone at the bottom of the cliff and congratulates the old man for having fallen unhurt from such a height, and Gloucester believes this fable. The scene is strangely poetical; it is, unless I am mistaken, the one Keats liked so much and that he used to read over on the Isle of Wight. Particularly the passage containing the word *samphire,* a rather mysterious word.

AUGUST 28. I don't want to drop *King Lear* without noting several things that have struck me. Act V, scene 3: this which is important: "And take upon's the mystery of things, As if we were God's spies." The idea was taken up by Browning. A poet is God's spy.

And this also: Act V, scene 3. Regan has just been poisoned by her sister Goneril. She is in great pain and cries: "Sick, O, sick!" Then Goneril, in an aside, makes a comment that cannot but be found extremely comical in its cruelty: "If not, I'll ne'er trust medicine."

Shakespeare often gives his language a familiar turn, not unlike current American speech. For instance (to be found in *King Lear*): "Shut your mouth, dame." And this, which is very fine, at the very end of the last act (Kent speaking): "Vex not his ghost. Oh, let him pass! He hates him That would upon the rack of this tough world Stretch him out longer." There would be better examples to find, however.

SEPTEMBER 4. BALTIMORE. Translated seven or eight pages of *Memories of Happy Days,* but don't know if I will go on with it. Certain naïvetés pass in English but would not be tolerable in French. This is because I am not the same person in both tongues; I knew it, I said it throughout a lecture.

* * *

SEPTEMBER 17. Read Auden's *Look, Stranger,* with deep admiration. Some lines make you feel like clapping your hands (I realize
that a critic might say: That's just what we find fault with! but
that is not the way I take it). I do not find in them the facility he
is accused of, what I see above all is a certain contempt for pleas-
ing everybody, of being understood by the many. He teaches
near here. If I followed my lead, I would go to see him. As it is,
to have a great poet in the vicinity is a great deal. I cannot resist
the pleasure of quoting a few lines where singularly beautiful
images remind one of Blake at his best:

> That later we, though parted then,
> May still recall these evenings when
>   Fear gave his watch no look;
> The lion griefs loped from the shade
> And on our knees their muzzles laid,
>   And Death put down his book.

SEPTEMBER 22. Read some of Auden's poems. They have a touch
of the Byronic irony adopted nowadays by so many English poets
with a sort of fervor. The pietism of unbelievers. It is character-
ized by complete nihilism, by contempt for everything that has
been handed down by parents, that is, for the nineteenth century,
for the Victorian era, a rebellion against venerable commonplaces,
against everything that has so long confined us in our political
errors and that produced moral circumstances apt to hatch wars
such as that of 1914 or of 1939. It must of course be admitted that
they are right, nine times out of ten. But also to be included here
are the snickers that greet the testimony of mystics ("night of
the soul, dry as a bone"), in short, the great desert known as "the
clean sweep."

There is a fact in my life that I have never so clearly understood
as today: for the last four years I have been running away from
the book I want to write. How can I not understand the meaning
of all those numerous attempts that were cut short so abruptly?
The reason is that I have not published *The Transgressor*. Writing
a book is not enough to set an author free, the public must read
it, the public must know. Everything that I have written for the
past four years, memoirs, diary, prefaces, lectures, has been written *instead of something else.*

* * *

SEPTEMBER 23. Reread Stekel again. The conclusions of his book on anxiety are fascinatingly interesting. Enough material there for ten novels. There is an excellent passage about the havoc created by tenderness in the souls of beings thus made incapable of facing life. But I can never reread Stekel without saying to myself as I close the book: "Yet the Church is right: sin is a terrible reality." It remains nevertheless true that what he calls repressed sexuality can be dangerous to a degree not always suspected, when a very strongly organized spiritual life does not provide the necessary counterweight, does not restore equilibrium. Wouldn't insisting on repressing sexuality, in a very moderately religious person, mean exposing him to serious accidents, body and soul . . .

Beyond these things is the world of mystics. I was struck by what I read in Eckhart this morning: a priest said to him: "I wish I had your soul in my body." And Eckhart replied: "That would be useless. A soul can save itself only in its own appointed body." (Fénelon said something similar: to save oneself by means of one's own particular temperament.) And so our instincts, which vary so much from one individual to another, would be the particular instrument of our salvation. Can one imagine, however, a part of the human race banned by society in the name of divine laws, and that on account of instincts which this banished minority cannot help? Must it go in a body to a convent? This seems absurd. And what does the Church say about this? The Church is silent. Mauriac, to whom I submitted these difficulties, merely shrugged his shoulders as much as to say: What can be done about it? An answer most Catholics make. And this argument: You wouldn't have the Church allow such things, would you! I note that in this case the Church follows the example of Jesus, who was silent. St. Paul expressed himself long and furiously on the question we are discussing. Christ did not say a word about it that has come down to us, and yet, in Judea, at the time, under Roman rule, in a great city like Jerusalem, the question must have been asked Him, anxiously asked Him. What did He say? He kept silent, as the Church is silent. This is in itself a sort of answer, but what an obscure one!

OCTOBER 1. A moment ago, I listened once again to George Gershwin's *American in Paris*. The opening theme, a young American on the boulevards around 1920, is so good-natured and at the same time *so faithfully observed* that I felt a little heavy-hearted. The Paris of 1920 (for me of 1922) is so far from us and seems so lovely and carefree that it is almost painful to remember it. Nightly walks along the Seine or the Champs Élysées, street lights shining through the horse chestnuts, mystery, gaiety, the smiling quality of it all, the absolute confidence in the future that swept me onwards, the exhilaration of being alive in the most beautiful city in the world and at the finest moment of my youth —I felt at times that my heart was not big enough to hold such happiness. This pretty theme, a trifle waggish and a trifle sad, brings it all back to me now. I hope never to be the man who thinks the Paris of his youth more beautiful than the present one, but it seems to me that between 1920 and 1928, life had a certain sweetness never since recovered. I feel heartily sorry for the boys born twenty years after me.

OCTOBER 8.   Read *The Tempest* for the sixth or seventh time, but was never so much struck as now by the character of Caliban. We are so used to seeing in him a brute in the state of nature that the author's intentions are obliterated by this preconceived notion. Trinculo and Stephano are just plain out-and-out drunks, but Caliban, with all his coarseness, often expresses himself exquisitely. It was Schlegel who noticed that he always speaks in verse. What Caliban says about the sounds heard on Prospero's island is exceptionally beautiful, and one feels keenly that it is not just a fortunate accident in Shakespearean poetry. No, Shakespeare wanted the lines to be beautiful because they were Caliban's:

> Be not afeard. The isle is full of noises,
> Sounds, and sweet airs, that give delight, and hurt not:
> Sometimes a thousand twangling instruments
> Will hum about mine ears . . .

And what follows. There is a delicacy in this conception of a completely and deeply natural being that could only be that of genius. Therein lies the surprise. A savage who talks of music like Byrd or Purcell! A second-rate author would probably have given him a base, rude speech. What makes me feel ill at ease in this play (although the defect is less apparent here than in many others of Shakespeare's plays) is the triumph of commonplaces, the royal vestments that clothe hackneyed ideas. But the music and color of the verse rank it among the finest ever written.

✳ ✳ ✳

NOVEMBER 8. Yesterday evening, Father Couturier came to see me. I no longer remember in what connection I said that sin gives an experience of life that can be turned to immense advantage, spiritual advantage; that sin educates the individual, is a sort of school where he learns to know humanity; that God allows souls that have lived in sin to escape from it and then grow closer to humanity than souls that have never lost their innocence. He allowed that I was partly right, remarking however that the danger of remaining in sin is far too great, and that very spiritual souls intuitively know sin to such a degree that it amounts to a perfect knowledge of all aspects of the problem. Such intuition, I said, would be tantamount to genius, that is, extremely rare. . . . At one moment, I seemed to justify sin and wish to prove the usefulness of evil, but Father Couturier understood me. I was thinking of a certain young priest whose complete ignorance of worldly matters turned him into a sort of child; I know perfectly well that the confessional is an admirable school of psychology, but before he has learned his lessons, how many souls will the young man have rebuffed and discouraged by his uncompromising harshness!

NOVEMBER 20. As we walked in the woods just now, I was telling Anne, in connection with an invitation I had just refused, that I never felt quite at ease with rich people. I have been like this since childhood. It is perhaps because I was brought up very simply; something in me disapproves of luxury (as much as it nevertheless admires it). To dine in a dining room that looks like a dining room in a palace plunges me into a sort of stupor that quickly turns to melancholy. Sumptuous surroundings depress me and I never feel quite happy with a gold plate before me.

In the life of the poet Hopkins by Eleanor Ruggles are quotations from letters exchanged by Hopkins with an Anglican divine, also a poet, but a completely unsuccessful one. Hopkins tries to comfort him. He tells him first of his own lack of success, then says this which I find deeply touching, because one feels he believes it (and also because it is true): "The only just literary critic is Christ, who prizes, is proud of, and admires more than any man, the gifts of his own making."

Reading the book on Hopkins reminds me of certain questions I have sometimes asked myself about physical beauty. Is beauty a sign of latent spiritual perfection, like the mark of a superior vocation? I have always thought that a faultlessly beautiful being who commits an evil deed betrays the man who is himself as he should really be, whereas an ugly being (of a particular ugliness, however, for there exists an ugliness that is almost a form of beauty) who perpetrates an evil action only makes the inner man conform with the outer one.

NOVEMBER 26. Read some of Yeats' poems with delight. An Irishman has a mysterious understanding with nature; you might think he had made a covenant with her, and when he talks about the country, the trees and the grass and the sky do the talking.

Reading the life of Hopkins, I can't help feeling that his personality was crushed by the discipline of the Order to which he belonged, but that is perhaps the impression that the author wants to give. Be it as it may, I wonder to what extent Hopkins accepted his vocation. He remained faithful to the end, but admitting that he never entertained doubts about the wisdom of decisions taken, he would never have fallen back, would never have owned up to a defeat, for to flinch in the face of a decision that involves a man's whole character would not be like an Englishman of his kidney. And in any case, there is no serious reason to believe that he was not an excellent religious although one suspects him of lacking enthusiasm.

NOVEMBER 29. Have thought a great deal about the beauty of human beings (perhaps Hopkins roused these thoughts in me, although I must say that they were only dozing). It seems to me that the beauty of the human eye alone is beyond all possible speech; and I remember that Father Couturier, who was very austere but most intelligent, once said to me: "Nothing in the world is more beautiful than the human body."

DECEMBER 15. At the theater last night to see *The Cherry Orchard*, a play that I admire deeply and whose meaning is more clearly apparent than ever over here, in 1944, for I think that America contains lots of cherry orchards, ready to pass from hand to hand. Behind me, a nasal voice said in an important, well-informed tone: "The play was written to show the corruption of the ruling classes." (!) Keenly sensitive to the beauty of certain scenes where, as in Shakespeare's theater, the characters seem suddenly *larger than life*. At one moment, the limits of sadness are reached when, in the big, bare room, empty of furniture and the large wooden shutters closed, the old, white-whiskered servant comes in and, finding he has been forgotten, lies down on a sofa that has been left behind and very simply dies while the cherry trees are being cut down in the orchard. I know of no one but Chekhov who could have produced such an effect; one almost resents such a form of cruelty even though it is accompanied by the most moving tenderness. The comic scenes I thought overstressed, but that is life's way of being funny, and life does not always have a light hand.

DECEMBER 30.   On reading a book like the *Imitation*, I am always struck by the intense reality of the spiritual world; a reality so powerful that it seems to shut out any other possible reality; it consequently appears quite natural to be captivated by an invisible world that offers us the only lasting goods. Things become more difficult later, once the book is closed and other realities present themselves. The answer could be, of course, that compared with spiritual realities, those of the physical world are scarcely more than shadows that seem terribly lifelike at times. The opposite phenomenon then takes place, I mean that the reality of our world of flesh is so commanding that it excludes even the idea of a contradictory reality.

1945

JANUARY 18. WASHINGTON.   I have often wondered why the sun makes me feel so sad. That is not the way it usually affects people. There are days when great splashes of light on a wall fill me with dreadful melancholy! People would probably cry out in horror against my irreverence if I said that I almost always feel happier when the sun disappears from the sky, and the time when lamps are turned on in cities has a very special charm for me. "Busie old foole" [1] gives me a headache. I never go out in the morning if I can avoid it. In my mind, everything tragic takes place in full

[1] See Donne's "The Sunne Rising."

sunshine. "The night shall be light around me." How often has that sentence from the Psalms come back to me! Night is to some extent my home. I have always noticed in my books that when some calamitous event is brewing, the weather is almost always fine.

FEBRUARY 1.   . . . I ask this without being able to answer: Does religious indifference afford a novelist greater freedom? What scruple can arrest him in creating the world contained in the pages of his book? A book without mortal sin? You would have to be Péguy to write such a book, and Péguy was not a novelist. Now, a real novelist does not reign over his novel, he becomes his novel, is immersed in it. The connivance between himself and his characters is even deeper than he thinks, and if they sin, he sins too, in a certain way. He is all that his book is, if he believes in it, if he allows himself to be caught; and if he does not allow himself to be caught, if he is not under the spell cast by the monstrous thing that issues from his brain—for a novel is a monster—he no longer writes novels, he manufactures them. Supposing this is the case, and it is, beyond the shadow of a doubt in my mind, I would like to know if the fact of writing a novel is consistent with the state of grace. I cannot and will not answer this question. I am above all afraid of the answers that could be given me, the ingenious solutions. A scrupulous man will never produce a great novel. For fear of offending God, he will write prudent platitudes and who knows if God does not wish a risk to be taken? Who knows if this is not the way to please Him and to fulfill one's vocation?

JULY 19.   I stopped just now before the stall of a man selling magazines and candy in the doorway of a building. I bought some magazine or other. The young man in a white coat who stood behind the counter looked smiling at his open hand and I held out a quarter, but he did not take it, went on smiling and looked down. A little surprised, I said then: "This magazine costs fifteen cents, so you owe me ten, as I gave you a quarter." He immediately handed me a dime without a word, but still smiling. He was blind. I had a strange feeling of his moral superiority over me, although it was impossible for me to explain why. Perhaps on account of a verse in Job that has played such a great part in my life, and where I cannot help seeing the solution of certain problems: "I have made a covenant with mine eyes. . . ." This blind salesman was safe from the weaknesses usual in those who see, he does not sin with his sight, and if ever he made a covenant with his eyes, he is now certain of keeping it. He looked joyful; a handsome sixteen- or eighteen-year-old face. An indefinable quality of poetry surrounded him because of his infirmity, he was *apart.*

JULY 22. Asked Father Couturier the other day if he had ever thought about the happiness of medieval men who lived in a world with so little room for doubt and where, generally speaking, everybody believed in the same thing. But all of us who live in a world where doubt is, to a certain extent, the general opinion, how can we not feel isolated and like lost children in modern civilization, we and our singular ideas about the incarnation and the transubstantiation (singular in the eyes of the world, but as natural to us as the sun in the sky)? He said that he too had had that feeling of solitude, but I did not encourage him to say more. I could have added that this feeling of spiritual isolation, so painful at times, historically precedes the joy of universal belief, for the first Christians, lost amidst Roman civilization, must have felt a little the way we feel today.

JULY 27. BALTIMORE. I have a passport and will soon leave America. These last days in Baltimore have been difficult. To go away is almost always for me an uprooting, even if it means leaving a place where one has suffered, and I was not always unhappy on Blythewood Road, far from it, in spite of the war. I have known moments of hope and real happiness, thanks to my cousin's kindness. . . . So the other day, I packed my trunks and watched a man put my books into crates. The room where I worked for four years has that look of disaster peculiar to moving, and the heat has added to the sadness of my preparations for departure. And yet, isn't this the moment I have been waiting for since 1940? It is, of course, but I can't help it; I am not leaving in high spirits.

AUGUST 7. CRAWFORD NOTCH. Day before yesterday, looked long at the sky, which happened to be exceptionally transparent. Except in Tunisia, I have scarcely ever seen so many stars and such bright ones, although they seemed larger to me in Africa. What could ever be said of such a sight? It reduces human speech to nothing. Even the effect it produces in us is beyond words. A great inner happiness, a deep feeling of the world's vanity, a more mysterious feeling akin to that of the presence of God, an enormous silence within us, like an echo of Heaven's silence.

AUGUST 14. NEW YORK. Took up *Romeo and Juliet* again. On reading it afresh, I discovered a wealth of beauty that had escaped me in the past. The love scenes are among the only convincing ones in the whole of literature or are even the only readable ones, because a love scene is what we anticipate in dread as it is almost invariably a flop, even with the greatest writers, even with Balzac and Dickens. Here love itself speaks its genuine, inspired language; it is really the heart's outpourings, the inimitable freshness of youth and its faltering amazement. There are strange weaknesses toward the end of the play, such as Juliet's soliloquy just before she drinks the sleeping potion; a few extravagances, one of which at least is funny; she is in a funeral vault and threatens to break open her head with the bones of a deceased relative!

AUGUST 28. At Suffolk, where I wanted to say good-by to Jim before leaving for Europe. He is married. I had scarcely sat down in the drawing room when he told me that he had had a letter from France and wanted to read it to me, in order to dissuade me from returning there. I answered, with a sharpness at once regretted, that I knew beforehand what the letter had to say, that I was as well informed as anyone in America of the state France was in. I refrained from adding: "When you love someone, you don't say: 'I'll come to see you when you're quite well again.'" But Jim was most hospitable and affectionate. There is a world of memories between us.

SEPTEMBER 19. AT SEA. To leave those we love is horrible; it is almost like dying. The last words exchanged, hands waving as the train slowly leaves the station, I can hardly bear to think of it and remain perfectly calm. We should never say good-by. I stayed in my cabin on the boat while New York grew distant and disappeared in the mist.

SEPTEMBER 29. AT SEA. Around eight this morning, my first sight of the coasts of France. They are a dull blue against the almond green of the sea and a smoke-colored sky. I was moved by these soft, mellow shades, for they seemed like the mellowness of France herself. In America, the sky has an empty transparency, the sea the hardness and sparkle of precious stones; nothing over there of the tender, misty effect I have before me, one so conducive to dreaming.

OCTOBER 6. PARIS. At the American Embassy, Keeler Faus, extremely agreeable as always, tells me he has just seen Gide, who talked to him about me. Would I like to speak to him? I should be delighted, and a minute or two later Faus hands me the receiver with Gide at the end of the line. When I gave my name, I heard, and everyone else in the office with me, a great cry, an "Ah!" that enchanted me and then this sentence: "Wait till I bring my armchair closer. . . ." An appointment is made for Sunday. "Now I recognize the sound of your voice, Green. It moves me, you know."

OCTOBER 8. I found Gide much the same as when I had last seen him. I say much the same, because, for all that, there was all the weariness of five hard years. He held my hand in his for a long time, made me sit facing him. The expression in his eyes is the same, an expression that portraits do not quite succeed in conveying, for they always give him a sharp look, whereas Gide's is above all attentive, with a depth of feeling. He wears a black cap, shaped much like those of Neapolitan fishermen. He talks to me about Paris, says I am going to suffer from cold and hunger. He himself is going to Egypt. Then he asks me what I have been doing and I mention my translation of Péguy, but he jibs at Péguy—although he used not to—and thinks his poetry bad. Is that his exact term? It seems to me it was. . . . He then tells me that Gabriel Marcel had talked to him about his own conversion in 1916, and also of mine. According to Gide, Marcel is mistaken, but what about my conversion? I tell him it is perfectly true that I was converted in 1939. He listens silently, nods, then reminds me of his "hostility" toward the Church. I have long known of it, but my friendship for Gide has never changed. I often thought of him in America. He answers by laying his hand affectionately over mine and says: "I knew it."

OCTOBER 11. Long walks through Paris. Very depressed by the thought that I have no place to live.

* * *

OCTOBER 15. I sometimes feel like Rip van Winkle, who slept a hundred years and returned to a changed world. The coin I hand a newspaper vendor is given back to me because she thinks it spurious. Yet the coin is like those now in circulation, with this slight difference: it is made of silver; I found it in the pocket of a prewar suit.

OCTOBER 16. Have just been to see Gide. He received me just as someone was leaving, someone who had helped him "revise his translation of *Hamlet*." Once alone with me, he complains of the innumerable difficulties he met in this work. *Antony and Cleopatra* was far easier. Shows me a passage where Hamlet says he killed Rosenkranz and Guildenstern "with these hands." For all the French translations render the word "arm" by "hands," whereas Gide is certain that the meaning is not hands (literally arm, in English) but a weapon. The English friends he has consulted think him right! But in the same passage, I notice the phrase "he whor'd my mother" that Gide translates by "he has dishonored my mother." I can't help saying that dishonored seems a weak term and smacks of high-flown speech. "And how would you express it?" I feel very much at loss. However, I hunt for a sentence and find this: "He turned my mother into a whore." That is literally the English meaning. . . . Gide then goes and sits in a corner by the window, exactly between the piano and the window, separated from me by a small polished wood table. How often have I seen him thus, huddled in a corner of the large room, talking in a subdued voice and listening as only a very few know how to listen!

He talks at some length about the attitude of all and sundry during the occupation. . . . Finally, as he hands me a copy of *Attendu que* . . . we speak about the *lama sabachtani*, which I refuse to interpret as he does, and later, concerning the mysterious sayings voiced at times by men and the irritating quality of these sayings because we are uncertain of having understood them right, he quotes these words of Valéry's, found among his notes, the last one he ever wrote. "By chance the last one," says Gide and then, correcting himself, adds: "We must not say by chance." Valéry said: "The idea of love in the divine was introduced for the first time by Christ." (Not at all sure of quoting correctly; this should be checked, but if the sentence is perhaps not exactly as he said it, I believe the meaning is just as I have given it. . . .)

As he asks me certain questions about my religious opinions, I reply that, maybe on account of my Protestant upbringing, I will always find it difficult to talk of religion, or rather, of *my* religion. Our personal religion is more of a secret than anything else. And then, my case is not such a rare one that much need be said about it. I am sure that God acts differently with each of us; yet, in one of George Herbert's poems, I find all that is essential in my conversion, even down to several very precise details. Wouldn't it be enough to read the poem? So Gide and I look it up in the *Oxford Book of English Verse* but, to my great surprise, without finding it; it was perhaps judged to be too well known; it is "The Collar." . . .

I said to him: "Whatever arguments can be opposed to Christianity, this is perfectly unanswerable: 'You spoke and I heard your voice' . . ."

As we were parting, he said: "So you have never been able to find your balance? I have always maintained that we must allow everything we have in us to develop freely. The crises you go through show how youthful you have remained, and to what an extent. I too have had such crises, but put a stop to them. They only tear you to pieces. I said to myself: 'Oh well, it can't be helped!' and ended the whole thing."

A little earlier, he told me that he had spent ten days with Mauriac at Malagar, and that the two of them read aloud to each other, Mauriac reading Racine and Gide the Bible. "I read the historical books, the story of David. . . ." We then launch forth on the subject of Catholics and the Bible, a subject I will return to some other time. "It should be admitted in exoneration of Catholics," said I a moment later, "that they have no fine French translation of the Scriptures. The equivalent of the English Bible does not exist: the Bible, in France, has never been the literary monument it is in England and in Germany. And this is most serious: it is not *quotable* in the French translations. When an Englishman quotes a verse from the Scriptures, he repeats the words and the order of the words with scrupulous respect for a translation that is a work of genius. In France, the words that come to one's lips are a more or less faithful recollection of . . . Crampon."

Gide makes this striking remark: "Even when faith changes or disappears in a Protestant, something remains of his early formation. When faith disappears in a Catholic, everything gives way." To which I reply that this may be true in France, or even in England, but not in America. I don't want to generalize, but it seems to me that over there, it is Catholics who are uncompromising and Protestants who are slack, because Catholics have the minority spirit, the "little flock" turn of mind that makes them hold tight. Puritanism has changed camps.

I don't think I ever saw him more alert, or more like himself.

OCTOBER 18.   May the world not destroy what is valid in us. I came home this evening to read the Bible, to try to shed some light on my darkness. There are times when you cannot help but have a horror of yourself, when you are in agreement with those who would condemn us, if they knew. But what the world knows least is what takes place in a soul, and I think that if I were to be judged by the world and not by God, I would be damned. Reread four or five times the poem by Herbert that I mentioned to Gide.

Gide was telling me this morning of a Catholic boy, a very pious and horribly deceitful boy, who serves Mass, goes to confession, etc. (by "etc." I suppose Gide means that he goes to communion) and whose confessor, "one of those holy, short-sighted souls," does not see his baseness. Gide is too ready to hold the Church responsible for such isolated cases.

OCTOBER 19.   Nothing leads me to believe I will find a flat. This is becoming a rather painful problem. I am thinking particularly about the moral aspect of the question. Last week, at the theater, I was overcome by the idea that I would not be able to find a roof in my native city; this aroused my indignation—rather briefly, to be sure—but violently. I might be told that I was unreasonable. I can't help it. I find it hard not to be able to say this simple thing, in Paris: "I'm going home." Yet I looked at a flat yesterday that had been offered me and refused it. It was almost out of town on the quai de la Gare, in a house that was to be torn down before the war and that will cave in of itself if steps are not taken to prevent it. One walks up a black and evil-smelling staircase that yells of crime. The view of the Seine is splendid, but would be ruined for me by the continual roar of trucks rolling past the windows. And then, a house that looks sinister in broad daylight must be inexpressibly sad when night falls.

UNDATED.   I sometimes hear it said: "Where there's a will, there's a way." But this is said thoughtlessly, as the minute one begins to

will, the problem is solved, no matter which way. So the real difficulty must be, not to will, but to have the will to will. For it is
so true that back of the will is another will that sets it working.

Thought a lot about physical pleasure and the way it attacks
faith. No theologian has ever been able to explain to me how the
errors of the body can reach the soul. The truth is that the body
is not the guilty party, but the soul that consents. There lies the
mystery. How, being spirit, can it consent to what it hates? But
the fact is there: a voluptuary makes a bed for the unbeliever.

OCTOBER 23. I found Mauriac in his study. You reach it by means
of a very steep inner staircase. I ran down it, both he and the
maid cried: "Look out!" I went up to him and kissed him. . . .
He talked about my diary, saying that he had valued it during the
occupation, but reproached me with having said too little. "But
you can't tell the whole truth!" I cried. "People wouldn't tolerate
it. . . ." In the dusk, his head seems quite white; he coughs. Talks
about "this poor country," of an exhausted France, of fears for
the future, and drops the word *revolution* (under his breath, as
though to keep it from waking up). . . . Later he mentions the
articles I sent the *Figaro* from America. "Of course your idea of
France was right, of course it was right, in spite of all these
changes." I understood that I had been mistaken. "Of course it
was right" informed me better than a long speech.

NOVEMBER 25. I wanted to hear Mass at Notre-Dame and went
there this morning. Strange to be forced to write that on seeing
the great, stark cross that is to be erected in the center of the
Weimar-Buchenwald camp, I was gripped by an unexpected emotion, more violent than any I have felt, it seems to me, since 1940,
for it was as though the France I am looking for said to me suddenly: "Here I am." This cross must be eight or ten yards high.
A French flag hangs from the crossbar so as almost to conceal the
foot. It is set in a heap of sand and gravel under the big rose
window on the right-hand side of the transept when you face the
high altar. I don't think the Middle Ages would have devised anything different. This cross will replace all those that could not be
put up over the tombs of the fifty-one thousand dead at Buchenwald and the annex camps for the simple reason that there were
no tombs, the disorder in which the victims' remains were found
allowing only for a single, mass burial.

* * *

NOVEMBER 29. I was telling Father Couturier how disappointing it is to meet certain authors, although their work is most deserving, because they appear to live on a lower level than their work. "The reason for that," said the Father, "is that they put all their spiritual energy in their books and that there is not enough left for them to live on a higher level." If this is so, it would account for the fact that so many conversions are paid for by an apparent decrease in talent. What should have gone into books pours into daily life. Let us hope that good authors who are bad Christians will find salvation through the books they write!

DECEMBER 5. Yesterday I took a young American officer to see Gertrude Stein, as he wanted to meet her. I am anxious for him to admire the quays at twilight, the rue des Grands-Augustins, the rue de Savoie, all the old houses. Why? I really don't know, but have always felt this to be a moral obligation; one should pass on what one has received. Be it as it may, we reach the rue Christine. A wide staircase for sedan chairs. A barking behind the door: Basket, the white poodle. We find Gertrude Stein and Alice Toklas in a room hung with Picassos and Francis Roses, the portrait of Gertrude Stein by Picasso placed over the mantelpiece mirror; near it, Picasso's young nude girl holding a bunch of flowers. A tribute to Le Nain by Rose: the portrait of a young ragamuffin in gray and black, rather fine, but when all is said and done, Le Nain directed the Englishman's hand. Gertrude Stein makes me sit by her on a big black horsehair sofa. She tells me that one day at Belley (not sure it was Belley) she turned on her radio "by chance," just as it was announced that I was going to speak and that it moved her to hear my voice. It was in 1942 or 1943. I sit and look at her. Her face, which is carved in rock, has become very beautiful; a great spiritual force has modeled the nose, mouth, and brow. Her very large, very black, very deep eyes sparkle with intelligence. She wears a gray skirt and a grass-green sweater. Her hands are short, square, and strong. Turning to Captain X., she asks him several questions and ends by making a big speech that is singularly like a dressing down. "Our soldiers like you so much," he says. "Yes, because I am frank with them and don't tell them lies. They have been told too many lies. One said to me: 'We have lost our illusions about the war and the newspapers, because we know what they make of the news, we have lost our illusions about ourselves, we have lost our illusions about God. . . .' " (Not to have any illusions about God would be the beginning of wisdom!) She continues: "It is very serious. They have lost faith. They are devitalized. All you Americans are devitalized, you have lost that something that drove the pioneers onwards, the founders of the United States. What's the reason for this? All Americans are job-minded, they think of nothing but their job. A job is the answer to all their problems. The soldiers go home with the fixed idea of finding a job. That is what is weakening the whole nation. What America needs these days is martyrs. Go home and be martyrs!" "But, Miss Stein, why don't you become our first martyr?" "No, I've shown my mettle, I've proved my courage."

1946

JANUARY 3. It is owing to Jacques B.'s great kindness that all my books were safe during the occupation. While I was far away, he had them placed in a small room, on the fifth floor of an old house in the rue Saint-Augustin. I found them there the other day. Many of them were piled against the walls, others lay flat on the long shelves that run around this strange library, and at first, I dare not put a finger on anything. If I pull out a book, twenty topple over. There must be six thousand of them and the room is not large. I recognize a book I often thought of in America. I take hold of it, pull at it very gently to extricate it from a tottering pile, and the whole thing slips down slowly, the whole thing collapses. Soon I am in a sea of paper. At my feet suddenly appears a great bundle of letters that I thought I had destroyed, and I throw myself on it to read the letters over, standing, in this icy room. How many memories throw me back into the past! A moment ago, I was almost happy. But not at present. With gloved hands, I replace the letters in their envelopes and go toward the door, for I have spent at least an hour stirring up the past, and wonder once again why we are always so eager to keep what can never be anything but a pain to us, after having been so much of a joy. To forget is no more, no less, than a grace.

* * *

JANUARY 14. I went to a Dominican convent today to attend a taking of the habit. André and I get there around half past six and are made to wait in the visiting room with some twenty people. At the far end of the room, double doors flung wide open allow a complete view of a rather vast room (the chapter hall?) that looks like a drawing room that has been turned into a chapel, the walls painted white, and a very plain altar with a great Christ above it. Four tapers have been lit. Silence. Along the walls, two rows of motionless monks face each other, and some seem to be praying. They all wear a black cloak over their white robe. I don't know if they realize the aspect they offer. With a complete disregard for size, the big ones stand with the little ones, the very tall with the very short, as though it had been done on purpose. They do not move at all, they even move so little that, in a few minutes, everything begins to look unreal to me. I myself stand among the others without budging, and the prolonged stillness finally produces a most peculiar sensation verging on dizziness, I mean a sort of fascination, like dizziness. It seems to me that I am gradually becoming a figure in a picture. I would like something to happen, I expect a great deal of what I am about to witness, and at the same time I dread this silence, this immobility, coming to an end. After ten minutes, a great clatter of shoes and two boys dressed like scouts pass among us to go toward the altar. We are then introduced into the chapel. The subprior is seated in an armchair, his back to the altar, an embroidered stole around his neck, and I see, stretched out before him, their brows touching the floor, the two scouts. "What do you ask?" says the subprior in Latin. They murmur something I cannot catch. The subprior then says: "*Levate!*" and they get up. Both are young, not over twenty, and one seems handsome. The subprior then makes a little speech, reminding both of the days they spent in a prison camp during the war, and talks very simply to them about their vocation, as though the three of them were alone. The boys then kneel and a white wool robe is slipped over them. I was very much surprised to feel a sort of indignation at that moment. To see such youth disappear under that wool, those slim, lithe bodies buried in stony whiteness, all that seemed terrible to me. I expected and secretly hoped for an exactly contrary emotion. I counted on some indefinable but great yearning for religious life, instead of which I experienced a spiritual withdrawal. Meanwhile the two novices embrace each of the monks with a tenderness both spiritual and human, recalling

for me a picture of medieval times that I thought gone for ever.
Next, all the monks go to another chapel and we follow, walking
behind them in the corridors. The subprior once more addresses
the novices, saying this in substance: "In two years, if we are
pleased with you, and you are pleased with us, we will keep you,
otherwise you will be free and so will we." I admired the clarity
of the contract.

After Compline André and I meet the subprior, who takes us to
his cell, which is large, well lit, full of books. He motions to me
and I sit on his bed, which, to my surprise, is made of planks with
a blanket thrown over them. A few minutes' talk and we go down
to dinner. Here we are, in the refectory, a long white hall in the
center of which some forty monks sit at a table that seems immense to me. Along the side walls, two other tables of the same
size, with a row of monks on one side only, their backs to the
wall, on an interminable bench. All their hoods are pulled down
almost to the eyes. At the end of the hall, a lector stands reading
a life of the curé d'Ars in a completely colorless voice. From
time to time, a monk corrects him: "Pronounce your words better.
Don't say tirrible. Say terrible." As for me, I sit on the subprior's
right, near one of the two doors that face each other at either end
of the refectory. We are served a good soup, a dish of rice, some
hare pâté (for André and me, not for the others), an apple, and
a biscuit. I am forgetting the beer, which would have had the
greatest trouble in intoxicating a baby. So much for the fare. From
time to time, a monk enters the refectory, flings himself down
before the subprior, who raps on the table with a small gavel, and
the monk gets up and goes to his seat. I cannot help finding great
beauty in this thirteenth-century life, kept up in the heart of the
twentieth. I stare, try to remember everything, I also listen. The
lector's voice is so intentionally toneless that it requires an effort
to follow it. I recall this: "An unbelieving woman once said to
me: 'If I had faith, your breviary would burn my hands.' Brothers,
does your breviary burn your hands?" Such fine and vehement
words spoken *recto tono* produce a strange effect; you have the
impression that the lector strips the clothes off the text and offers
it naked to the listeners' intelligence. I keep wondering what all
these men think. The monks who serve us come and go in their
wonderful white robes, as in Fra Angelico's predella at the Louvre.
When the meal is over, the subprior raps the table with his gavel
and the lector stops. Everybody gets up. André and I are asked

into a drawing room with some ten monks and seat ourselves in armchairs. As could be reasonably expected, the conversation turns on literature and I wonder what meaning literature can have for men in black and white robes. Perhaps they pretend to be interested in it out of courtesy, but what can it matter to a religious if such and such a novelist does or does not go through his little tricks? This struck me as a sort of revelation. It seemed that each book discussed was, at one fell swoop, emptied of its contents. I wished I had been able to say something worth saying (and also worth listening to); no indeed! As ever, under such circumstances, not a word passed my lips. And then the others, all the others, are so delighted to talk that I would hesitate to deprive them of this pleasure. I prefer being silent. There are enough people in this world who give tongue for one of us to keep quiet and no harm done.

A little later, the subprior speaks to a brother whose innocent face is truly that of a child and wishes him a happy fête day. The subprior says something like this: "We all love you. You're like a little boy." At which the brother nervously wiggles his fingers under his scapular. That very morning, it seems, his companions, in kindly fun, had slipped a bag of marbles into his shoe as a fête-day present. André and I leave shortly after.

I could not get to sleep this night before two o'clock. I thought about the refectory, of all those cowled heads and then of the after-dinner conversation. I should have said something, but what I heard disagreed too strongly with what I was thinking deep inside me. And also, if I had spoken, they would probably have listened, and I can't talk if people listen to me. This sounds like a joke, but I can't help it. If I find a man driving nails into a bit of wood, or shining his shoes, or laying colors on canvas, I can easily tell him what I am thinking about, if he appears more attentive to his work than to my talk. In any case, when more than two people are present, I am dumb. Yet I have talked to almost a thousand people, and that, several times. But it was not at all the same thing. To begin with, I read my text, and to read before a thousand people is as good as being alone in a desert. What seals me up tighter than anything else is to see three or four people looking at me and waiting. Why is this so? I have never known. I believe I much prefer saying what I have to say in writing.

JANUARY 16. Heard a priest discuss the Christian idea of love.

He said some very fine, very bold things on the subject, but what he lacked—and I say this very gravely—was physical experience of love . . . and of sin. A virgin soul that is called on to direct men and women can lead them to disaster through an ignorance of the passions. Theoretic knowledge, even accompanied by prayer, is not sufficient. Among the American clergy, I have seen boys fresh from their seminaries, with resolute faces and heads full of answers. A contempt for the flesh could be clearly read in their eyes; if they had tried to understand, these alarming children would have believed themselves lost.

JANUARY 20.   Late this afternoon, I went to see a friend who lives on the boulevard Beauséjour. The dining room is packed. The guests throng the buffet showing all the less shame because, the electric light having failed, no one can see them. A candle or two shed a poor light on all these people chattering unceasingly like children at playtime. Someone pushes up to me: "Do you recognize me?" Do I! It is Gaston Gallimard. A stage director assures me that he wants to put one of my novels on the screen, whereas in 1930, he told me he was waiting for the first snowfall to film *Leviathan*, for he *had* to have real snow. . . . A former comrade also looms up in the darkness. He was redheaded, still is, and his voice has not changed. I feel a trifle bewildered by all I see, by all I hear. Can all this be true, can this crowd, lit up by flickering candles, be the Paris I used to know? Isn't it a dream from which I'll wake up in a moment? But also present is a Paris I do not know. In the half-light, youngsters with carefully tousled hair talk in lisps about their poems. A young man who was at Buchenwald for months tells me that the prisoners belonged to different categories. The old ones, those of 1933 or '34, had a right to the movies and . . . to the brothels. The last-comers are regularly illtreated by the earlier prisoners. To be told of all these horrors in a drawing room has an extraordinary effect on me. The same man told me that he had known Father Leloir very well; he had a respect for him but thought he showed immoderate zeal for conversions. According to him, the Father talked a great deal about marriage and in such a manner that he seemed to have an unconscious yearning for matrimony. I think this true of a certain number of monks. Sealed up inside them is an excess of tenderness that their words unwittingly betray, and in a most pathetic manner. Went home tired and exasperated. I was told lots of things that I could not hear, but no sooner am I in a drawing room than I seem to go deaf and my sight dim. I was like that at eighteen and am still so today. The very word *drawing room* has something about it that makes me feel depressed and gloomy.

JANUARY 24. It sometimes occurs to me that all I receive in this world, my relatively comfortable life, the pleasure I take, for instance, in reading in bed before going to sleep, all that is perhaps my *reward*, in the sense given it by the Gospel, when it declares that those who have been favored in this world will be told: "You have had your reward." And so, no Heaven. Or rather, I will have had my Heaven, and what a shabby, stupid heaven! So much so that I write it without a capital. Yesterday, in the subway, I read almost the whole of St. James' epistle, where I stand condemned thirty times at least. "Thou shalt love thy neighbor as thyself" is called "the royal law" (2:8). Struck by verse 19, Chapter 2, which I should have used as an epigraph for my pamphlet against Catholics: "Thou believest that there is one God; thou doest well: the devils also believe, and tremble."

What really counts is to fight, even if it means being defeated each time: to accept, to knuckle down, is horrible. Something inside one should say no, even if the body says yes. And how could the body say anything else but yes? That is its language. It is acting true to part. But the soul's silence can only be the silence of death. Spiritually, my life is a disaster. I insist on writing this sentence down in black and white to see how it looks. Yet I wonder who would have the nerve to write: "Spiritually, my life is a success." One would have to be an idiot. However, I stick to what I have said.

FEBRUARY 1. Lunched in a house on the faubourg Saint-Honoré. Bénouville was there. Nothing particular to note, but in ten years, how interesting a conversation I have already forgotten would seem! What wouldn't I give to know the trifles that a few people discussed at dinner, for instance, in this same house, around 1780 . . . or 1900!

At the British Embassy day before yesterday. Much admired the great drawing rooms, particularly the white and gold drawing room where dinner was served. The house once belonged to the duc de Charost, who was reading a book when he was taken to the guillotine and marked the page by turning down a corner before having his head cut off. I sat by Louise de Vilmorin, who was at her loveliest. She and Lady Diana Cooper discussed Bresson's *Anges du péché*, a film that they had just seen. The scenes of convent life enraptured them and, not content with describing them, they decided to act one for us. Louise was the mother superior and Lady Diana threw herself down flat on her stomach to ask forgiveness for her sins.

Had lunch with a young painter yesterday. Éluard was there, tall, almost majestic. He speaks slowly and gravely, with a courtesy that we are beginning to forget. His face is the face of a poet. Around him spreads a zone of solitude that I did not attempt to breach; people talked to him a great deal, but it seemed to me that even the most talkative were never able to get at him, and I admired a haughtiness that managed never to lack politeness.

FEBRUARY 2. I never meet anyone without being told that we are racing headlong toward an era of fresh disasters. I had a long fit of insomnia last night, during which many thoughts stirred in my mind, most of them very gloomy. Then I remembered St. Teresa of Ávila's prayer: "Let nothing trouble you, let nothing terrify you. God only." And I once more found peace. The wish to leave the world has crept into my heart again, but what would I find in a convent, seated in my cell, in a black or white robe? Myself. Yourself is the one that you must cast off.

FEBRUARY 10. Mass this morning at the Benedictines', rue de la Source. The church is bare, gray and pink, not too ugly, and the monks' black robes create a great impression. The beautiful hymns have a beauty that wishes to please God alone. They really turn away from the world and are intended for God. None of the operatic cooing and winking of music for degenerate times, like ours. The liturgy, gestures, and minutely ordered movements, all this is for God. Then what am I doing here, what is this crowd doing here? A low Mass would be far better for us. Aren't we in this church to feast our eyes and ears rather than to pray? Why trick ourselves? Let us leave the monks to their business, which is to praise God by singing true, with a pure heart, and let us go elsewhere to pray.

FEBRUARY 12. A young man, both very handsome and very ugly, sometimes the one and sometimes the other, was talking in my

presence of his conquests in Stockholm and Copenhagen. This re-
minder of an easygoing, delightful, and poisonous life made me
very sad and I wondered whether it were possible to be saved
without withdrawing from the world. No doubt one can. The
world is a sort of novitiate for many people who will pronounce
their final vows in Heaven. Thought of the wonderful youth I
had. We did not have the frantic excitement of the boy I have
just mentioned, but we had joy. There wasn't that confusing of
pleasure with happiness then. We were happy. What more could
we wish for? I think that if these people had *one hour* of the unutterable happiness we then enjoyed, they would never forget it
and would remember it as the supreme event in their lives. No one
suspects that during the years when I was writing those inexplicably gloomy books, I was so happy that such bliss sometimes
kept me from sleeping and I wept with joy.

"From disaster to disaster, we are heading for victory." This
sinister 1940 saying came back to me. I believe that this is just
simply the way we are heading for Heaven. Thought a lot of a
sentence by Father Lallemant: "God is more interested in governing a single heart than in governing the whole of the natural universe." I have been upset by so many things these days, the rue
de Presbourg lunch, for instance, and, that same day, what an unknown priest said to me with extraordinary simplicity, after hearing my confession: "You are saved." "How does he know?"
immediately asked the inner voice I know so well. But he may be
right, after all. If I believed the opposite, I would go mad.

FEBRUARY 18.   Disturbed by the problem that I am in the habit of
calling the problem of two realities: the carnal reality and the
metaphysical reality. Am I to be their battle-ground to the end of
my life? So that is to be my fate, the fate I so often speculated
about around my thirtieth year: the particular question that will
have been asked me in this world and that I will have to answer.
But in what way do these difficulties differ from those of all
human beings? In a great many ways. Each of us is a special case.

MARCH 22.   Yesterday afternoon, at Saint-Médard. The air was
inexpressibly sweet and the doors of the church left open to let
in the warmth, although the apse still held a little of winter's cold
mingled with the first breath of spring and the peculiarly heady
odor found in very old churches. Lots of memories came back

to me, memories of walks through the old parts of Paris when I was twenty and crazy to improve my mind. At that time, the idea of pleasure did not even occur to me. I was so ignorant of sensual matters that a nun could have given me pointers! None of that interested me in the least; I imagined, for instance, that men and women came together only once a year. School had not taught me anything; I found out only much later what took place there when I was a student. This protracted innocence seems disastrous to me, in many ways: it is always paid for very dearly later.

APRIL 10. I went to see Lucien Daudet yesterday afternoon. He received me in his little, dark, low-ceilinged room. Both legs paralyzed, he sits at a table littered with books and papers. Over his shoulders, a shawl and a black *veil*. His delicate, suffering face is wasted, but his expression gentler than it used to be; the bitter lines at the corners of his lips have disappeared. On the mantel-piece, a gilt wood statue of Mary, and facing him, on a level with his eyes, a photograph of his father, Alphonse Daudet, whose face is ringed with a sort of fur made up of his hair and beard. All around, portraits, souvenirs, knickknacks, a horribly melancholy little world—all that remains of happiness. He talks with admirable preciseness. I remember what he said about the youth of 1946: "They don't know what life, such as we knew it, is. They don't even know what a good cake tastes like, but they don't care, they are happy, they don't care a fig for anything." He also said: "I hear of nothing but sprees and roistering." I maintain that we were happier. "And yet," he said, "you never knew the days before 1914." And to give a good picture of these times, he adds: "Times when shops did not shut between noon and two!" Nothing could be more like an episode in one of his father's books than this life ending in an old Paris house. As I was getting up to go, a lady just back from Switzerland entered. "How is her Majesty?" asks Lucien Daudet. He was speaking of the Queen of Portugal. It was like an echo of *Kings in Exile*, one of his father's novels, and on that echo I took my leave. A stifling sadness falls over one in this little room pervaded by the heavy odor of the nineteenth century. In the hall, before shutting the front door, I glanced at a fine photograph of the Imperial Prince (Napoleon III's son).

MAY 4. I thought I knew this Beethoven quartet (Op. 59, No. 2) by heart and yet was upset last night by all I found in it: such splendid violence, such explosions, such sudden tenderness, the beauty, the tangled network of its themes, the quivering of wings, the throbbing of fountains. Debussy's quartet moved me on account of the happy memories it recalled, the inexpressible happiness that was mine around 1930.

MAY 9. Alone in a chapel at Saint-Sulpice, a young man kneels on the edge of his *prie-dieu*, arms crossed, body erect, a big black rosary mended with string and hanging from his elbow; very simply, almost poorly, dressed in black, a very handsome face, pink shading into brown, tousled hair with a lock sweeping his eyebrows, large, deep eyes. He yawns from time to time and, when anyone approaches right or left, turns his head sharply in that direction. After a while, he grasps his rosary, carries it to his lips with a sort of violence, crosses himself, puts his rosary in a pocket and, always very straight, continues praying. His distractions, his weariness, his good looks all made him a very mysterious person and as passionately interesting as a fictitious character. And there was this too: faith, the strange spectacle of faith. I went out of my way to leave without going past him.

JUNE 10. I went to Gide's day before yesterday as he wanted to see me alone. He talked to me about religion, in connection with Bloy's book (*Ici on assassine les Grands Hommes*). What struck him particularly in the passages about Hello were those relating to the writer's last days and, at the very end, this pathetic cry: "Make the little ones pray!" What disconcerted Gide more than anything was the despair that appears to have attended the poor man's death, but what do we know about it? Who has ever been able to tell what takes place in the soul of a dying man? He then talked about a mother superior ("Is that what they are called?" he asked), a relative of Edmond Jaloux, who also died "in despair" among her nuns. But the temptation to despair almost always lies in wait for a believer on his deathbed. I see very clearly that that weakens religion in Gide's mind, for he seems to believe that the object of religion is to give unshakable confidence to whoever is about to cross the great borderline.

JUNE 14. Sins of the flesh teach some people what they would never have otherwise known, and I mean this in a widely human fashion and not only an erotic one. Experience of physical love

goes far beyond the body; it includes a world of valuable knowledge, where much good mingles with much evil. I sound as
though I were justifying pleasure, which is not at all my intention,
but I have known very sensual men and women with a far more
developed sense of humanity than souls obviously more virtuous
and innocent. To know, in the physical meaning given the word
in the Bible, is no vain term.

UNDATED. The more improper parts of an intimate diary are far
less the erotic passages than the pious ones. A Carthusian monk
would understand me! Exhibitionism of the soul is more difficult
to admit than that of the body. I have that feeling each time I go
into a so-called religious library and am so disgusted, not only
with all those books, but with myself, that nausea does not seem
too strong a term to describe it.

JULY 13. When I hear certain Frenchmen talk—among those I
value most—I feel a little sad not to be as quick-witted as they are.
No doubt I have been given gifts they do not possess, but there
is something wonderful about their nimbleness of mind. They
cut figures of eight on the ice with the greatest ease. But when
I cut figures of eight, I almost always hear the ice cracking ominously. Yet these men can be reproached on two scores: firstly,
they think too fast; they are deeply ignorant of the fact that the
shortest way from one point to another is not always the straight
line. Secondly, they can see only in broad daylight and go all but
blind at twilight. This said, I have said about all there is to say.

JULY 21. Read Auden, at first with admiration, then with a certain weariness. His extraordinary felicity of phrase reminds one of
a man who always wins in a lottery. There is something about
this that annoys and finally irritates me. He is so obviously proud
of his verbal nimbleness; he says all he wants to say with never a
stammer, he says everything one thinks and was on the point of
saying, and saying far less well than he does. He rarely shows
emotion, but when he does it is exquisite (in the poem about the
two refugees, for instance).

AUGUST 4. The day when a man realizes that he will never be
able to know everything is a day of mourning. Then comes the
day when he vaguely suspects that he will not even be able to

know much, and finally comes the autumn afternoon when he sees that he never even completely knew the little he thought he knew.

AUGUST 22. Worked as usual this morning, but felt discouraged. Who will like this book? Thought today that one of the only things I am proud of is never having written a quarter of a line for money, nor even tipped my hat to obtain a prize.

How vain everything is but love! Just as a sailor senses a storm in a clear sky, I feel that my life is about to change.

AUGUST 25. A moment ago, read André Gide's *Theseus* at one sitting. It gave me a feeling of irritated pleasure. How can I deny my admiration for its style and, to begin with, why should I deny it? But this goes much further than style, for here style clings to something very precious, which is human flesh. Most beautiful and noble is Oedipus, who puts out his eyes to see more clearly into the inner world, more noble perhaps than Gide himself thinks; and at the end, Theseus takes leave of us after a wonderful speech which might be, I believe, the author's last will and testament. . . . What a jumble he makes of all the judgments one is tempted to form of him! I think him mistaken as to the meaning that his work will have in the eyes of posterity, those distant generations that he strives to reach beyond present generations (and this is precisely what I would most admire in him: the care he takes to find words within the knowledge of those who will come later).

AUGUST 26. Robert lent me a copy of *André Walter* with a photograph of Gide at twenty, a long rather full face, long black hair, the eyes of a Chinese, a drooping lily attitude, a somewhat "arty" pose. I was staggered by the changes time has wrought in him. I think I could have talked to the youth he was then. I would have discussed things with him. We had a few uncertainties of opinion in common, but now it is sometimes difficult to talk to Gide. As Americans say, he knows all the answers, and what attracts me is indecision, a certain wavering, a "well, I don't know . . ."

AUGUST 27. A long, passionately interesting conversation with Béguin. He talked about death, and when I said that all the dead I had seen looked as though they knew something we don't know, he made a remark that I think extremely curious: "No one can have any idea of life without having looked at the face of a dead man."

SEPTEMBER 23. The man I am will always raise a protest against the man I wanted to be and the two will live together to the end, but the man I wanted to be will be the one on whom judgment will be passed.

OCTOBER 1. Dropped in on Gide late this afternoon. I said in substance: "Although I am far from sharing your views in *Theseus*, yet I don't think I ever read anything of yours that I thought finer as to style." . . . He told me he had written the book in two months with a glad heart. The simplicity with which he talks about it appeals greatly to me, and I went so far as to say that Theseus' last soliloquy left me with a feeling of melancholy as I could not help but seeing it as a sort of farewell, like that of Prospero in *The Tempest*. "Why yes," says Gide, "it is a farewell." However, he adds immediately that he wants to write "one more book" and the words are said with a sort of enthusiasm that take forty years off his age at one go. He then declares himself sick of our present world and of the growing flood of totalitarianism, which he loathes. A moment later, he tells me confidentially that he is going away in January. "To Egypt?" "Much farther." "To America?" He looks at me for a second. "To Tahiti," he answers finally, stressing each syllable. "And it might be," he adds, "that I will never come back. . . ." As he talks about my diary, where "too many things are passed over in silence," I ask if he means physical problems. "Yes, those," he says. I then ask: "But do you know of a diary, of a single published diary, that is not silent about these questions?"

OCTOBER 16. Spent the day in a large monastery near Paris. . . . I was left by myself in the library for a moment and asked for a book written by Melchor Cano for Philip II of Spain, who wanted to have him as his confessor. The author very simply states his own defects. I read for half an hour. I was to be fetched at five, but at six I was still alone in the vast room into which night was slowly creeping. Yet outside, the sky was still light, a pale blue. Workmen were hammering in the vicinity. Immense sadness of the countryside at that hour. I felt cold. I wondered if I could bear shivering twenty years in a monastery for the love of God. Suddenly, I fell into a sort of despair. I thought: "If the religious life is not true, nothing in this world is true, and then it's finished, I have nothing left." I stood motionless, horrified by the great black tide that rose toward me. Doubt went through my mind and I was frightened. I did not move, but all I felt capable of doing was precisely not to move and to remain as I was. It seemed to me that death itself could not have been sadder or blacker than this exceptional moment, one that I believe unequaled in my life. I had a violent distaste for religion, for myself, for everything. This lasted about half an hour, but it was only some time later that I grasped the reason for all this and the presence of whom I had felt within these walls.

DECEMBER 3. Last Sunday, to the Latour-Maubourg convent to hear Camus. There are far too many people and the two drawing rooms on the second floor are crowded. We are placed in the first row. Camus is seated a couple of yards away from us and faces us at a small table. By him, Father Maydieu in a white robe. In the next room, a Dominican stands *on* the mantelpiece, peacefully smoking his pipe. Ill and visibly weary, Camus talks however in what I think a most moving manner about what is expected of Catholics in the France of 1946. He is moving in spite of himself, without the least attempt at eloquence; his integrity is what stirs one. He speaks rapidly, simply, with notes. In his rather pallid face, his eyes are sad, his smile is sad. The lecture over, Father Maydieu asks me if I have anything to say, and I shake my head, unable to answer without a few minutes of reflection. A few in the audience ask questions, but such blundering ones that it would be better if they had held their tongues. One of them, an ex-revolutionary with an ingenuous face, says this and it makes us all start: "I am in a state of grace and you, Monsieur Camus, I tell you very humbly that you are not. . . ." Camus's only answer was the smile I have just mentioned, but he said a little later: "I am your Augustine, before his conversion, I am struggling with the problem of evil and can't get to the end of it." Indeed, one is reminded of Augustine by this Latin from North Africa who is trying to find out how we would behave in the presence of the Vandals. Someone else in the audience who had listened attentively to Camus gets up and says: "Monsieur, I can't make up my mind in forty seconds about the way I would behave if the

Church were persecuted. I want to think it over all my life."
"Monsieur," replies Camus, "you are just about five years old."

DECEMBER 6. Many a time since childhood I have tried to seize
upon the moment when I fell asleep, when I could tell myself:
"I'm going to sleep." I have never succeeded, but the instant just
before the sort of drop into unconsciousness is marked by a phenomenon which I call the dissociation of mental pictures. For no
sooner do I put out the light than I begin to see. This is one of the
only gifts remaining to me from a time when I could scarcely
talk. To imagine, for me, is to see pictures, and when I am not
able to see, I won't write any longer, for it seems to me that the
starting point of all my books is the bolster where I lay my head,
but I find it impossible to say how I see. At any rate, there comes
a second when these sometimes startlingly clear pictures suddenly
dissolve and slide into one another. There results a sort of chaos
that invariably announces sleep.

DECEMBER 9. Yesterday, I was quoting this saying of Father
Dehau's to Robert: "Faith is the cross where intellect is cruci-
fied." And I said that Bossuet would have liked this sentence.
Robert asked me if I was sure of this. For Bossuet, faith continued
intellect in an unbroken line. And he quoted this sentence of St.
Augustine's: "Faith is the fruit of intellect."

DECEMBER 27. It was thirty-two years ago this morning, St.
John's Day. I thought once more of my mother's face as I saw it
on her deathbed. Twice I went to look at her, staying each time
for a few minutes that have meant a great deal to me. She seemed
far from this world, far from us all, with the air of having been
entrusted with an uncommunicable secret and of moving away,
gliding straight toward unknown spaces. Her extraordinary grav-
ity made an impression on me that the years have not obliterated
and that has marked me for ever, I think. It was then that she
really taught me all she knew of the invisible, of religion, and she
pointed it out far better then than when she taught me the cate-
chism. Her face was extremely noble, particularly the high,
rounded brow, the somewhat mysterious mouth that smiled, it
seemed to me that morning, *but intermittently*. Around her, an
enormous silence; yet she did not frighten me. The dead do not
frighten.

1947

JANUARY 8. Lunched with Cocteau. Talking about the theater, he said that it is always a curious thing to watch the audience, particularly "at the moment of hypnosis" which comes sooner or later. The moment when everyone is spellbound, a rather brief moment, "for," he says, "in France the house is always empty. Everyone is on the stage. Everyone is the queen." One feels like applauding when he says such things. Struck by what he says about "the conspiracy of the plural against the singular," signs of which he sees everywhere. Extremists have told him that his play was *insulting*, because it did not conform to the pattern approved in their set. "Your books are insulting," he told me. "*Midnight* is an insulting book." (I am truly thankful that it is.) He talked to us about his house at Milly, the so-called bailiff's house, which he is already attached to; says he wants to be buried in the garden, "and may the dogs piddle on him, if they feel like it!" Talks sadly of France, which he finds so changed, of its wretched and ambitionless youth. . . . Nowadays, he thinks, holiness is the only thing that creates a worthwhile ideal. Monasteries have taken all that was best. . . . Struck by his pessimism: "We are like the people who used to say: 'Ah, if you had only known that great actress, Rachel!' We say: 'Ah, if you had only known 1920!' And we are right."

JANUARY 9. The carnal man lives with the spiritual man. One tries to slit the other's throat. To give up pleasure means throwing the carnal man into jail, but none the less, he goes on living, tied up, and gagged as tightly as you please; yet he is there, and what is strange, he changes, follows a completely personal evolution. What he longs for today is no longer what he longed for at twenty, or at thirty, or even at forty. An inflexible determinism forces those furious appetites to *develop in nonsatisfaction*. Thought sadly about all this. How is it that we are what we are? We scarcely ever know it. I am completely ignorant about my great-grandparents; even my grandparents never told their secrets (they had some, we all have some). Between these unknown people and myself, my exceptionally good parents formed a sort of moral barrage, but behind them, some way behind them, what a number of neurasthenics walled up in their *idée fixe*, and to put it more frankly, what a number of lunatics! Often thought that I have kept my balance by writing my stories.

UNDATED. I was talking to Robert about the irritating problem of translations. Sticking to the literal meaning is the more often a mistake, as the author who is being translated would certainly have used other words and said different things if he had written in the translator's tongue. So you should try to discover the book he would have written in that language. With a swiftness of thought I have always admired in him, Robert summed up the whole question in a single sentence: "A good translation is not a glove turned inside out; it is another glove." Nothing could be better expressed.

JANUARY 28. Yesterday to Véfour's, where a farewell party was given for the ballets that are leaving for some place or other. I went there to see Bérard, who had agreed to illustrate my diary.[1] An enormous mob under the charming painted ceilings, and in the mob, two or three faces I thought handsome. Bérard took me into a corner, sat with me at a table, and talked about this edition of my diary: "I thought at first of featuring American soldiers. That would have been very pretty. Then I had the idea of showing Paris as seen through your own sadness." His beard is touched with silver under the chin. His fat pink face is at times extremely dignified. I thought of the dreary day when I looked at a self-portrait of Bérard in a New York hotel bedroom. The painting stood on the floor, propped against a wall, a picture in exile that looked as though it knew itself to be in exile. If I could have been told then: "In six years, at Véfour's, Bérard will tell you how he expects to illustrate one of your books," I would have taken many a trial with a lighter heart. Around us, lots of very smart people, what is called society. I did not stay long. I wanted to talk to Laurence Olivier, but could only have made myself heard by shrieking, and felt so ill at ease that I went away.

FEBRUARY 4. . . . I have been reproached for what are discreetly termed my reticences. Yet, to give the public my intimate

[1] This illustrated edition of my diary never came out. Bérard assured me that the publisher had kept the gouaches; they were exceptionally fine.

diary is an idea that has never entered my head. One would have to be crazy. . . . I notice, however, that the most impatient, the most eager, the most vexed not to *know,* those who most loudly accuse me of not having said enough, are always the most guarded and the most timorous. The zeal for truth burns them up when it means having others speak it. "Come on, be bold! Go ahead! Go ahead!" they cry, shoving one by the shoulder. And then, they sit down.

FEBRUARY 20. I finished my book at midnight, yesterday. Three full pages in two hours, which is not my usual speed, but I was determined to end it that night. Around eleven o'clock, I felt my room grow cold and threw a log on the fire. I don't know why I note these details, except that the very last hour devoted to a book nearing its end is a specially grave one in the author's eyes. The book does not finish at all in the way I imagined it would. The idea of Fabien wrapped in his sheet and going to answer a knocking at the door is probably an unconscious reminiscence of the episode where John-Mark, clad in his *sindon,* runs away naked when he is arrested (Mark, 14:52).

APRIL 24. Today at last I am back again in the setting that our furniture creates for us, the setting of my whole youth, which I regard all the more fondly because I have been deprived of it since 1940. Impossible to write for more than a month. Worked from morning till night to put a little order in this flat, to attempt to bring it out of chaos. For we were obliged to move in with workmen on the premises: masons, plumbers, painters, electricians, locksmiths. An indescribable disorder. Gaping floors, torn partitions, plaster everywhere, and a fine gluey dust that stuck to fingers and went down our throats. No baths. Meals hastily eaten in a room that looked as though it had been shaken up by an earthquake, bits of furniture piled one on top of the other, all the suitcases heaped in a corner. . . . All that is over now. I am writing these lines in my study, the window of which looks out on Embassy gardens. Deep peace.

MAY 21. At times I have such a keen feeling of the world's emptiness that it seems as though my mind will not be strong enough to stand the weight of such a truth. This sounds a strange thing to say, and I think very few people ever think of it. Some days, I can't open a book, even one of poems, without saying to myself: "What's the good?" God alone exists, He is the only one that *is*, and to feel separated from Him is horrible, for apart from God I can see nothing but vanity. If such is the case, how can I be interested in what interests the world?

JUNE 20. Someone just back from the United States tells me that America is recovering from the war "like a giant from a scratch." So much the worse and so much the better. It means that the lesson has not been learned.

JULY 12. The inexorable reality of the material world, its stones, its voices, its faces, its great beauty, its thought even, everything that, in a certain way, *seems right when spirit seems wrong*, because this world offers nothing that is not provable and almost tangible, whereas the world of spirit, of faith, remains interior, mysterious, *nonprovable*—how would it be possible to avoid suffering from this eternal contradiction? A man who lives by his faith is necessarily isolated. At every hour of the day, he is in acute disagreement with his century; at every hour of the day, he is alone and, in a certain fashion, appears to be mad. This is one of the most peculiar aspects of the tragedy our conscience is going through in Europe. No matter how numerous Christians still are in this world, no matter how close their mystical union, they cannot help but have at some time or other a feeling of terrible solitude. . . .

JULY 19. A feeling of nothingness. Indescribable. It is familiar to those whose lives have been bared of all *divertissement*, in Pascal's sense of the term. For to certain souls, no longer to believe in the need for *divertissement* means losing their mainstay. There is nothing like it to make you rush to God, as you would cast yourself into an abyss, for the problem that now faces you is: God or nothing. Living in a large, well-furnished room does not alter the question in the least. Comfort, music, books, the pleasures of conversation change nothing and, above all, add nothing, because it is impossible to add an iota to nothing and that *nothing* remains all-powerful back of all the appearances that it destroys. But what is instructive in such contacts with nothingness is the growing conviction that the sole possible reality is God. One knew it, of course, but not in this manner, not to the marrow of one's bones.

JULY 21. Went to see Gide. He had written me a most cordial note, but I thought, for the first time, that nothing good would come of this visit. He received me in his little bedroom, where he was at work writing. Above his bed, a mask of Goethe. Gide wore a green-checked thick woolen shirt. Almost at once, he talked about my novel, which he judges very unfavorably. "You want to save your soul," he said, "but just look at what a cost!" I then replied: "You oblige me to quote the Gospel: 'For what is a man profited, if he shall gain the whole world . . .'" "Yes," he answered rather quickly, "but in spite of that, see . . ." He next developed the idea that a convert loses his talent and that the Church is responsible for this. Suddenly, he seemed furious with me, as though I were guilty. "Wait until I have done wrong before judging me," I then said. "But you'll never do wrong, Green!" he cried. "You are far too honest for that, and it's because you are honest that I am fond of you." So he has it in for the Church. He flew at her again. He had seen Curtius in Germany, and the latter is "more of a Protestant than ever since seeing the evil done by the Church." I must say that this argument does not move me, but the following remark seemed graver: "I find that converts are never bettered by their conversion. The proud remain proud, etc. There is no improvement." And he asked me point-blank: "What about you? Do you feel you've improved?" As though anyone could answer yes to such a question! "Copeau," he went on, "is what he was before his conversion, only more so." He dwelt at length on this point and, pursuing his criticism of Catholics, reproached them with always having a ready answer for all occasions, like the Communists. (I myself have always raised the same objection, but did not breathe a word of it this morning. The replies they furnish to all problems deprive them of any feeling of mystery, to my mind, but that was not what Gide was talking about.) When our conversation was almost over, he began luring me with a magnificent literary future: "You are capable of great things. You have behind you a whole series of remarkable books. . . . You carry a heavy responsibility. You will cause many people to draw away from the Church, once they see what harm she has done a man like yourself." (Why so anxious for the welfare of the Church?) He showed me the place I could occupy and suddenly darted this question at me: "Why don't you have *a try at the devil for a while?*" I told him that I would never be on the devil's side. And then, this from Gide: "You could pretend . . ."

Once more, I said no. Going back to my journal, which he had mentioned a moment before together with my novel, he told me that my diary was full of reticences, that I had only recorded *"proper* things." "Yes," said I, "but the omissions are very clearly indicated, as well as the nature of what I have omitted. Now haven't you yourself published a journal that contains many blanks? What a lot of things you don't say!" "I'll see to it that the blanks are filled in," he replied simply. An hour and a half had passed. I thought we had said all we had to say to each other that day and stood up to leave. At that moment Gide did something that went straight to my heart and far more deeply than he believes: he also got up and kissed me.

JULY 22. That conversation with Gide stirred me so deeply that I had to lie down when I reached home. My heart thumped for almost an hour. And now, I wonder if his kiss did not mean that he was saying farewell to me. He told me confidentially that he thought "constantly of death" and watched it approach "with serenity." One sentence in particular comes back to me: "I think of death with complete indifference, if that is understood as serenity." Regarding the Catholic faith, he said that he could see nothing in it but a phenomenon caused by autosuggestion and heredity. Forgot to note that at one moment he asked me why I did not write a book anonymously, as Jouhandeau did in the case of *De l'Abjection.* (That, I imagine, meant having a try at the devil for a while, but a try without too much of a risk.) "That is impossible," I replied, "my books are of such a particular nature that their author would be immediately recognized." He agreed with me on this score. I have also forgotten to say that at the beginning of our conversation he asked: "Why don't you take holy orders? How is it you haven't left the world?" I answered that one doesn't take holy orders without a vocation. "That's just it," he continued, "with your Christian vocation, I don't see why you don't go into a monastery." "But a vocation is something very definite," I replied. "You can be a very earnest Catholic and not have one." I was convinced as I listened to him, and am still more so on thinking it over, that he talked to me as he did because he thought it his duty, an imperative, inescapable duty.

JULY 24. Yesterday morning, in the faubourg Saint-Honoré chapel of the Dominican Fathers, Anne abjured the Anglican heresy at the hands of Father Couturier. A very long, meticulous, but beautiful ceremony. First came the exorcisms at the side door of the church, not the main one. Anne could not enter before the *spiritus immundus* of heresy had been driven out of her. I thought this a little hard. When I was converted in 1916, the heretic that I was entered the rue Cortambert chapel without any ado. Nor was I made to read the act of abjuration on my knees, as took place yesterday. It was standing, and my hand on the Gospel, that I read Pius V's confession of faith (in a loud, ringing voice, I was told later). Yesterday, I could not help protesting in my heart, for to see her kneeling, you might have thought poor Anne was accusing herself of a crime. Is that the way one knocks at the door of the Father's house? The Church behaved more leniently to me. I was moved, however, and very much moved, as I am always by the presence of something real in violent contradiction with the world: water, salt, an immense sign of the cross that seemed to cut the sky in four, beyond the walls of this sorry chapel. . . .

AUGUST 26. BERNE. Arrived here at twilight. It is the best time. To slip into an unknown town at the moment when the light begins to waver and soften, not quite at dusk, but just before it, gives a secret joy: I don't know what I am hoping for, but my hopes are high. . . . After dinner, a walk down a long and beautiful street, probably one of the strangest the world affords, lined with old houses whose ground floors jut forward a little, like the roots of very ancient oaks, and whose roofs have the outlines of hats; and the street is so long that it resembles those one walks down in dreams and that never end. In the middle of the street, at intervals, are fountains with Renaissance figures. A setting that could not be used in a novel: too fine. One would have to be Hugo or Hawthorne. Strolled around the cathedral this morning. Market day. Fruit, vegetables, cheeses, delicatessen, an overabundance here of what is cruelly lacking in other parts of Europe. There is so much of everything that it doesn't seem true. One has the impression that what is true, what is serious, is misery and that the happiness seen here is an illusion.

AUGUST 29. Last night, one of the most curious dreams I ever had. I had gone to sleep in anguish. . . . After a moment, I saw myself (which never happens to me in dreams) in our rue Cortambert flat, the one where I spent part of my youth. In the hall was a glass sentry box, very much like the telephone booths to be seen in the streets here. Motionless in this glass sentry box was a man in a raincoat belted in at the waist; his hat was pulled down and almost hid his eyes, but his expression could be guessed. His face expressed nothing but extraordinary brutality, with something blind about it that made him most alarming. I knew that he had been living with us for years and years and that he usually stayed in his sentry box. . . . I also knew that he possessed superhuman strength but had only the intellect of a child of five, a brute who had always obeyed me, although he had obeyed less perfectly for some time, because it had dawned on him that he was stronger than I. If I told the man to go here or there, he carried out my orders, but with an ever-increasing and threatening sullenness. Usually, I chased him from my room and he returned to his sentry box, but I was afraid of him and my fright grew greater by the second. Finally, I saw him coming toward me, to kill me. Having taken refuge in my room, I turned the key in the lock, but when I awoke, my heart thumping, he was already shaking down the door with his powerful shoulder. How can I see anything in this brute but the personification of instinct? The whole dream was intensely real, far more so than everyday life because nothing besides action was given any importance. This confirms my belief that a man who dreams is sometimes a far more gifted artist than the man who is awake. Words cannot express the length of time passed in a vision that lasted a few seconds. Years of horror followed one after the other.

OCTOBER 8.   There was a brief moment in my life that I have never told anyone about, although I think of it at times, and it still remains perfectly mysterious to me. It must have been in 1932 or '33, at the end of a very fine afternoon in May. The sun cast spots of light on the wall at the far end of my study and I watched them as I lay on a sofa. There came a moment when these spots, which moved very slowly, reached the edge of a frame. I don't know why I then had a feeling of the world's immense sadness; it was like a kind of revelation. What meaning can such words convey to anyone who has not felt exactly what I felt then? But I can add nothing to what I have just written except that I was seized for *the first time* with a melancholy I have never been able to shake off entirely. Since then I have sometimes said that a spot of light on a wall seemed to me one of the saddest things in the world; but who could understand such a peculiar remark and one so apparently unreasonable?

OCTOBER 25. At Solesmes Abbey. Very deeply touched by the hymns I heard in the chapel. An *Ave, maris stella* that, according to Father X., goes back to the twelfth century, makes you feel like leaving the world then and there. But what century are we in here? Certainly not the twentieth. The monks in their black robes seem to glide over the surface of the floor like ghosts. On their faces, *pax*, as everywhere in this place. Peace and joy. On this cloister's threshold, the hideous agitation of the century dies away. It seems to me that Benedictine life is one hymn of happiness and love, in a rather slow mode, true enough, but what charm in this slowness and how precious it is to me in a world that a passion for speed has made almost idiotic! A hymn, that's what it is. All these hours, from Matins to Compline, are sung softly, almost tenderly. And how carefully the music is handled by voices that are so humble and so true! *Bis orat qui cantat*, says St. Augustine. It occurs to me at times that these monks live in a sort of great liturgical dream, whereas, in reality, they are the ones who see things as they are, and we are the ones who live in a dream always on the verge of turning into a nightmare.

NOVEMBER 3. A young author has sent me a copy of the work he is writing about me, in which he believes he can prove that all my novels have been written under the devil's influence! This view seems to me very systematic. . . . But what is true is that my novels allow glimpses of great dark stirrings that I believe to be the deepest part of the soul—and that always escape psychological observation—the secret regions where God is at work. These books could not have been otherwise than as they are. I could not rewrite them and change them. I think that each is in itself a chapter of a very large book that I will never end writing. If I must be judged, I should be judged by my work as a whole.

NOVEMBER 5. Excellent remarks about the translations of the New Testament, in Goodspeed. What he most clearly brings out is this, which I knew but had forgotten because I wanted to forget it: the King James Version is difficult to accept, as much on account of its mistakes as of its obscurities. The English public, which continues to prefer it to the Revised Version in which all

the errors were lopped off at the end of the last century, understands it all the less for knowing it almost *by heart*. We should
pause before this term whose magnificence is hidden because it has
become a commonplace. A Protestant knows his Bible by heart,
he knows it from the heart, from love. This bond of charity exists
between himself and his Bible: it is really *his* Bible and it is his
because he loves it. A Catholic, when he reads the Bible, when he
happens to read the Bible, reads the Bible and not his Bible. In
general, he does not read it at all, he prefers to believe that the
Church forbids him to, which is false. But to go back to Goodspeed, he thinks that a too literal knowledge of the Scriptures is
an obstacle to understanding the texts; you end by never asking
yourself the meaning of the words you quote—and which sometimes have none in the old translation I am discussing. (The only
example I can remember at the moment is not the least picturesque: it is found in Matthew 23:24, where a misprint that makes
the sentence incomprehensible has passed, together with the context, into the memory of English readers. I have never heard this
verse quoted, and it is among those most often quoted, without
the mistake turning up, doggedly faithful.) Goodspeed is in favor
of putting away the 1611 translation among the great literary
works of the past, and reading the Scriptures in modern versions
that are more literally accurate. Knowing all this, a sort of instinct
makes me revert to the book that revealed the word to me when
I was a child and whose old language will always move me. I have
this to say in its defense: every time it agrees with the original,
it is admirably faithful and is, I believe, unequaled in English;
where the Old Testament is concerned at least, it does not seem
to me possible to translate better than when the translation is
good, I might even say that it does not appear possible to translate
in a more Hebraic manner (it has introduced Hebraic construc-
tions into the language). And then, it will always be right in my
eyes because it is the most beautiful.

NOVEMBER 8. Yesterday and this morning, spent my time ar-
ranging books in the large cupboard that I have turned into a
bookcase. One of these cupboards has already been converted to
such a use in my study. Now there are two of them, side by side,
forming a single wall of books, facing a longer wall. So one of
my oldest dreams has come true: to work surrounded by books.
One always ends by getting what one wants, one gets it a little

late, more often too late, when one scarcely wants it any longer, but one gets it. Those rows of old bindings made a brave show in my eyes, but as I displaced all the books and replaced them on other shelves, I heard the voice, the mental one we all possess, ask the eternal question: "What's the good?"—a question that darkened part of my youth. What's the good since nothing lasts? What's the good since we have to die? A question asked repeatedly that sometimes directs us toward the absolute; and that perhaps comes to us from God.

NOVEMBER 25.   Anne was talking to me yesterday about one of our sisters, whom we lost in January, 1918, and the circumstances of her death. "Why, didn't you know?" (In 1918, I was on the Italian front.) "She suffered greatly" (meningitis), "but always smiled when anyone joked before her. This lasted two weeks. The time came when she seemed very low. I felt her pulse and knew her life was ebbing away. Perhaps she realized it too, for suddenly in a loud, clear voice, she said: 'Now I lay me down to sleep . . .'" (I knew the little prayer that children are taught:

> Now I lay me down to sleep,
> I pray the Lord my soul to keep.
> If I should die before I wake,
> I pray the Lord my soul to take.)

"She only managed to say the first line and died. She did not know many prayers." She was very beautiful, a little silent, but not sad; she was twenty-three.

DECEMBER 8.   I don't know of a prettier landscape in Paris than the one I see from my windows. A moment ago, under a stormy gray sky, I had a glimpse of the little Dutch Embassy through black trees and, suddenly lit up by a last sunburst, these colors began to shine softly behind a faint mist. I looked long at the narrow gardens that can be picked out here and there, with their lawns, ponds, flower beds all so discreetly designed; one makes out a touch of green that stands out faintly against the pebbled walks, the whole effect being one of faded, washed-out colors, like the wools in an old carpet. I don't think a sheerer quality of melancholy could be found anywhere. At the far end of a murky, rainy sky—for here comes a shower—the twin steeples of Sainte-Clotilde

seem to waver, then grow dim, and the squat little dome of Panthe-
mont gleams softly like a big black pearl.

DECEMBER 16. . . . Some days, life appears to be a very thin and
yet invincibly opaque veil behind which roars a huge fire, but
this is not only hell-fire. The veil I speak of is everything that
the senses teach us: the color of the table on which I write these
lines, the cheeping of birds under my windows, the sound of a
neighboring convent's bells, the gardens I catch sight of when I
look up, and the noise made by this pen as it runs over the paper,
all that I see, hear, touch, and taste all day long, and not only
that, but the thoughts of people who talk to me, and also my own
thoughts, in fact everything that is not God. When the veil's appearance is too beautiful, it forms a trap where souls are snared
(*"Species decepit me,"* says one of the elders in the story of
Susanna). Men spend their time in "agreeably blinding themselves," as Pascal has it, and hide from the immense fire of God's
charity.

1948

JANUARY 18. Speaking of false memories (the impression of having seen a place where one has never set foot, the impression of
having lived in a house whose threshold one has never crossed), I
told someone that this must be a manifestation of hereditary memory. The idea was once developed by Jung. I remember the lecture he gave around 1935 about the drawings of madmen, many
of which bore traces of millenary memories: an illiterate patient,
for instance, produced an extremely complicated drawing whose
equivalent could be found only in Tibetan art. It is highly prob-
able that in writing the preface to *Varouna*, I recollected this
theory of humanity's memory, the great common source at which
we all constantly draw. I wrote the preface in an attempt to make
it clear that my novel was not a story about metempsychosis, but
what use has a preface ever been? About twenty years ago, I was
in a small Austrian town for the first time. As I was about to go
by a large house with an open gateway, I thought suddenly: "A
little uphill street and at the end of the street, the sky." This was

exactly what I saw less than a second later. The house bridged an alley, a rather usual thing in Austria, and this alley climbed steeply to a flat piece of ground where the sky was visible from top to bottom. The shock this gave me made me feel pensive for the rest of the day. Unquestionably, I had never set foot in this street, and all the fables about the transmigration of souls returned to me. The truth appears simpler to me now. Humanity is but one man and is to be found in its entirety in each of us. For a second, in an unknown town, I had memories of this town. I had lived there with generations of men and women. How and why we are suddenly enlightened as to the past, I don't know, but the experience is profoundly disturbing.

FEBRUARY 9.   The silence of the room where I write is one of the greatest treasures of my life; it is also a luxury, and I wonder if I won't be one of the last men to enjoy it. In a quarter of a century, will a writer's life such as mine be possible? I sometimes feel as though I already belonged to a bygone age.

FEBRUARY 20.   Had lunch in a restaurant with about ten people. Camus sits facing me and I try to talk to him. I am deeply touched by his very sensitive, very human face. There is such obvious integrity in the man that it almost immediately inspires respect: simply, he is not like other people. Malaparte and his book *Kaputt* are discussed. Mme X. tells us that on meeting the author, she said: "I have read your book. I would have very much liked to read the other." (That is, the one he would have written if Germany had won the war.) Mme X. says that Malaparte did not reply. Whereupon, Camus exclaims: "If you had said that to me, Madame, I would have left the room!" "Oh! the French are so sensitive," answers Mme X. "Italians aren't like that."

FEBRUARY 22.   I was told of a recent convert who exasperates everyone around her by her uncompromising zeal. Any conversion is, in fact, a tacit reflection on one's neighbor, but who would not lose patience on seeing these proselytes monopolize St. Thomas, put on deep airs to which they have no right, because their wisdom is a brand-new wisdom, much like a borrowed garment obviously not custom made. At fifteen, I used to see a mounting fury in people's eyes when I brandished some scarlet sentence culled from Bloy's diary.

* * *

FEBRUARY 28. An ever-increasing horror of the spiritual indis-
cretions such as are published nowadays, unasked-for confidences,
illuminations, ecstasies! The "humble" tone—which saints, real
saints, have never had, theirs is different—the dull, pious chatter
that tends to be "edifying" and is simply scandalous. And if ever
I have been guilty of this—I hope not—I here pass final judgment
on myself! For this is not true religion.

MARCH 4. Paris this morning was wrapped in a pure white mist
behind which shone the spring sun, and the mist was like a veil of
snow stretched across the sky in front of a huge, blazing diamond.
In writing this, I remember something I saw in a small château
in the north of France, in 1935. I was in my room at three in the
afternoon of a very fine summer day, watching tiny specks of
dust pass slowly through a sunbeam. One of them, caught in the
rays of this dazzling light, began to shine like a tiny sun; this did
not last long, but when the diminutive star was extinguished, it
was replaced by others that glittered in their turn. This sight held
my attention for some time, but if it seemed beautiful to me then,
in the sky of memory, today, I find it richer still, decked out like
a constellation. The soul must shine like this in the presence of
God, for it is a mere speck of dust compared with the great sun
and the light in which it moves is what gives it life. I remember
having read in St. Teresa of Ávila that a soul in a state of grace
is so beautiful that anyone who could see it would, if that were
possible, take it for another God.

MARCH 10. Very much struck by one of Keats' letters in which
he describes a trip to Scotland and particularly Fingal's Cave,
which he talks of enchantingly: "Suppose now that the giants who
came down to the daughters of men, had taken a whole mass of
these columns and had bound them together like a bunch of
matches; and then, with immense axes had made a cavern in the
body of these columns." How well one sees what he means. . . .
He has the precision peculiar to poets that novelists possess only
inasmuch as they are poets. On reading these pages, I was seized
with a renewed love for Keats, whom I consider pre-eminently a
poet and place ahead of all the others, with Hölderlin. But it is
not only the poet, it is the man himself who fascinates me. I like
to think that a young man who was anything but a softy, and even
proved pugnacious and a little rough at times, should have written

the woman he loved: "The world is too brutal for me—I am glad there is such a thing as the grave." During his last illness, he said: "I can feel the cold earth upon me—the daisies growing over me."

MARCH 18. Read a most informative article by Father Bouyer about psychoanalysis in Switzerland. One passage was like a flash of light. I formerly taxed psychoanalysis with suppressing the freedom of the individual by making him the tool of circumstance and, above all, of heredity; now I understood suddenly that circumstances and, in particular, those caused by heredity are like a sphere of action chosen by God, where our freedom is exercised in a measure known to Him only. ("Circumstances are God," a Dominican father once said to me.) This tallies with the thoughts suggested to me by Gide's remark about faith, "the result of auto-suggestion and heredity." Although I know very little about psychoanalysis, what has always seemed curious and attractive about it is that it penetrates to the core of the soul's mystery without throwing much light on it; the further it advances, the more things become obscure; once a question is solved, another appears behind it and the newly revealed question hides an even greater one.

MARCH 29. Have thought a great deal about the problem of the novel, lately. A fact of cardinal importance is that I no longer feel like writing one. Why is that? I am discouraged, perhaps, by the threat of another war. But that threat will always exist, even if war does not break out. We should behave *als ob*, as Adler says. But there is something else: fighting oneself, fighting against the physical instinct, paralyzes a novelist's imagination, for the simple reason that the talent of a novelist is rooted in sin. The source of a novel is impure. I am summing up and, in summing up, simplify what would be very lengthy to say and also very complex.

APRIL 12. A novelist is like a scout commissioned to go and see what is happening in the depth of the soul. He comes back and reports what he has observed. He never lives on the surface but only inhabits the darkest regions. Such has been my experience. I admit that it is not necessarily that of other novelists. Thought about it this morning in connection with the ties that exist between the novel and faith. The idea of writing novels in defense of

Christianity has something about it that horrifies me. I would rather give up writing than trump up a piece of fiction tending to prove anything whatsoever.

MAY 21. A long conversation with Father Couturier on the subject of the novelist. The latter feeds on everything he sees, on everything he reads, on everything he hears. If he is a believer, the difficulty begins when he sits down at his table to write, for he is obliged to become each one of his characters and plunge with them into their sins. I used to think this a false problem, but the fact is that no novel worthy of the name exists without a complicity between the author and his creatures, and far more than complicity: a complete identification. I think that is why no one has ever heard of a saint writing a novel. When I read novels whose source has been "purified," I marvel at the wealth of poisons to be found in each character! Delete the poison and you kill the novel. And if God wishes works of art to be created, as Father Couturier said to me, would one dare to condemn *Les Liaisons dangereuses*? Once expurgated, what would remain of literature? Depressed and annoyed by this question.

MAY 30. Called up Gide yesterday morning: "Why, of course, come to see me. You are always welcome." I suggest tomorrow: "That's too far off. Come this afternoon." He wanted at first to come to see me in my new flat, but was afraid to climb my four flights of stairs. I dropped in on him around six o'clock. He is in the usual corner between the window and the piano, and each time I see him there I am reminded of a great bird in its eyrie. He is dressed today in white flannel and wears the black cap so amusingly described by Guth ("a photograph where he is seen wearing a convict's cap and gaily playing the piano"). I have brought him a present which I put on a table, and he gazes at it, in his own words, "with emotion and devotion." For it is a cast of Chopin's hand. He looks attentively at the plaster hand, turns it over, regrets the lack of lines in the palm, admires the extreme slenderness of the fingers, the vigor of the wrist; while the hand is delicately feminine, the wrist is a man's wrist; the whole strength of the hand is sheltered there. Besides, says Gide to me, it's not the hand of a pianist: the stretch of the fingers is not wide enough. Listening to him, I am struck by his pallor, but he holds himself very straight, his eyes shine, and both his speech and thought are admirably clear. Conversation glides from one topic to another, and I can't remember in what connection he asks me if I know about the Kinsey Report. I was about to say that I was ill informed about politics (he knows that, anyway), but something held me back and I simply answered: "No." Great amazement, a rather scandalized amazement. "What! Then I'll go and fetch it for you." He leaves the room and returns a few minutes later with a thick volume, crammed with notes, and makes me read several passages, in particular a series of questions put to twelve thousand Americans by three professors over there. I marvel that such answers could have been obtained, for the questions concern sexuality and acts, certain ones of which are punishable by the laws of the country; now, Americans as I know them are somewhat reluctant to tell such secrets, dreading above all that people might *know*, but it would appear that the professors in question knew how to go about it. According to the author, says Gide, seventy-five per cent of Americans should be in jail, if the law were applied. Interesting. As to American women—for the first volume is about men alone—the women will also have a Kinsey Report, and I don't think they lose much in the waiting. What annoys me a little about this bulky volume is, I must say, the mania for statistics. I refuse to believe that twelve thousand Americans, no matter how skillfully chosen, can inform us accurately about the mentality of the entire male population. "Figures don't lie," as people so often say in the United States. That remains to be seen.

JUNE 9. Yesterday, a visit from Béguin. He talked about Bernanos, who is very ill and had had his gall-bladder removed. I remember how generously the man behaved to me early in my career and how much he encouraged me then. He suffers greatly from being unable to write novels. "I have a dozen novels to write," he told Béguin. And if he does not write them it is because he wastes his energy on magazines and newspapers: the times are responsible for this. He suffers from not being able to be Bernanos. . . .

JUNE 10. I sometimes wonder if it is possible to work out one's salvation while remaining in the world. Some heretics have thought not, but the starting point of almost all heresies is a truth misunderstood. Day before yesterday, Béguin talked to me admirably about the grace of sin. I always benefit by listening to him. When he left, I thought about this: some people go naturally to God, and those are the saints. The rest can only return to God, and that means all of us, but in a certain way, those who return to God know a little more than the ones who have never done anything but go straight to Him; they are infinitely poorer, but have received a special grace that saints have not had. "Return . . . Return . . . Return . . ." is the word continually found in the prophets. The gold ring, the best robe, and the feast are for the soul that returns.

JUNE 13. There is a curious letter of Voltaire's about instinct. The following sentences throw a wonderful light on a great problem: "It must be admitted that, in art works of genius, everything is the work of instinct. Corneille wrote the scene between Horatius and one of the Curiatii as a bird builds its nest, save in this particular: a bird always builds it very well, whereas we weaklings do not." Too many authors nowadays build their books with their brains, at the expense and to the detriment of their instinct; now, instinct in many cases is genius, but they dare not give in to it. Fear of being ridiculous.

I saw a bird build its nest. It happened in Baltimore. A blue jay lodged in a corner of my cousin's window. One day, she came to fetch me, opera glasses in her hand, a finger on her lips. I approached on tiptoe and looked at something five yards off, my eyes glued to the glasses. To be truthful, the fat bright blue and light blue bird had already built his nest, but he shaped it, trampled it, rounded it out, and—I almost burst out laughing—accomplished this last feat with his cerulean bottom. For he stood in the center and turned around slowly, pushing at the edges of the little skiff. This took a good fifteen minutes, but the bird was finicky and patient. Finally, he sat down, looking extremely satisfied, made himself as large as possible, and filled his home to a nicety.

JUNE 15. I was in a bookstore a little while ago and skimmed through a reissue of Gide's diary, which I had never read entirely, but after a few pages I was once more convinced that I would never be able to finish the volume. Why? I am not quite sure why. He writes beautifully and every page is crammed to overflowing with a wealth of ideas, yet, while he gives all he has to give, he chills the heart, and the more you read, the less you believe, the less you hope, and—I say this regretfully—the less you love.

UNDATED. At times, I remember an unkind, lucid sentence of Stendhal's: "In a seminary, there is a certain manner of eating a soft-boiled egg that denotes the progress made in religious life." I care so little for this man—although I can never open one of his books without falling on a few pages and devouring them—yet how much I admire him, in spite of my dislike!

JUNE 21. Saw Gide, a moment ago, in his little study. He offers me a tumble-down armchair over which he has thrown a folded blanket. Removing the blanket, he shows me that the armchair is losing its horsehair stuffing. "I sometimes think of having it repaired, then I tell myself that it will last out my time, so what's the use?" He says this gaily. I don't believe I have ever seen him downhearted. . . .

JULY 10. ASCONA. Perhaps it may do me good to write down what is worrying me. But indeed I can't. I am ill. With every appearance of health, I am ill. Yet this is where everything will be decided, I know it for certain. However, you know perfectly well that nothing is ever decided. The final assent is never given in this world, excepting in the ear of death. We never are, we continually become. And how could this conventional setting be the one for a tragedy? From my window, I see a garden and at the end of the garden mountains, and in the garden, a gardener. Can everything end in a postcard?

JULY 12. These hideously memorable days . . . The religious crisis I am going through began on June 30th. I wonder how far one can go without losing one's mind. And in the midst of all this, a strange happiness. Drove to the Madonna del Ponte, which is almost on the Italian border. The waters of the lake are two sharply contrasting colors: turquoise and navy blue. A clump of huge cypresses, some so old that they are dying and only remain standing thanks to props of masonry.

Felt very sad to hear that Bernanos had died. He knew all the things that grieve us. And it was this very fact that made up his greatness. No matter if we saw him dressed in a suit like the rest of us, he was a man out of the invisible.

* * *

JULY 22. MERANO. I spent a couple of hours dreaming in the big public bathing establishment. Above the cabins, a purple mountain wore a thick bonnet of white clouds. As I saw all those bodies running about happily, or loafing in the sun (none was very beautiful except those of children), I was struck once again by the chastity of nakedness and, in a roundabout way, returned to the irritating question of soul and body. People talk about the body *and* the soul, as though the body were the container and the soul the contents, as if the two could separate at will, be distinct, whereas more often they mingle, a little as earth and water mix in mud. There is no perceptible borderline between the two, or at any rate no borderline that is not breached continually at every minute, as though it did not exist. The soul is reached through the body and the body through the soul, and therein lies the whole tragedy of the human lot, which makes us such deeply mysterious beings. "Oh, body, thou art the soul!" cried Whitman.

AUGUST 8. PARIS. We all have a dark angel with whom we must struggle. Yesterday, I was seized once more with a wild desire for earthly happiness because a lunch with friends, a walk with Paris as a setting, everything talked of my too happy youth, too happy for me to bear remembering today. In my Jansenist moments, I come to wonder whether one can live a Christian life in the world and if an insuperable contradiction does not lie there, but it is impossible that Christ should have come to save only the religious in their convents. I have known men who could not accept the fact that they were sinners, and even great sinners, and who were furious not to be saints.

AUGUST 20. Writing books comforts the author for everything that life has refused him. It might even be that an overgratified, successful life could have proved a sterile one for him. A surfeited man does not write.

AUGUST 23. I woke this morning at dawn and *saw* my book[1] from beginning to end. It roused me from sleep. Facing me, in the darkness, stood that motionless character. As though the whole thing had been given me, as though the whole thing had been given back to me. Not much in common with the story of Célina

[1] *Moïra*.

as I had intended writing it. A moment ago, I really recovered my taste for work, for life, and felt the pen between my fingers racing over the paper, as if it wrote of its own accord. Happy in spite of the physical problem that darkens my life, but all that will also pass into my book.

SEPTEMBER 25.   I was sent into this world to write. Not to write would kill me by slow inches. To say that this book helps me to live would be saying very little—it helps me to breathe.

SEPTEMBER 27.   Yesterday evening, I read the second chapter of the Epistle to the Ephesians. It contains this strange verse: ". . . and sins, wherein in time past ye walked according to the course of this world, according to the prince of the power of the air . . ." What echoes this rouses from the depths of the reader's soul! There are times—I hesitate to say so—when I resist a temptation to open the Bible, because I know the power of its spell. For me, it is far more than a book, it is a voice and a person.

Thought over my novel at dawn this morning. I must keep it from tending toward eroticism—it is only too eager to do this of its own accord—because the spiritual counterweight will not be strong enough to assure its balance. What should not be too clearly expressed is that everyone is in love with the hero. What I have against eroticism is, above all, its facility. It is no longer daring now, but a sort of triteness, and that it has become fashionable is enough for me to loathe it.

There are strange remarks in Havelock Ellis about the connection between religion and sexuality. Did we ever wish for such a thing? I should think not! If the religious element in us heightens the sexual one or, to talk like bygone moralists, if what is good heightens what is evil, where is the solution of the problem?

OCTOBER 6.   A long fit of insomnia last night, during which I thought about religion. That is the other side of my nature, the stronger. I have taken a loathing for books that speak of God as though He were someone who could be questioned and who obligingly satisfies our little curiosities. God likes this, prefers that, thinks such and such a thing. The truth is that we know practically nothing about this. What, exactly, God wants of us, why we are born in this period and not in another, why here and not there, are so many mysteries. No one in the world has ever shared God's secrets. Religion should be brought back to something very simple, to the Eucharist and the Scriptures. To abide by the articles of faith, no more, no less. All the rest is conjecture. Three lines of Dante come back to me, the Italian so clear that one might be reading French:

> *Avete il vecchio ed il nuovo testamento*
> *ed il pastor della Chiesa che vi guida:*
> *questo vi basti a vostro salvamento.*

OCTOBER 19. I said to a religious: "Chastity is the body's night-mare. The soul is certain of its vocation, but the body's vocation is physical love. That is its mode of expression, the way it fulfills its part; that is all it thinks, that is all it thinks about. How can you expect it to understand the soul's cares? That body and soul are forcibly wedded is a mystery. The body hates the soul and wants it to die." I add this: "To remain chaste does not necessarily make a saint of you, but chastity is one of the hallmarks of holi-ness, and if you wish to be chaste, you also wish to be holy, with-out daring to admit it, perhaps."

OCTOBER 24. I said to myself this morning, in church: "Listen to what your conscience says." But my conscience said nothing. I thought about the book I was engaged in copying, of my early diary whose fate seems so doubtful. I think that four religious out of ten would have told me: "You are committing a great sin." Yet, at certain times, I hear a voice deep within me that urges me to continue. I cannot express this otherwise. The voice is not like those we hear *through memory*, it is something both silent and confused. This strange book will cease someday from appearing to be so, and will accomplish its mission, which is to be useful to a few people, to guide them, to teach them to avoid certain mis-takes, to help them to a better knowledge of a lonely man's heart. Of course evil is mixed into this work, but it cannot exist with-out evil. That is where it is human. Evil, in the present case, is like a vehicle for the good contained in the book, and what is good in this book—which I will never see in print—is an endeavor for a truth which is my truth. I have tried to tell the truth at all costs.

NOVEMBER 9. Read some of O. Henry's short stories. They are written by a semi-barbarian, fascinated by words, who handles them much as a savage would turn over a handful of bits of colored glass. His stories are very ingenious, but as they are invariably written in view of a final surprise, you must wait until the very last lines to judge of the merits of what has preceded—and this is a most questionable form of literature because of its mechanical process. O. Henry has had enormous influence over American short-story writers and appears to have broadly outlined a model for their tales. He has a wonderful imagination.

NOVEMBER 13. I wonder where I get this passion for telling the truth honestly, without choosing or altering. As a rule, one doesn't say everything, one tries to obtain a certain unity of character, but on what plane will such unity be carried out? On the spiritual or the physical? Whichever the plane chosen, one will cheat: one is willing to tell the truth about the soul, but not the truth about the body; or that about the body and not . . . etc.

Read the Book of Esther in my Hebrew Bible. What confusion there is in my life! If I were to put all that into a novel, people would think it impossible, would say I had invented it.

NOVEMBER 20. Called up Gide's number. Great difficulty in obtaining it. The person who finally answers is incomprehensible and, what is more, does not understand me. I was about to hang up when Gide comes to the telephone: "I was told that M. Scribe wanted to speak to me. I hesitated to answer!" Tells me that he is too ill to see me, that he had left his bed to come to the phone when he realized it was I, but that he is going back to bed and hopes to be "fit again" in two or three days.

NOVEMBER 27. In Jefferies' *The Story of My Heart*, there is a very curious passage on the feeling of worship that the sight of a beautiful body arouses in the author, who is intensely pagan. I have often experienced this and said so. Something religious. And I believe that Jefferies is right in saying that ascetics are the real impure, although I would have preferred him to say the puritans.

DECEMBER 19. Had a friendly telephone call from Gide, this morning. He receives me a little later in the small room where he works. A big leather cushion has been thrown over the broken-down armchair that he has given up all idea of repairing. On the mantelpiece, a bronze head of Gide on which is tossed, no, most carefully placed, a fine green velvet beret. Gide himself wears a fisherman's hat under which his face seemed to me extremely pallid and his eyes a little weary behind his spectacles; his voice is softer, lower than usual, but as clear and distinct as it was twenty years ago. I give him the passages about him in the fourth volume of my diary and ask him to read them. He reads the first page and declares himself touched that I don't think he has a sharp expression—such as photographers give him—but an attentive one. When he asks for the following pages, I tell him that I would prefer to leave them with him: "You can return them to me later. I would feel cheated if you read them now; I would much rather talk to you." He laughs and agrees. Tells me he is going to publish his correspondence with Claudel. . . . When he asks me what I think of *Le Partage de midi*, I make no bones about expressing my admiration for the play. "But," he says, "the text has been modified in the name of orthodoxy. . . ." I left soon afterwards.

DECEMBER 20. Gide said to me: "Claudel is a man who thinks one can go to Heaven in a Pullman."

DECEMBER 22. Read Thomas Merton's autobiography with great pleasure. He is a young poet, now a Trappist, in Kentucky. Almost all his loathings are mine, but his led him to a convent. He talks roughly and brutally of worldly life and of all the foolishness that amuses us. He is often right, but it seems a little easy to be right in this manner, I mean in exposing the inaneness of worldly pleasures. Intelligent worldlings are perfectly aware that all this is vanity, but nevertheless enjoy it. "Turn away from it all," they are told, "for everything will pass away." They think this the best possible reason for hanging on to it! However, the book is a great fisticuff through a papier-mâché setting.

DECEMBER 30. What meaning can I give to this dream and what does it want to tell me? I was in a vast Romanesque church and, holding a child by the hand, led it to the doors of two adjoining prison cells, each with a grilled peephole in its door. I raised a lighted candle and said to the child: "Look, this is for your good." The tortured faces of two men appeared at the peepholes. I then said: "These two men are going to be burned on Tuesday. . . ." The whole thing is all too clear, down to the detail of the peepholes, but why two men? They are my own self. Perhaps a tendency to see myself twofold. And who is the child? Myself also?

1949

JANUARY 2. Two forces face to face and equally formidable: spiritual energy and sensual emotion. There is sensual emotion in everything we see, and in everything we don't see, spiritual energy, but in everything we see, spiritual energy penetrates like the waters of a river that bursts its barrages and overflows into the meadows. And in everything that we don't see, sensual emotion rises like a great overwhelming flood. There is sensual emotion in a prayer so innocent that a child could not pray it better, and in the transports of physical love enters something like a blind longing for Paradise lost. Nothing is quite pure, just as nothing is quite impure. A Sister of Charity's humble heart may be swollen with sensual emotion, which our Manichaeism alone prevents us from seeing, because we will not admit that sensual emotion is also a work of God, and that it is essentially many-sided. In the same way, a frenzy for pleasure does not take on its full meaning and cannot be wholly understood, unless one recognizes that it contains something divine, a nostalgia for holiness.

JANUARY 16. A Catholic talks to me about what he calls the delights of communion, but I know him to be very sensual and, like many men who are more or less allured by mysticism, he transfers his sensuality, bag and baggage, to the religious plane. He has no idea of this, but I see it so clearly that I cannot help dropping a hint about it, as discreetly as possible; I have known him long enough to do so. . . . He tells me confidentially, a moment later, that he has never experienced remorse for carnal failings. And what true-hearted man would talk otherwise? Remorse of this kind is almost always obtained, I was going to say trumped up, when conscience stings us—if it still lives in us—as soon as we sin against love.

FEBRUARY 2. What a strange profession is mine. I am working well, with a passion for forgetting, plunging into an imaginary world. And what do I meet in this imaginary world? My own problems immeasurably enlarged to the point of reaching terrifying proportions.

* * *

FEBRUARY 5. Worked a lot at my novel. How alive that Joseph is! He fascinates and at the same time horrifies me. What a monster of sensuality one must be to possess such modesty, such outrageous modesty!

FEBRUARY 12. Had a long talk with Elie-Anne about Marcel Proust, who sometimes came to see her with Lucien Daudet. "He always seemed self-conscious and said very little. His appearance was so queer that Lucien had to assure us that he was really somebody. When we read his books, they irritated us. They were so wrong and at the same time contained enough truth to make them plausible, but we knew very well that things were not at all the way he showed them, because he had never known *the real dukes and the real duchesses.* He had only second-hand information. The people he should have known would never have received him, because they lived in a closed circle and never saw outsiders."

FEBRUARY 26. The truth I have reached, after years of struggles and thought, is that I hate the sexual instinct. I recognize its importance, I admire the gigantic force that has achieved so many works, but hate desire, that force that throws so many wise beings at the feet of fools and makes them rave, like lustful children. I wish it was not so.

Devoured Gourmont's *La Physique de l'amour.* Chastity, "the strangest of all sexual aberrations," he says. The amours of moles, tragic amours, of a surgical character. Frightful the hit-or-miss methods of nature, "that good mother," Gourmont says with a snicker.

FEBRUARY 27. Just as I returned from Mass this morning, I had a telephone call from Gide asking me to see him. I went at once. Gide is better, after a heart attack. I find him at his usual place, in the library. The small table he sits at is littered with books and papers. An open copybook where I recognize half a page of his handwriting and a volume of his collected works. He stoops a little, his face very gray, his cheeks covered with a white stubble, for he seems not to have shaved for two or three days. Shakes hands and makes me sit opposite him. "You're going to find me intellectually diminished," he says, laughing. I laugh too and reply: "You say that very friskily!" Turning serious, he answers: "No, I feel diminished." "No one would think so . . ." "But I am." "Yet I find you working." "I'm just pretending to. See, my pen is dry." (He points at it.) It takes a lot of courage to talk so about oneself, to be so clear-sighted. A little later, he tells me that he has received a *thirty-word* cable from America (his voice supplies the italics), asking him to go over there to receive the Goethe Prize. "What's the Goethe Prize?" "I have no idea. I've been offered five thousand dollars and all my expenses paid." "How magnificent they are!" "Yes, magnificent, but I'm not going, I'm too tired." He speaks of a letter from an American called Henson, who mentions me. "But who is he?" asks Gide. I tell him. Henson has a great admiration for Gide, and I speak highly of the young man, whom I met when I served in the American army. "Yes," says Gide, "there are some very fine people, no matter what is said to the contrary. There are lots of them. I don't care for people who run down this one and that and who play the pessimists. I'll leave this earth thinking that there are very fine people in this world. I say this without sadness. There's no sadness in me. No, I don't like people who take pleasure in spitting in the soup." "Oh, neither do I!" I answer, disgusted by the picture conjured up. "Neither do you, I know it. That's why we see each other. And then, have you noticed that it's always in other people's soup . . ." But I have been with Gide for half an hour and must go. In connection with Scandinavia, where I intend to go this summer, Gide asks questions and sighs: "If I followed my inclinations . . . No, it's impossible. You're going there this summer? Well . . . I can't." That was the saddest thing he said that morning. I get up and he shakes my hand. As I am about to cross the threshold of the library, he asks me what I am reading at present and if I know of a book to recommend for Catherine. I think for a moment. The books I read are so serious that I hesitate to mention them. However, I have been rereading Montaigne and say so. "Ah," says Gide, "what edition are you reading?" "The small Jouaust edition that gives the 1588 text and that of the second edition." "I am asking this to know if you have the variants. That is most important." (Forgot to say that when I mentioned Montaigne, Gide exclaimed: "That surprises me, from you!" "Because I'm a Catholic? Why, Pascal read and reread him." "Merely to refute him." That remains to be proven. Pascal admired and hated him at the same time. I might have answered, but thought of it too late, that St. Francis de Sales took the keenest pleasure in reading the *Essays*.) Gide is near me, asks me to take down one of the four big volumes he points to on a book-shelf. It is a magnificent Montaigne with broad margins. The variants are in italics. "You know the famous sentence about La Boëtie . . . Well, 'because it was I' was added later." "Yes," I replied, "it doesn't figure in the first edition." "The sentence is held up to us as something wonderful, coming straight from the heart," continues Gide. "But it took thirty years to come straight from Montaigne's heart!" He suddenly becomes the Gide I used to know, and during those last few minutes I find him exactly as he used to be. He shakes my hand again. "It was nice of you to come over right away." I don't think he ever showed himself more affectionate than in that little sentence. What I admire in him is a never-failing lucidity, a desire to see things as clearly as possible, not to be fooled by his own self.

MARCH 20. Father Couturier called me up the other day and said: "I want to *reassure* you about Hell." I had to make him re-peat the sentence, which I didn't catch at first (surprised as I was by the word *reassure*). He reminds me that last week, during lunch, he had expressed doubts about the large number of lost souls. I had said: "No one ever preaches any longer about our latter ends. The clergy dares not speak of Hell. All the saints believed in it and talked about it." Today, he says: "I want you to know that I believe in it, like all good Christians." "But, Father," was my reply, "I believe exactly all that you believe." Strange to think that he should have said that to me, of all people. My very first book was partly based on this subject. He had much better talk about Hell to such Catholics as seem not to believe in it at all, but this trait in Father Couturier's character pleased and touched me. It is truly that of a spiritual man, centered on the invisible world, and a conscientious one. Nevertheless, it made me laugh.

APRIL 10. Claudel was told of Gide's witticism: "Claudel is a man who thinks one can go to Heaven in a Pullman." To which Claudel replied: "Well, Gide is going to Hell in the subway."

APRIL 18. A visit from Father Couturier. He came to ask for some information and has no idea of the extraordinary impression he made on me. One dares not write the word *holiness*. Do I know what a saint is? Yet I thought that it must be something very much like this. There was an inimitable radiance about him, a real humility that seeks neither to hide nor to show off, a gentleness that is the gentleness of a violent man. At one moment, I could not understand what he was saying and thought I saw him through a sort of shining mist. . . . Thought of the tomfoolery I hear. Writers outdo themselves at it: "My customary sincerity . . ." "My honesty . . ." "My terrific modesty . . ." Poor things.

Listened over the air to Messiaen improvise. Music that sounds as though it had been composed *after* the end of the world. It has monstrous beauty, makes you see vast caverns where rivers flow, where piles of precious stones glitter. You have no idea where you are—in India, perhaps. The composer was playing the organ in Trinity Church. Never have the vaultings of that hideous building heard more disturbing sounds. You have the impression at times that Hell yawns open. Cataracts of strange noises *dazzle* the ear.

APRIL 24 OR 25. AT SAINT-NICOLAS-DE-VÉROCE, IN SAVOIE. Read the *Introduction to Kierkegaard* by Jolivet. Few books have upset me so much since I came into this world. It is horrifying at times to discover oneself in another man, and this happened to me when I read this book. But isn't it the role of very great men to reveal us to ourselves? I mean that they teach us what we knew without knowing that we knew it. In this sense, Kierkegaard's sentences are like so many magic mirrors where the soul is reflected and sees itself for the first time. Thought once more about Descartes's dream, which has engaged so much of my attention lately. Are books merely an aspect of this dream? Wouldn't it be, rather, that the reader imagines what he reads, or thinks he is reading? In the flashes of Kierkegaardian thought, one has glimpses of great depths that are singularly like a revelation. "Christianity has not materialized," he writes.

MAY 2. As long as something inside us protests against ourselves, there is room for hope. It is when one accepts oneself as one is, and gives up, that the game is in danger of being lost. In other words (if I wanted to be funny), one can set one's mind at rest so long as one feels uneasy!

MAY 5. Alone today. I took a path that runs down into a valley, through the meadows. I followed it to a wood of fir trees where

I spent the better part of the day, for this is one of the most beautiful spots in the world. One finds oneself there on a sort of spur that advances to the middle of the valley and cuts it in two. Thicknesses of moss and fir needles give the ground a wonderful springiness, as though the soil bore one up. Inside the wood, the ground goes up, goes down, with green-carpeted ravines from the bottom of which loom very straight firs taller than the pillars of Notre-Dame. A dim light, a silence broken only by bird songs, a complete stillness everywhere and solitude are what is found in this spot. I dreamed, I thought of our life, of what Robert said to me about Kierkegaard the other day, on the road: "The older one grows, the more one wants to provide for one's inner life." Thought about what the philosopher says concerning the necessity of "choosing your choice." He sums up almost all my problems in three words.

MAY 21. PARIS. Read Kierkegaard's *Fear and Trembling*, which affected me like a thunderclap. I know what faith is, I have grown up in its shadow, for, seen on this side of death, it is a shadow. My parents handed it down to me, by God's grace, and it goes so deep within me that it lends its color to everything, to good and evil alike. Without a feeling for the absolute, we would sink like a stone. We are all like the church of Philadelphia, in Revelation: weak, but protected on account of our weakness.

MAY 22. If few people go to Heaven, how will *you* go there? How would you form part of the elect? What is duty? To count on a miracle. I am not afraid of Hell and never was, in spite of desperate efforts to obtain this fear, but I think that what would be more grievous than going to Hell would be annihilation after death and not to see God. I must admit that reading a sermon by Newman on the small number of the chosen disturbed me very greatly.

JUNE 15. The other day, as I was tidying a large cupboard, I found a plaster cast that I used to be very fond of: the head of the charioteer of Delphi; and next it was the cap I wore in the American army, and I put the cap on the charioteer's head, just to see; the effect was so likely that it made me laugh. Nothing more Greek than a young American's head, when he is handsome.

* * *

JULY 1. . . . AT VERRIÈRES. I enter the world called real as one enters a mist. I would like to pause and explain what I mean, what I believe I understand. It takes very little for the outside world to lose its reality in my eyes. No doubt it is not with impunity that since 1924 I have thrown myself deliberately, and at the price of great effort, into a state known only to novelists, in order to believe and *see* what I describe. Following which, the world does not always appear to me as something completely real, and there are moments when I clearly feel that I'm going to lose my footing. Consequently, when I see a large number of people who have to be talked to, I shrink back and don't quite hear what is being said to me. I take refuge in temporary deafness. I am present, but like a somnambulist. I may perhaps seem at ease, but a somnambulist also gives that impression. . . . I went the round of the guests, I saw a splendid garden in the sunset, very big trees, long stretches of grass, and, in a setting fit for childhood memories, lots of very well-dressed men and women, society in fact, what is called society. I looked at the bright pink sky beyond black trees. . . . During dinner, I talked to my neighbor about this feeling of unreality. She was English, she understood. I told her of having seen, in an American university, sapphires and rubies lit up by "fluorescent" light, and that these precious stones were just pebbles picked up on a road. It might be that this light showed them to me as they really are. God, perhaps, sees them so. Poets and saints are the only ones to guess that a veil is stretched between us and the world (I kept these ideas to myself). Then I talked to my left-hand neighbor. Her Christian name, Evangeline, is written on a cardboard four-leaf clover, but the name only suggests to me Longfellow's poem. She speaks French, and so well that I wonder where she comes from. She is interested in literature and asks lots of questions about my work (this happens only once every ten years); I am amazed to be sitting next to someone who forgets to talk about herself. I ask her if she writes, but she waves aside the question as though what she did had no importance, and asks me about a book that I wrote in English. We talk about America. One of the most beautiful streets in the world is the main street in Salem, where Hawthorne lived, and it is now exactly as it was two centuries ago, with its large eighteenth-century houses set back a little from the road behind rows of trees. Does she know it? Why yes. She also knows Concord, where Emerson, Thoreau, Hawthorne, and Melville lived. She has seen everything that Europeans

never see, they who form such a hasty and often oversimple opinion of the United States. She smiles when I mention Baltimore
and gently says that she is Dr. Fisher's niece. Now I lived for three
years facing Dr. Fisher's house, and my cousin and sister know
him well. I suddenly emerge from my haziness. My neighbor is
the wife of Ambassador Bruce.

JULY 2. To know everything no longer interests me. To know
everything is a young man's dream. What interests me passionately today is to understand, and I no longer wish to know except
for the sake of understanding more clearly. Anyway, what value
has knowledge in itself? What Bayle knew over two centuries ago
seems debatable to us. How much error can be found in Erasmus'
knowledge! In fifty years, our books will make schoolchildren
smile.

JULY 17. Yesterday, an exceptionally happy and beautiful walk.
We went to Versailles and at once walked to the Grand Trianon
and passed through it to see the gardens, delighted by their design
and color schemes, and from there to great empty avenues, overgrown with nettles, grass, and brambles, but still most majestic
between rows of huge trees. We were quite alone, and I had a
feeling of indescribable happiness, a human but not carnal happiness, a happiness free from shadow. . . . I would have liked the
walk to continue till nightfall, but everything always has to end,
we must always go farther on, we must always turn back. No
doubt there will be other walks like this one, but not quite like it.

JULY 18. Novel. I must not allow the action to bog down in
conversations, as it might have done in psychological develop-
ments. As soon as a character listens to himself talk, he must be
made to shut up. From time to time, I take up the book from the
beginning, that is, I skim through it to look over the contents of
each page in a few seconds. In this way, I can see if it is making
headway, if it is moving, or if, on the contrary, it is marking time.
The beginning of the second part, which I am tackling today,
must have the same impulse as the beginning of the first part had.
The characters themselves furnish the action and I leave it to
them. As soon as I try to direct the action myself, I am almost sure
of making a false move; they *know*.

* * *

JULY 19. Last night, listened over the air to a part of *Don Giovanni,* which is being given at Aix. After an hour, I went to bed, no longer *hearing* a music I know too well and am so deeply fond of. I might almost say that I was familiar with the leading airs before knowing how to read, for my sisters used to play and sing them in our old rue de Passy flat. All my life, these delightful themes have been with me, following me in joy as well as in sadness; they have already lost their novelty for me, and it is a pity; I fear to hear them too often, not to find them each time lovelier, fresher; I dare not write that I fear to tire of them. The passages that touch me most are in the second part and reach one when the ear is already a little weary. What wouldn't I give to hear *La ci darem* for the first time! That intoxicating *first time* that in all spheres gives us something we will never find again . . . I have always thought that our joy in Heaven will be made up of this, that we will see God for an eternal *first time*; there will be a one and only time that will never cease, there will never be the sad thing linked to duration: repetition.

JULY 20. How keenly one feels whether a book is necessary or not—and this holds good less for the reader than the author! Is the initial impulse powerful enough to carry the story to its end? At every page, one should have the feeling of an irresistible pressure from within; instead of which, more often one has an impression that the author is ridding himself of a chore. It sometimes happens that the book undergoes this mysterious pressure at the beginning, but that the pressure loses vigor on the way and stops short, leaving the book to follow as best it can. Those sluggish words that cover page after page, those long sentences written by a man in a hurry to get through with it all . . . I have always had the greatest distrust for an overlong book, because it is often the sign of a lack of energy and not, as is thought, the mark of great labor.

AUGUST 10. Violent efforts to learn Danish.

Read John Addington Symonds' *Michaelangelo* with admiration. It now appears obvious to me that the man had the same horror of the sexual instinct as is found in Leonardo. Perhaps he dreaded the very thing that attracted him. His work is not that of a satisfied, surfeited man. It is in itself one of the most powerful sexual acts ever produced by art, but would seem to be that as an act of compensation. I can easily imagine that this somber, violent, timid man was chaste. None of his contemporaries, so far as we know, ever definitely proved that he was not. I believed the opposite for a long time, although without the least proof.

AUGUST 15. . . . What meaning can there be in all this? Our life is a book that writes itself and whose principal themes sometimes escape us. We are like the characters in a novel who do not always understand what the author wants of them.

SEPTEMBER 24. The carnal episodes I sometimes describe express a part of the truth that I carry in me and that is my truth, but they weigh on me and I hate them. All this will, one way or the other, get into the novel I am writing at present. Thought once more about the problem of sentences among which one must choose, those it is necessary to discard, but whose presence must make itself felt. All this subjacent, nonwritten book . . . the mistake that many transatlantic authors make is precisely to want to write it. Most of them do not choose.

A religious upbringing has shown me only too clearly the vanity of the world. That is what paralyzes ambition in me. I have never quite believed *that the game was real.* I would die of shame if I were to push myself forward as some people do. And let's not talk of modesty. It has nothing to do with the matter. I work exactly like a bird or a bee, because that is what I was made for, because it is my instinct and I would suffer too much in going against this instinct. I don't believe there can be the least question of literary fame nowadays, on the threshold of such a strange world as opens before us. I am completely indifferent as to whether my name will be remembered or forgotten. In eternity, this will not be of the slightest importance, but I want to fulfill my destiny, which is to express what is in me.

SEPTEMBER 28. Marveled as I read the Book of Esther in Hebrew. A reward for more than ten years of effort. I can at last get at the text that is back of translations.

SEPTEMBER 30. Sometimes I feel so happy to be alive that I sing when I am alone. I even think I would be perfectly happy were it not for the sexual problem, which I don't want to talk about. This morning, I was obliged to stop working on my book after thirty minutes. No one will ever know until after my death how much

I have had to fight in order to continue being myself, to be present until the end.

OCTOBER 1.   Read Lafuma's *Études Pascaliennes*. I always find it moving to be with Pascal again; he has had such an influence over me that I cannot even imagine what I would have been if I had not read him. His terrible sentence about sensual pleasure has sounded more than once in my ears this entire summer. "May they get drunk on it and die."

OCTOBER 5.   . . . As we were speaking of applause, of the sound of applause, I said that I very much disliked this violent, brutal noise, and Mme Bourdet, a theater fan to the core, exclaimed: "Oh come! It's the most beautiful sound in the world!" I stuck to my guns, I said that nothing was more beautiful than the silence that follows a Passion by Bach, at a concert of sacred music, a silence through which linger the last chords, the very last note where music dies away and disappears as into an abyss, instead of shattering against the sort of resounding wall built by hand clapping.

OCTOBER 9.   Abbé Omer Englebert's book on St. Francis of Assisi contains interesting remarks about the Poverello's virginity, a virginity very delicately questioned by his latest biographer. The first ones had rather clearly pointed out the sensual nature of the failings of the youthful Francis. After the saint's death all this was quickly glossed over and we were led to believe that his errors consisted in singing and dancing farandoles through the streets of Assisi. Farandoles indeed! I would much rather know that Francis made a few mistakes. He becomes all the dearer and more human to those who love him and his merit can only be that much greater. But I have always preferred saints of fire (such as St. Augustine) to saints of ice whom temptation did not even graze. That St. Francis of Assisi should have stumbled, revives our hope. There he is, very close and very vivid. As the Lord liveth, he sinned like the rest of us.

OCTOBER 12.   A priest who is enamored of mysticism tells me of his horror of theology: "It's nothing but straw! And who said that? St. Thomas. What do you say to that?" And speaking of St. Clara, who instructed her daughters to admire creation and look at the trees when they left their convent, he makes this remark: "What she really said was: 'Look at men and look at trees,' but the author of the book you mention did not think fit to say 'men.' " It seems, however, that in a future edition the quotation will be given in its entirety—and in Latin. A fine saying of St. Francis', who, when he once heard himself called a saint, exclaimed: "Don't canonize me too quickly! I am still quite capable of begetting children!" When I ask my visitor if he thinks that the Poverello's spirit is still extant in his Order, he replies shrewdly enough: "It's as though you asked me if the spirit of Christ still prevails among Christians." We next talked about Father Damien. My visitor had been to Molokai and told me that one day he had been to visit the lepers at Saint-Louis, in Paris. There were about ten of them. The nun said: "Don't let them touch you." A missionary from Molokai came up to him and, holding out his hand, said: "As you see, I haven't got leprosy." "And yet," continued my visitor, "the lower part of his face was eaten away by this terrible disease. But I shook his hand. Could I have done otherwise?" This is very much in the manner of the first Franciscans.

OCTOBER 16. I write what I see. If I had to sum myself up as an author, I think this sentence would say all there is to say. If I don't see, I can't write, I mean that if my mental eyes do not have a very clear view of the scene I want to describe—I designedly say scene, as one speaks of a scene in a play—I can do nothing. I am not like writers who can invent at will, without seeing anything, who invent with the help of words and not with their mental eyes (and this ends by being felt). I have said in the past that all I could do was to invent, but I had not sufficiently thought over the problem when I expressed myself so inaccurately. The truth is that I do not know how to invent. There is something or someone in me that makes me see my characters and makes me see them in action. In my case, such intensity of vision has never been greater than when I wrote my first three novels. It decreased in *The Strange River* (the influence of surroundings and an incomprehensible desire to go against success). The gift was given back to me in *Midnight* and *The Dreamer*, almost totally failed me in *Then Shall the Dust Return* and in *If I Were You* (excepting the scene with the child and perhaps also the one that takes place in the passage du Caire). In the novel I am writing at present, the vision is so clear that it prevents all explanations of a psychological order; so much the better.

* * *

OCTOBER 21. Reread Rilke's *Notebooks of Malte Laurids Brigge*, but am going back a little on my former admiration. Too many pages are spoiled for me by an obvious desire to intensify the author's native melancholy, to "pile it on," to make a show of anguish in and out of season, about a woman who sells pencils, a building that is being torn down, about some word pronounced in a certain fashion, about a draft. I know, unfortunately, what anguish is. It is not gratuitous to that extent and, when it appears, has solid reasons for doing so. From subtlety to subtlety, one becomes the prey of literature, literature of the most spurious kind. But there are passages of outstanding beauty (a description of the reading room at the Bibliothèque Nationale, for instance). I admire this great artist, but don't like his way of telling us: "Look out, I'm going to suffer, and you're going to see in what a subtle fashion."

OCTOBER 24. Once more obliged to reconsider my opinion of Rilke. Having opened his *Notebooks,* I happen on the wonderful story about the epileptic man. There is so much sympathy in this account—I give the word its literal meaning—such a great and genuine compassion that I scarcely see any but a Russian writer capable of approaching love of such quality (how can this be expressed otherwise? It is really a question of love, the gift that distinguishes saints from the rest of humanity). Yet I was exasperated a little earlier by the list of fears that the author says he feels or has felt: fear of a small woolen thread, fear of the button on his nightshirt, fear of a crumb, but in order to judge him, one should remember what he had set out to do, namely, "to discover among visible things the equivalents of interior visions."

. . . Reading Rilke enchants me. Almost everything in these extraordinary Notebooks should be quoted: the sentence about his dead father's face, which looked as though it "remembered out of politeness"; the description of the Reverend Jespersen, the portrait of Margaret Brigge, the piercing of the father's heart and the wound that lets out two drops of blood, like a mouth pronouncing a word of two syllables. I take back everything harsh that I may have said about this great writer, not without maintaining a few reservations about certain mannerisms such as the hypersubtleness that spoils for me the first thirty pages of the book. Among the letters that I have received is one written fifteen years ago by a friend of Rilke's; someone will find it someday; it said that he had liked my first book. I realize today the very great value of such a testimony.

OCTOBER 29. My novel is getting on slowly, too much so perhaps, but it seems to me that clearness of vision is obtained at that price. I could cover a larger surface of paper each day, but then I would be *inventing* and, to a certain extent, lying instead of describing as truthfully as possible whatever it is that I see. Often it seems to me that I see only a bit of an apron, a gesture, the lower part of a face, and can only catch a word or two; at other times, I am given a whole scene, with a superabundance of details, details that I don't know how to dispose of and among which I must choose. Anyone examining my manuscripts would notice that all the suppressed passages were invented in order to hurry on to reach the real truth that I knew was waiting for me further on. Who works in this manner nowadays? The other day, that was the question I asked a young Belgian critic, M. Théo Louis, because I thought it interested him. He said that, as far as he knew, the fact of visualizing characters does not seem important to present-day novelists, who are far more preoccupied with ideas than with images, "but," he adds, "although it is true that your characters rarely express ideas, your books hold a view of the world, a philosophy." I replied: "If you like. What I have against certain novelists of today is not that they make their characters express ideas. No, what I have against them is that their characters' ideas are not part of those who voice them, but part of the author. When a character in a great Russian novel confides his ideas, what speaks is his flesh and blood and we believe what is said, but how is it possible not to see that the characters of such or such a modern writer are no more than his mouthpieces and that their speeches are interchangeable?"

. . . Jacques Maritain has always maintained that my books were those of a man living on the mystical plane (he means this in the broader sense), and I think, as a matter of fact, there lies in all my books a deep uneasiness that an irreligious man would never have felt. I am not trying to say that my books are Catholic novels. The very idea appalls me. But I believe that all my books, no matter how far they may seem from an ordinary, accepted religiousness, are none the less essentially religious. The anguish and loneliness of my characters can almost always be reduced to what I think I called a manifold dread of living in this world.

NOVEMBER I.   I have spent many an hour reading that I could have given to my books, but that is my way of building what I call the dike and holding fast. Studying too much is laziness, said Bacon. Not in my case. I devote three hours a day to reading, plus an hour and a half to studying the Bible. To my novel, about an hour and a half; that is all I can do, I mean that what I write after an hour and a half invariably has to be rewritten the next day. Twenty lines, sometimes thirty, that is all. I write only in the morning because my critical sense is most wide-awake then. The evening is a time for a lyrical frame of mind. I write letters only when obliged to and consider the practice a mere waste of time. What I have to give, I would rather put in my books; my books are my letters.

NOVEMBER 4.   I asked Father Couturier: "If you were a pagan, would you let yourself be converted by Claudel?" He started: "I should think not!" We were talking about the correspondence between Gide and Claudel that is now appearing in the *Figaro*. Even when Claudel is right, he is right in an aggressive manner. With him, goodness assumes a condescending air, and in spite of oneself one is tempted to side with his adversaries. And yet, I repeat, he is right, but how often have I noticed that the more zealous the defender, the more clumsily truth is defended. . . . You could swear that truth does it on purpose. What can be said about the effect such bludgeon strokes might have on an unbeliever? However, the poet of genius appears here in some very fine passages.

NOVEMBER 6.   Today, as so often happens, a fit of indescribable melancholy as I walked about the rooms I have taken such pains to furnish. What is the origin of this sadness? I don't know. It is the sadness of being in this world and of feeling the threat that hangs over all that one loves. I can never be completely happy in a world where death always has the last word and where it can step in at any moment. And even at that, if I were the only one concerned . . . I marvel that we can laugh so often, that we can behave as though *it* were not there.

Gide once told me that if he ever wrote anything about me, he would stress the fact that I draw without ever allowing my pencil to leave the paper. This unbroken line is plainly visible in the novel I am writing at present.

NOVEMBER 10.   Somerset Maugham's *The Summing Up* is a book
that delights me. The author's honesty and common sense make
the work rare and unexpected, and he talks of his profession with
a deep understanding of all its difficulties. What he reveals of himself is all the more arresting since you feel it is true. Nothing
extraordinary; his experience of life does not differ much from
what we all know, but he says things as they are, very simply,
with a first-rate choice of words, and that is enough for each
sentence to hold one's attention. The recipe is so simple that I
wonder why it is not used more often, but then I think that the
sort of parade called literature would no longer exist. And yet,
how interesting truth is, and that solely because it is the truth!
Even in small things, it has an inimitable ring, it has a charm and
a strength of persuasion that all the trickeries of style can only ape.

NOVEMBER 11.   I was thinking, a moment ago, that certain difficulties would not have existed in my life if I had not been subject
to ungovernable fleshly appetites. My books would have been
quite different. Better? I don't know, but different. My books
are the books of a prisoner who dreams of freedom. . . . The
novel I am writing is one long cry of anger against instinct. . . .
I am not saying all this to complain but to put the question correctly. I think that my case will appear very strange someday,
when all is known, and yet I am inclined to believe it is a com-
moner one than would be supposed. Faith is the cause of this
bitter conflict.

Reading Maugham. I can't always find him right, particularly
when he says it is stupid to reread books, that to learn languages,
dead or living, is a waste of time; but I agree with him when he
writes that England and France are the only countries to own a
literature: the others only have great writers. True enough, these
two countries are the only ones where one finds an unbroken line
of great works, the river that runs flush to the brim without
ever drying up.

NOVEMBER 16.   In spite of feeling so weary tonight, I want to try
to give an account of my visit to Gide. I went to see him this
morning to ask his consent for Biblio-Hachette to publish a letter
he wrote me in 1934 about *The Dreamer*. He showed me into the
little room where he works, which has a view of roofs. We sat
down opposite each other; between us, a small table covered with

books and papers. Gide's face looks pinker than I have ever seen
it since my return from America, and he seemed young and alert,
just as he was before the war. He was never so charming to me
perhaps, so simple in manner, so cordial. I believe he was really
happy to see me, for he said so several times as though he were
bent on convincing me of the fact. When I told him why I had
come, he appeared a trifle surprised, which leads me to think that
people do not always behave so scrupulously with him. He read
the letter, his letter, most attentively and paused once to exclaim
under his breath: "Why, my letter is very good! I'm glad to have
written it!" I then handed him a rather long, separate postscript,
which is a list of errata he had noted in my book. "Have that
printed too," he said good-naturedly. "It will show up my school-
marmish side! . . ." We had a rambling conversation and I can't
remember in what connection I told him that I don't sleep well.
"Do you know Descartes's letter on insomnia?" I do not know
it. He led me to his study and, taking out the Pléiade edition of
Descartes, sat in a corner by the window. The letter is addressed
to his friend Guez de Balzac. Gide read it slowly, in a beautiful,
distinct, sonorous voice, not at all like the weary, toneless voice
he has at times over the air (I am thinking of his radio conversations with Amrouche); on reaching the passage where Descartes
talks of his dreams and says—I am quoting from memory—"I walk
through formal boxwood gardens, enchanted palaces . . ." he
lowered the book and looked at me with an enraptured smile; he
felt an almost sensual joy in reading this beautiful language.

NOVEMBER 17. . . . This too I did not mention in the account
of my visit to Gide: as we sat facing each other, he told me that
he was reading the last volume of my diary and, owing to this,
thought of me every day and talked to me (those are his very
words). Told me again how very much touched he had been by
what I wrote about him in 1944. He made several unsuccessful
attempts at lighting a cigarette, holding the lighter far too much
to the right. Yet he reads with ease.

NOVEMBER 21. Perhaps God wishes certain souls to live in a state
of unbalance. There are times when I believe that a great many
men will be saved in spite of their faults, and even through their
faults, because they remained steadfast in faith and charity, amidst
the most violent crises.

DECEMBER 3. Simone Weil. I knew very little about her works and am reading them at present with astonishment. She touches on all the subjects that move me most and seeks what is deepest in us. Her passion for the absolute makes her kin to the best, and her contempt for what is relative is, I think, unequaled except by St. John of the Cross and Pascal; they are the ones she reminds one of sometimes. How many books that were mere literature does she convict of vanity! How many things does she outmode and reduce their contents to nothing! Robert tells me that her conclusions are nonhuman, and I think so too, but that means she climbs to heights where we find it hard to breathe. A monster of intelligence. There is something about her that horrifies.

DECEMBER 4. Too sensitive to the voice of human beings. I think it reveals them more than their expression or their hands, although the latter own up to almost everything.

DECEMBER 8. Reread in Harris the (authentic?) account of Wilde's frightful death, the body that burst open, and later the disinterment. Wilde seen in his coffin with a beard, still recognizable in spite of, or because of, the quicklime that merely succeeded in drying the flesh instead of devouring it, and Ross' wonderful charity, waving aside the gravediggers and their shovels to go down into the grave himself, to pick up the horrifying remains with his own hands and reverently place them in a coffin. Ah, how glad one is that such a gesture was made, that there should have been one Englishman to make it, that not everyone should have been hardhearted, and that a really Christian soul should have been present at that moment, by the grave!

1950

JANUARY 8. Went to Gide this morning around ten-thirty. I ask him if he has read Wilde's *De Profundis*, which has recently appeared *in extenso*, and he says he has, and what disturbed him most in the book was the way Wilde composed an attitude for posterity (even more than the accounts he gives of large sums spent to satisfy

Douglas' whims). . . . He looks for a file and opens it before me to take out a letter from Lord Alfred Douglas, dated 1929, and asks me to read it aloud. It is violent, extremely coarse. Douglas had just read *Si le grain ne meurt.* . . . I recall this sentence: "You would never have written such a book if you had been a gentleman. It shows what an awful cad you really are. . . ." He denies that there had ever been any physical intercourse between himself and Wilde. All things said, he forgives Gide "because I am now a Catholic" but nevertheless shows overwhelming contempt for him. The letter is an extraordinary piece of hypocrisy. It is not so much a letter as a scene, one of the scenes that were so frequent in Douglas' life. Gide tells me that he was not handsome, but pretty, "yes, pretty is the word." He relates the scene between Douglas and Wilde (see *Si le grain ne meurt*), Wilde trembling with anger but remaining silent and saying to Gide, after Douglas had left: "It's like that every day. . . ." We then talk about English poetry. Gide fetches his copy of Milton in the Tauchnitz edition (he noted on the flyleaf that he had bought it in Florence, in 1912, but had had it bound later and that he had been particularly struck by the beauty of a passage in *Paradise Lost*, Book V, lines 25–75; it is Eve's speech to Adam: "O sole in whom my thoughts find all repose . . ."—a beauty that seemed to him unsurpassed in any tongue). He shows me a number of passages underscored in pencil and says that he had lately reread Milton's two great poems "with rapture." Also talked about Marlowe; Gide is particularly fond of *Hero and Leander*, and I quote a few lines from the poem that make him smile. John Donne is also a favorite with him, but when he speaks of the two portraits of the poet, one when he was young and very handsome, the other when he was dead and in his winding sheet, I call his attention to the fact that the second likeness was made during Donne's lifetime, when, no doubt to satisfy his strange obsession with death, he had himself painted with his eyes shut and his face enclosed in a winding sheet tied in a knot at the top of the head, according to the fashion then prevailing. In discussing Marlowe, we agree that if one compared him with Shakespeare, Marlowe would probably have been the greater of the two if he had not died so young. Gide is the only Frenchman with whom I have ever had the opportunity of talking at such a length about English poetry, with which he is very familiar. However, he did not ask me to come to see him in order to discuss literature. A priest is to call on him. . . .

* * *

JANUARY 27. At Gide's . . . One of us talked about chastity, saying that at first it was easy to remain chaste, it even gave one a feeling of unutterable freedom, but that after a year or fifteen months, obsession appeared to play havoc, the whole energy of body and soul seemingly employed to beat off assaults of the sexual instinct. . . . In connection with Denmark, where I expect to go soon, Gide talks about Andersen, of whom he is extremely fond: "People do not fully realize that he is one of the only men who ever created myths. The story of the little mermaid is a marvel." "And the Emperor's new clothes." "The grand duke's new clothes, Green, the grand duke's, but no matter, it's wonderful."

FEBRUARY 23. Came back to Paris feeling very ill. Influenza. Continued *The Red Badge of Courage,* a book that I had till now found consistently admirable. The soldier is seized with panic during his first battle, runs away, wanders here and there, is caught in the turmoil of the fray and carried from one side to another by the ebb and flow of armies. Enormous confusion. The men's disarray, their sufferings, all this is shown with extraordinary vigor. It reminds one of the greatest writers, of Tolstoy. I wonder if anything more eloquent has ever been written against the crass stupidity of war. Yet the author composed his book with accounts he had had from Civil War veterans. What genius it took to bring to life the big monster called battle!

MARCH 6. Yesterday, talked to Anne about *The Red Badge of Courage,* which she admires, just as my mother admired it, and which I too admired extravagantly at the beginning. But look! The coward of the first two-thirds of the book turns into a hero at the end. The young man whose panic fright was so wonderfully described is seen, as the book finishes, proudly bearing the Union flag into the thick of the battle. He has unwittingly become a hero, like a character in one of Erckmann-Chatrian's novels. What puts a finishing touch to disgust is that the author is a writer of quality, but he is the one who had "cold feet," he sacrificed to the public's taste. A true civilian book. A soldier would never have flinched.

MARCH 7. We are constantly told that the world is coming to an end. I can't say that this makes much of an impression on me, first because I am getting used to it and then because death is for each of us a little end of the world. Yet, this idea of a possible and general annihilation finally creates a peculiar state of mind. There isn't an author nowadays who can any longer think: *non omnis moriar*. A concern for fame has been given such a blow that it is no longer possible to pose for posterity.

MARCH 17. Looked at photographs of the War between the States. I remembered Mr. Brooks, an old Virginian colored man, my grandfather's last slave whom he freed long before the war and gave a field and a small house by the roadside. We used to go to see him in a carriage or on horseback. My pretty cousin would wave her hand and cry: "Hello, Mr. Brooks!" And he would appear in his doorway, his charming old tobacco-colored face framed in a white beard. On being told that I was his master's grandson, he took both my hands in his and smiled. This doesn't sound in the least like *Uncle Tom's Cabin*! All the misunderstandings in history arise from the fact that the winning side's theory always prevails. If Germany had won the 1940 war, France and above all England, not to mention the others, would have appeared to be the great culprits.

MARCH 24. A long conversation about the devil. Lots of things that I will never repeat, but Father Couturier told me this, which is something to be remembered: the devil cannot perform miracles. Yet he can bring about circumstances that assume a supernatural appearance. No pacts, such as we hear of in time-honored stories, but a gradual paralysis of the will. I know that, just as Bernanos knew it. A man who gives in to the temptations of the unmentionable one, ends by no longer wishing for God, and there lies the real danger. Physical temptations count for nothing in comparison with spiritual ones.

Enraptured last night as I listened to Monteverdi's *Orfeo*, relayed by Berlin. Orfeo's voice had the beauty of a beautiful body, it turned into something physical, something tangible. Jacques Février, the pianist, asked me the other day if music was important to me, but I don't think I would write if I could never hear music. I have always come up against words, as one runs into a wall. Music alone says what I want to say. There are writers for whom words are accomplices, but this is not the case with me.

MARCH 29. Heredity. Between my great-grandparents and myself, during the whole of my childhood, a sort of barrage was set up by my father and mother, who led admirable lives. In their way, they were saints. They protected, concealed me from myself. When they died, I was delivered to the being that I have become, and this is not the finish, because one never gets to the end of discovering oneself. At one period, a sort of massive irruption of heredity invaded my being. Religious mania and the rest. I am the outcome of all these instincts. On certain days I have a feeling of being crushed. God knows all that, has allowed all that. . . .

MARCH 31. Sometimes one must walk about in the depths of the abyss. Even if I go down as far as Hell, God's arm is long enough to bring me up again. Those are His very words in the Scriptures. He is there. Not only do I know it, but I *believe it.*

The human body in all its glory, the human body clad in its nakedness, like a royal vestment, the soul clad in the royal vestment made for it by God, the vestment that is flesh. Ah, how silly we are, we and our morbid ideas about modesty!

PALM SUNDAY. "They know not what they do" would be the definitive words that would end all our problems, if we understood those words rightly; they would induce us to forgive our own selves. I have been reading Havelock Ellis, now very much outdated by more recent works. Yet, what pleasure Montaigne would have taken in reading him! Heredity. If the individual has the whole of the human species back of him when he seduces a woman, where is his sin? What resistance can he offer to a countless multitude that takes him by the shoulder and pushes him forward? Is instinct then allowed complete license? No, the individual remains free, in spite of everything, because grace is present and will act, unless he refuses it, but if he stumbles, I cannot help thinking that he will be shown boundless clemency, God's clemency. Heaven is paved with good intentions, not Hell, as is somewhat foolishly said. If the exhibitionist gives in to a deeply mysterious instinct that he inherits from a very ancient past, where the most obscene forms of worship were favored (that explains, according to Havelock Ellis, the solemnness with which he carries out an act that he himself cannot understand), how can one judge him? Will it be necessary to go back to Adam? One might cite as an example a very well-known English statesman who could not resist the desire to expose himself to women, if ever he was alone with one of them for a moment. This might raise a laugh; I think it tragic, considering the merits of the man.

APRIL 3. Last night I read a little book by D. H. Lawrence: *Obscenity and Pornography*. With his usual violence and intemperance of adjectives, the author dashes off at top speed along a road that can only lead him to absurdity, but as he can't help being the man he is, he says brilliantly things that invite thought, even when they seem questionable. Came across this: "For every man has a mob-self and an individual self, in varying proportions. Some men are almost all mob-self. . . ." "The worst specimens of mob-self are usually to be found in the professions, lawyers, professors, clergymen, and so on. . . ." "The public, which is feeble-minded like an idiot . . . is always exploited." He inveighs against puritans who reprove the sex-appeal of certain books. According to him, half the beauty that the world has produced is beautiful because of sex-appeal. "Even Michelangelo, who rather hated sex, can't help filling the Cornucopia with phallic acorns. So we can dismiss the idea that sex-appeal in art is pornography." Very well, but he can't prevent himself from going too far and says this, which raises a smile: "Boccaccio at his hottest seems to me less pornographical than *Pamela* or *Clarissa Harlowe* or even *Jane Eyre*. . . ." He calls puritanism the gray disease. "Without secrecy there would be no pornography," and he adds this which is extremely curious, for by dint of running away from puritanism he ends by rejoining it and himself talks like a puritan: "And the mass of our popular literature, the bulk of our popular amusements just exists to provoke bad habits." (It is I at present who play the puritan, for Lawrence expresses himself more crudely.) He censures these habits on account of the shame, the anger, the humiliation they cause. He talks at great length on the subject. Very deep truths mingle with enormous naïvetés.

APRIL 5. Last night, listening to Flagstad sing in the *Götterdämmerung* (relayed by the Scala in Milan), I realized that I was no longer in the least the enthusiastic Wagnerite of twenty years ago. No more today than in the past can I recognize any of the sensations described by the composer. In this respect, to mention completely different musicians, I feel in perfect agreement with Bach, with Gluck, with Brahms. Wagner still stuns and dazzles me, of course. One can still enjoy watching what Verlaine called "the great white barbarians" thunder by, but what does this music appeal to? The heart? Certainly not. The brain? No indeed. It is the strangest case I know of in music. One is moved, but why? I dare not write that one is moved through the senses, but am inclined to think so. Beauty of form always ends by acting on the nervous system. Although this immense show of strength produces its effect, I don't believe that a more inhuman music can be heard.

UNDATED. If I were to die tonight and were asked what moves me most in this world, I would perhaps reply: It is the way God passes through men's hearts. Everything is swallowed up by love, and although it is true that we shall be judged according to the degree of love we possess, it is also beyond all question that we shall be judged by love itself, which is none other than God. I believe that if lack of charity were called Evil, instead of weighing down the wretched human body under this curse, the whole of false Christianity would be turned upside down and at the same time the kingdom of God be opened to millions of souls.

MAY 24 OR 25. SALZBURG. Hotel Traube, in the Linzergasse, just where the Kapuzinergasse runs into it. Here for the last four or five days. Too many happy memories cling to us to prevent a shade of melancholy from overshadowing our walks through a town that has always been dear to me. It has changed, the world has changed. Salzburg is not quite the same person it was in 1930. I read Faulkner's *Sanctuary* in the Schloss Mirabell gardens. A book of extraordinary intensity. Not a trace of rhetoric, not a sentence that does not carry; I devoured it in two days, reading over certain passages to make sure of extracting all their pungency. One can't skip a word. What is admirable above all is the choice of details, the quality of the dialogue, the command of the narrative, which so skillfully wanders from the point.

MAY 27. *Crime and Punishment.* What can I say that hasn't already been said? For thirty years, I have hesitated to read Dostoevsky. I distrusted him, and rightly so. Had I read him earlier, a whole portion of my work would have been different. We sat down to read by the Wolfgangsee. Robert laughed aloud as he read Shaw's *Doctor's Dilemma* and I read *Crime and Punishment.* When Raskolnikov kills the old woman, I could not help giving a scream. When he killed Elizabeth, I put the book down on the bench and walked about to recover. What modern author is capable of writing such things? Not one. I was bowled over and still am. I see very well why Conrad would never read Dostoevsky. An instinctive and perfectly legitimate jealousy.

Most important conversations with Robert. The yearning to leave the world is so strong at times that I don't know how to resist it, but am nearly sure that this is the great temptation that must at all costs be warded off.

JULY 21. PARIS.   Just as some people continually wish to go south to sunny countries, I unceasingly hear the call of the north. It is more than a wish, it is the German *Sehnsucht*, a sort of perpetual languor deep in my heart. That is why the sight of a sea's milky waters, or a birch wood, affects me so powerfully. Hedwige, a character in *The Transgressor*, sprang from this. "Your name is like wind over the snow," someone says to her in an unpublished part of the book. Beauty, for me, is above all a thing of the north. I wonder what can be the cause of this.

. . . I found this, too, among my old papers, a prayer that I transcribe without comments. A trace of it can be found in *Moïra*. I had forgotten all about it. The awkward little text is dated May 8, 1924: "Lord, give me peace, silence, a quiet heart, a quiet mind. I did not ask this world for joy. The world came to me and offered me its joy. Its joy is bitter, Lord, and I do not want it or do not want to want it. Yours is the power to destroy my flesh, but I know that You will not before my hour has come, and my hour is a long way off, for great is my imperfection. Look, however, on the wretchedness of my flesh. Longings at dawn, longings at noon, longings at dusk. Did You ever suffer such wretchedness, Lord? You never mentioned it. No one ever mentions it. Can it be that it is shameful? Does everything great and noble belong to the soul, can it be that the body is nothing?"

JULY 26.   Father Couturier came to see me the other day. Regarding Michelangelo, no doubt "a godly man," according to the Father (who sends everyone to Heaven), he considers the Last Judgment in the Sistine Chapel to be "an entirely and absolutely religious painting. Of course, there are the naked men and women, but this does not alter the fact. The ceiling is another matter." "The ceiling," say I, "is the dream, no, the ravings of a man repressed." "Yes," answers the Father, "without any doubt, but one can suppose that Michelangelo hadn't the least idea of it." This is possible, everything is possible where a man as religious as Michelangelo is concerned. I would willingly believe him to have been very chaste. Otherwise, he would not have thrown over the ceiling those great muscular, disdainful *ignudi* who represent an extraordinary compensation for a devouring hunger. He possessed, in his mind, the most beautiful human beings that a painter's brain has ever conceived.

JULY 27. Robert was talking to me a moment ago about this diary, of which he has read large extracts in the complete text. He regards it as a book that, to his knowledge, has no equivalent, because it shows the whole of a man passing from one extreme to the other. I would very much like these pages to be published. I think it will be possible someday, because people will then be able to stand the truth better than we do in 1950, but I may be mistaken; one should always credit human beings with great stupidity. In the world's present state, this diary would dismay the very people it is made for. It is nevertheless my best book. (I am talking, of course, about the unexpurgated text.) That is why I want to save it. The one person I fear is myself and that mania I have for burning papers, every ten or twelve years.

AUGUST 27. SALZBURG. Read *The Brothers Karamazov.* Very deeply touched by Alyosha. He thinks that nothing evil can ever happen to him. Very beautiful. But what would Alyosha produce, if he were a writer? I might be told: "Alyosha could not be a writer." Writing is already evil, but evil is also action and act we must, because good almost always mingles in some way with evil. Does pure white exist among us? White is no more of a color than black.

SEPTEMBER 14. Visit from a young American Quaker. I look with enormous curiosity at a man who cannot lie. American law dispenses him from taking the oath because he is a Quaker. As in St. James' epistle, his yea is yea and his nay is nay. I find myself full of respect for this youth of twenty-five! He has a narrow face and intensely black eyes, almost too bright at times, I mean that when we get on a subject that moves him for some reason, his eyes begin to flash, like Joseph's in *Moïra,* and as it happens, he wants to know if religious feeling can reveal itself with the violence it has done in my book. At that moment, he looks so much like the character I have just described that I have to struggle with myself not to tell him so. A little later, he asks if French Catholic publishers, and mine in particular, exert pressure over their authors to obtain books that will serve the Church's cause. I thought for a moment before replying that my publisher is not what is called a Catholic publisher, seeing that he has printed numbers of works by unbelievers or non-Catholics, by Gide, for instance, and that, to my knowledge, no publisher exercising pressure over writers exists on this side of the Iron Curtain. The question was put without malicious intent, but it affected me queerly and I had to make an effort to answer calmly. The ideas we form of one another from continent to continent are so discouraging at times, and so strange, that one wonders whether they are worth refuting. Yet, one should.

SEPTEMBER 20. Father Couturier came to see me yesterday. He was white as a sheet and looked very ill. He suffers from asthma. It took him almost ten minutes to climb my stairs. He spoke openly of the Church, seen from an administrative angle. "It is," he says, "a continuation of the hateful Roman Empire." He had refused to say the Mass of the Chair of St. Peter. "After all," he goes on grumpily, "the Pope is only the Bishop of Rome. The Reformation was necessary (not in the way Luther understood it, however . . .). There is no trace in the Gospel of this ecclesiastical government. The Gospel is, on the contrary, an anarchical book, almost tending to destroy family life ('If any man come to me and hate not his father and mother . . . ,' 'I am come to set a man at variance against his father . . .'), most marriages are a failure, children who live too long with their parents are good for nothing. . . ." By separating these sentences, I risk giving them a sound they did not have, but I am quoting his very words, and he spoke with a vehemence that struck me. As regards our latter ends, he is inclined to think that not *all* Hell is necessarily the place of suffering that people take pleasure in describing, and that Christ may perhaps return there once more to save what has been lost. Finally, on the subject of the wrong done to God by the wicked, a wrong that demands infinite punishment since it offends an infinite being, I tell him that such words are meaningless to me and he says I am right: according to him, that is the reasoning of theologians and he has a horror of theologians' reasoning, as I have. That is the very reason why I can talk to him. He brings peace, he gives it on behalf of God, without always being aware of it.

SEPTEMBER 23. Went to the movies yesterday to see a sort of documentary of our times. Gide, Jean Rostand, and several others speak. Picasso appears for a moment. It is explained to us that the world we live in would be a paradise if mankind applied its recent discoveries to the progress of peace instead of trying to use them for wars to come. Who doubts that? None of the atrocities of atomic warfare are spared us. St. Peter said that "the elements shall melt with fervent heat" and that "the heavens shall pass away with a great noise." This is something like what scientists prophesy, and they haven't read St. Peter. Sartre puts in a brief appearance, giving vent to a few truths regarding the responsibility each of us has toward the others. One of these days, if he isn't careful, he'll discover the Gospel.

SEPTEMBER 25. Last night I looked through Dante's *Inferno*, illustrated by Doré, an old tome that belonged to my grandfather and that has had such enormous influence on me. These pictures acted on my senses with a delay of ten or fifteen years, and the poet's atrocious theology left its mark on me. I used to take those frightful tortures literally. Curious to see that all this finds an echo in me, even at present. A voice whispers in my ear: "And supposing it were true?" I can't manage to silence it!

SEPTEMBER 26. Ever since I was fifteen, I have lived with a feeling of danger that has scarcely even ceased. I say scarcely. For I have had moments of complete security, but God alone gives them. Hence the delirious joy of converts. They think themselves safe, at last, they are saved. Unbelievers cannot have the least idea of what happiness this means.

SEPTEMBER 30. A moment ago I was in my room, looking at a big spot of sunlight on a door, when suddenly I was seized by that something I don't know how to name that I call happiness. It lasted at least five minutes. I fell asleep and, on waking up, once more felt that extraordinary emotion compared with which nothing in the world seems real. I don't know how to express it.

I believe that if all men lived according to the Gospel, they would experience what I am trying to describe. Deep, complete security: death no longer exists, nothing remains but love. All this in unutterable sweetness. Strange that it should not depend on a state of grace, as everything in me shrieks that I am not in it. It is none the less a grace sent by God. Spiritual authors would talk, I suppose, of natural mysticism, but I am convinced that the happiness of Paradise is not made of any other stuff . . . in an infinitely higher degree!

OCTOBER 2. This vague feeling of danger that I have always had from the mere fact of living in the world . . . Is it that the world is dangerous? Perhaps this is why monastic life used to attract me so powerfully. Returning from Saint-Jean-de-Beauregard, the same feeling of danger as we neared Paris. I have always had it, without knowing why. Once safe in my own quarter, the feeling abates without quite disappearing. A great confused threat.

OCTOBER 4. Yesterday, a visit from a young Dutchman who talked to me about my books in such a way that I wonder if he doesn't know them better than I do. He prefers *Moïra* to the others and has something curious to say about each episode, recognizes the white apron worn by Joseph as the one I had given Serge in *Midnight*! He sees a certain likeness between Claude in *L'Autre sommeil* and Praileau in *Moïra*, and I tell him that he is perfectly right, the two characters were drawn after the same model, with a few modifying details. And feeling I could trust him, I tell him the whole story of B., which has had such a deep effect on me. We were walking along the Seine, one morning in 1923. I had said to myself: "I'll tell him what is in my heart before we cross the Pont-Royal." Taking his arm, violently moved, I said to him: "I have something to tell you, something most important." He often laughed at my serious expression: "All right, go ahead, I'm listening." We reach the bridge, I thought I would drop to the ground. I then see clearly enough that if I speak, I will immediately lose B.'s friendship, and for ever. I said: "I've thought it over. I mustn't." It was one of the painful moments of my youth. B. never knew anything about it. He is still as gay, as good as ever, always pokes a little fun at me when we meet, which is seldom, for he lives a long way off. He once gave me a terrible talking to, on seeing me with a volume of Baudelaire in my hands.

He was puritanical to the backbone. We were twenty. I looked at him in despair. How could such a gulf be crossed?

OCTOBER 24. Yesterday afternoon, went to see Jouvet at the Athénée Theater. You climb two flights of very narrow stairs, then you enter a low-ceilinged room, so dark that the lamp on the long table is lit at three in the afternoon. On the end wall, a painting representing, I think, the actors of the Commedia dell' Arte. On the desk, a photograph of Giraudoux smiling, with a slightly mocking expression behind his tortoise-shell-rimmed spectacles. Jouvet has scarcely changed since I saw him in 1932. A little heavier. Black hair brushed away from the brow. Dressed with rather British elegance in dark blue. He tells me that I have not changed and I return the compliment. "Oh," he says, "it's my business not to change." His voice is smooth, even, a trifle low, the sentences cut short, as though with a knife. We talk about his Tartuffe. He makes several bitter remarks about the obtuseness of critics, wails over the poor quality of the modern stage. *Le Maître de Santiago* finds favor in his eyes, and he is sure that *Port-Royal* will be a fine play, but he is ill disposed toward F.M. "He doesn't like the theater or actors, he doesn't like Molière, he only grants that, having paid his actors to the end, the gesture will be put to his account. But he thinks that Molière is damned, in spite of this. . . ." I can't help laughing: "Does he share God's secrets?" Jouvet looks at me with shining eyes: "God? He has put Him in his pocket." I change the subject at once, feeling he is moved. He asks questions about *Moïra*. "Why did Simon kill himself?" he says abruptly. "On account of Joseph." I explain that Simon walked into my book of himself and almost forcibly. He listens attentively (he listens wonderfully, like Gide, like Simone; he listens like Robert). Then he says: "You are a born playwright. This is your opportunity. So everything is settled. We rehearse in February and I put the play on in March." I laugh once more and tell him that not a single scene has been written yet, that my mind is still very vague about the play he asks for. He looks at me severely and says in his strange, colorless voice: "It's time you gave us a play." I leave shortly after.

OCTOBER 29. Having read half of *Armance*, I closed the book to avoid dying of boredom. For at that point, sparkling conversations and ultra-subtle complications begin. . . . What I don't care for is Stendhal's personality, his affectations, his terror of being taken for a bourgeois, his passion for getting on in society. On the other hand, what is captivating and genuine in this great creator is his admiration for youth and his rather pathetic efforts, in each of his books, to disguise himself as a good-looking young fellow and to imagine himself as fascinating, agreeable, a lady-killer. That he should play a losing game in *Armance* is very significant, for he comes to grief but, in spite of all, retains the qualities of physical beauty and intellectual superiority.

November 6. At Antwerp, a walk through the zoo. Profoundly sad to see all those caged animals. It is perhaps one of our greatest sins to put an antelope or an eagle behind bars, but we are all of us such barbarians that we are not even aware of it. A couple of crows from the Congo, sleek and fat, shiny as freshly polished boots. Brown zebras striped in black; their rumps look like magnificent agates. An immense condor, its head hooded in a sort of white woolen bonnet and with black, spreading wings, motionless except for the tips of the wings, which stir imperceptibly, wings of a terrifying size, made to thrash the air at dizzy heights. It stands like a man being measured for a suit. The polar bear and its sinister waddle, its head shaking ceaselessly and, without ever interrupting this motion, opening its jaws at times to show, in a huge yawn, a dingy mauve tongue. I left after a few moments. I loathe zoos almost as much as I do concentration camps, which they very much resemble, anyway.

November 9. Paris. If one only thought it over for a second, who is not ashamed of his life? I am ashamed of mine very often, but I do work. Very much struck by a visit from poor G. The suffering written over his wretched face. A strict moralist would tell me that his is a wicked suffering, that of ungratified desire, but I don't think there is such a thing as wicked suffering or one kind of suffering for the devil and one for God, there is simply one suffering, the one that life is made of, the stuff that life is made of. I used not to think so, I think so today.

An astounding article in *Life* about the present state of our astronomical knowledge. A subject I know nothing about, but that always enchants me, because it puts everything in its proper place with staggering authority. According to Einstein, if I understand aright, which is not sure, we are inside a virtually immeasurable sphere, the universe; and outside this sphere there is nothing, an unimaginable nothing. The stars, in vast groups, rush through space, moving away from each other with incalculable speed. Reading such things, you wonder what meaning our little worries can have. What does all this signify? The earth is so small, so lost in these abysses, that it would be quite as reasonable to say that it does not exist. And yet, at this very moment, poor Georges Poupet is suffering in his rue Garancière bedroom and telephoning his friends in that woebegone voice of his. This is only one instance in a hundred thousand. If the earth exists, it is because it is peopled with souls, and if God sent his only son to mankind, in this infinitesimal spot, it is perhaps because there are no souls anywhere but here. This bears out my idea that we are far more of souls than of bodies and that what we do is most important, in spite of everything, because we are souls. What overwhelms is the notion of space, because no matter how much we enclose the universe on all sides, it is impossible that space should not continue farther on. Be it as it may, I wonder what becomes, in all this, of literary ambition, fame, and the world's gimcracks.

1951

JANUARY 20. Went to the theater last night. *Les Mouches,* by Sartre, an astonishing, very powerful play and not without beauty. Electra's speech to Jupiter's statue: "Heaps of filth! etc." The author's atheism is given a free hand, and I don't doubt it might perturb many in the audience, but the god shown us by Sartre is so mediocre and so limited that one can easily imagine the playwright's atheism in regard to a god of such paltry dimensions. If God were Sartre's God, God as Sartre sees Him, I would be an atheist twenty times over, I would be the atheist of such a god and a fanatical one too, but this is a case of mistaken identity.

JANUARY 28. I called up Gide this morning and went to see him. Another visitor was there before me, Jean D. Gide says he is very tired, thanks to a *good night* obtained with the help of a sleeping pill; he explains that a sleepless night leaves him rather alert sometimes, but that after a long sleep, he is occasionally "stranded," as Valéry used to say. A little later he turns to Jean D., who is a Catholic, and says: "We must ask Green where to find the sentence we were talking about just now." And staring me full in the face, looking rather severe, he asks: "Where is this taken from: 'You would not seek me if you had not already found me'?" I can't help murmuring: "'. . . if you had not found me.'" And I add aloud: "The sentence is in Pascal's *Mystery of Jesus*." (I concealed my amazement as best I could. Can it really be Gide asking me such a question?) "Ah!" he cries. "So it isn't in the Gospel!" Then I tell the story of Father B., one of the most learned men I know, who said that as a student he had looked high and low in the Gospel for "These particular drops of blood were shed for you." All honor to Pascal for being able to cause such mistakes! But Gide tells me that he prefers reading Bossuet to Pascal. And he adds this, which shocks me: "In Pascal, there are only ten cries from the heart. One could quote them. The rest does not attract me, except the letters to Mlle de Roannez." I then mention Bossuet's letters to Sister Cornuau, but Gide has not read them. Is this possible? Perhaps he has forgotten them. What he says next is what people almost always say when Bossuet's name comes up: "I read Bossuet for the style." He passes very quickly from one subject to another, picks up from the table a small, very badly printed book: "Here is a book I used to be fond of that I now find disappointing." It is a copy of La Bruyère. However, he likes La Bruyère's *Dialogues on Quietism*, which has just been reprinted, although he doubts the work's authenticity. He suddenly exclaims: "A writer I don't at all care for is Chateaubriand." "Not even *Les Mémoires d'Outre-Tombe*?" I asked. "No, I don't like that either." "But the parts about his childhood?" "Ah, people always mention those! But all the rest bores me." I remember the day in 1937 when, as we walked down the boulevard des Invalides, we talked about Chateaubriand. Gide had noticed the word *chauvir* (to prick up one's ears) in one of my books, and I quoted a sentence from *Les Mémoires d'Outre-Tombe*: "My luck sometimes pricks up its ears." He told me then that he had never read the *Mémoires*, which greatly surprised me. . . . Today, I feel that he is trying to talk as he used to. He does not want to disappoint us, but in 1930 he would never have spoken as he does now. Sadly, I am obliged to note that what he says is poor and cold and that he has had to cudgel his brains to say it. He is very old and knows it perfectly well. "Old age is a horrible thing," he says. "Aren't there a few compensations at least?" I ask. He collects his wits and, as though to contradict what I have just been thinking, finally murmurs what I consider · a very fine thing. "It is harder to carry one's glass to one's lips, but one feels less thirsty." "And what about serenity?" (I ask this.) He turns to Jean D. and then says: "There is no serenity except in cloisters, the one that faith brings." (But what a contempt he probably has for that kind of serenity!) Jean D. gives a very good account of a taking of the veil that he had witnessed. Gide smiles and tells a story about a child who, on seeing a nun behind a convent grille, after a similar ceremony, asks: "What would happen if they let her loose?" He goes off into gales of laughter, tells us that as far as he can learn, the Church is not at all the same as she was at the time when she was attacked and that she has become more tolerant. "Father Valensin once said to me: 'You have a sense of mystery. That is sufficient.' " Gide adds: "Everything was going smoothly, and then came the Encyclicals!" (He says the last words with such emphasis that one feels tempted to write them in capitals. He sounds as though he were saying: "We were peacefully picnicking on the grass and out came the rhinoceros!") Neither Jean D. nor I say a word. I ask him if he is planning a journey and he tells me he is going to Morocco. "A rather long trip," I then remark. "Yes, but such long journeys tire me less than walking from here to the dining room. It's my heart that is weak." He spoke affectionately to us both.

JANUARY 30.   The other day, at the mention of Pascal, Gide exclaimed: "Ah, that makes me feel wide-awake! Yes, Pascal . . ." He needs literature as a stimulant. I noticed this once before in 1949, when we talked about Montaigne.

FEBRUARY 23.   Went to Gide's for the last time. A silent crowd in the dark entrance. I recognize Roger Martin du Gard, Gallimard, Jean Lambert, Marc Allégret. All of a sudden, I see Gide in a room adjoining the drawing room. He lies on a small iron bed, the tips of his fingers joined. Not quite a prayerful gesture, although it reminds one of it. His head is thrown back and looks very majestic. He seems to be thinking rather than sleeping. As I went downstairs, I met Jouhandeau, all keyed up at the idea of seeing a corpse. . . . "I can see that you feel very badly," he said to me, "for he was so fond of you." Did not answer. In the street, to my great shame, I cried. Strange. It has always surprised me to find how much attached I was to him. Mauriac writes, in the *Figaro,* that Gide chose evil. What does he know about it? What do any of them know about it? God alone knows.

FEBRUARY 28.   Great hilarity in Paris over a telegram received by Mauriac a few days after Gide's death, which read: "There is no hell. You can go on a spree. Inform Claudel. *André Gide.*"

Noted this in St. Jerome: "Our sins are what makes the barbarians strong. . . . Our vices are what bring about the defeat of Roman armies. . . ." This reminds me of Calvin's sentence: "God will speak to us with great blows from halberds, with great blows from pikes and harquebuses: we will not understand a word, the language will be most strange." Thought a great deal about the carnal problem. If an unreasoned phobia for the body existed formerly, we are certainly in danger of swinging in the opposite direction at present, and not only us laymen, but some part of the clergy (I am thinking of the priest who went to see Gide and so wholeheartedly threw St. Paul overboard). "I have not lost faith," says someone in Bernanos's *Diary of a Country Priest,* "because God has been pleased to preserve me from impurity." Now chastity is simply too heavy a burden for present-day humanity, because faith has weakened. Less and less are we Christians. We rebel against the New Testament when it irks us (particularly St. Paul). It is a sort of heresy that is gradually taking shape. Is my case different from that of millions of Catholics? But I don't want to be a heretic. As time goes by, I realize the importance of every hour that falls into everlasting nothingness.

MARCH 3.   Long conversation with Robert about music. I was telling him again that the least song by Schumann wrings my heart and that Bach's music is like an invasion of the soul by faith, whereas Wagner remains mysteriously *exterior,* no matter how much admiration, how much surprise he provokes.

MARCH 7.   Reading Emerson again. "The Oversoul." Some sentences are so beautiful that they should be able to change our life. That, at least, is the impression one has for a few minutes. After which, they return to the general current of ideas. He says that man is a river, the source of which is hidden. Magnificent. A source that escapes psychoanalysis.

* * *

MARCH 16. A letter from Allen Tate telling me that he has read *Moïra* and sees it as "a parable of the great Protestant neurosis of our world." But I wanted to go beyond denominational borders and get at puritanism under any religious form, Catholic as well as any other. In connection with this, I note a statement made by a group of American bishops: "Sex is one of God's endowments. It should not be ignored or treated as something bad."

Quennell's *Byron*. The constant suffering inflicted on his pride by a misshapen foot, the gliding walk he invented to conceal this defect, what a cross it must have been to a nature like his! This delicate, sensitive man none the less rented a window to see a man hanged (in front of Newgate jail). I have always thought him to have been misunderstood. The disappearance of his diary is an irreparable loss. There was in him a religious man. All that one sees is the lady-killer.

MARCH 21. Still reading Quennell's *Byron*. Impossible to pass judgment on Byron, because the outer man had taken on inordinate importance, concealing an unknown one, probably terrorized by his nurse's Calvinism. His bad taste, his ignorance, the legend that has established itself in lieu of the truth, as sometimes happens.

MARCH 24. Finished Quennell's *Byron*. That great rustling of skirts leaving the drawing room when the poet took up his stand there, an elbow on the mantelpiece . . . England had had wind of his sexual eccentricities (his sister, his wife). The unfortunate Annabelle Milbanke had confided the most amazing things to Dr. Lushington. One woman remained in the drawing room, a carrot-head who said to Byron: "You should have married me. I would have known how to manage you." Life is a novel of most unequal talent, but this scene is admirable. The account of Byron's flight to Dover, a prey to the creditors who came to seize him. Nothing remains to him but his carriage, which the bailiffs, much to their regret, were not able to seize, having arrived too late that morning. His despair when a few gray hairs stray into his lovely curls. And he is getting fat. All this is strangely melancholy. Nothing so much resembles a life that fails as certain successful ones.

Read an essay on my works. It has sometimes been said that the two great literary influences in my life were Poe and Hawthorne. That would be counting for nothing the first eighteen years I spent in France, which molded me. One would think that

I was born at nineteen, at the University. In this same essay, the Bible is not even mentioned.

Placed end to end, my conversations with André Gide might lead people to think that we saw each other frequently, but a more attentive look at the dates will dissipate this illusion. To tell the truth, I have never been able, so far, to give the public anything but small fragments of a long conversation that never took place, because circumstances were never propitious. The necessary element would have been, for instance, the opportunities afforded by a long journey, and this journey, which we both wished for, was put off from year to year until it was too late. I always had the impression of seeing Gide by fits and starts, and he probably felt the same, as he often told me that we had a great deal to say to each other but lacked time; now it has gone for ever. However, I think that the essential was said.

True, I might have seen more of Gide, but I made it a principle never to ask for an invitation, but to go to see him the moment he asked me to. In this way, I was sure that if he saw me, it was because he wanted to see me. For I knew him to be badgered by visitors and dreaded not so much to be importunate as inopportune. I have suffered too much myself from what Montherlant calls *biophages* (or people who devour the lives of others); nothing would have induced me to be the caller for whom a clock is placed well in sight.

No matter how incomplete the notes I took on Gide, they will, I hope, give as fair an impression of him as possible. I have described him as he appeared to me, but the Gide we saw on his deathbed carried away the secret of one of the most complex personalities of all times. What attached me to him even more than his talents was an all but fanatical fidelity to the truth as he saw it. Even the ancient world never produced a man who stuck more firmly to his opinion when he believed himself right, and at times he reminded me of an old Roman.

My return to the Church was, in his eyes, a sort of scandal to which he was never reconciled. Our friendship was obliged to round a Cape Tempest on several occasions, but now all that is in the far past. I can't help thinking that if I had given in to his arguments I would perhaps have lost some of his regard for me, and that it interested him to see if I would hold fast. Summed up in this manner, the question appears simple. With him, however, nothing could be entirely simple. How I hesitate to write the following sentence, convinced as I am of the misunderstandings it will give rise to! Since my return to France in 1945, I never had an opportunity of seeing Gide without his attempting, one way or the other, to aim a blow at my faith. In my case, conversion for him meant yielding to the force of heredity, and Gide would not admit that anyone could yield. It would be understanding him very badly to say that he played the part of Satan. Quite the contrary, his purpose was to *save* me. He wanted to win me over to unbelief and exerted all the zeal of a Christian trying to convince an infidel. That is what perturbed me. Any means seemed good to him in order to make me doubt, because that was the price of salvation. And what was religious in him lent a particular form to his atheism, and to his nonbelief the aspect of a religion. On the other hand, his extraordinary intuition of human beings allowed him to sense how much I was upset by our talks on Catholicism, no matter what pains I took to hide my state of mind. I sometimes eluded this trying subject; he brought me back to it gently, firmly, with the obstinacy of a missionary. Finally, he realized that he was wasting his time (I could no more fall back than a man with a wall behind him), but he never quite gave up trying to *convert* me, and did so visibly for conscience' sake and sometimes against his will. The last time I saw him, he asked me a question, from which I am wary of drawing any conclusion, but that in my mind assumes the particular character of *ultima verba*. In that serious voice of his that agreed so perfectly with his expression, he asked if I read my Bible every day. At another time, I would have smiled at words that reminded me of my Protestant childhood, but I did not feel like smiling that morning. I answered yes, that I always read it, and he fell silent for a moment. Did my reply please him or not? I don't know. I record this incident to show to what an extent it would be difficult for me to judge him, if ever I felt like it. But judging does not interest me. . . .

MAY 16. One of the most complicated problems of my literary life has always been that of letter writing. I think that a writer should keep up a constant fight against people who prevent him from doing his work and, I say it sadly, against those who write to him and expect an answer, an answer that will never come. What they don't know is that the time and sometimes the energy devoted to answering them would be more profitably used for a book; now, what they want, in fine, is a book. Be it as it may, I remember a friend's indignation on seeing a file on my table thus inscribed: "Letters demanding an immediate answer." For he knew very well that no matter how demanding those letters were, they would obtain nothing but a deep silence, and perhaps he thought there was a touch of cynicism about that superinscription, but I am not at all cynical and, on the contrary, these words meant something like this: "Aren't you ashamed?" I no longer feel the least shame nowadays; I am resigned to a state of things that I cannot help. After writing for a couple of hours, I am no longer fit for anything but a walk or for jotting down a few notes in this diary. The very few letters I have written, except the five or six that have really counted in my life, are of no interest to me. Yet how eagerly I throw myself on the morning mail! I believe I would be sorry if no one wrote to me any more.

MAY 17. A formal lunch at the Ritz. I am seated next to Pierre Brisson. Facing us, Claudel, Guéhenno, David Rousset. Claudel talked admirably about the earthquake at Tokyo, in 1923. A horse finds itself on the second floor of a bank. A lady, stark-naked in her tub, on top of a wall and around her, nothing. In the dirty water of a sewer, on a roadside, the Italian consul. A policeman paces calmly up and down (no sign of panic anywhere). He throws a contemptuous glance at the Italian and says: "Well, you have earthquakes in Italy, don't you?" The first quake was felt at five minutes before noon. At noon, in an appalling din, the sound of a cannon shot announcing noon, as usual, could be distinguished. Someone asked Claudel: "What impression does an earthquake make?" Answer: "It's like seeing a most respectable lady suddenly raise her skirts and dance like a lunatic." He next talks about Vergil and calls him "the greatest among all poets." Quotes from memory rather long passages but recites them without scanning, as though they were prose. . . . Guéhenno speaks passionately about Greek and Latin and the poverty of classical education, as it is now understood.

JUNE 8. The day is drawing in. This is the hour when, some twenty years ago, I simply could not stay indoors. I left my room as soon as the city lamps were turned on in my street. Those interminable walks, the source of so many of my books . . .

* * *

JUNE 12. Last night, saw Sartre's play *Le Diable et le bon Dieu*. The author talks to us about God for almost three hours and tells us why he does not care for Him. This is a most questionable form of atheism. The play is somewhat sharply criticized by a number of spectators who declare themselves unable to stand such an avalanche of blasphemies, but I prefer blasphemy to luke-warmness, and certain scenes are admirable, particularly that of the wager. There is enormous strength in the play, together with great incoherence. I think the group of scenes in the second part are badly connected. Here is a very Sartrian line: Götz says in the presence of a priest (this should be checked as I am quoting from memory): "If God exists, man does not exist" (incidentally, what mystic has not felt this: "What am I in Your presence, Lord? A nothing"), "but if man exists"—and here we have a consider-able piece of roguishness—"then God does not." The priest rushes away shrieking before hearing the end of the sentence. I stayed till midnight, leaning out of my stage box, listening to every word of this strange drama that touches on the only interesting ques-tions in this world.

JUNE 14. Had lunch yesterday in what is called society. After lunch, a young pianist sat down at his instrument and played a few measures of different pieces. "Whom is this by?" he asks. Silence. I am amazed. Not to recognize Schumann's "Nussbaum" and to mistake one of Mozart's concertos for Chopin, as some-one did . . . After hesitating slightly, I answered and answered right, for a musical memory is, together with a visual memory, the only one I possess to a rather unusual degree. No memory for words, alas, or a weak one acquired only at the price of great efforts. I learn languages easily, but can't remember ten lines of verse for more than a month or two.

JUNE 24. There is a certain benefit in looking long and very at-tentively at objects that we see every day and no longer notice. My eyes suddenly light on a wastepaper basket and there it is, called to life. I had never observed the delicacy of its wicker sticks, some of which are honey color when the light strikes them, and the three rings that hold them together shine like ivory. Soon, nothing in the room exists but the basket, and this lends it con-siderable importance. Caravaggio or Zurbarán or Dali would have faithfully reproduced its beauty, would have known how to give it a place to itself, to make it stand out clearly in the material universe. For more than twenty years, it had waited humbly for the moment when my eye would unexpectedly light on it. And so it is with everything.

JUNE 26.   Had lunch with a religious to whom I said: "In each of us is a sinner and a saint. One and the other develop, each on his own plane. The one and the other, and not the one or the other. Both at the same time. While the saint develops—if the man is a saint—the sinner in him develops on the imaginative plane (the temptations vary from year to year, following a curve peculiar to each individual's temperament), and meantime the saint develops on the spiritual plane. If the man is a sinner—that is, if the sinner gets the upper hand of the saint—the saint develops as best he can on the imaginative plane (a yearning for holiness). That is why a converted sinner never starts from scratch. He has progressed during his life of sin. The saint that he was to become has progressed. In the same manner, a fallen mystic becomes an out-and-out sinner, because the carnal man had continued to develop all along, in spite of the saint's efforts." The religious listened attentively. He too had gone through moments of great suffering. Now, why is it needful to suffer? We too often forget that the symbol of Christianity is an instrument of torture, we forget it because crucifixion is no longer in practice. To realize this, we would have to imagine a religion whose symbol would be a guillotine or a gallows. That would frighten us. We would run away from it. No one runs away from the cross. We buy pretty ones that are worn as jewelry. Some are made of diamonds. Let us think this over a little. This superannuated instrument of torture no longer makes anyone shudder. There must have been a time when it made the bravest quake.

JULY 1.   The minutes of Wilde's trial make very strange reading, for they show that his biographers have not turned all the facts of this business to the best account. From a psychological point of view, some of the evidence is extremely picturesque. Witness what William Parker relates about the supper to which he and his brother Charles were invited by the author, the latter feeding Charles with his own spoon and fork and this, which is even more unpleasant when you think of the man's age and physique and particularly his bad teeth: he held a cherry between his lips and young Charles was supposed to take it with his own and swallow it. All this is painful reading. Didn't Wilde see himself as he was? Pages and pages of questioning. His sheets are constantly examined and hotel maids report on them. . . . And also, those slips of paper that were handed to the judge, slips on which names were written, names that should not be pronounced, names of important people, too important to be troubled by the police. The trickery, the hypocrisy of the whole business; the unfortunate carouser hedged in by judges and lawyers who talk as though they were as white as the driven snow. This trial is what has given me the most serious doubts of present-day justice since my university days. "If that's their idea of justice . . ." I used to think.

JULY 3. A visit from André Parinaud, a newspaperman, who questions me about the sources of my novels. As I listened to my replies, I thought: "Why don't I write all this?" But I have, in my notebooks, and the whole thing is scattered through my diary. The War between the States, in which my childhood found an inexhaustible source of melancholy. Why teach children history? My twelfth, my thirteenth year were tinged with gloom by the accounts my mother gave me of the South's crushing defeat. My country no longer existed as a nation, it had been suppressed by history. This was the cause of a first and powerful feeling of isolation, of a circle traced around me. At the lycée, little Roger Laubeuf said to me: "You belong to a nation that no longer exists and to a religion that no one ever heard of." For I had tried to explain to him that although my religion was Protestant, it was neither Lutheran nor Calvinist. Even at that age, I could not talk like other people. No more than I can now. As a child, I wanted to be like the others and never succeeded. In short, I acted like a simpleton. I was alone, among all those clever little French boys. Something of this remains in me. Almost all my characters are solitary and cannot climb over the wall that separates them from their neighbor. *"Der Menschen Worte verstand ich nie."* This line of Hölderlin found an extraordinary echo in me when I read it for the first time.

JULY 6. Ran into Malraux in an art photographer's shop, rue Bonaparte. He is very pale, asks me at once what I am looking for, and the question strikes me, for to tell the truth I am not looking for anything in particular. I walked into the shop much as one opens a picture book. Malraux launches almost immediately into what I can only call a magnificent speech on the pages I wrote about Gide in *La Table Ronde* ("It is," he says, "the only accurate portrait that anyone has ever made of him"), but I find it impossible even to give an idea of the brilliant way in which he lengthily enlarged on the subject. A summing up would only impoverish and denature it. How often have I felt this in talking to Malraux! His thought is so swift, so numerous are the ideas he suggests, that an attempt to fix it all in one's memory overcomes one with despair. A little depressed to think of everything that is lost, of everything that Malraux deprives us of by not writing what runs through his mind instead of just saying it. I had the feeling several times of standing face to face with Thomas De Quincey.

JULY 9. As I get on in years, I believe more and more that I am going to die, and, at the same time, I believe more and more that I am not going to die. Death to me seems both inevitable and impossible. This is no doubt because the body's machinery has been working too long for me to be able to conceive of its stopping. At twenty, one is not really used to existing. One continues to be surprised by it. At my age, one is so accustomed to it that a state of nonbeing becomes almost impossible to imagine (naturally, I am speaking of the body's nonbeing).

OCTOBER 25. Give me pen, ink, and paper and I will always find a way of entertaining myself, if it is only a question of entertainment. For I can create for myself an enchanted country in which I wander about at ease.

NOVEMBER 4. I was talking to a priest about all that is inexpressible in us. He quoted a saying of St. Thomas' that I thought very fine: *Omne individuum ineffabile*. I was reminded of what Fénelon wrote: "I have never said anything that did not seem to me untrue a moment later."

DECEMBER 4 OR 5. A visit to Colette in her little red drawing room at the Palais-Royal. She had written me: "If I were Julian Green, I would go to see Colette." Her face has not changed since I last saw her at Mme de Polignac's, before the war, and no one could look at her without loving her. Her large eyes are the most beautiful ones I have ever seen in a woman, eyes as beautiful as an animal's, brimming over with soul and sadness. She scolds me for not having been to see her sooner, when, she says, she was in better condition. On the long table that bridges her bed is a great jumble of letters that will never be answered, she tells me. She picks one up at random and murmurs: "What dirty dog is this who talks about my 'long experience of life'?" Picture books make her scream with admiration, like a child: "Oh, what lovely birds! Just look . . ." She hugs the copy of my diary that I have brought her and says: "I'll save it for tonight. . . ." No, dear Colette, neither for tonight nor for any other time, but this little fib touches me as much as a great compliment. She tells me the story of two swallows that she used to take to school with her, as a child, and that have to have . . . "Worms?" I ask. "Worms! Of course not, my boy! Live flies. You don't know swallows. Their contempt is superb, superb. . . ." At that moment, in comes an old gentleman who talks to us about pornographic books. He leaves and Colette says pensively to me: "How young you look! You're right. Old men are lousy."

DECEMBER 22. Jean Duché was talking to me about culture. I told him that in my opinion culture was not so much a question of knowing and remembering as an aptitude for receiving, for being able to recognize beauty and to enjoy any great book. I told him what an enormous influence the literature of the Far East had had on me: the choice of details in narratives, the omission of everything that should not be said. When we say everything, we write like barbarians.

1952

FEBRUARY 2. An evening reception. I have a horror of this kind of party. Several times I lost all sense of what is called reality and lapsed into silence. Toward the end of the evening, a nightmarish scene. All those old men, all those old women, came up to the sofa where I was sitting with two ladies. They approached like babies, clinging to their armchairs. We all of us stayed for three hours, and nothing curious, or amusing, or important was said. What good is this idiotic worldly life?

FEBRUARY 15. Spent the evening with a religious. He told me several things that struck me, as much for the meaning they assumed in my eyes as for the answers I heard myself make. It happens that we ourselves say things that surprise and inform us. I don't know how that can be, but I noticed the fact years ago. This religious was talking about a priest who killed himself because of an uncontrollable passion. "He had," I said, "a very poor idea of God's mercy." "But he was insane." My guest's own face had a sorrowful, noble expression as he talked about all this. . . . I think that God does not want the paltry little order we sometimes build up so carefully, with Bible readings and prudent little prayers; He saves us in a disorder which is His order and whose laws we don't quite understand. "We go to Him in the midst of all this verbiage," says Father L. Everything is jumbled up in an inextricable confusion. How can this be made clear to anyone at all? One always seems to be saying the opposite of what one thinks, or to be trying to justify evil, or to floor sinners. It is best to keep silence, although there are times when one suffocates. I could not sleep last night.

FEBRUARY 16. Vice can be depicted, but love can no more be described than light itself. The idea we give of ourselves is always simplified and contradictory.

FEBRUARY 28. "The terror of loving what one loves . . ." This sentence of Valéry's (essay on Stendhal) is a good summing up of my play (*South*). A play written in a strange way. I am discovering the real subject as I am about to reach the end, as has so often been the case with my other works. I must go on with it to the finish in order to explore its whole meaning. Knowing about it from the start would bore me so that I could not write another sentence. When I wrote the first act, I had no inkling of what it was all about. I am always outdistanced by my characters. They are so crafty. . . .

MARCH 12. Have begun reading Lancelot's [1] *Memoirs*, which

[1] Dom Claude Lancelot, a seventeenth-century writer of the Port-Royal community.

plunge me deep in thought. There is an almost irresistible force in our lives that drives us forward, but where does it come from? I have had the vague idea, at times, that perhaps it does not come from God but at this point we wander in darkness! For it may be that God wishes us to give in to a force whose effects will be useful to some people. Our books originate from this force, and I think that God wishes us to write our books, but if we continue to do so, will we be saved? Can God wish anything for us but salvation? This would be inconceivable. Strange to have to write that, with years, personal salvation seems me less important than universal salvation, and I don't know whether this is right or wrong.

MARCH 17. Yesterday, a visit from one of Gide's friends. He talks about what he calls this writer's coldness of heart. I remember that Gide once said to me: "Love has never made me suffer." This seemed to me so strange that I finally believed that I had heard wrong, but my visitor confirmed the statement. "Your feelings will be your undoing," Gide often said to him.

MARCH 20. A great longing to write a book. I was talking to an English poet the other day and, as Eliot's name was mentioned, I said that I was very fond of the poet, without being very sensitive to the music of his verse, even in *Four Quartets,* and doubted if there were any. "Yes, there is," he replied gently, "but it is everyday music." This struck me. It was aptly said and in a most precise manner.

APRIL 2. MONTE CARLO. Called on Somerset Maugham in his villa at Cap Ferrat. Renoirs and Toulouse-Lautrecs on the walls. I greatly appreciate his courtesy. He is broad-minded, simple-mannered, attentive to what is said to him. He talks a little about Gide, thinks *La Porte étroite* is not a good novel because the actions of his characters are not "sufficiently motivated." He is very keen on motives. They are one of the strong points of his stories. In his opinion the best style is "an easy conversational style," and he cannot understand the agonies of style, such as Flaubert describes them to us. . . . I think I could have confided in him, a thing I could never have done with Gide. There is something indomitable and honest about him.

* * *

APRIL 4. PARIS. Unquestionably, I buy too many books. I buy them every day, new and second-hand, French and English. What a pity one can't, at the same go, buy the time to read them, says Robert. At this very moment, I am almost certain of not being able to take all this in before dying, but I cull a few pages here, twenty there. I reread. When I travel, I take five or six books along, even when it only means going away for two days, as happened quite recently. At Monte Carlo, I had my Bible, a Baudelaire, a Verlaine, and a volume of Plutarch's *Lives* translated by Amyot. I don't want to be reduced to reading one book only, for I might not be in the mood to read it that day. I must be free to choose. This sometimes makes my suitcases rather heavy to carry. "There can't be anything in this but a corpse, alcohol, or books," an American porter once said to me as he lifted my big suitcase.

I had a vision of Hell at Monte Carlo. In the main street, standing at a newspaper stall, was a poorly dressed old man, his white locks straying from under his cap. Inside the stall, a perfectly motionless saleswoman. With trembling fingers, the old man turned the pages of a magazine that he was allowed to look at without charge: an album of naked women.

HOLY SATURDAY. I have never known a Good Friday when I was completely free from all anguish. As early as two-thirty, unutterable sadness wells up in me. Yet an incident took place at Saint-Thomas d'Aquin that would have seemed funny at any other time. I was standing by a *prie-dieu*. The church was packed with people. A beadle came up to me and touched my *prie-dieu*. I understood, wanted to argue, felt myself choke with anger. The man said: "It is for M. le Curé," and that leaves me speechless. I let him remove my *prie-dieu*, thinking that M. le Curé really needed it, which is ridiculous, for M. le Curé is naturally in the choir, with the clergy. I moved away, genuflected before the high altar, and went to the chapel at the back of the church to attempt to calm down. For I had seen the beadle give my *prie-dieu* to a very old gentleman. He had lied to me. How joyfully would I have broken that piece of furniture on his head! I tried to pray but was upset by this silly business and also by the words that fell from the pulpit, for they were remarkably feeble. After quite an effort to recover, I walked out of Saint-Thomas and went to the little Ukrainian church on the rue des Saints-Pères. It was empty.

I stayed there for a moment. What an army of *prie-dieus*! I had only too many to choose from. I quieted down, pulled myself together, and went out. How often have I not thus choked back my anger! Yet people think me gentle. My only reason for noting an absurdity of which I am ashamed is that it amuses me now.

MAY 12. One of the greatest encouragements that I ever received came from Rilke, but I was only told of it many years after his death. After reading *Avarice House*, he said this to Mme de W., who noted it: "You'll see, he will be a poet." I never wished to be anything else. I think I am a poet who has strayed into prose.

MAY 28. I met Auden, a poet I have long admired, at Mme Gillet's. Also present was Professor Delay, to whom Gide had once sent me with the idea, I suppose, that he would cure me. Cure me of what? Of faith? I had a perfectly frank talk with him at the time, one that I recall with pleasure, for Professor Delay's delicacy and intelligence led me to tell him things that I would certainly not have confided to just anyone. Later, much later, Gide talked to me about this conversation, of which he knew nothing but the broad outlines. He had asked Professor Delay if he thought I would be cured. "But suppose the patient does not *wish* to be cured?" answered the professor.

MAY 29. A visit from an American writer whom I knew when I was young. He is the same as he used to be, but his hair is quite gray. Says he had a very serious disease of the mouth and that it was the way God had punished him for having talked too much and been too fond of physical love. He has given Kinsey his private diary and advises me to do the same, thinks one should never burn anything. He had a terrible shock when he was told that he was ill and might die, and stamped with despair, alone in a field, at the idea that, for instance, he would never again hear Bach's cantatas. Talks about Melville's intimate papers, which have been made away with. He himself has written things of the same type, but, he insists once more, nothing should be burned. I have the impression that he has a great deal to say, is conscious of great interior wealth and wishes to give it all away before leaving this world.

*   *   *

JULY 16. Why do you make gestures that are not your gestures? Why do you say things that do not come from the truest part of you? Why this make-believe? There is a certain kind of make-believe which one acts to deceive other people. This one is of no interest to me. There is another which one acts almost automatically because it has become a habit—whether it is a question of passions or courtesy. This one is more serious, it means playing the world's game, to all intents and purposes the devil's game. I cannot accept it.

JULY 19. A moment ago I saw Praileau, the Praileau in *Moïra*, a novel he will never read. He is in Paris with his wife and two small daughters. He makes gentle fun of me, as he used to. If he knew me as I know myself, what would he say? Nothing unkind, but he belongs to the race of the righteous. When I look at him, I have no difficulty in seeing him exactly as he was when I knew him in 1920. I asked how he had obtained my address, as we have not corresponded for years. He said that he had entered a bookshop and had asked to see some of my books. He was handed a copy of *Moïra*. He noted the publisher's name and the latter told him where I lived. What irony lies in all this. . . .

JULY 21. Yesterday, on the sidewalk outside a café, I caught sight of S. A tragic, resolute face. What a hell he makes of his life! But he knows what he wants, he really wants it, whereas I don't in the least want what I want. There is always someone in me who says no. Looking at S.'s face, I wonder if the pitiless obsession that hounds him from one place to another at all hours is not a sort of madness, but his features have a dignity that is very foreign to the idea that people form of vice, there is an accepted suffering; for him, the game is worth the candle. He is unaware of the sympathy I feel for him, and this sympathy can be explained only by the fact that, in his way, he has a sense of the absolute.

AUGUST 18. MUNICH. Munich's ruins are dreadful. Cocteau used to say that Paris would make beautiful ruins, but ruins cannot be improvised. It takes centuries to give them the loveliness we admire in Hadrian's Villa, for instance, or at the Forum. Towns suddenly transformed into ruins are simply hideous: Hamburg, Bremen, Le Havre. Stones should crumble down one by one, under the onslaught of time, and grasses flourish in crannies, with the sun to gild the whole thing. I cannot see any beauty in the great blackened debris that now strews part of Europe.

AUGUST 31. CORTINA D'AMPEZZO, IN THE DOLOMITES. Read an article against capital punishment. There are things that we should know. Descriptions of executions. A man being electrocuted: his horrible leaps within the leather thongs, the dreadful sound of the air escaping from his lungs, the smell of roasting flesh, the oil that streams down his charred face. A man who has been hanged and whose head is sometimes torn away, because of the weakness of his neck. I was almost sick, but forced myself to continue reading. We are not civilized, that's all there is about it. That slim little book, the Gospel, beams over our barbarity, but scarcely anyone takes it to heart. . . . I would like to be free, not free like people who are surfeited and no longer hungry, but free as the children of God are free. When one writes such a sentence and then lays down the pen to think it over, can it be possible that one is lost? I want to believe in certain signs. I sometimes try to reassure myself by interpreting them favorably. I wonder if the sensuality that lies in each of us is not a kind of accident and if something is not concealed in our heart of hearts that will get us out of trouble.

DECEMBER 14. PARIS. Sometimes, when I think of my life and see in it all the contradictions that sadden me, it seems as though a voice I know so well says to me: "After all, haven't you got what you wanted? What could you complain of?" But that is precisely what worries me. Is that violent desire to quarrel with the world ever followed by a result? Can one go on living like this until death, in a constant state of rebellion against one's self?

DECEMBER 23. First auditions of actors on the stage for *South*. Slept badly because one of the actors I counted on most for the part of Ian did not live up to my hopes, and I will have to make him understand this. On the other hand, a peculiar thing happened that I will not forget for a long time. We had listened to six or eight actors, when a skinny, sickly boy appeared on the stage, holding in a shaky hand his role, of which he had not read a word. I think that I shall always remember that gaunt face, those sunken eyes, those white cheeks. What's the use of hearing him? But the

stage director, Mercure, comes and tells me that the young man
is in great difficulties, that his child died the night before. He is
only twenty-one. He stammers appallingly, and all of a sudden, a
kind of miracle takes place: his admirably well-pitched voice
begins to give sentences a meaning and a depth that make us all
prick up our ears. He was merely given this direction: "You are
acting the part of a very simple, very pure character" (for the
role was that of MacClure). Quite soon, I felt very much moved.
It is impossible to understand how a boy who hasn't the least idea
of what all this is about, and who, I am assured, has never been on
the stage, can manage to put so much soul and intelligence into
a rather difficult part. Before five minutes have gone by, he has
complete mastery over himself. He says and does what he wishes
with supreme self-assurance. Mercure then asks him to read a
passage in Ian's role and he does so with wonderful ease and authority. We will certainly take him. He is, I believe, of Flemish
origin and is called Vaneck.[1]

1953

MARCH 23. I have not kept this diary for almost a month, when
it would have been interesting to note certain things that will
gradually escape me. It is still too early to know whether or not
my play will succeed in finding its public. So far, we have had
almost full houses, in spite of a partly hostile press, or so I am told,
for I have scarcely read anything that has been written about
South. After the dress rehearsal, I locked myself into an office at
the Athénée and within an hour made cuts that Mercure approved
of. During the dress rehearsal, I was in a sort of waking dream. I
saw lots of anxious faces, but the fact did not worry me at all.
There was a single moment of anguish—but a horrible one—when
I felt the audience waver. A few days later, however, I admit to
having been frightened for a minute—it was quite paralyzing—but
no one ever knew of it. I go to the theater every night and stand
behind a bit of the scenery. Vaneck is excellent. All this has

[1] 1963. Vaneck is now a very well-known actor.

stirred me deeply. So many childhood memories suddenly coming up to the surface, as though they rose from the bottom of the sea, and the South there, on the stage, under my very eyes.

MAY 14.   I have gone back to reading Montaigne with delight. At twenty, I couldn't. Such continual vacillations between yea and nay irritated me. I detested fine shadings of thought, I was passionately fond of downright statements that fell like blows of an ax.

MAY 26.   Listening to Bach's Cantata No. 32, I realized how very near the invisible world is to us, if we do not drive it away. When I heard his cantata for the first time, around 1926, it stirred me so deeply that I foresaw it would be necessary for me to change my whole life, but that I should remain in the world. Impossible to express how great a part Bach has played in my life; it is he, more than any other, who has reconciled me to the idea of dying.

NOVEMBER 10.   Thought a great deal about death, about my own death since it is waiting for me at the hour appointed by God. For several months I have had a pain, slight, to be truthful, but persistent. This morning, as almost every day, I had taken a volume from my bookcase, thinking it to be the Vulgate (I wanted a little change from the English translation of the Bible), and by mistake pulled out the Book of Isaiah, translated and annotated by Father Condamin. As I was about to replace it, I thought: "No. If you took it out, this must have a meaning." I opened the book at random and chanced on the following verses, which struck me: "I shall go softly all the years of my life in the bitterness of my soul. O Lord, by these things men live and in all things is the life of my spirit: *so wilt thou recover me and make me to live.*" From that moment, I did not give my pain a thought.

UNDATED.   A long talk with Robert about music. I had been very much impressed by Monteverdi's *Beatus vir.* He speaks a tongue that has disappeared, a divinely serene tongue and so sweet that, after him, there is something rude and harsh in the greatest composers, who seem to create havoc and to throw furniture out of the window. Sunday morning, I listened to Bach's wonderful cantata: *Ach wie flüchtig, ach wie nichtig* . . . A marvelous prelude showing the world's agitation, a music of extreme violence that filled all three of us with admiration and gave me a great longing to change my life. But what does changing one's life mean? To leave the world? And what if one shouldn't?

NOVEMBER 17. It is sometimes in watching the fire that I find what I have to say. All my books have sprung from my dreams. They are not for the many, but I think there will always be a few readers to be fond of them, and these are the ones for whom I write.

Too many books in my flat. I was obliged to sell some, those of no interest to me and whose pages I hadn't even cut (if people only knew all the books I haven't read). . . . In the case of Gide, I was interested only in his personality, with the exception of *Thésée,* the *Journal,* and *Si le grain ne meurt* (also the *Retour du Tchad,* but that he called a *Nebenwerk*). My bookseller tells me that all writers sell the autographed copies that are sent them, and he mentions a poet who even adds a few words of his own to the inscription, to increase the value of the book. Léautaud makes no bones about lighting his fire with the books he is sent. It seems that Valéry did the same during the Occupation, saying that the blaze gave him at least fifteen minutes of welcome heat.

NOVEMBER 26. Virginia Woolf's diary is beyond doubt an event (in England, at least). At first, one is dazzled, then defects begin to be apparent. "I, the greatest woman writer in England," is what she more or less says. A stupid conversation with Lytton Strachey that is supposed to be brilliant. Somewhere else she talks very well about the "pinch of essential dust that the French put into their books." She speaks a little foolishly and, if I may say so, Britishly, about Americans. Her opinion of them in no way differs from the usual commonplaces. And with it all, she has gifts that the greatest writers might envy her. I saw her only once, in 1929, at a literary gathering that took place in a London drawing room. She and I were being awarded a prize. May Sinclair presided, poor terrified old lady, who knew neither what to do nor what to say, pausing after the first sentence of her little speech to murmur: "Oh, I'm so frightened!" I then asked Virginia Woolf if she wanted to speak before I did. She was very nervous, her hands in constant motion and beating like wings. She threw me the glance of a hunted animal and said: "No. You go first." And I went, a little as though I were going to my death. I remember talking about my English grandfather. Virginia spoke next and said in-significant things, but she created a great impression. There was a mixture of disdain and fright in her long face.

DECEMBER 3. Sad to think that a very distant threat of death, a very light roll on the drum, as the Chinese poet says, is necessary to show us the true face of those around us, for we do not quite see beings as they are; what is luminous and good in them is too often concealed by daily life.

1954

JANUARY 5. Went to the rue des Plantes yesterday to see Father Couturier in a hospital. He is very thin, sits up straight in bed, tells me that he has been ill for a year and will be for another, if he recovers. An American specialist sent him word that the first stages of his sickness were the most dangerous and that, once he had weathered the first year, he stood a good chance of getting well. He is serious, smiles seldom, but is very calm. We talk about the world of the senses, and I ask him if it has ever occurred to him that the world as we see it does not exist. "No," he says firmly, "it is too beautiful as it is not to exist as we see it." That is the way a painter would speak, as he himself agrees. I then remark that the world is still more beautiful than we suppose and go on to describe the pebbles I once saw in a glass cabinet, in America, ordinary pebbles picked up on a road, but under a fluorescent light each pebble became a precious stone, a big sapphire, a ruby, a huge diamond. The whole of creation may have been thus be-fore original sin. Traces of this splendor can be seen here and there, in the human face, which will always be the marvel of marvels. A little later, I tell Father Couturier that it grieves me not to be able to write at present, that this has always been the case since I was twenty-five, and that the interval between two books was always very painful to me. At such times, I have a feel-ing of having lost my gift. On the other hand, it is useless to urge myself on, it does me no good. I have to remain idle, because this idleness later becomes fruitful. The Father told me that all artists go through such phases. Just before leaving I asked him if he thought it unreasonable to believe that I could work out my salvation in writing books, and he answered that it seemed natural to believe this.

Read the Bible. If the story of David and Jonathan were told in transposed form, how many people among Catholics would cry shame!

FEBRUARY 11. Stopped keeping this diary because I felt sick at heart. Father Couturier's death was a great blow and I don't know what to say about it. The world seems to me poorer now. The poor Father had a difficult end, struggled for breath for ten hours, finally offered up his life immediately after receiving Extreme Unction. What life has ever had a happy ending? Always the same dreadful tragedy. Thought of him, of his charming smile, his extreme simplicity of heart. Having written this, how is it possible to talk of anything else?

FEBRUARY 13. Went to the Faubourg Saint-Honoré chapel for Father Couturier's funeral. A great many people. I have rarely seen such distress in the faces of so many men and women. The Brothers in black and white robes going to fetch their dead brother, the coffin covered with a stole, six tapers around the bier, the *Dies Irae* sung very softly as though to tone down its terrible threats—there was so much grief and affection in all this that I was very much upset.

MARCH 15. Listened with Anne and Robert to two cantatas by Bach, *Ich bin vergnügt* and *Gottes Zeit ist die allerbeste Zeit*, marvelously sung. With Bach, feeling is seldom on the human plane, but a few notes are enough for him to carry us to the world of the absolute, which is his world. I wonder how it is possible to listen to him and not believe. Yesterday, someone told me that I was too serious. But serious does not mean sad. I am not sad, on the contrary, I feel a supreme joy rise within me that makes me deny death, old age, and nothingness.

MAY 3. I wonder if I dare write what I think. Yes, I do. I believe that in the very depth of sin, God watches over us with extraordinary attentiveness, as though over a prey, but not as devotional books usually say. Drag a writer away from his sin and he no longer writes. This, I admit, is a horrible statement to put into words. Is sin necessary to his works? Who would dare say such a thing? But remove sin and you remove the works. Are the works necessary? You might as well ask if a writer is necessary. He is inasmuch as God wishes him to exist. Purify the sources? But it does not seem evident that writers who have tried to do this were successful and that their works were improved by it. One must be pure from the start and remain so. That was the case with Bernanos. I don't know if present-day Catholic writers are pure. There are moments when I doubt it, but I know that I am not, hence all my difficulties. I can withdraw from the world, as I have so often been tempted to do, but then, no more works. Now, I believe that I came into this world to write books and to reach a few people.

MAY 9. I was telling someone here who asked me certain questions that I had suddenly stopped smoking in 1944. And why? Because I smoked too much and, above all, too fast. I had fits of giddiness that were rather unpleasant, but not always. Once, sitting in an armchair, I had a very distinct impression of being at the far end of the room. My body was seated, but I (if such words have a meaning) was some distance away. That was the day when I gave up tobacco. I sometimes dream that I am smoking. The man I was talking to said that thus to resist a habit corresponds perhaps to the wish we sometimes have to punish ourselves, and that this wish finds expression in various ways. Montaigne says very sensibly that sexual moderation is more difficult to practice than total abstinence.

MAY 22. This morning, the Ascension cantata by Bach. When the "great" are right, they are right in a way that verges on the miraculous, I mean that when they assert something, as Bach does, the rest of the world, everything outside that assertion, ceases to exist for the time being. These are the "tremendous statements" spoken of by Auden, in connection with a city orchestra, it is true, but the term holds good for those I call the great, the elders of our race. Thought today that I would die at the exact minute that God has chosen for me, and that He has chosen lovingly, for He does all things lovingly, otherwise would He be God? And He knows that the minute of my death will be the one when I will be with Him, at last.

* * *

JUNE 26. Had lunch with Béguin, who tells me several important things, for he is among those—how many are they? Four? Five?—who talk to say something that one remembers. We were speaking about prayers, which are all granted, sooner or later, but one has to reach the age of fifty to discover this, with the necessary perspective. Youth does not know it. One ends by getting everything one wanted, which is not always a good thing. Béguin tells me that all the longings of youth are so many prayers, unconscious prayers, and prayers that are granted. In connection with this, I quote a sentence from Racine about God, who, in His wrath, sometimes gives us what we ask. Real Jansenism. A little later, I say to Béguin: "What makes my strength as well as my weakness is that I am both younger and older than the men I have to deal with. I have kept my childhood and have intuitions that they do not possess, because they have lost theirs. I am clumsy in a struggle. I lack weapons."

JULY 2. Listened to Couperin's *Tenebrae*. The title is sung at full pitch by the contralto. Magnificent. The extremely severe, lovely modulations go to the soul, brush aside the sensuous world, give you back to God for a few minutes.

JULY 23. Very much impressed by Father Bouyer's book, *Du Protestantisme à l'Église*. One must search one's own heart, seek God at any price; it is the only thing that counts. I felt deeply anxious as I turned the pages of this book. In this study, where waves of silence seem to break one after the other, I think that God has spoken to me more often than anywhere else. I have followed the carnal instinct against my heart and often with such horror that no man could have an idea of it unless he had experienced the same dread. I do what I don't want to do. Copied my diary for 1953. That will keep me busy and prevent me from falling into discouragement. I realize better that God holds me firmly by the hand, and will not desert me in the darkness.

JULY 25. Asked to be given a horror of sin. It is a great gift, and I don't see how else to keep out of trouble. Passions darken the soul. We live like madmen.

JULY 27. Yesterday, a visit from a young Englishman who is choirmaster in an Oxford college. He speaks disdainfully of John

Blow and contemptuously of Handel. "He reminds me of a country squire. And then, he is so facile. . . ." *Facile* pronounced with a shade of disgust. After he left, I listened to a few of the "English Anthems" by the incriminated composer, as well as *Acis and Galatea*, which I like so much, and, true enough, facility can be found there and, what is more serious still, Handel is never satisfied, once he has said something, until he has said it again, in the same terms, and that is not enough for him: he has to say it again. There are repetitions in Bach, but you always feel that they differ a little one from the other, even when he changes nothing in his phrase. A phrase by Bach repeated twenty times becomes more and more profound. Handel usually remains on the surface; but I still remember the extraordinary effect produced on me by the *Messiah*, at Salzburg, two years ago, and I will always admire this very great man.

AUGUST 7. GENEVA. Colette is dead. Last night, wishing to be with her a little, for I am very fond of her, I picked up *Sido* and, opening it at random, found this. She has just described in a masterly way—for no one has her gift for taking you where she wants, with the help of a few sentences—two lost springs of water that she remembers with the deepest enjoyment, and she says: "Just by talking of them, I hope and wish that their taste will fill my mouth when all is ending, and that I may carry away with me that imaginary swallow. . . ." How can one not believe that Colette is at this moment drinking the waters offered to the Samaritan woman?

AUGUST 16. Today, for the first time in my life, I regretted not being fifteen. I was lying on my bed after lunch, reading Montaigne, when this unreasonable regret seized me. I thought about the sweetness of those distant years, of all the time that lay ahead of me then, and that I was inwardly certain of having ahead of me, for contrary to what one so willingly imagines at an age when one is so romantically inclined, I did not believe in the least that I would die young, I even thought that I would live quite a number of years and felt rich because of all this future time, whereas now, each day as it ends leaves me a little sad, for I know very well that it counts.

AUGUST 26. Copied a number of passages from Calvin's *Institu-*

tion Chrétienne, for I have to return the book. There are things
in it that could not be believed unless one saw them in print, for
they might have been invented by spiteful Catholics. . . . Every
sentence tells. At times, one is reminded of a ruler hitting the edge
of a desk, at others, of a sword stroke falling on a rebel neck, but
the marks of literary greatness are there. The passionately interesting thing about Calvin is that he almost always goes too far.
Where others would not dare to venture, he charges at a gallop.
And with it all, through the sheer force of reasoning, he is monstrous. He is reason gone mad. This said, he has a feeling for the
divine to an extremely rare degree. One can imagine the saint
he might have been. On the other hand, one can easily see what
a choice place Dante would have reserved for him in his Inferno,
but it is far simpler to condemn the reformer than to appreciate
the exceptional majesty of certain pages where he speaks of God
as a doctor of the Church might have done. Why should he have
become the doctor of despair? He has done a great deal of good
and a great deal of evil in quickening a sense of sin in certain
souls and in giving others a panic terror of damnation. One could
not assert that God did not wish Calvin to be Calvin. And anyway,
what can one assert?

Around the middle of the last century, there were cases of acute
melancholia (I might simply call it insanity) in my family; a
melancholia caused by the idea of predestination as conceived by
Presbyterians (to all intents and purposes Calvinists).

Yesterday, in a small street that leads up to the cathedral, I
bought another very nice copy of the Book of Common Prayer,
in a second-hand bookstore. It was the book my mother used and
through it, I must say, she left quite a strong mark on me. The
young American Quaker who wrote a thesis on me would take
this for a sure sign of what he calls my Protestantism, but I am
nothing of a Protestant and what I seek in the Book of Common
Prayer is the best that Catholicism has left in it.

AUGUST 27. Dined at Mies, yesterday. We were a large party,
and that invariably makes my head swim. I say what I feel I
shouldn't say and, once at home, am angry with myself—but
enough of that. One of the guests, a French psychiatrist, talked
to me in an interesting manner about the dreams of the insane. He
has studied them for years, has often heard words pronounced by
lunatics in their sleep, and, as far as such things can be known, it

appears that they have *reasonable dreams*. It would seem that a madman who dreams, dreams only of normal life. Our own dreams are our form of madness, and if we did not dream we might possibly become insane. As the psychiatrist asked me certain questions, I said this to him: "My books are my dreams. They are what have allowed me to keep my balance." Their symbolism, if they are symbolical—it seems that Stekel said they were—all these strange themes provided by the subconscious act in accordance with secret laws of which I am ignorant and wish to continue to ignore. The man I was talking with said that a psychiatrist could easily cure me of the anguish that is so apparent in my books, but, I replied, if you remove the anguish, you remove the books, and if there are no more books, who knows if the former anguish will not be replaced by another? There was no answer. I talked very indiscreetly about myself, a thing I scarcely ever do. As a rule, I listen and the others are the ones to give themselves away.

Thought about predestination. God has honored us with the freedom to choose between good and evil. Hell is the risk we run, although it seems to me difficult to lose your soul if you don't want to, and who, with a full knowledge of the case, would want to? If the risk is removed, man's salvation is assured, but he can no longer be said to be free, as God is free, and this diminished creature would no longer be in the least equal to its fate, which is an admirable one.

Thought about the idea I had of Christ when I was a child, then the one I had later, at twenty, and so on to the present time. It was the same Christ, but I always saw Him differently, for as a child I saw Him as my elder; and once I had lived beyond His years, I saw Him in a certain fashion as my junior. I changed but He did not, and yet He did. He changed in an astonishing way. This should be developed, but of course avoiding the pietistic tone that is the devil's most ingenious invention, since nothing pulls one away more violently from religion. One should have outlived youth, I think, to begin to understand Christ a little.

Who could help being attached to this house, with its big, low roof, its bright rooms, its air of happiness? From my window, I see a large square lawn sloping down to the lake, bordered with clumps of shrubs. One can catch a glimpse of water through the trees and, in the distance, of Geneva crowned by the cathedral. At nightfall, the garden is extremely beautiful, moving, lovely as something about to die; the greens are deep, the air seems motionless. I must own that it makes my heart ache to think that this holiday is ending. That everything must end used to make me despair as a child, and thanks to an intuition so frequent at that age, I have distrusted all that passes away and unceasingly sought for the invisible that never ends. We sometimes see traces of it in the eyes of those we love.

AUGUST 29. Today's walk, the last one, was the most beautiful of all, but it would require other gifts than mine to talk about it. I am as fond of trees as it bores me to describe them, because I feel that others could do it as well as I, if not better. A subject at which one excels should be found and stuck to, otherwise one resembles too many novelists.

I happened on a passage in Gide's diary that concerns me. He imagines that when I told him that my characters led me at their will, I said this to please him, but I had already said it long before knowing him, to Frédéric Lefèvre and others. What should be known is that Gide had just presented me with a fine copy of his *Journal des faux-monnayeurs*, in which he wrote that he followed his characters' lead, but what he was ignorant of is that I didn't read his books often and that I had not read that very one, because I had not read (and still have not done so) *Les Faux-monnayeurs*. I am sure this must seem scandalous to certain people, but I can say it now that Gide has gone. I admired what he had to say to me, but far less admired what he wrote, although I kept this to myself. I liked *Si le grain* (as he called it) and also, much later, his *Theseus* and many parts of his diary, but his novels disconcerted me; I had tried to read them and as quickly dropped them. A whole portion of his work was inaccessible to me. I could never talk to Gide about what he wrote, and for a good reason. His book on the Congo held my attention, not because of the Congo, but because of what he told us about himself. He was passionately interesting when he talked about what he thought, about what he was, but he did not correspond to the idea I have of a novelist and certainly not of a poet. I was writing my fourth book when I met Gide and opened one of his works for the first time. He never talked so well as when he talked about himself, but there, he excelled. He once read me a speech from his *Oedipus* which I found terribly labored. I kept silent and think that this annoyed him a little.

* * *

SEPTEMBER 6. PARIS. This is my birthday and it is also St. Julien de Brioude's day, or was, I think, when I was born, although my mother had no idea of it. I can't really believe that I have reached the age I am, for it seems to me that I have been the same person since I was twenty. No matter how much my mirror gives me the lie, I look in it and believe what it tells me, but immediately after, forget what I saw, like the man in St. James' epistle.

OCTOBER 30. "The waters of Babylon flow, fall, and sweep on." This sentence from Pascal delights me. Apart from the meaning, its softly muffled music, its movement, its pace, all seem to me to possess the magic quality of certain chords that haunt the mind, without one's quite knowing why.

The truth should be acknowledged: if we read the Bible today in the vernacular, it is because the Church allows it, but it is also because certain courageous Protestants desired it and went to the stake on that account. Without the great Reformation movement, when would the Church have permitted the translation of the Bible into common speech? We are free to believe that we would have waited a long time. At the present day, many Catholics still think that the Church forbids reading the Bible. Those Catholics hold to the times when the Church forbade a layman to own a copy of the Bible in the vernacular. Why this interdict? Did the Church foresee the heresies that might spring from a close scrutiny of this book? The reformers forced her hand. Nowadays, she multiplies the number of translations to be used by the faithful, but isn't it very late? Modern France bypasses the Bible. You can't spend an hour with an Englishman without some allusion to the Bible slipping into his conversation, at times unconsciously: he will quote it, without always being aware of what he is quoting.

NOVEMBER 4. A few days ago, as I was filing letters, I came across one from Father Couturier written a short time before his death. He had insisted on reading *South,* and I had taken him a copy. The answer came quickly. These lines are an extract: ". . . You have dealt with this delicate subject without one's being able for a single instant to forget and disregard the seriousness and grandeur of such a tragedy: no one has ever done this before. Please God that it may contribute to increase charity among us and a greater respect for grieving hearts."

Yesterday morning, went to the place du Parvis Notre-Dame to say good-by to the actors who are going on tour with *South* (in the provinces, then in Switzerland, Belgium, and finally North Africa). The cathedral is a very great personage who prays, her head lost in the sky. I wandered under the lofty vaultings. Very few people, except around the statue of the Blessed Virgin, where I paused for a moment. Also went to Saint-Julien-le-Pauvre, where I asked for the theological virtues, no more no less. The silence of this marvelous little church where Dante perhaps prayed. Outside, the cries of children.

NOVEMBER 15. A few sentences about me in a recently published book. It is said that my childhood was not spent in France, that I am a Virginian. This is most interesting, for ever since 1924 I have said and never ceased saying that I was born in Paris, in the Ternes quarter, that I pursued all my studies at the Lycée Janson up to the *baccalauréat* (the school-leaving certificate), that I had great difficulty in learning English, that my nurse, Jeanne Lepêcheur, taught me the first words that ever left my lips, that I had gone to America for the first time at nineteen, etc. I have written all this in my diary, in articles, and in a somewhat detailed account of my childhood called *"Quand nous habitions tous ensemble,"* which appeared a few years ago in a Paris weekly. Nothing can be done about it. Gide died with the idea that I was born in New Orleans. I had rid him of the notion that I was born in Canada. And then, what importance can it have? But it amuses me to watch a completely false legend being trumped up under my very eyes. If people are mistaken about me, how many errors are made about other men, dead or living? It is apparently hard to imagine that an American can be born elsewhere than in America, can be born and brought up in Paris.

NOVEMBER 25. I had a bad night after a long conversation with Béguin, because he is one of the very rare men with whom one can go to the bottom of things and reach the essential. My heart beat violently several times during our talk, which lasted almost two hours, I think. As I was speaking to him about the apparent futility of what is called a self-examination, as all one sees lies on the surface, while all that is most important remains hidden, Béguin told me that it is perhaps better so, that if we could know how God works within us, we would not be able to bear it. I believe that most men live in deep ignorance of themselves, of the riches that they turn to no account, of an unutterable happiness that they pass by wailing over the sorrows of this life. . . . Only in prayer does one have a feeling of the deep reality of all this. The world's futility is overwhelming at certain times, but one has to pretend that everything is real; indeed, it is even a duty to act this sort of comedy, but one should never lose sight of the fact that it is a comedy.

UNDATED. There is someone within us who *knows*, whereas the person who speaks and whom we take for ourselves does not know. I could give numerous instances of this. I can remember two that made a strong impression on me. The last time that I saw André Gide, he was certainly not in good health, but he moved about much as usual, it seemed to me, and I think he would have been surprised to be told that he did not have three weeks left to live. When I was about to go, he looked at me gravely and asked me a question that I could not help finding singular: "Haven't you anything else to say to me?" I answered no, and we parted. Only after his death did the question assume its full meaning. I certainly would have had something else to say to him, had I known, and I am convinced that in Gide's mind the little, apparently insignificant question had nothing of a foreboding: he did not *know*, any more than I did. Something of the kind, although more moving, happened when I saw Father Couturier for the last time. (Incidentally, he admired André Gide and would never allow him to be attacked in his presence.) I had gone to see him in his hospital room. As a rule, I stayed only half an hour, knowing that visits tired him, and he never pressed me to remain. This time, as I rose to go, he asked me to stay, and I sat down again. Fifteen minutes went by and once more I got up. "No!" he cried, and asked me so insistently to stay that I neither dared nor wished to refuse. I resumed my seat and he smiled at me with that almost divinely kind expression that lit up his face and endeared him to me so much. My hand lay on the bed and he touched it with his. I can't remember what we said to each other, but in actual fact and without having the least idea of it (for he hoped to recover and I wanted to believe that he would get well) we were saying farewell.

"Each human life is a path that leads to God." This was said by Husserl, unless I am mistaken. Blessed be the men who say such things, for they help us to live and to stave off despair.

* * *

NOVEMBER 29. Since I was fifteen, I think that I have never felt closer to the Church nor more deeply in agreement with her. I particularly wish to say this so clearly and in such a manner that no doubt can remain in the mind of whoever reads these lines—if this diary is published. Generally speaking, I am rather indifferent to everything that can be said about me, but this does not hold good for the faith that I have received and wish to keep until the end. For I am extremely sensitive on this point. . . .

DECEMBER 15. Sometimes, when I blow on my fire, which won't catch, I hear street noises that come to me through the chimney, and it wrings my heart a little because I remember my childhood. We weren't well off, but how happy we were! Then, from my mother's room, I heard distant street noises, as I hear them now, stretched out on the carpet and blowing on the embers. I wonder how one can possibly live believing that we will never again see those we have loved. It is enough to drive one crazy. But we who have faith know very well that they are waiting for us.

DECEMBER 17. Had lunch with Béguin and his wife the other day. She says this, which I think very fine: "Human love changes, sometimes ends. With God, you can always begin again, nothing is ever ended, no break is ever final. . . ." God is very vulnerable, as Jacques Maritain so admirably says. But He is always there, asking us to come back to Him. Come back, a term that runs through the Bible like a long-drawn-out cry of love. Come back to Me who love you. That is what God never ceases to say to the soul.

One of my very first childhood memories is, I think, rather curious, because it gives one of the keys to my whole life. I am alone in the garden of the cours Sainte-Cécile. It must be eight in the morning. I don't know why I am alone in the garden, which seems to me immense and which I have attempted to describe in *The Dreamer*. The air is fresh. I hear someone playing the piano in a neighboring house. A tune I know, because my sister Mary plays it at home: Mozart's "Turkish March," and it occurs to me that all this is queer, queer to be alone in this place. I am happy—I always was at that age—but wonder what I am doing in this garden. Now this garden is the world, the earth, and the feeling I had then has never completely left me. I will always feel a stranger in this world and it will always be impossible for me to understand why, but I am sure that others must feel as I do.

* * *

DECEMBER 22. This evening, irritated beyond measure by a number of things that I don't even wish to mention, I opened the *Divine Comedy* at the beginning of "Purgatory." A delicious breath rises from these pages, great happiness possesses the soul and hope returns, that hope of salvation that will carry us to the bright shores. Dante and Vergil have come up from Hell and stand by the waterside. A great skiff advances toward them, moved by an angel who stands at the helm with lightly beating wings, and in the skiff, a hundred souls who come from Earth singing *In exitu Israel*. They land, and as they go closer to the two poets the first soul to recognize Dante is the musician Casella. They are about to suffer, the mount of purification must be climbed, but they are saved, they are blessed. How much truer all this is than theological treatises and their somber reasonings! It grew late, but I could not tear myself away from a book that restored peace in me. I went as far as the three steps at the top of which stands an angel holding two keys that open the great door shown us by the poet. The first step is white and like a mirror; one looks in it and sees oneself: this is the sincerity of the soul. The second is made of a black and very hard stone; it is broken: this is the contrite heart. The third is flaming red: this is love. The angel has been given the keys by Peter, who says that it is better to open the door by mistake than to leave it shut. Now, it opens more noisily than the Tarpeian Gate, for it is the penitential door, and rare are the times when it turns on its hinges. At this point, I closed the book, filled with a new happiness.

1955

JANUARY 3. If the devil wrote music, it would be Tchaikovsky, seductive, skillful, and vulgar. Its languishings would excite the coldest listeners for a moment. Suddenly, it goes crazy with pleasure, for no known reason, and who would not follow it, who would not let himself be carried away by this whirlwind? It ignobly titillates. All at once, it puts on the grand airs of an exiled queen and goes its way, sad and contemptuous. Then, with a dirty wink, it begins jiggling again. Yet one listens. It has extraordinary charm.

* * *

JANUARY 17. The autobiography of St. Theresa of Lisieux has been in the house for the last three days. I mean the *very copybook* [1] in which the saint wrote the story of her life. I examined it one evening when I was alone. It was there on the table where I am writing these words. A buff cardboard cover; nice neat lines allowing no space for margins. Some sentences have been crossed out, others erased. Strange to think that this precious manuscript should have found its way to my study.

JANUARY 31. The faces of people who have something to hide are like a wall. Better still, they are like a bricked-up door whose outline can nevertheless be vaguely distinguished. I thought this as I observed a very proper and aggressively respectable old gentleman. And yet, everybody knew only too well . . . He imagines that this cannot be seen, because he has taken pains not to let anything appear, but his poor face shrieks the truth. Nothing, to my mind, is sadder than such a farce that takes in no one except the man who acts it.

MARCH 3. What I have against a life of pleasure is that it kills in a man all aptitude for love. It gives him the heart of a eunuch. I said this to someone who was piqued by my remark, but I feel strongly that I am right. Nothing is colder than a pleasure-loving man. This is perceptible only in the long run, because during youth there exists the eternal misunderstanding about desire and love, which are taken one for the other. Love is not necessarily linked to desire; it surpasses it continually, but love is not to be met every day, it does not run about the streets: in fact, that is precisely what it never does.

APRIL 2. I keep this diary far less regularly than in my youth, when everything was new to me and it seemed a duty to describe even the shape of a flame in the hearth. Not that the beauty of a fire no longer touches me, far from it. The older I grow, the more sensitive I am to the splendor of the visible world, of all that God shows us, and that we scarcely glance at, but my time is running short. I use my days sparingly, which is foolish as duration is an illusion among others. We are going to die in a couple of hours, said St. Teresa of Ávila.

---

[1] This copybook had been entrusted to my sister, who, under the direction of a Carmelite Father, was doing some collating.

Yesterday, a party in what is called society. I could not avoid going without hurting some people's feelings, and, I don't know how, rather late in the evening a discussion arose about religion and more particularly Purgatory. A man I like very much and see very little talked of his horror of death: "Never leave a dying man unattended. . . . The loneliness of the dying is horrible." Although he is not a Catholic, he spoke in a touching manner of the dying who leave this world supported by the Church's solicitude and love: "The Church prays for them, comforts them with the last sacraments." I said to him: "A Protestant dies with a certainty of salvation, as this forms part of his faith." (I thought of my grandfather, who, just as he was about to give up the ghost, said: "Give me my stick; I am going to Heaven.") He smiled sadly: "For two pins," he replied, "some people would say to God: 'Lord, here is a very choice soul. You must take great care of it.'"

APRIL 7. Someone asked me if he should answer a rather low attack from a weekly magazine; I advised him to keep silent. Silence is a wonderful weapon, but it has to be handled with great care. One must know whom it is being used against, and what meaning it will assume in the mind of whoever is answered in this way. There is an indignant silence, or a wounded, disdainful, contemptuous, amused, sarcastic one, one that is full of sorrowful reproach, or one that is pathetic, jeering, jovial, teasing, furious, vengeful, etc., etc. But it always ends by being rightly interpreted, unless it is the mysterious silence that leaves the opponent in doubt, and this last is exasperating. Bossuet used it against the Protestant minister Jurieu, who accused him of being father to several children, or it may perhaps have been the silence of baffled rage, or that which we have all used and misused: the silence of indifference. To complete the list, let us finally mention the silence that says yes and the silence that says no, and the silence that would almost justify murder, because it says neither yes nor no.

APRIL 9. Faith means walking on the waters. Peter himself had begun to sink when Jesus stretched out His hand, reproaching him for doubting. Now, we must believe. In an atheistic world, we have received this exceptional gift. In wind and in darkness, if the ground gives way under our feet like water—and who has not felt this at some time or other?—we must go straight ahead, in spite of all, and grasp the hand that is stretched out to us.

APRIL 10.   What is love? There is a letter from Keats to his sister Fanny in which he, the unbeliever, the pagan (dear pagan, may you be in Heaven!) explains to the youthful Protestant what she will have to say and do at her Confirmation, and he explains at length, he tells everything he knows, everything he remembers of a faith that is his no longer. He refers her to passages in the Scriptures. He thinks that the Extreme Unction of the Church of Rome is called thus because of "anointing the extremities of dying persons with holy water" (letter of March 31, 1819). He cannot help writing God with a small "g" through a sort of upside-down bigotry, but there is more love in this letter than in many a pious speech that one reads with disgust.

How is one to pray? I have read quite a large number of works on methods of prayer and was never able to derive any benefit from them. It seems to me that to place oneself in the presence of God and to know that He is there would be enough in most cases, but is that praying? I think a great many people would say no, and yet it does one good to remain before God in silence, to keep silence before Him. Talk to Him? Why, I believe that when one has said the *Pater* and the *Ave*, nothing else is worth while, except silence.

APRIL 12.   Yesterday, a visit from a journalist who asks me lots of questions about myself, my works, my views of Christianity. This continues for a couple of hours, and I feel weary. I think that what men say, no matter how well or how fully, does not ring like the Gospel. They wish to prove to you that the sins of the flesh are not sins, and they do so brilliantly. No sooner have they left than you pick up the Bible and it speaks a very different language. One is free not to read it, but one cannot prevent it from existing in our world and continually saying no when the modern world says yes. Because of this, I feel a little lonely at times and a little sad.

Later, a visit from a Pole whom I like very much although we rarely meet. He talks extensively of my diary and thinks it rash of me to have revealed graces that were granted me. Why? Because God might not grant me any others? But there is no such keeping of accounts with Heaven that I know of, and also I have only hinted at what is very vague and very usual. The question would be, rather, to know if it is not a duty to bear witness and if it is not a sort of injustice to keep to oneself what has been received. I told my visitor that I was happy to be alive and, above all, indescribably happy that God existed. This feeling is very powerful and also obscure, and words do not express it properly. I admire, yes, I admire the strength of character of atheists who can live and bear the burden and heat of each day without the Almighty on whom to lean. It has never appeared to me possible to live without believing.

UNDATED. The conversion of a little quite ordinary soul seems to me as miraculous as the conversion of a great soul, and a slow, almost imperceptible conversion just as admirable as a sudden conversion that fires the imagination. I even wonder if a man very gradually attracted to God does not offer a better example of the power of love. A man prostrated by Grace who then and there breaks all ties with the world, that is indeed an extraordinary sight, but a man fettered and bound by the world's pleasures, to such an extent as to seem impossible that he could ever be able to leave them, and who manages, in spite of all, through the infinite patience of Grace, to destroy the snare, thread by thread, and suddenly free himself from all these deadly complications—what is more astonishing, if one thinks this over?

MAY 26. I scarcely fear death any longer. (And supposing it were there, all of a sudden, what would you say? Would you talk in the same way? I wonder.) The earth is the womb of our mother who bore us and which we leave to be born. This should only terrify people who refuse the word of God. Yet, I was thinking the other day of what I had written about the Church sorrowing over her departed children, a sorrow I can't understand, because it means they have gone to God and that the earth is shown us as a land of exile (nightmarish funerals, black draperies, doleful hymns, etc.), and remembered that when Jesus heard that Lazarus was dead, He wept, just the same.

Read with dreadful sadness the accounts of tortures inflicted during the sixteenth century upon Protestants by Catholics, or upon Catholics by Protestants, for none were more cruel than Protestants (they sawed Catholics in two by sliding them naked over tautly stretched ropes; and who can forget the martyrs of Gorcum and their long-drawn-out agony on the gallows?). Human cruelty is practically limitless, because it would seem that our imagination tends more strongly in that direction when the devil allows it full play. Beyond eroticism, but in the same direction, lies the hell of cruelty, and the further one goes in eroticism, the closer one gets to this hell. That is why excesses in the sexual sphere end by creating terror, crime being the natural result of eroticism.

MAY 29. One must make up one's mind to be badgered by the devil until one dies. I sometimes hear it said: "He has faith, he has found peace once more." But Christ came to bring a sword, not peace. I had a letter from Jacques Maritain this morning and it contains an idea that I think very fine: having so often wished to be removed from the world, I should consider that I have left it, because faith isolates us. I too believe that faith isolates us, not from the humanity for which Christ died, but from the world for which Christ did not pray.

WHITMONDAY. A desire for literary fame was very keen in me until I was about twenty-five. It lessened at the time when I discovered that the world did not exist at all in the way that we imagine it, but that desire of mine for fame did not die without a struggle. I can say today that practically nothing of it remains in me. In 1955, I can write with assurance that I no longer have any worldly ambition. The desire that my books should live on would seem to me ridiculous, if I fostered such vain imaginings—for in me, one part of my being always judges the other. A writer's fame—I have already said this elsewhere—has become a paper glory . . . and our paper is worthless. That of the seventeenth century, the fine, laid paper on which I read so many books that I love, this fresh, white paper has kept all its pliancy, whereas our paper turns quite yellow within thirty years' time, and in reading a book printed around 1925, one runs the risk of actually breaking its brittle pages, just by turning them.

JUNE 1. Last night, I was telling Anne: "Since 1938, I have never had the shadow of a doubt concerning faith. The Catholic faith with all its mysteries and obscurities seems to me evidence itself, but evidence viewed from a world of darkness." Such a complete absence of doubt sometimes makes me pause, for the greatest of us have had doubts, and terrible, harassing ones (St. Paul of the Cross is one example among many). Our responsibility is all the greater for our having a vigorous faith. Thought a great deal about these things because of a letter I received this morning. It came from a man for whom I have a great regard, and I wish with all my heart that I could answer him, but when confronted with atheism I am as mute as I would be facing a phenomenon that is impossible to understand or to believe real. My correspondent cannot imagine that a believer might be anxious about his salvation, but the uncertainty in which we live justifies such apprehensions to a large degree. Protestants are the only ones who are certain, according to their views. We Catholics can only hope, but to hope is a duty. This said, I wonder if, in reading this diary as one would read a novel, with the author as its hero (?), a believing reader might not be led to ask: "How will this end? Will the hero be lost or saved at the end?" The question would seem to me quite an apt one. I wish it were for me the most actual of questions, one that would disturb me a thousand times more than it does. Of course I have not the least certainty of being saved, but then I do not feel the terror of people who think themselves lost. I could be told that this is meaningless, that you can agreeably put your eyes out, as Pascal says. I know that perfectly well. I even add that my qualms are not great enough concerning all this and the few I do feel have been obtained only by cudgeling my brains and searching the Scriptures for passages best fitted to make me quake, and that's the truth.

JUNE 16. Sometimes I am seized with such a deep and perfectly inexplicable sadness that the whole world suddenly appears void of any meaning. Void the present moment, void the words we utter, void all our motions and all our efforts to accomplish anything whatever. Those are the hours that I dread most, those where nothingness asserts itself. I felt this powerfully once in Naples and once again in Stockholm. It is the wind of despair rising to lay everything flat. The devil, the face of the devil.

JUNE 18. Abbé Pierre said this, the other evening, on the air: "Love must precede love. To go to the poor with pockets full of dollars is nothing. They must be loved. I refused money offered me by Americans and asked them to spend it on their own poor; they have plenty. What I ask them for is love, before anything else. I don't want France to look like a beggar in American eyes." I think I have noted his words accurately.

Anne and I went to see the Maritains yesterday. We found them just as we had always known and loved them, and when I say the Maritains, that includes Véra, Raïssa's sister. No one will ever quite know what their affection has meant to me. One of the greatest favors ever granted to me by God was to place Jacques on my path in 1924. I particularly want to say this.

JULY 3. Long conversation with Robert on the subject of music and in particular of Beethoven, whom I no longer care for as much as I did, except his chamber music, which is quite obviously the peak of genius. His symphonies (all but certain parts of the Ninth, which I avoid hearing because I like them too much and don't want to tire of them), his symphonies I simply cannot listen to, and this holds good for his overtures. Why? Alas, something in me no longer echoes these heroic aspirations. This juvenile enthusiasm wearies me, these cavalry charges, this continual cry of "Forward!" Stimulating music, yes indeed, but not to me. On thinking it over, what I have just written seems to me perfectly ridiculous. I can't hear *Egmont* without a pounding heart. And *Fidelio*, in spite of the opera's being inacceptably conventional to my mind . . . What bothers me, in all opera, is an effort toward realism that can only be ludicrous. Opera singers are almost always wretched actors. Monteverdi's *Combatimento di Tancredi e di Clorinda* seems to me far less false: here the characters declaim without budging and are so conventional that they finally escape conventionality.

I was telling Robert that so-called gay music can be heart-rending, and that, for this reason, I find it difficult to listen to some of Schubert's allegros (and those ghostly scherzos where death has already joined the dance), whereas, when Bach says "Remember that you must die," it is stimulating, but Bach has never saddened me. An agreement should be reached about the words *sad* and *gay*. I can't listen to Schubert when everything is going wrong. His tenderness demoralizes me.

JULY 7. At twenty, I believed in my elders' answers, I thought they knew. Now that I myself am an elder, when people come to me full of questions, I don't know what to answer. The more I go, the less clearly I see; but the thicker the night, the greater faith must grow, otherwise how can one live in this darkness?

OCTOBER 17. There are days when one avoids writing because

nothing good could come of it and the words shaped by the pen are simply too carnal. It is odious to be the threshold of sin for others. . . . I think that if I had been twenty in a period of such extreme facility as this one, where morals are concerned, nothing much of what is solid would have remained in me. I would perhaps have been incapable of loving, and who knows if faith would not have been shipwrecked along with the rest? I must say that I used to live in amazing ignorance of what went on around me. This kept me in a state that ranged from enthusiasm to melancholy and allowed many feelings to develop in me, feelings unknown to present-day youth. They lack a certain ingenuousness without which no real love exists. What they call love, as far as I can see, are affairs that last a few weeks or a few hours. They believe in nothing.

OCTOBER 19. More and more attracted to chamber music, that of Mozart, of Beethoven, of Brahms. Everything interior that can be said—two violins, a cello, and a piano can say it; the rest, the great orchestral ensembles, are often only there for decorative purposes. Bach needs only a voice and a flute to open Heaven to us.

OCTOBER 28. That sensation of danger, so strange because it is both so vague and so powerful, that fear lessens and calms down in the presence of certain people one is fond of. My father reassured me completely. I have often wondered if his goodness and innocence did not verge on a sort of holiness of which he had no suspicion. We seldom talked together, but there was a drawer in my room where I kept confessions that it never occurred to me to lock. One day, returning from a journey, I discovered that the drawer was empty. I was so casual and carefree that I had forgotten all about it the next day. I was twenty-three. The idea simply crossed my mind that someone had read and destroyed these papers, but I never opened my lips about it and no one ever mentioned the subject to me.

NOVEMBER 4. *The Transgressor* has had a good press, contrary to my expectations. Five or six times in my life, not more, not many times more, I have wondered what would remain of all my works; I would like this not to be indifferent to me, but then so many things are indifferent to me since 1940 and more particularly since Hiroshima, which has separated us all, every one of us, from a great part of ourselves. . . .

Yesterday a visitor asked me the name of the stove that heats this room where I am writing (it has a long pipe that comes out into the room and is called, I think, a *cheminée à la prussienne*). He had never seen anything like it, and I believe that in another twenty years, all such heating appliances, wood or coal fires, will have disappeared. We will have rooms without mantelpieces, commonplace and decentered, for in a sense the hearth is somewhat like the soul of a room, toward which one goes and sits. A blazing fire is wonderful company. It helps one to think, it flickers, it blazes, it is there. I look at it whenever I raise my eyes. There is an affinity between us.

NOVEMBER 5. Yesterday, a visit from an Italian professor. He talks to me about his country's spirituality, such a curiously moving one. An unlimited trust in God that fits in with the *mala vita*, prostitution, etc. An unmarried, pregnant woman throws herself out of a window, grasping a crucifix. He tells me that he once rented a room in a southern Italian town, in which to work during the day; he discovered that it was rented to lovers at night and, complaining of this to the lodginghouse-keeper, who was very poor, she said: "Yes, they live without benefit of clergy, but they love each other." We next talk about charity, and I remark that rich men's charity is often a mere form of condescension and that they rid themselves of the poor by giving them money. "Yes," he replies, "in Italy the poor give alms to the poor, and they do it lovingly."

NOVEMBER 13. One should try to remain alone. To be able to do this, one must refuse success, I mean easy success, for in going from one easy success to another, one ends by being lost. Come honors and all is over. . . . I am a Catholic, but a suspicious one in the eyes of certain Catholics because I read the Bible. All this apropos of a doctor who said to me yesterday: "You are no longer free because you are in the public eye." But one has to remain free, even at the price of solitude.

NOVEMBER 16. So few men are in their proper place in this world. . . . This strikes me more and more. Am I in my proper place? It doesn't much matter now that the game has been played.

(How I love the sound of bells brought to me on the November air, through the drawn curtains of this room, so far away from the world! The presence of such a quiet and beautiful hour is worth noting.) If I gave up painting long ago, it was no doubt because I was afraid of not excelling in it. I was unconsciously ambitious. This seems strange to me now. The first time that I saw my name printed in a newspaper, in a stationer's window, I ran away. Yet, I think that I was born to write books. What books? This one, perhaps.

NOVEMBER 19. . . . This morning, I had a letter from a priest who writes: "You are alone." And he adds: "You are saved." Saved—how does he know? But alone, yes. To be truthful, and strange as it may seem, I do not know a priest to whom I dare tell, in this very room where I am writing, even a quarter of my difficulties. We talk about books, of course, but for goodness' sake, what is a book and what reality can it have? Now, the soul is real, is cruelly, sorrowfully real. My correspondent also says: "One obtains from God as much as one hopes to get." Yes, and in that case, I want everything. This is what constitutes the deepest part of certain lives that are so disconcerting on the spiritual plane. Perhaps, then says a voice I know so well, but what about that black notebook? There is always a black notebook in every man's life. Ought I to say all this? Beyond any doubt, there are days when one ought to say what one doesn't want to say. It was not without uneasiness—why not write "not without dread"? —that I reread the last chapters of Isaiah yesterday. Such anger directed against me, against any man who receives the word, since no man is pure before God, but also those marvelous promises of a universal conversion . . .

NOVEMBER 21. I wanted once more to hear *Schlage doch, gewünschte Stunde* with Robert. Only very great men can reach this divine simplicity, divine because it comes from God. Compared with this, the enormous and magnificent intricacies of a composer like Wagner . . . Yet I don't think I will ever tire of listening to the *Meistersinger*, even the overture, too well known, but as beautiful as the sun breaking through the clouds and beaming light in all directions. This is genius in all its wonderful self-assurance, I was going to say: insolence.

* * *

NOVEMBER 26. A priest was telling me of his indifference to graves, for those of his own dead. "I go to visit them out of politeness," he says. This devotion to the dead, according to him, corresponds to a very ancient idea that the neglected dead wreak vengeance on the living. But then, to appease them once a year with a bunch of chrysanthemums . . . My own particular cemetery lies in morning and evening prayer. That is what counts. And also, there is no cemetery because there are no dead. The departed live in God, and God said that He was not the God of the dead but of the living.

DECEMBER 2. Talked about Gide with someone who knew him very well. I told him that he would not perhaps have had that very bitter and very stubborn hostility to the Church if it had not shown itself to him under the features of So-and-So, if we Catholics had been different and above all better, I mean better Christians. We have our responsibility in this matter. And also, in regard to believers, there was something in him akin to the resentment that old men harbor for young ones who still have a heart to love with, whereas old men no longer have one. I have felt more than once that he was vexed, and very much vexed, not to be able to believe. Hence that acrimony and the constant malicious teasing to which he subjected my visitor and myself.

DECEMBER 9. Satan's power is enormous, his subtleness extraordinary, but God with one breath knocks all that down. Then what is the power that works on us unceasingly and that patiently leads us toward our end, even through evil? We recognize God in the darkness, His voice which is not a voice like ours, His voice which has the same quality as silence and which makes the heart beat. . . .

DECEMBER 20. My sister Eleanor writes us from London that everyone is getting ready for "the great Christmas bacchanalia." Indeed, what other name could be given this feast? It no longer has any really Christian meaning for the immense majority of gluttons and spreers who celebrate Christmas Eve with parties. The birth of the little Jewish child who saved us has become the pretext for extra debauchery.

DECEMBER 23. "Back of nature lies a dreadful power," said

Father Pouget. Whoever has not felt this intuitively, at least occasionally, at least once before dying, does not know the meaning of life. That power is God, and it may indeed appear dreadful, because of the enormous force it implies. It is legitimate to be frightened. The Scriptures even think this to be a very wise thing, but that dreadful power is love. O You whom we do not see, but whom we feel around us and whom we constantly offend, how could the man who knows You are there manage to resist You? Words are suddenly dumb when such things are to be expressed. In such a case music alone speaks, and great writers are great only in so far as their thoughts blend with music and they speak its tongue. Away with a man who has no music in himself!

DECEMBER 27. A sermon by John Donne on death. He turns sleep into a daily death and declares that we deliver ourselves to our enemy when we lie down to sleep. What a good time those puritans unconsciously had! For this is nothing but a sinister play of images, the fancy of a great poet who was both fastidious and obsessed. Death wreaks vengeance on Donne's own self. This is the favor that Donne asks of it. Donne the preacher kills, and kills over and over again, the young profligate he was at twenty, he slits his throat with ferocious joy, he tramples him, he delivers him to the worms, he damns him.

1956

JANUARY 4. This, in a letter from Keats: "I carry all matters to an extreme—so that when I have any little vexation it grows in five minutes into a theme for Sophocles." Suffered a little from this all my life, with the difference that my imagination, without enlarging facts, tends to distort or denature them. Maybe this is the novelist working in me! Now, the novelist in me is none other than the madman I would perhaps have been if I had not written novels. I am probably exaggerating a little, but I owe my equilibrium to ink and paper.

Bremond. Oh, Abbé Bremond, how you annoy your reader when you give him to understand that you think him well in-

formed about all sorts of things, when you know perfectly well
that he knows nothing at all! That allows you *modestly* to show
off your knowledge.

JANUARY 21. I burned quite a number of papers last night. I
hated to do it, I admit. As I stood before the fire, poking at these
pages, I thought that behind me, helping me to make this difficult
gesture, were generations of believers, all the members of my
family who firmly believed, those whom we rather lightly call
fanatics, and they whispered to me: "Far better to burn all this
than to burn yourself."

JANUARY 22. To slip a few papers under blazing logs—such a
simple gesture. An impossible gesture to make, seemingly, but
once it is over you realize it was nothing. . . . Many of these
pages would have been considered harmless by most people, but
I am so constituted that at certain moments everything is poison
to me.

JANUARY 24. It is useless to attempt to get ahead of divine action.
Our soul is an abyss into which we vainly peer. We scarcely see
anything, but something is happening there—a great drama, surely;
the drama of Adam's salvation. The Church puts these things to
us as best it can, but in a necessarily imperfect tongue, that is, the
human tongue. It makes us familiar with extraordinary ideas that
lose much of their strength with time. Happy the man who, in
growing older, can feel the mystery increasing beyond all expression. . . . In the Second Epistle to the Corinthians, chapter
4, it is said that the Gospel is hidden to those who lose their souls.
It is also said that visible things are temporal and the invisible
ones alone are eternal. This chapter, together with the Gospels,
Psalm 23, Psalm 50, the whole of Psalm 68, the last chapters of
Isaiah, and some in Ezekiel (notably the thirty-third) are the great
lights that shine in my darkness.

FEBRUARY 6. It is childish to cling to what we have learned, for
what we know is of little weight, but I admire people who know
what they know thoroughly, who don't know it in a slipshod way.
With time, I must admit to having lost the taste for learning just
to acquire something that I will not retain. What becomes passionately interesting is to exist. I don't mean hanging on to life,

but to break away from all things transient. Let things drop, Fénelon often said.

An article by Cartier about the most recent astronomical theories. The universe breathes. After a period of expansion (which is ours at present) will come a period of contraction to annihilate us in fifteen billion years. Creation incessantly renewed, galaxies wandering off into space beyond frontiers that our curiosity cannot cross. . . . In disappearing they are replaced by others—and that endlessly. We were brought up in a universe where everything was still in its place, the earth, the stars, and instinctively we put ourselves in the center of all this, we had the illusion of a certain peace amidst infinite spaces. . . . We would look at the sky before going to bed. Orion is there. Way up high, the Great Bear. And now we have figures and a rumpus that make our heads swim. The truth is that the Middle Ages continue within us, although we are not aware of it. We are gradually struggling out of it, but we drag after us great fragments of the story of humanity and it is not easy to get free of them. This article is worth many a so-called religious book.

MARCH 8. We are growing old and our decaying civilizations are going, one after the other, but God is always new, He is always there like a beautiful, fresh, clear morning, and that is how we will meet Him again after the night and storm of sin. His wealth of forgiveness is without limits. He is youth eternal.

MARCH 9. Reading is a form of laziness in so far as one allows the book to think for the reader. The reader reads and imagines that he thinks; hence a pleasure that flatters vanity with a delicate illusion.

Nothing seems to me more demoralizing than certain works on sexuality. I am thinking of the confessions that are sent to specialists who publish them. All these things said in cold blood, couched naked on paper, these horribly precise words, the clinical sentences bereft of frenzy, for nothing but sensual frenzy could make them pass. On reading these pages, how could one help from longing for the absolute?

Music lends beauty to the places where it is heard. Wicked words make ugly and sadden the places where they are uttered. Blasphemy makes the walls totter, coarseness sullies them; everything turns poor and shabby, through some unknown and strange magic, in a room where people express themselves badly and boredom creeps into a man's heart.

. . . There are moments in our lives when madness bursts in and triumphs, be it only for a few seconds: first, in sleep, through the gate of horn of dreams; second, in sexual intercourse.

UNDATED. Late this afternoon and much against my will, I went to a reception held in gloomy drawing rooms where despair walks sumptuously to and fro, the despair that follows wealth like its shadow. Men in uniforms. A member of the French Academy, whom I used to know, passes by me, glides by me like some gigantic fish in his green uniform. Princes of the Church. I remained almost dumb in this strange place and left after a short time, wondering what it could all be about. We are told that our dreams are absurd, but I have had many that seemed to me more reasonable than these queer fifteen minutes.

GOOD FRIDAY. Thought of a sentence that I once read in an English book. It seems to have no meaning and yet has a very great one: "How close I was to God when I was far from Him!" An illusion, no doubt, but nothing gives me a keener longing for God than sin.

APRIL 9. The act of photographing a face is a sort of magical operation. The reason why so few photographers faithfully reproduce the face that I see every morning in the mirror is that they do not know it. An unknown man comes to my house and photographs an unknown man (unknown to the photographer). The result is null. The camera has seen me but has understood nothing, guessed nothing. The photographs taken of me by people who know me well are quite different, for they show what these people think of me, and the camera sees what the photographer sees. An American came here and took some rather poor likenesses of me, for he had at his disposal a highly—too highly— perfected camera that spared him the trouble of looking, not with the eye, but with what should think and understand within us. I say this because what happens to me in this respect happens to everybody else. A photographer cannot dispense with also being a painter.

MAY 5. The only books that count for me are those of which

one can say that the author would have choked to death if he had not written them. Namely, those by Dostoevsky. The rest is scarcely more than brilliant stuff and nonsense such as we are offered nowadays. In talking about all this to a young writer, I thought of what the Flemish drapers said in the fifteenth century when a war with England deprived them of the wool they needed: "You can't make cloth without wool." Where is the wool in all these novels, and of what stuff, of what imitation cloth are they made?

MAY 20. In growing older, we become our parents. Their principles end by getting the better of the ones we had in our youth, which were perhaps those they had in their own. When one has had parents like ours, there is room for hope, but we should choose our parents carefully!

MAY 26. I have been asked questions about *The Transgressor*. To my mind, Jean, like Hedwige, is a victim, without her innocence, but nevertheless a victim. He is a transgressor in the eyes of those who dare to judge him. So I might be told that the title is ironical. Yes, of course, but bitterly ironical. What I condemn in this character is what I also condemn in all the men and women who cast a stone at him. One's hands should be clean indeed to cast a stone, but what is remarkable about clean hands is that they don't cast stones.

MAY 28. In a corner of one's room when the day is closing, when the sounds of the city and of life die down a little, when in us lies the silence of twilight where God is perhaps more perceptible than at other moments—that is the time to open the Bible and listen to what it is going to say to us. To talk to God with a heart still warm with happiness. How He must love to be told that He is loved! And the more we tell Him so, the more He loves us.

I think that nothing in the Old Testament surpasses the beauty of the third chapter of Jeremiah, no matter how terrible, how disquieting it may seem. The Bible is a book that stays open for ever, since it speaks only of the eternal present.

MAY 30. A young man who almost took orders said the other day: "I prefer pleasure to God." And I prefer this alarming sen-

tence—alarming for him—to lukewarmness. That is the way violent, headstrong men speak. The lukewarm rarely return to God.
The violent suddenly return to God, and for ever.

JUNE 14. A letter from Germany blames me for Jean's suicide
in *The Transgressor*, even more than for Hedwige's, because
Jean believed in God. "God's purposes should be obeyed and life
should not be cut short," writes my correspondent. This is un-
doubtedly true, but a novel is not a handbook on morals, it is a
mirror in which we see life, and if what I see is tragic, isn't the
story of humanity tragic on every page, and daily newspapers as
well? Give us newspapers that contain good news only and I will
write optimistic novels (as a religious asked me to do). Let the
condition of man be changed, let life be changed. "Life is not so
black," old Mme Alphonse Daudet said to me. How often have I
heard this remark, and heard it from people whose families could
vie with the Atridae.

JUNE 15. Not to forgive oneself anything is a kind of sin. There
is a great deal of pride in being, or wishing to be, more severe
than God. That man within us is the one we ought to kill.

I was told the following story. It concerns a man who was very
close to me, one of the best Christians I have ever known. Long
before the 1914 war, he had an exporting business in Savannah.
One of the men who worked for him proved most unsatisfactory,
in spite of all admonishments. He was a slightly unbalanced Spaniard. The manager finally decided to discharge the man, who refused to go. Things dragged on from bad to worse. One day there
was a row. The Spaniard, on being told once more that he was
dismissed, declared that go he would not and clung to his desk.
This article of furniture was carried out of the house and set down
in front of it, on the wharf. There stood the Spaniard, behind his
desk, in the open air, haranguing the passers-by. He shrieked, he
cursed his former boss, he prophesied that not a cent of the money
inherited by the latter from his father would be left. And this
came true literally. God took away all the money this man had
been left by his father. Perhaps this is the way God saved him. I
knew someone who had witnessed this strange scene in the port of
Savannah. I think it rather fine. The novelist called life is sometimes well inspired.

* * *

JUNE 21. Among Mozart's works, *The Marriage of Figaro* is the one I like least, and I wish I knew why. It is a shadowless opera, and this no doubt is why it does not charm me like the rest, where, at some time or other, you always find the exquisite melancholy that makes me so fond of Mozart and that distinguishes him in my eyes from composers with unalloyed high spirits. I except the Countess' aria, through which runs a regret for childhood and lost innocence. The *Marriage* is in broad daylight, a blinding Italian light, *deafening* at times. Such aggressive gaiety makes me feel like running away, no matter how much admiration the music's formal beauty arouses in me.

JULY 5. At Mareil, near Paris, which we reached a moment ago in the finest possible weather. The house is rather old. The staircase must have been built at least two centuries ago. The large, fine semi-Romanesque, semi-Gothic church is separated from us by a path on the other side of the garden wall. The garden is a stretch of lawn hedged in by clumps of flowers, and at the far end is a sort of terrace buried in trees. All this is quiet, secret, a trifle dark no doubt at certain times of the day, but how much I enjoy being within these walls! I have a beautiful room with two windows facing each other. The sun passes through the muslin curtains as through a mist. Here, life pauses for a moment in its hectic race. You can breathe, look around you. Anne will be with us in a few days. Yesterday, as she was putting sheets in a suitcase, happy at the idea of going away, she said to me: "This is like old times, when we went to Andrésy, in July." And she carries the sheets as my mother used to carry them, but it is no longer quite like old times, alas, too many of us are missing. Mother packed the sheets in a big wicker hamper, and the creaks of the lid as it closed were like shrieks of pain. All that is far away. And the children, the others, where are they?

JULY 6. It would bore me to have to describe this house, except in a novel, I mean that it would take too much time. Its façade is covered with red roses. The house is so old that you feel it would be impossible to make a gesture that it has not seen made thousands of times. In the room where I am writing, the sun stretches over the floor the same golden rectangle that it laid there in 1700 or earlier. What strange thoughts have moved to and fro within these walls, how many prayers too, perhaps, how many unacknowledged ambitions have ripened under its long black rafters, only to be disappointed later. . . .

I am plunged resolutely in Jane Austen's *Emma* for a change of atmosphere and to prevent my being bewitched by Port-Royal. Miss Austen's world is a very quiet one. The heart's beat is steady, there is no screaming, but hidden emotion lies under these appearances of calm and uniform good breeding. The author's subtlety of observation might easily go unnoticed these days. Everything is said with bated breath. Compared with this novel ours seem very ill bred, very vulgar, and very heavy.

JULY 8. Just now, I was talking to Robert about Proust and trying to make myself understand why I admire this writer so much, although I like him so little. What I have against him are his characters, his innumerable models, several of whom I know and who have attempted to make me love Proust as much as they did and who irritated me on account of their pretensions to intellectual refinement, which was an imitation intellectual refinement, and their fashionable jargon, their sham simplicity, their spurious enthusiasms, their search for psychological complications, the crashing boredom they exuded because it was all intensely false. I except the most Proustian of Proustians: Lucien Daudet (son of Alphonse Daudet).

JULY 9. Alone in the house, I continued reading Jane Austen in the charming and tiny ground-floor library. She overrefines feelings, but with such a firm, light hand that she makes us seem gross and bearish. How pleasant it is to be plunged into a world so peaceful that the arrival of a letter is a sort of event!

JULY 14. How can one think oneself pure when the ancient corruption of the human race is felt to the core of one's being? Who has not experienced the horror of knowing himself deeply enslaved by human beauty, even if only for a second, a flash? What's the good of deceiving oneself? Could one possibly imagine that, by imitating the actions of saints, one becomes saintly? This is false. Everything is different inwardly. Holiness that is only an outward show is perfectly ridiculous, and if we believe in it we are silly. I have the feeling of never having gone beyond outward appearances, that I have been satisfied with fine semblances. What's the result of these idiotic efforts? I secretly rebel, not against faith (God forbid), but against myself who understand nothing about matters of faith, who do not even know what faith is—and in that I am not alone; I have hosts of Catholics with me, and particularly, theologians.

JULY 15. The secret is to write just anything, to dare to write just anything, because when you write just anything, you begin to say what is most important. You must let your hand run along the sheet of paper for a while. Then someone guides it, someone you don't know and who bears your name. How old can he be? A thousand years, I think.

An expression that I like in *Emma*: "To be in charity with oneself," to be at peace with oneself and, better still, to love oneself, to forgive oneself. Why not? ". . . I love my neighbor *as myself* for love of You," says the act of charity. Then may this terrible, homicidal, and constant struggle against oneself cease!

JULY 26. Read Jane Austen. I am glad to have undertaken to read *Emma* but am impatient to get through with it. The guiding thread is a little tenuous and it requires very great attention to prevent its slipping out of one's fingers. The dialogues are often admirable, but the action boils down to very little. At one point, a young man asks a girl to play on the piano a waltz that he has just heard. "She played," says the author. And that is all. Not another word. This is not dryness but an exquisite restraint that might wrongly pass for poverty in 1956.

JULY 30. Robert was telling me that it was probably owing to reading the Bible that I had become, as he says, nontemporal (with the serious inconveniences that can result from it in everyday life), and it is true that the Bible has freed me from some of the fascinations of this world. I know the devil's old spells only too well. I can no longer believe, if I ever did, in the reality of honors, of reputations, of pleasures. But I feel lonely. This crumbling world has never been more convinced of its own existence.

AUGUST 1. I was struck by a book about Gide and his wife. If Mme Gide was as intelligent as her husband believed her to be, she could not have ignored how much she would hurt him by burning his letters to her. On the other hand, if she thought it her duty to punish him, taking the place of God, I cease to understand her, no matter how admirable she was in other ways. Who knows if she didn't kill in Gide a better man than the one we knew? Didn't he say himself, and most explicitly, that if this correspondence disappeared, nothing would remain of him but an incomplete, inaccurate, caricatural, grimacing picture and that what had been his true representation would be wiped out for ever?

AUGUST 3. A walk in the forest of Saint-Nom-la-Bretèche; the earth is black and the light is such as is found in a cellar. I remembered what St. Bernard said: "In woods, you will find something more than in books." But what do books give us? We gradually forget them. Most serious of all, if we aren't careful, they end by thinking for us. They ask nothing better. Yet what they have to offer us is immense, they teach us to find within us the truth that God has put there and that is God Himself. Nothing else on this earth is of any interest but the discovery of God within us. Now, He is there, whether we know it or not, whether we feel it or not.

An excellent chapter in *Emma* where the heroine publicly insults a poor old lady whose intemperate chatter exasperates everyone. Once at home, she is filled with shame and remorse and weeps secretly. Mysterious Jane Austen! How I would have dreaded living with her! Not one of my weaknesses would have escaped her, for she saw everything with a pitiless eye. Emotion, with her, is always delicate, but then everything is delicate in this woman, cruelty like the rest. One can say that she is almost unknown in France because translations only thicken and coarsen such a very light and very subtle prose.

Why do you want to be a better man? (This question could be asked of every man.) Because you would love yourself more if you were better, you, always you, black or white. You will be a better man only when you have completely lost sight of yourself and will then think of your Creator. No more diary, no more mirror, no more self-complacency. A fly, after long wanderings over a windowpane in search of the sun it sees but cannot reach, being separated from it by this sheet of glass, will fly out of the window when death opens it.

AUGUST 11. We are returning to Paris day after tomorrow. What a number of walks, of villages lighted on, with their little Romanesque churches that, in solitude and silence, pursue the great

Catholic dream! Houdan, Nonancourt, Herbeville, Orgival and so many others. Immense fields framed by woods, hills as far as the eye can reach, the most beautiful landscapes in the world, those of my childhood, those of happiness.

AUGUST 17. To many men, the horror of going to confession is an insuperable trial. To be thrown like a criminal at the feet of a judge before whom one shakes with fear, that's what it is. Afterwards only do you realize that the judge loves you so much that He died for you and died for you on the cross and that, of course, He forgives everything.

AUGUST 24. A certain man I know is devoid of real humility, but he has a showy modesty, an ostentatious modesty that is worse than anything and fills me with the most violent disgust. I prefer bare-faced pride, pride in all its foolishness and vulgarity. How difficult it is to save a man of letters! But nothing is impossible to God, since He manages to save even the rich.

AUGUST 29. Thought last night of the sight presented by humanity. It is wounded, crippled. This escapes our notice, but an angel ignorant of earthly matters and of the state of mankind would be horrified. What a sorry sight we are! One need only observe passers-by in any street. They all bear the stamp of a frightful and most ancient catastrophe. We are told of the havoc an atomic bomb would wreak, but there has already been an atomic bomb: the punishment of original sin that has left us in a state of woeful inferiority in comparison to what we should have been. Yet there are human beings who resemble the idea we can form of humanity before the Fall. One sees faces and bodies so beautiful that they surpass what words can say of them, but this does not last and no sooner do they reach the age of twenty or thereabouts than something fades. In the reckless admiration inspired by a beauty that is both frail and marvelous and is the cause of such great tragedies, one cannot help but see what is pathetic and pitiful in all this. The expression and the whole person of those whom life has not yet touched, has not yet disfigured, hold a reflection of vanished glory.

SEPTEMBER 28. Pascal said almost all there was to say about one side of Montaigne when he wrote: "He inspires a certain unconcern for salvation." Of all the things with which a man I like so much could be reproached, this one is to my mind the most serious. It is nevertheless true that St. Francis de Sales delighted in him and read him with other eyes than ours. The Bishop of Geneva would have been astonished to hear that the time would come when one of his favorite authors would be placed in the Expurgatory Index. Be it as it may, it is characteristic of a huge part of modern literature to inspire this unconcern for salvation. The Gospel's urgent, burning message is passed over in silence. People write as though there had never been a Gospel. The Gospel's voice is not heard in the books we are given to read, love is dumb. In literature, everything that does not lead you to God imperceptibly detaches you from Him. The great scandal is that pietistic literature turns you away from God more forcibly than does the unbelieving kind.

OCTOBER 5. Read some of the Psalms in Monsignor Knox's translation. I don't hesitate to call it simply scandalous. Scandalous because of its ugliness. Psalm 23, *Dominus pastor*, is horribly badly rendered. His prose has neither the rhythm, nor the metrical number, nor the music that such a text demands, and moreover it is *unsingable*, whereas the Protestant version (in the Book of Common Prayer) possesses this quality to an eminent degree.

OCTOBER 13. The devil is a great moralist and a great puritan. He suggests great austerities which he very well knows will bring about spiritual disasters. He never suggests small sacrifices, he aims at what is grand, sensational, at everything striking, at everything that stirs the imagination. And with it all, he is the most skillful, the most crafty of artists. Music is a great help to him. A beautiful voice serves him wonderfully well, for he manages to turn it into a beautiful body, no less. He is very sentimental, very tender, and speaks with exquisite gentleness. And every one of us is taken in by this. We spend a good part of our lives in letting God rescue us. Sad to have to say that every day, perhaps, we pass by our own self, by the self that we might have been.

God alone can understand you perfectly, you who read this. The words we use in attempting to explain ourselves serve only to confuse things. The French imagine that everything can be understood, can be clearly explained ("What is not clear is not French"). They make an exception for the Creator, faith obliges them to, but if the Church were not there to keep a watch on them, they would define Him.

OCTOBER 14. The West has never produced the founder of a religion. It has received its religion from the East, and we Christians as well as the others. This is a fact that we should not forget. We are Occidentals faced with an Oriental conception. Hence the bewilderment of certain among us.

OCTOBER 17. I can no longer speak except in a whisper, and there is too much noise for me to make myself heard by a great number of people. I don't complain of this.

OCTOBER 19. Yesterday, I had an appointment with my publisher. As usual, I was a little early and waited in the entrance hall, seated at one end of a long table strewn with books. At the other end, a woman, youngish, well dressed, with a modest air, her hands clasped over her handbag. A door opened. The publisher's secretary went up to the lady, gave her a manuscript in a folder, saying: "We're sorry. It's a little too pornographic." The lady took the manuscript, smiled, and left. What struck me was that these few words were spoken in a quiet, commonplace tone, as one might have said: "We're sorry. It's a little long. Too long by fifty pages." A whole aspect of our times was shown up in this short scene. Even *porno*, as it is called, has lost its prestige. Maybe, in a not too distant future, we shall once more have novels where all the characters will always keep their clothes on.

OCTOBER 21. . . . Which of us is really represented by what he writes? Which of us does not surpass his letters, his works? Is there a writer who does not live and breathe between the lines of his books? Yet you can't shut up a man inside his sentences. He will always escape, and only a close examination of texts can give you an intuition of what has not been written and what is often the essential part of what you want to know. I know only too well to what an extent this is true of me and all the more so of the greatest writers. . . .

OCTOBER 24. We don't give much to God. We even give Him so little that I wonder what name this little can have. It is nothing, and even less than that. We are ourselves. The saints are a different matter. As regards us, we would willingly accept a halo, but energetically (or slyly, or subtly) refuse the cross that is offered us, the hard, dry, cold, bitter, bloodstained cross. Yesterday, a Carmelite Father was telling me that the eccentricities of saints can be explained by the fact that they feel they are saved and that nothing in this world matters to them, except the love of God and the love of one's neighbor; so they give themselves up to their whims. They are not great conformists.

DECEMBER 14. That the body can suffer and the soul be happy, and very happy, is an aspect of life that unbelievers cannot even imagine.

DECEMBER 15. Kant said that the sight of a starry sky annihilates us as physical beings. It annihilates us, tears us away from the earth, and throws us into the infinite. I have often wondered if it were possible not to feel the tremendous attractive energy of the firmament. How I loved the word firmament when I was still a child! To me, it seemed filled with light. My first purely religious emotion, so far as I can remember, goes back to my fifth or sixth year. I think I have mentioned it elsewhere. I was in my parents' room, rue de Passy. The room was dark, but through a windowpane I saw thousands of stars shining in the sky. This was the first time, to my knowledge, that God spoke directly to me, in that vast, confused tongue which words have never been able to render.

DECEMBER 17. Someone I am very fond of told me that he had great difficulty in going to sleep, because anguish grips him the moment he turns out the light. It is the anguish of solitude, the fear of dying in the night. A short time before, he spoke to me about the extraordinary effect produced on him by the cantata *Schlage doch, gewünschte Stunde*, which immediately carried him away to another world filled with unclouded serenity. I told him that this was the real world, and the one that frightens and makes us suffer is a world of terrible delusions; it must be quitted at all costs, but what keeps us there are covetous desires of all kinds, which are our tyrants. Our real master is Jesus. He alone will free us from the terrors of this life. The first step is to leave pleasure behind; the rest follows of itself.

1957

JANUARY 4. Do I really know the Bible well? The truth is that I wander through it like a blind man in a palace where he has lived since childhood. I feel along the walls, I find my way. Yes, that is it, but a ready memory of the texts fails me. I locate and rediscover them pretty well, if I am given time enough.

A young foreign student told me that he can find no pleasure in reading a book that does not belong to him. It may be shameful, but I have the same feeling without being quite able to explain it. I get no benefit from reading a borrowed book, which I am afraid of losing or spoiling. Similarly, it is as painful for me to lend a book as it is agreeable to give one away, and I have given many a one in my life, but it is enough for a book to disappear from my shelves to feel an urgent, cruel need of it.

JANUARY 15. Yesterday evening, in the chapel of Foreign Missions, rue du Bac. There were present a very old white-bearded priest, four nuns in black, and two or three laymen, all absorbed in such deep meditation that for twenty minutes I did not hear the least sound, and had I closed my eyes, I might have believed myself completely alone. There was something magnificent in this silence. Father Surin says that God visits souls only when they are *still and empty*.

JANUARY 23. AT GSTAAD. Everything in our lives being, it seems, of a sexual nature, our gestures, our way of sitting down, the most innocent of our little manias, the good and bad books we read, the manner in which we soap our bodies, everything, in fact, how can we not see that when a man gives up physical pleasure, he replaces it instantly and unconsciously by thousands of small things that are a sort of compensation to him for what he misses? Am I wrong? I don't think so. I believe that taking a nap, or eating a cake, or settling into a comfortable armchair simply means cheating one's hunger. A hunger that one doesn't even wish to name. Mortal sin is sent packing, escorted to the city gate with a great beating of drums (the devil does the drumming), but sensuality tiptoes back, creeps in at the back door, duly disguised. Saints who sleep on the floor and fast so severely have understood this. You don't win the game by confiscating the body's sexual organs, to speak plainly. Sexuality looks elsewhere for shelter, it can even conceal itself in mortifications.

. . . A religious said to me: "You can't talk to a dying man of Extreme Unction. You run the risk of hastening his end. You must show mercy. . . ." Is it really being merciful if the man is truly at death's door to let him leave for the next world without a sacrament that would be of such immense help to him? For my part, I beg that the truth will not be withheld from me when the time comes. I don't want to be shown that kind of mercy.

JANUARY 26. In Milton Waldman's *Elizabeth and Leicester* there are interesting remarks about the art of the theater, which is so often impersonal, whereas a novel delivers up the author, body and soul. Thirty-seven plays and two long poems have been attributed to Shakespeare, but what do we know about the man he was? Nothing, except that he was a great genius and that he worked a lot and quickly. He was so much the lover and the loved one, so much the traitor, so much the king, the faithful knight, the clown and the gravedigger, the drunk and the scholar, the dotard and the nurse, that one no longer knows where to find him, or what his beliefs and thoughts could have been. What stands out most plainly, I think, apart from a certain conventionality that I cannot admire, is a frantic love for beauty and youth.

FEBRUARY 11. PARIS. Saturday, an anniversary Mass for Father Couturier. About forty persons were present. I was glad to see Mauriac as well as Jouhandeau and Cassou, but was unable to talk to them as I wished. A religious read fragments of Father Couturier's letters between the Gospel and the Creed, at the altar. "*Faites ce qui vous chante et cela chantera en vous.*" (This sentence remembered among several others.) Father Couturier writes that he has called on Matisse and on Colette and "that both are going to Heaven without the shadow of a doubt." This would seem to exempt us from praying for them, a drawback to the rapid canonizations habitually decreed by the Father in the goodness and pureness of his heart. He sent everyone to Heaven. Thought of him affectionately. How I wish he were here.

FEBRUARY 13. Another morning spent in useless efforts. That is exactly the way it was when I wrote *The Dark Journey* or later when I wrote *Midnight*. Experience does nothing, brings nothing, gives no facility. Finally there will be a book, but at what a price! To want to work and to be unable to, as this morning, is a sort of tragedy for me. The power is there, but not released, for some unknown reason. If I force myself to form words on a sheet of paper, I fall into abstraction, and when I fall into abstraction, it means that I *see* nothing; now, if I see nothing, it is better not to write. Today, I feel that words resist me. This is such a frequent experience that, having noted it, I won't refer to it again.

This, in Montaigne: "Some make the world believe that they believe things they never do. Others, and they are the greater number, persuade themselves they do so, being unable to conceive what it is to believe." Unable to conceive what it is to believe. Can this be better expressed? The quotation is from Book II, Chapter 12. Nowadays, many are atheists without knowing it and would be dumfounded if told so, but what effect has their so-called faith on their daily life? Does it make them give up a single pleasure, a single meanness? Does it disturb anything? Montaigne is right when he says a little further in the same chapter that we are only lip Christians.

MARCH 5. . . . I have the ever-increasing conviction that in each of us lies someone unknown to us on whom God keeps His eyes fixed from our birth to our death. That someone is ourself, it is you who read this. When you do right you think yourself good, and when you do wrong you think yourself wicked, but the one you really are is quite different and you do not see him. When death comes, there will no doubt be happy surprises; there will also be terrible ones, the happy surprises being for the sinners, I hope. The other surprises . . . I won't dwell on this.

MARCH 15. It is an illusion to believe oneself to be alone. One can't be a Catholic all by oneself. One is a Catholic in the mystic body of the Church, or not at all.

If anyone ever had the idea of writing my biography, which will not happen during my lifetime, what should be pointed out is the enormous influence that Byron had over the first years of my youth, not the Byron of the poems and the attitudinizing, whom I don't care for, but the Byron at whom I guessed and who was revealed to me by Peter Quennell's books around 1950. I thought

about him so much that I almost imagined having known him. Today this seems peculiar to me and yet it is true. Until the age of
twenty-four, I was under this strange spell.

MARCH 29. To begin a novel, the adventure that a fresh ex-
ploration of the outside world represents, is also a long journey
inside oneself. There is, I know, the problem of the evil one is
led to describe, but what is a novel made of, if not of evil? Remove evil and what remains? Good—that is, white. Black also is
necessary. It might be said that this is where one runs a risk. I
take that risk. It forms part of my vocation.

APRIL 9. Yesterday, I laughed when someone said in my presence that saints have no physical desires. Perhaps they have more
of them than we do, we who are nothing but sin from head to
foot. I remember the expression of a priest as he once said to me:
"Deprivation of pleasure is a cross one never gets used to."

APRIL 13. One loses all in losing grace. Many a time have I heard
this said, but it is curious to observe that a single sin *disenchants*
the whole of the spiritual world and restores all its power to the
carnal world. The atrocious chaos immediately *reorganizes* itself.
How does this happen? I don't know, but it becomes impossible
to understand the book one enjoyed the day before; I don't mean
impossible with one's head, with one's reason, but with the heart,
with the soul if you like, it is no longer possible. A veil stretches
over the page. The book is the same, the reader's soul has grown
dark. Suddenly, the sensuous world becomes unquestionably right.
One must give in to every desire, have a good time, the best
possible, possess all sorts of things. This is the dreaded breach
through which the devil enters, but a single act of contrition is
enough for this wretched phantasmagoria to vanish and for the
marvelous presence of the invisible to return. A man who has not
felt such things does not know one of the greatest happinesses to
be had on earth.

MAY 2. Have taken up Fénelon's letters again. His great letter
to Louis XIV will never cease to astonish me. If it is true, as Saint-
Simon says, that Fénelon reminded him of a water tap, one must
admit that the day when he wrote that letter, the tap let out scald-
ing water. If anyone ever foresaw the 1789 earthquake, it was
Fénelon, Archbishop of Cambrai.

* * *

MAY 5. In all books, in all painting, in all music, I can't help seeing two kingdoms, one constantly invading the other. It has to be
so, it has to be that light rushes upon shade and that shade throws
itself on light to blot it out, but this takes place within us. Outside, nothing moves, nothing changes. This might even lead us
astray.

MAY 6. Yesterday evening, someone I am very fond of made me
listen to Brahms' *Requiem,* and I don't know which I found more
beautiful, the very grave, very luminous music, or the face of
the one who listened to it. In eyes that have looked at me for
more than half my life, I read deep attentiveness to all that is invisible. That is religion. I don't know why it is sought for elsewhere.

MAY 12. A young Catholic tells me that he is disturbed by
the thought of the harm he may do by writing the novel he has
in mind. That is thinking up trouble! I am not the one who should
be consulted on this point. Racine endangered many a soul. Should
he not have written *Phèdre?* (Whom would he perturb nowadays? Some poisons evaporate.) Baudelaire is infinitely more dangerous. Should he not have written *Les Fleurs du mal?* That seems
absurd. Yet words wreak terrible havoc. They have a shape, a per-
fume, a contour, a warmth, a sweetness, they take the place of what
they describe and create in the reader a sort of hallucination, because they are produced by a poet's hallucination, if he has genius.
    Reread some pages in Dante. He meets Latini in Hell (this is
a little harsh, but we'll let it go at that) and the latter looks at
him "like an old tailor as he threads a needle." Ah, to be able to
write like that! One of the elements of Dante's genius is a scrupulous truth of observation and an inimitable gift for everyday
imagery.

MAY 15. Someone told me with wonderful humility: "Unfortunately, I am an erotomaniac." But there is nothing surprising in
this. Almost all men are erotomaniacs, from the most dissolute to
the holiest. A seventeenth-century writer informs us that St.
Jerome and St. Bernard (I wouldn't have believed it of St. Bernard) were continually harried by "dirty thoughts." I don't know
what an idea we form of saints. Yet, they aren't born with wings.
St. Alfonso Liguori was a martyr to certain carnal obsessions.

I listened to Mozart's music. His very lightness is not free from sadness, his joy is shrouded, but human joy is always shrouded, because death exists. It is impossible to have any lasting happiness in a world where death exists.

MAY 21. This morning, I went back to my novel, which takes place in America (I hesitated a long time as to where the action should be situated). Not without melancholy do I remember America in 1920. I suffered a great deal there but finally became deeply attached to it. My holidays in Savannah came back to me. Those wide avenues were where the devil lay in wait for me with the poetry of night, the scent of night, and a setting of white columns and black shadows on the silvery streets, the mystery of squares filled with the odor of shrubs. I knew nothing, suspected nothing, but poison was already stealing into my heart—how, I don't know. At times, I thought of what one of the rue Cortambert nuns had said to me, all in white behind the grille of the little parlor that smelled of wax: "Beware of the world . . . The world . . . The world's poison . . ." All that is far away. From the armchair where I am writing, through the white curtains, I can see the big tree, each of whose leaves flutters in the sun, each one living, palpitating, and the tree bends forward and straightens, like a pitching ship. What a silence in these rooms, in the heart of a city haunted by noise! By straining the ear, all you can hear is a long murmuring, like a very distant storm. That is all.

JUNE 6. A long walk along the quays, but in the Paris of 1957 continuous noise spoils what used to be delightful strolls. Only five years ago, you could enjoy sauntering through the streets; this is no longer possible. I examined with interest the celebrities of yesterday in the boxes of the second-hand booksellers that line the quays: the charnel house of literature. That is where we shall all be thrown. What an atrocious little farce is literary glory! The most disappointing of all. "What makes you write?" was the question asked before the war. In my case, I don't know. Something drives me to, and it is certainly not a desire to be known and praised. I want at all costs to express myself, that's all.

JUNE 11. Yesterday afternoon, around five-thirty, I put down a volume of poetry and thought that never, in the future, must I remember the minute when God's grace was so clearly offered me, a grace which I did not make use of—that the memory of that minute should never find its place in an eternity of despair. One should not remember the moment when, in a room in Paris, on a fine summer afternoon, one heard the call of God, the repeated call of Christ, and never should this instant return to one's memory . . . at what place, Lord? Parted from You for ever.

JUNE 18. An American poet sent me the account of a crime committed in New Jersey by a most pious young Protestant, a great hymn singer, a great reader of the Bible, one of Billy Graham's most ardent listeners, scrupulously clean, handsome, who raped little girls (eight to ten years old) and who recently murdered a girl of twenty by strangling her with her belt after having raped her. When he went home, *hearing* of the murder, he knelt with his parents and prayed for the murderer to be discovered. He is to die in a few weeks and, it seems, prays most fervently. What takes place in this unfortunate soul? (How can I help being reminded of *Moïra?*) To kill him is useless and barbarous and will not frighten future murderers, because a man who commits a sexual crime is incapable of reasoning at the moment when he perpetrates it. He is a lunatic who should be cared for.

JULY 10. A visit from a young Catholic who talks to me about physical passions. He believes that they calm down with age. I said: "If this were so, we would all have heard of it." The truth is that if one could enter a seminary only at forty instead of at twenty, there would be only half the number of applicants. No matter how strong passions can be in a boy of twenty, they are not yet too deeply rooted, they are not yet too cumbersome and leave him free. It is only with time that they take root and everything feeds them, good as well as evil, a taste for beauty, a love of music, of books, even the satiety that creates a craving for novelty. A young man can control, transcend himself, a mature man slowly becomes obsessed.

JULY 22. "Whore!" cried Savonarola on seeing a provocative and handsome boy. I have always imagined the boy with the looks of the young man painted by Botticelli (some say by Ghirlandaio) that hangs in the Washington museum of art. He has the insolence of his years. You can't hold that against him, but his cold, cruel, calculating, and appraising eye is that of a woman of fifty who knows how to size a man up. He has perhaps sent many a soul to the fire that is never quenched and no doubt continues to act on souls through the fearful magic of art. You can understand perfectly and of course be glad that the painter did not throw the picture into the bonfire of vanities, although that is none the less its proper place. Shelley could not see Michelangelo's Bacchus without uneasiness and thought it the image of vice. Hawthorne found something diabolical in Praxiteles' Faun (but the blood of witch burners ran in the great American's veins). What would one and the other have said about the young unknown in Washington? There is fearful power in him and he defies what is best in man. Savonarola's enemy was that boy.

JULY 31.   I have been asked to write the scenario of a film about *Dr. Jekyll and Mr. Hyde.* I accept in theory. The subject is almost too good, and I have thought about it so often since I first read the book at the University. . . . I read it again recently. It is very profound at times, but Hyde, who is the wicked side only of Jekyll, dies, and because of his death, Jekyll dies too. This seems neither convincing nor fair. If what is bad in us brings about the death of what is good, it would be too horrible. The truth is that good and evil are inextricably mingled and the one cannot cause the death of the other. One does not kill the other. One is not alternatively all the one or all the other. The story is very clumsily told. There are too many repetitions, too many returns to the past, too many letters, too many envelopes to be opened later, etc. But what a great book!

It sometimes takes an almost superhuman effort to absolve oneself, to plead not guilty in one's own eyes. Charity will give us the strength for that, charity for that neighbor of ours who is our own self.

AUGUST 5.   The reasons that make a book like *Romola* unreadable nowadays teach us something about novels in general. Handsome Tito and handsome Romola get married, but no matter how much they are enamored of each other's beauty, the author gives no indications of a carnal bond existing between them. They quarrel and part on account of some business of a bookcase being sold without the consent of one of the pair. Victorian puritanism will not allow any sensuality whatever to be expressed. No matter how much of a positivist the author was, she believes in the devil, and, for her, the devil was sex. It is fetishism in reverse. Since then, we have seen authors made idiotic by the fascination of sexuality. Both phenomena are to be distrusted.

AUGUST 10. Looked at my notes on *Romola*. One made me smile. Speaking of Tito, George Eliot says: "his loathsome beauty." This is indeed the sort of reproving gluttony I mentioned earlier. The characters stop at the waist. At about the time when George Eliot wrote her tiresome book, Dostoevsky was working on *A Raw Youth*.

AUGUST 12. Moral theology textbooks are often exasperatingly ingenuous. It is a mortal sin to look at certain parts of the bodies of men and women in the street, but this is not so of legs and faces. And supposing legs and faces are what disturb one most? How can such balderdash continue to be printed?

AUGUST 22. Yesterday, at Larchant, I saw a magnificent church, half demolished by Protestants in the sixteenth century. What remains is very beautiful. A spiritual force assembled these stones, threw these towers into the clouds. In our times, what is spiritual can be found only in books, and even so . . . In the old days, the smallest village church said its prayers with commanding majesty.

AUGUST 30. In a life of Pope by Edith Sitwell, I note the story of Wycherley, who lost his memory at thirty and died at seventy without having recovered it. He read Montaigne and Molière, and a little later imagined that such or such a sentence or scene was his, which explains the plagiarism of *L'École des femmes* in *The Country Wife*, a first-rate comedy, anyway. At bottom, the man who lost his memory had an astonishing one.

NOVEMBER 20. Listening to Chopin the other evening, with all the pleasure I usually feel, I wondered suddenly: What can be lacking in him? And the answer came at once: Heart. This sumptuous show of melancholy, these cries of despair, these sobs of sadness are not heart, but a counterfeit heart for the use of sensitive souls—who can be so very hard. This takes away from the admiration I have for the composer. He can be heartbreaking when he is simple.

* * *

NOVEMBER 27. A visit from an American friend of Kinsey. He talks to me at length about the latter, whose work is, and I don't doubt it, most important. Also talks about an author who can no longer write (this can happen: *homo unius libri*) and who keeps copies of all his letters, which he considers of great importance. How queer such literary preoccupations seem to me! Our world is ending and still we worry about our sentences, about the fate of our letters. This kind of madness allows us to live in surprising tranquillity.

DECEMBER 6. In one of his sermons, John Donne says that man is "a sick god." Nothing could better describe present humanity. It is a sublime cripple. It holds an immense power in its hands, such means of doing good and evil as perhaps it never had before.

DECEMBER 16. A priest told me that he was against wearing a cassock. He would like Catholic ecclesiastics to dress like Protestant clergymen. "The cassock," he says, "is conspicuous and prevents visits to people who dare not receive priests."

Regarding the novel I am now writing, I would like to say this, which is true of all my books: there comes a time when great breaches are made through which passes something that does not come from me, but from another who frightens me, as might another self more imperious, more commanding, and more assured than the self I know. What writer has not experienced this? Having said these things, I won't mention them again.

INDEX OF NAMES

Adler, Alfred, 196
Alfonso Liguori, St., 301
Allégret, Marc, 8, 239
Allégret, Yves, 32
Altermann, Father, 24, 52
Amrouche, Jean, 222
Amyot, Jacques, 252
Andersen, Hans Christian, 225
Angelico, Fra, 133, 169
Aristotle, 107
Arnim, Achim, 77
Ars, Curé d', 169
Auden, Wystan Hugh, 152, 177, 253, 261
Augustine, St., 129, 180, 181, 190, 216
Austen, Jane, 32, 40, 111, 290, 291, 292

Bach, Johann Sebastian, 15, 119–20, 216, 228, 240, 253, 257–58, 260, 261, 263, 278, 279, 281
Bacon, Francis, 220
Balzac, Honoré de, 5, 134, 160
Balzac, Jean-Louis Guez de, 222
Barna da Siena, 99
Barrès, Maurice, 63
Baudelaire, Charles, 18, 91, 117, 234, 252, 301
Bayle, Pierre, 213
Beaumont, Étienne de, 25–26
Beauregard, Pierre Gustave Toutant, 48
Beethoven, Ludwig van, 30–31, 56, 93, 175–76, 278, 279
Béguin, Albert, 178–79, 198–99, 262, 270
Béguin, Mme Albert, 270

Benincasa, Lapa (mother of St. Catherine of Siena), 133
Bérard, Christian, 22–23, 31, 48, 183
Berl, Emmanuel, 5
Berlioz, Louis Hector, 94
Berman, Eugène, 37
Bernanos, Georges, 198, 200, 226, 240, 261
Bernard, St., 292, 301
Beyle, Marie Henri, see Stendhal
Blake, William, 24, 152
Blow, John, 262–63
Bloy, Léon, 120, 126, 176, 195
Boccaccio, Giovanni, 228
Boniface VIII, Pope, 12
Bonney, Thérèse, 25
Bossuet, Jacques Bénigne, 119. 181, 238, 273
Bost, Pierre, 23
Botticelli, Sandro, 303
Bouguereau, Adolphe William, 10
Bourdet, Mme, 216
Bourdichon, Jean, 44
Bourget, Paul, 62
Bouyer, Louis, 196, 262
Brahms, Johannes, 228, 279, 301
Bremond, Henri, 283–84
Bresson, Robert, 173
Brisson, Pierre, 244
Brontë, Charlotte, 32, 228
Brown, George Loring, 117
Browning, Robert, 146, 151
Bruce, Evangeline (Mrs. David K. E. Bruce), 212–13
Byrd, William, 154
Byron, George Gordon, Lord, 95, 143, 241, 299–300

Calvin, John, 240, 263–64
Camus, Albert, 180–81, 194
Cano, Melchor, 179
Caravaggio, Michelangelo Amerighi da, 245
Cartier, Raymond, 285
Casson, Jean, 54–55, 298
Catherine of Genoa, St., 107
Chamberlain, Neville, 87
Charost, Duc de, 172–73
Chateaubriand, François René, Vicomte de, 238
Chaucer, Geoffrey, 133
Chekhov, Anton, 72, 156–57
Chopin, Frédéric, 94, 197, 245, 305
Christus, Petrus, 118
Clara, St., 216–17
Claudel, Paul, 6, 27, 80, 205, 209, 220, 240, 244
Cocteau, Jean, 8, 37, 147, 182, 254
Colette, 8, 248–49, 263, 298
Condamin, Father, 257
Conrad, Joseph, 27, 230
Cooper, Lady Diana, 173
Copeau, Jacques, 6, 24, 186
Corneille, Pierre, 199
Cornuau de Saint-Bégnigne, Sister, 238
Costa, Uriel da, 69
Couperin, François, 262
Courbet, Gustave, 148
Courtauld, Stephen, 94
Couturier, Charles, 123, 133, 154, 156, 159, 166, 188, 196, 209–10, 220, 226, 230–31, 232–33, 259–60, 267, 269, 298
Crampon, Abbé, 67, 129, 163
Crane, Stephen, 225
Crashaw, Richard, 132
Crété, Father, 4–5, 56
Creuzer, Friedrich, 90
Crevel, René, 36, 113
Curtius, Ernst Robert, 10, 11, 61, 186

Daladier, Edouard, 87
Dali, Salvador, 35–36, 245
Damien, Father (Damien de Veuster), 217
Dante Alighieri, 114, 115, 203, 233, 264, 268, 271, 301
Daudet, Alphonse, 175
Daudet, Mme Alphonse, 288
Daudet, Lucien, 175, 207, 290
David, 163, 260
Debussy, Claude, 176
Dehau, Father, 181
Delacroix, Eugène, 65
Delay, Jean Paul Louis, 253
De Quincey, Thomas, 130, 248
Descartes, René, 210, 222
Dickens, Charles, 37, 40, 62, 134, 160
Donatello, 130
Donne, John, 132, 138, 157, 224, 283, 306
Doré, Gustave, 233
Dostoevsky, Feodor Mikhailovich, 229–30, 231, 286–87, 305
Douglas, Lord Alfred, 224
Doumer, Paul, 36
Dow, Gerald, 117–18
Duccio di Buoninsegna, 17
Duché, Jean, 249
Dumesnil, René, 33
Dumesnil de la Tour, 57
Dürer, Albrecht, 132

Eckhart, Meister, 153
Edward VIII, King of England, later Duke of Windsor, 70
Einstein, Albert, 236–37
Eliot, George, 304–5
Eliot, Thomas Stearns, 142, 251
Ellis, Havelock, 16, 202, 227
Éluard, Paul, 173
Emerson, Ralph Waldo, 212, 240
Englebert, Omer, 216
Erasmus, 213
Erckmann-Chatrian, 225

Esther, 104–5, 204, 215
Evans, Maurice, 123
Ezekiel, 284

Faulkner, William, 229
Faus, Keeler, 161
Fénelon, François de Salignac de la Mothe, 90, 153, 248, 285, 300
Février, Jacques, 226
Fisher, Dr., 213
Flagstad, Kirsten, 228
Flaubert, Gustave, 23, 33–34, 90, 95, 251
Fourier, Pierre, St., 123
Francis de Sales, St., 92, 208, 294
Francis of Assisi, St., 57, 136–37, 141, 216–17
Freud, Sigmund, 42

Gallimard, Gaston, 171, 239
Garrett family, 99
Gershwin, George, 154
Ghéon, Henri, 6
Ghirlandaio, Domenico, 303
Gide, André, 5–7, 8–9, 10, 13–14, 19–22, 23, 24, 25–26, 31–32, 33, 37–38, 53–54, 56, 61–63, 67, 69–70, 71, 75–76, 79–81, 82–83, 84, 85, 89–90, 91, 95, 161, 162–64, 176, 178, 179, 186–87, 196, 197–98, 199–200, 204–5, 207–9, 220, 221–22, 223–25, 232, 233, 237–40, 242–43, 248, 251, 252, 258, 266, 268, 269, 282, 291–92
Gide, Mme André, 21, 80–81, 291–92
Gide, Catherine, 81, 208
Giles, Brother, 57
Gillet, Mme, 253
Giorgio, Francesco di, 17–18
Giotto, 18, 114, 117
Giraudoux, Jean, 235
Girolamo dei Libri, 44
Gluck, Christoph Willibald von, 228

Goethe, Johann Wolfgang von, 8, 13
Gogol, Nikolai Vasilyevich, 84
Goodspeed, Edgar Johnson, 190–91
Gosse, Edmund, 80
Goudeau, Mlle (seamstress), 140
Gourmont, Rémy de, 207
Graham, William Franklin (Billy), 303
Green, Anne, sister of Julian Green, 71, 155, 187–88, 192, 225, 260, 276–77, 289
Green, Charles, brother of Julian Green, 148–49
Green, Charles, grandfather of Julian Green, 46, 48, 273
Green, Edward Moon, father of Julian Green, 112, 148, 227
Green, Eleanor, sister of Julian Green, 282
Green, Mary, sister of Julian Green, 27–28, 270
Green, Mary (Hartridge), mother of Julian Green, 22, 25, 49–50, 181, 227, 264
Guéhenno, Jean, 244
Guth, Paul, 197

Handel, George Frederick, 77, 94, 263
Harris, Frank, 223
Hartridge, ——, grandfather of Julian Green, 48
Hartridge, ——, grandmother of Julian Green, 48
Hawthorne, Nathaniel, 116–17, 149, 188, 212, 241, 304
Henry, O. (pseudonym of William Sydney Porter), 203–4
Henson (American admirer of André Gide), 208
Herbert, George, 132–33, 163, 164
Hewlett, Dorothy, 142
Hitler, Adolf, 37, 60, 78–79, 87

Hölderlin, Johann Christian Friedrich, 195, 247
Holland, Vyvyan, 68
Homer, 120
Hopkins, Gerard Manley, 139–40, 155–56
Hugo, Victor Marie, 8, 79, 188
Husserl, Edmund, 269

Ingres, Jean Auguste Dominique, 25
Isaiah, 257, 284
Isenbrandt, Adriaen, 117

Jackson, Thomas Jonathan (Stonewall), 48
Jaloux, Edmond, 24, 54–55
James, St., 172
James, Henry, 34
Jammes, Francis, 22
Jefferies, Richard, 204
Jefferson, Thomas, 47, 52, 72
Jeremiah, 76–77, 79, 287
Jerome, St., 240, 301
Job, 82, 158
Joergensen, Johannes, 136
John, St., 55, 121
John-Mark, 184
John of the Cross, St., 56, 58, 106, 223
Jolivet, Régis, 210
Jonathan, 260
Jouaust, Damase, 208
Jouhandeau, Marcel, 187, 238–39, 298
Jouvet, Louis, 54, 235
Joyce, James, 10
Julien de Brioude, St., 267
Jung, Carl Gustav, 54, 193
Jurieu, Pierre, 273

Kafka, Franz, 53–54
Kant, Immanuel, 296
Keats, Fanny, 274
Keats, John, 37–38, 78, 142–43, 151, 195–96, 274, 283

Kierkegaard, Sören, 210, 211
Kinsey, Alfred Charles, 198, 253, 306
Knox, Ronald Arbuthnott, 294
Kreutzer, Friedrich, 90

La Boëtie, Étienne de, 209
La Bruyère, Jean de, 238
Lacretelle, Jacques de, 33
La Fontaine, Jean de, 15, 62
Lafuma, Louis, 216
Lallemant, Louis, 174
Lambert, Jean, 239
Lamy, Father, 133
Lancelot, Dom Claude, 250–51
Latini, Brunetto, 301
La Tour, Georges de, 57
Laubeuf, André, 247
Laurens, Jean-Paul, 6
Lawrence, David Herbert, 146, 228
Lazarus, 275
Lear, Edward, 68
Léautaud, Paul, 258
Lee, Robert E., 48, 74
Lefèvre, Frédéric, 266
Leloir, Father, 171
Le Nain, 166
Lenin, Vladimir Ilyich, 68
Leonardo da Vinci, 85, 214
Lepêcheur, Jeanne, 268
Le Poittevin, Alfred, 90
Lincoln, Abraham, 48, 137
Longfellow, Henry Wadsworth, 212
Lorrain, Claude, 33, 117
Louis XIV, King of France, 300
Louis, Théo, 219
Lourié, Arthur, 132
Lourié, Mme Arthur, 132
Lull, Ramón, 107–8
Lushington, Stephen, 241
Luther, Martin, 232

Malaparte, Curzio, 194

Mallarmé, Stéphane, 85, 134–35
Malraux, André, 5, 10, 11–12, 14, 247–48
Manet, Édouard, 94–95
Mantegna, Andrea, 44
Marcel, Gabriel, 161
Maritain, Jacques, 8, 16–17, 24, 58, 84, 105, 107, 126, 133–34, 219, 270, 276, 277–78
Maritain, Raïssa (Mme Jacques), 57, 133–34, 277–78
Marlowe, Christopher, 224
Martel, Thierry de, 10
Martin du Gard, Roger, 20–21, 33, 80, 239
Masseo, Brother, 57
Matisse, Henri, 148, 298
Matthew, St., 191
Maugham, W. Somerset, 221, 251
Mauriac, André, 153, 163, 165, 240, 298
Maydieu, Father, 180
Melville, Herman, 212, 253
Mercure, Jean, 256
Merton, Thomas, 205
Messiaen, Olivier, 210
Michelangelo Buonarroti, 214–15, 228, 230–31, 304
Michelet, Jules, 54
Milbanke, Annabella, 241
Milhaud, Darius, 147
Milhaud, Mme Darius, 147
Milles, Carl, 148
Milton, John, 35, 224
Molière, Jean Baptiste Poquelin, 235, 305
Monet, Claude, 118
Montaigne, Michel Eyquem, Seigneur de, 208–9, 227, 239, 257, 261, 263, 293–94, 299, 305
Monteverdi, Claudio, 226, 257, 278
Moses, 77
Mozart, Wolfgang Amadeus, 122, 214, 245, 270, 279, 289, 302
Mugnier, Abbé, 75

Murillo, Bartolomé Estéban, 8
Mussolini, Benito, 87

Neumann, Teresa, 17
Newman, John Henry, Cardinal, 143, 211
Nietzsche, Friedrich Wilhelm, 13

Olivier, Sir Laurence Kerr, 183
Oumansoff, Véra, 278

Parinaud, André, 247
Parker, Charles, 246–47
Parker, William, 246–47
Pascal, Blaise, 23, 193, 208, 216, 223, 238, 239, 267, 277, 293–94
Pater, Walter, 34
Patinir, Joachim de, 117, 118
Paul, St., 3, 10, 68, 75–76, 78, 143, 153, 240, 284
Paul of the Cross, St., 276
Paulding, C. G., 133
Péguy, Charles, 122, 123, 126, 143–44, 158, 161
Pepys, Samuel, 3, 91
Perrin (publisher), 134
Peter, St., 233, 271, 273
Philip II, King of Spain, 179
Piazzetta, Giovanni Battista, 114
Picasso, Pablo, 25, 166, 233
Pierre, Abbé (Henri Antoine Grouès), 277
Pinturicchio, 117
Pius V, Pope, 188
Pius XI, Pope, 58, 80
Plato, 34–35, 107, 148
Plon (publisher), 7
Plutarch, 252
Poe, Edgar Allan, 51, 72, 73, 84, 85, 105, 148, 241
Polignac, Mme de, 248
Pollaiuolo, Antonio, 65
Pope, Alexander, 305
Porter, William Sydney (O. Henry, pseudonym), 203–4

Pouget, Father, 282–83
Poupet, Georges, 236–37
Poussin, Nicolas, 33
Praxiteles, 304
Prime, Mr. (seminarian), 144–45
Proust, Marcel, 207, 290
Purcell, Henry, 154
Pushkin, Aleksandr Sergeyevich, 84

Quennell, Peter, 241, 299

Rachel, 182
Racine, Jean, 83, 163, 262, 301
Ramakrishna, 64
Rembrandt Harmenszoon van Rijn, 69
Renan, Ernest, 24, 52, 83
Renoir, Pierre Auguste, 10, 33, 95, 148, 251
Reynolds, Sir Joshua, 46
Richardson, Samuel, 228
Rilke, Rainer Maria, 218–19, 253
Rimbaud, Arthur, 7
Rivet, Charles, 53
Rivière, Jacques, 7
Roosevelt, Franklin Delano, 126
Rose, Francis, 166
Ross, Robert, 223
Rostand, Jean, 233
Rothenstein, Sir William, 100
Rouanez, Charlotte Gouffier de, 238
Rousseau, Henri, 10
Rousset, David, 244
Ruggles, Eleanor, 155
Ruth, 112

Sade, Donatien Alphonse François, Comte de, 101, 129
Saint-Jean, Robert de, 5, 14, 19–20, 24, 38, 44, 48, 61, 75, 79, 85, 130, 134, 142, 145, 147, 178, 181, 183, 211, 223, 229, 230, 231, 240, 252, 257, 260, 278, 281, 290, 291

Saint-Simon, Louis de Rouvroy, Duc de, 300
Samuel, 82
Sartre, Jean Paul, 233, 237, 245
Sassetta, 17
Satie, Erik, 147
Savonarola, Girolamo, 12, 303–4
Saxton, Eugene, 126
Schiffrin, Jacques, 5, 19, 81
Schlegel, August Wilhelm, 154
Schliemann, Heinrich, 35
Schopenhauer, Arthur, 19
Schubert, Franz, 93, 278
Schumann, Robert, 9, 51, 93, 240, 245
Seneca, 138
Seurat, Georges, 95
Shakespeare, William, 19–20, 47, 69, 70–71, 122–23, 150–51, 154, 160, 162, 224, 298
Shaw, George Bernard, 229
Shelley, Percy Bysshe, 304
Sherman, William Tecumseh, 25, 48
Sinclair, May, 258
Sisley, Alfred, 118
Sitwell, Edith, 305
Skinner, Cyriack, 35
Sodoma, Il, 89
Sologub, Fedor (pseudonym of Fedor Kuzmich Teternikov), 24
Spinoza, Baruch, 148
Stalin, Joseph Vissarionovich, 68
Stein, Gertrude, 22–23, 36–37, 166–67
Stein, Sarah (Samuels) (Mrs. Michael Stein), 148
Stekel, Wilhelm, 32, 33, 41, 42, 124–25, 137–38, 153, 265
Stendhal (pseudonym of Marie Henri Beyle), 129–30, 200, 235–36, 250
Stevenson, Robert Louis, 12, 27, 137, 304
Stimson, Henry Lewis, 128

Strachey, Lytton, 258
Suarès family, 89
Surin, Jean-Joseph, 297
Susanna, 193
Suso, Henry, 118
Swift, Jonathan, 83, 101
Symonds, John Addington, 214

Tate, Allen, 241
Tauler, Johannes, 118
Tchaikovsky, Piotr Ilich, 271
Teresa of Avila, St., 92, 173, 195, 272
Teternikov, Fedor Kuzmich (Fedor Sologub, pseudonym), 24
Thackeray William Makepeace, 50
Theresa of Lisieux, St., 272
Thomas à Kempis, 157
Thomas Aquinas, St., 194, 216, 248
Thoreau, Henry David, 212
Tintoretto, 134
Titian, 69
Toklas, Alice B., 166
Tolstoy, Leo, 225
Toulouse-Lautrec, Henri de, 251

Utrillo, Maurice, 97

Vaillant-Couturier, Paul, 38
Valensin, Father, 239
Valéry, Paul, 85, 162, 250, 258
Van der Weyden, Roger, 118
Vaneck, Pierre, 255–56

Van Eyck, Jan, 118
Van Rysselberghe, Mme, 81
Vasari, Giorgio, 89
Vashti, 105
Verdier, Jean, Cardinal, 80
Vergil, 22, 141, 244, 271
Verlaine, Paul, 228–29, 252
Vianney, Jean Baptiste Marie, St. (Curé d'Ars), 169
Vigouroux, Fulcran Grégoire, 130
Vilmorin, Louise de, 173
Vincent Ferrer, St., 92
Vivekananda, 102
Vlaminck, Maurice, 9–10
Voltaire, François Marie Arouet de, 199

Wagner, Richard, 228–29, 240, 281
Waldman, Milton, 298
Washington, George, 25, 52
Weil, Simone, 223
Weill, Kurt, 31
Wells, Herbert George, 68
Wells, Thomas, 126
Whitman, Walt, 137, 201
Wilde, Oscar, 223–24, 246–47
Windsor, Duke of, *see* Edward VIII, King of England
Woodward, William E., 52
Woolf, Virginia, 258–59
Wycherly, William, 305

Yeats, William Butler, 156

Zurbarán, Francisco de, 245